Praise for *Slay In Your Lane*:

'Tackling representation and self-belief in almost every area of life, it's wise, witty and insightful'
Emerald Street

'Reading *Slay In Your Lane* is like talking to a very intelligent, articulate, and hilarious girlfriend – one who is able to recount a microaggression by finding the humour in it without making light of it . . . *Slay In Your Lane* comes at a time when "diversity" is a hot topic, yet nothing about this particular book is faddish . . . it stands at the forefront of a new wave of publications, TV shows, and podcasts that meaningfully explore the lives of black women'
Roundtable Mag

'A serious contribution in flaunting the achievements of black, British women who have made their mark on society, despite the obstacles in their path . . . the most engaging analysis ever to have reached publication of why it is that black British women still feel "tattooed with our otherness"'
Daily Telegraph

'A place where statistic comes alive, angles on the everyday melt and change. It is neither a sermon nor an indictment, but the passionate making of a case. A highly effective one'
***Sunday Times Culture*, Book of the Week**

'The synthesis of a thousand conversations about how to navigate career, love, family, racism and unattainable beauty ideals as a black British woman'
The Times

'An essential read for black women who want their experiences validated and for young British teens to see the inspirational women who have come before them'
Victoria Sanusi, *iNews*

SLAY IN
The Black

YOUR LANE
Girl Bible

Yomi Adegoke & Elizabeth Uviebinené

4th Estate • London

For Yem, who taught me to 'Slay In My Lane'
before I knew what it meant to,
and for Yinks, who inspires me to do so daily,
and more than she will ever know.

Yomi

....

In loving memory of
Ingrid & Sidwell,
thank you for everything.

Elizabeth

CONTENTS

INTERVIEWEES

Ade Hassan MBE

Afua Hirsch

AJ Odudu

Alexis Oladipo

Althea Efunshile CBE

Amma Asante MBE

Dr Anne-Marie Imafidon MBE

Bola Agbaje

Charlene White

Clara Amfo

Dr Clare Anyiam-Osigwe BEM

Cynthia Erivo

Dawn Butler MP

Denise Lewis OBE

Estelle

Florence Adepoju

Funke Abimbola MBE

Gemma Cairney

Irene Agbontaen

Jamelia

June Sarpong MBE

Dr Karen Blackett OBE

Keisha Buchanan

Lady Leshurr

Lakwena

Laura Mvula

Dr Maggie Aderin-Pocock MBE

Malorie Blackman OBE

Margaret Busby OBE

Melanie Eusebe

Dr Nicola Rollock

Patricia Bright

Sarah-Jane Crawford

Sharmadean Reid MBE

Sharmaine Lovegrove

Susan Wokoma

Vanessa Kingori MBE

Vannessa Amadi

VV Brown

FOREWORD

Teacher or nurse?

These were the only jobs that my career advisor at school thought I would be able to achieve. Both vocations are admirable and worthy, but come on, just two career options for a working-class girl from Reading?

I had several passions growing up in the UK as the second daughter of two Bajan immigrants. I loved sport, specifically athletics, and I loved travel. The excitement of going to the airport, getting on a plane and flying to a new destination was a very special and rare occurrence in my household. I treasured it. I also loved TV advertising as much as I loved the TV programmes. I would critique the ads, think about whom they were trying to talk to, and think of better ideas as to how they could get their message across.

I ended up running for my athletics club, and I was good, but not good enough to pursue a career in it. When I was eight, I wanted to be an air traffic controller or an air stewardess, but I rapidly went off both ideas as I got older, when I realised that I would just be staring at a screen all day (or night), and I might not get time to enjoy the exotic places that I would be flying to. But my love for advertising never wavered. Back then, though, advertising was (and to a certain extent, still is) a very white-male, middle-class domain. So how would I carve out a career for myself as a young, black, working-class woman?

My dad was a very wise man. He knew nothing about the industry that I entered, nor did he know anyone in this field. My dad wanted myself and my sister to be doctors, lawyers or accountants – vocations that had a high standing back home in Barbados. These were professions that would earn us respect and, most importantly, a salary that meant we could have a good life. My older sister became an accountant and is now a university lecturer. She inspires me every day; she is strong-willed, bright and has a joy for life. I am the black sheep of the family. I didn't go into medicine, law or finance. I pursued my love of advertising.

My dad knew how difficult it would be to be successful in the UK. It would be a marathon with many obstacles and challenges. He would often say,

'You're black and you're female, you have to try twice as hard as anyone else.'

I did. I worked extremely hard. My athletics training made me focused. I am naturally competitive.

My dad would also say,

'You have two ears and one mouth; use them in that proportion.'

I listened, I learned, and then I spoke up. I progressed.

I was fortunate to have my parents as role models and to influence me. So few young black women have role models outside of their immediate family and friends to help them navigate the inevitable hurdles that do exist. To give them valuable advice, encouragement, and support. I firmly believe that you need to *See it to be it*. It is no wonder that my careers advisor, all those years ago, thought that my future ahead was as a nurse or a teacher (in fairness, I do a bit of both in my current role!). They couldn't *see* anything else for a young West Indian woman. Black female role models were just not visible then to inspire them or me.

It is no coincidence that I personally know so many of the women featured in *Slay In Your Lane*. There are too few of us who are visible and known. I admire and respect all of them. A number of these amazing women I count as my cheerleaders, and I am theirs. They encourage and support me in my journey, and I try to do the same for them.

This book needed to be written. It is a book of inspiration, a book that tells the story of struggle, of resilience and, most importantly, of achievement. It answers so many questions that I had when I started my own career journey and looked around and had few people to ask. I wish this book had existed then, I am so glad that it exists now.

If you are a young black woman you should read *Slay In Your Lane*. Elizabeth and Yomi have put together an incredibly valuable resource for you. They have collated the stories of women who have pioneered and gone before you. These women give their honest reflections and pearls of wisdom.

We are your cheerleaders. Now go SLAY!

Dr Karen Blackett OBE

INTRODUCTION

'It's Always a Race Thing With Her'

ELIZABETH

'Work twice as hard to be considered half as good' was a saying that I, like most black women, grew up with. But it was only as I began my twenties and started to experience more of the world that it really started to hit home.

Slay In Your Lane is the love child of exasperation and optimism. I can't pinpoint the exact incident that tipped me over the edge – the various microaggressions start to blur into one after some time – but after one particularly frustrating week at work, I realised I was done. Done with feeling conscious of my blackness and femaleness and apologising for *just* existing. Like me, my black female friends have the ambition and drive to succeed within spaces that were not initially set up for us to excel in, but we have all found that navigating them has proved to be a challenge at times.

I sought advice where so many women do: in books. I bought Sheryl Sandberg's *Lean In*, and although there were parts that I learned from and related to, I felt it failed to address the uniquely challenging experiences faced by me and women like me. And why would it? Sandberg can only speak to one facet of my being, my womanhood, which, for me, is wholly intertwined with my identity as a black woman.

So I went looking for black women at networking events who *could* speak to my experience, and advise me on how best to navigate my way through the challenges I saw ahead of me. I still felt optimistic and positive about the black female experience and I met successful and inspiring black women from a variety of industries – from a tech entrepreneur turning over six figures to a Magic Circle lawyer carving out her place in a male-dominated field. We shared stories about the challenges we encountered and the triumphs we could see on the horizon. These women were not the finger-snapping stereotypes from a TV series, to which society often reduces the black female experience. They were not monolithic; they were awe-inspiring, amazing and relatable. But something just didn't add up: why were they only celebrated at ticketed events with limited numbers of seats?

I would leave these events feeling reassured that I wasn't alone, but also saddened that this sense of sisterhood ended with the event. This longing led me to call my best friend, Yomi, who is a journalist, to persuade her to be the one to take on the challenge of amplifying these women's voices and utilising their priceless advice on a bigger scale. I asked her to write a book that spoke to me, and other young, black, twenty-something women navigating life. Later, we decided to work on this campaign together.

Role models matter to the next generation more than ever, and black British women and girls have them in vast amounts, but you wouldn't guess that from a glance at the shelf of your average book-store. We need a movement that amplifies the voices and increases the visibility of black women who have been made thoroughly invisible by the mainstream. That's what *Slay In Your Lane* hopes to be; we hope to offer confidence and inspiration, but also, most importantly, support to other black women who are in the process of building their own foundation and who will, if the world has its way, be constrained by the limitations society tries to place upon us.

There is a saying: 'It takes a village to raise a child,' but how about 39 of the most trailblazing black women in Britain? *Slay In Your Lane* is the personal-development course I never knew I needed; as you read this book I hope it gives you the tools and support to be in the driving seat of your life and not a mere passenger. *Slay In Your Lane* is #BlackGirlMagic personified. It is exactly what we've been waiting for: a chance to revel in the achievements of those who ran so we could fly, as well as to encourage those who are just about to take flight.

3

YOMI

I owe a great deal to the TV medical comedy, *Scrubs*.

In an episode in Season 3, the white female doctor Elliot Reid turns to the black male doctor Christopher Turk and says he has 'no idea how hard it is' being a woman in their profession. 'I have no idea?' he says, eyebrow raised. 'Look, I'm not gonna fight about whether in medicine it's harder being black or a woman,' she responds. 'Black!' Turk shouts. 'Woman!' Elliot retorts. At that very moment, a black female doctor passes them slowly. 'Much props, Dr Rhodes,' says an awkward Turk. The pair shuffle on the spot.

Something that my then 13-year-old self had already frequently experienced but had never been able to articulate was perfectly captured in a 30-second skit: that the different facets of my identity – being black, being a woman – impact on who I am, and what my experience in this country is. It explained why I only somewhat related to stories focused on black men and white women. It highlighted why seeing my identity and my experience reflected mattered. *Scrubs* had just explained what, years later, I would realise went by the name of 'intersectionality' – and I immediately felt seen.

Being black and British, people know our parents are from somewhere else before we even open our mouths. Or if not our parents, our grandparents. Or great grandparents. We are tattooed with our otherness. We are hypervisible in predominantly white spaces, but somehow, we often remain unseen. Growing up, I felt keenly the dearth of visible black British women in the stories our society consumed and it made me feel all sorts of things. It made me feel as if I was invisible, too. It made me feel frustrated. It made me feel annoyed, upset and, most of all, restless. Restless, because I knew (or at least hoped) that when I was old enough, I'd one day be a part of changing things.

I attempted to do something about it when I turned 21, breathlessly starting up a publication aimed at young black girls in the UK. *Birthday Magazine* was the primordial goop from which *Slay In*

Your Lane was indirectly spawned. Its aims were similar: to outline the black female experience as well as excellence, and offer equal amounts of realism and optimism. It was a small-scale attempt to uplift; its distribution was local and the team was small, but its impact was larger than I expected. *Slay In Your Lane* was the next logical step that I didn't see coming, but Elizabeth did, animated by the very frustration, annoyance and restlessness that my younger self had felt.

Now, at 26, the same sense of restlessness has begun to set in, but this time it is without the anger, or even the upset. The current overriding emotion I feel is unbounded hopefulness, because black British women in 2018 are well past making waves – we're currently creating something of a tsunami. From authors to politicians, to entrepreneurs to artists, black women in the UK continue to thrive against all odds and well outside of the world's expectations. Women who look and talk like me, grew up in similar places to me, are shaping almost every societal sector, from the bottom and, finally, from all the way up at the top. All a younger Yomi would've wished for was the ability to learn from them; an older Yomi wishes for pretty much exactly the same thing.

If white women fear the glass ceiling, black women fear a seemingly impenetrable glasshouse. We're blockaded from all sides and there is little to no literature on offer to advise us as to how we're supposed to push on. So much is currently happening on an individual level to combat this, and it's of paramount importance that it is recorded, noted and passed on. We almost never hear of the persistence, perseverance and drive that fosters such success. Perhaps more importantly, we rarely hear of the failures, the flops and the insecurities that black British women have managed to push through to get to where they are today. We rarely hear about black British women, full stop. And this silence can be just as damaging as the negativity of which we're so often on the receiving end.

Throughout my teenage years I was a keen reader, and I am no anomaly – findings from a 2014 study by the National Literacy Trust show that black girls are more likely to read than any other ethnic group in the UK.[1] Yet books rarely touch meaningfully on the black British experience – and even less so the black British female experience. As a part of this group, I have a vested interest in *Slay In Your Lane* that goes beyond simply wanting to write a book. I guess you could say that Elizabeth and I are writing this as much for ourselves as we are for other black women. Just like our peers, our friends and our sisters, we are still learning how to navigate the workplace, the dating world and life in general.

We're not here to tell you that if you simply go for gold, put your mind to it and believe, that you can will yourself out of systemic racism. As pointed out by Elizabeth, even your parents would've no doubt once said that you'd have to work 'twice as hard' and meritocracy is a myth – and stats continually prove this. But what we *are* saying is that there is much empowerment and inspiration to be gained from the many women who have jumped over the very hurdles that you too will find yourself up against. There are practical ways to aid you to win, and admitting that there will be difficulties and challenges along the way doesn't mean submitting to defeat. It means coming to battle armed and prepared.

EDUCATION

'I also remember thinking that there was often
a double standard between the black girls and white
girls in school. We were punished when they
would be given second chances.'

Elizabeth

....

'For instance, there was the time the
cheerleading club decided to give its annual
"slave auction" a *Django Unchained* theme . . .'

Yomi

Lawyer, Doctor, Engineer

ELIZABETH

....

'Even today when I get into a taxi and
someone says "What do you do?" and I say
"I'm a space scientist", they do a double take.
I'm a woman and I'm black. "How come you're
a space scientist? That doesn't add up."'
Dr Maggie Aderin-Pocock MBE

....

When I was 16 I thought I was going to fail all my GCSEs. The grades
I had been predicted suggested that wasn't going to be the case, but I
still had a deep and looming fear that I wasn't going to pass a single
one. At home, the pressure to do well in school and in my exams was
immense. Results day in my household was set to be an unfair cup
final between two rival football teams: on one side were my parents,
armed with all the best players and expecting straight As. On the
other was me, with my mediocre players and a subpar defence, trying not to crumble under pressure and get annihilated. As the weeks
passed and results day got ever closer, the tension increased, and
so, to mitigate what I felt sure would be my parents' imminent dis-
appointment, and rather than wait to be caught out on the big day, I
naively started to job hunt. With no GCSEs and no experience, I knew
I was probably fighting a losing battle, but it still felt less frightening
to me than the *real* battle that I was convinced I had coming my way
on results day.

I partly grew up in Dulwich – a suburb of South London, home
to Dulwich Picture Gallery. I would often pass the gallery, so I had
noticed that they hosted a range of events aimed at their usual
demographic – middle class, middle-aged and white – nothing that
16-year-old me particularly fancied. But I needed work experience,

and I had an idea, so I went on Google, did a quick search and found the email address of the person who headed up the gallery's events and marketing and sent her an email. In it, I said I believed their events could do with appealing more to young people. I asked to meet her and, much to my surprise, she agreed – obviously she had no idea she was arranging to see a teenager. On the day of the meeting, as I sat there waiting for her to arrive, I was so nervous. To say I felt out of my depth is an understatement. I was thinking, 'This middle-aged white woman is not expecting some inexperienced 16-year-old black girl asking to be involved in her events.' But when she did arrive she looked pleasantly surprised. It just so happened that during that summer the gallery was introducing outdoor cinema screenings, and she wanted my input to help bring the idea to life. And that's what I spent my summer doing. It became my first experience in marketing.

Results day came and, much to my surprise, I did well and my parents were pleased. My panic had propelled me into finding work experience that would go on to prove valuable in my career, so I don't regret that move, but looking back on that summer, what I do regret, and find depressing, is how I let my crippling fear of not doing well and letting other people down take over my life. Instead of making the most of those weeks I spent them waiting anxiously and fretting about my future. Why? Where did my lack of faith in myself come from? On balance, when I look back on it, the work experience was a good thing for me to do, it was just the circumstances that drove me to do it that were far from ideal.

In my school, unless you were identified as a gifted and talented student achieving straight As and exhibiting model behaviour, it was almost inevitable that you would fall through the cracks and be forgotten about. By the time it came to making decisions about your future, you could find yourself in a no-man's land, caught between your parents' very high expectations and the lower opinions of the teachers who doubted your ability – not forgetting the usual teenage peer pressures. For me, this self-doubt then developed into a loss of self-esteem, and anxiety crept in about what I was good at and how I could translate that into a future.

When the time came to take the exams, I had noticed that some of my friends didn't believe they could possibly do well, so they just started to give up and misbehave – because this seemed to be what was expected anyway. This tension often became a 'one-way ticket' to disengagement, and so they began to succumb to that feeling – whether they had started out well-behaved and ambitious, or not. Being doubted by your teachers and put under great pressure from your parents created a sometimes toxic combination. The truth about educational achievements is often more complex than the stats suggest.

When the topic of race and education is covered by the media it is usually cast in an overwhelmingly negative light. When they aren't focusing on the low achievement of white working-class boys, the experiences of ethnic minorities are characterised by low aspirations, high exclusion rates and subsequent underachievement. With black children, the spotlight tends to be focused on black boys – perhaps understandably, because their educational attainment levels are shockingly low compared to black girls. As a result black girls are largely rendered invisible within the education conversation, so there has been little contemporary research and literature that looks into their experience of our education system, asking the question: how are black girls in the UK *really* doing in school?

....

'My friend, face your books, not this Facebook.'
Unknown African parent

....

It's not hard to see why an extremely high value was placed on education in my childhood home and in the homes of my friends, as well as in those of many of the women we interviewed for this book. We are a generation of people who grew up with parents – or grandparents – who had gained professional qualifications in the countries they had migrated from, but who often found it difficult to get jobs in the UK that reflected their skill sets because those qualifications weren't always recognised when they went to job interviews. Educated though they were, they often faced discrimination as they entered the labour market, and many had to take jobs for which they were overqualified.

Our parents appreciated the value of education and the opportunities it could bring. As mine would often remind me: 'Back home we do not have the same opportunity that you children have here. Education makes a way for you.' Despite this, they also weren't in the dark about how difficult it was going to be for us to navigate our future in Britain, and so they would also make us aware that 'this isn't our country; we have to work harder'. My parents had extremely high ambitions for me and my siblings. In their eyes, 'the sky's the limit'– if you worked hard, you would go far. I would hear them talk to their friends in true Nigerian style about how I would be doing a masters, when I hadn't even got into university yet. They believed that education led to job opportunities, and, perhaps unsurprisingly, as Karen Blackett's father did, they often steered us towards careers such as law and medicine – professions in which no one can deny your qualifications, regardless of the colour of your skin and the prejudice you might come across. From our parents' perspectives these traditional professions would give you job security.

Bola Agbaje, Olivier Award-winning playwright and writer, had a similar experience growing up: 'For African parents, I think it was just that thing that they wanted stability. A lot of parents who are first generation, they want their kids to be lawyers and doctors and things like that because those are the jobs that create stability, and also you can be wealthier with those type of jobs. So for them, they want their kids to have better lives than they had, so that's why they push their children into those types of careers.'

Educational researchers acknowledge that, of all factors within the home, parental values and aspirations have the largest positive effect on children in school. However, the high aspirations and motivations of ethnic minority parents do not always translate into the greatest achievement in the classroom, and there has been little research into why this might be the case. When black children enter the school system at five they perform as well as white and Asian children in literacy and numeracy tests. Their results are largely in line with the UK average, with literacy at 67 per cent and numeracy at 75 per cent, compared to the national averages of 69 per cent and 76 per cent respectively. However, by the end of primary school as they enter secondary school, aged 11, black pupils' attainment falls behind.[1]

When we look a little deeper, it's noticeable that there are differences in achievement levels between the different black groups. In the 2013–14 academic year, 56.8 per cent of British African students achieved A*–C grades – slightly above the national average of 56.6 per cent. This attainment level places them alongside Indian and Chinese pupils as the country's highest ethnic achievers. However, in sharp contrast, Black Caribbean pupils have a 47 per cent pass rate, trailing by nearly ten percentage points. On the whole, black pupils achieved the least in the five top GCSE grades out of all ethnic groups, but it is the performance of Caribbean pupils that averages out at 53.1 per cent.[2] There has been a corresponding lack of research into the differences in attainment levels between Black African and Black Caribbean pupils.

Not enough has been done to try to understand why a disparity exists between different black groups. Instead, the two groups are often amalgamated into one, which means we are unable to see emerging patterns and there's a tendency for many children to be left sidelined unless they are doing really badly. This lack of substantial research is especially apparent when it comes to the attainment levels of black girls. Althea Efunshile CBE, former deputy chief executive of Arts Council England, explains: 'I have sometimes wondered if black girls who don't do as badly as black boys are invisible in the education system. Because if you compare them to black boys, they're doing better, and so people say, "Right, okay, we don't need to worry about them so much." But if you compare them to white girls, they're not doing as well.'

Young black girls appear to value education highly: they want to succeed and try their best to navigate the school system. But as they progress through secondary school it seems that factors come into play that often lead to them not fulfilling their potential. Heidi Mirza is Professor of Race, Faith and Culture at Goldsmiths College, University of London, and has written extensively on ethnicity, gender and identity in education, most notably in her book *Young, Female and Black* (1992). As she pointed out when we spoke to her, 'Everyone says black girls do well, there's no problem for them. They do better than the boys, they do better than black boys, they do better than white working-class boys, and they're doing better than white working-class girls, what's the deal? We don't even need to look at them; in education they're kind of sorted. But actually, when you look down and you drill down, as I did for *Young, Female and Black*, what I found was that there are so many mythologies around black womanhood, and the fact that there's always the "strong black woman that survives narrative". All the theories and studies were saying was that, because they've got that inner strength, they do well, and what I found was, yes, they have that inner strength, yes, their parents really valued education enormously, and pushed them to do well – some did, some didn't, but at the same time there were structural things like racism, schools with not very good teachers, issues around poverty, resourcing, government policies, that they had to contend with, and the fact that they do well is because they overcame that, they learnt to navigate the system.

'They had very high aspirations, but as they got a bit older and they realised that they weren't getting the support at school to get through, they would make very strategic choices, so they would say, "I'm not going to get my GCSE, but I will go to college and I will get it in another institution, and I will go for nursery nursing because I can get on that course, but I don't necessarily want to be a nursery nurse. I want to go to university and study sociology, that might be a stepping stone for me."

'They knew the system didn't work for them and so they made many choices to accommodate – I call it the "long, backdoor route into success" – so they have to make many, many more different steps to sidestep the racism and the lack of support in the system by making strategic choices. So it takes some much longer to get into higher education, into university. They're usually older; nearly all my students when I was teaching at places like Southbank and Middlesex, all the black women were, you know, already in their mid-twenties, where the white young people would be 17, 18, 19. They were much younger because they didn't have to navigate the system as much.'

If black parents do notice that their kids are struggling in school, they often look for alternative methods to compensate for the failure of mainstream schools, rather than trying to effect change in the schools themselves. Some black parents choose to send their children overseas during their secondary school years as soon as they start to see a pattern of bad grades or disruptive behaviour. When I was in Year 9 in secondary school, I was constantly warned that I would be sent to Nigeria if my grades didn't pick up in maths and science, and my brother and sister were sent to boarding school there for a few years. This was in contrast with the faith they placed in the education system in the UK. I had friends who were in class on a Monday morning but by Friday they would have been taken out of school.

Private school is another option for parents who can afford it. Dr Nicola Rollock, Reader in Equity and Education at Goldsmiths College, University of London, started off in state education but her parents soon made the decision to send her to an independent school when they realised she wasn't being stretched academically. 'We used to read Peter and Jane books and they had a sequence – 1a, 1b, 1c – and I would get through the sequence quite quickly. Then, rather than being allowed to go on to the next sequence, 2 or 3 or 4, the teacher would ask me to go back to the beginning, so I was incredibly bored.' Rather than move her into a higher class, Nicola was expected to wait for the rest of the class to catch up: 'There was one black teacher who advised my parents to move me because I wasn't flourishing there. I had been held back by my class teacher, a white woman, so my parents moved me and I went to an independent all-girls school.'

Some black parents supplement their kids' education with tutoring. I went to a Saturday school for many years, run by two black women who employed highly motivated black teachers. There, parents had a say in the curriculum and the school was committed to raising the achievement levels of black students whose mainstream schools had often given up on them.

Attitude gal

So what *do* we know about why so many black girls are underachieving at school? We know that institutional racism plays a part and that bias in teachers' perceptions and expectations contributes to some black pupils' underperformance and attainment. Studies have revealed that bias can manifest itself in a number of ways. There is evidence that teachers have routinely underestimated the abilities of black students and that assumptions about behavioural problems are overshadowing their academic talents. In essence, low achievement among some black students is made worse because their teachers don't actually expect them to succeed. Dr Steve Strand from Warwick University, the author of one study, said: 'After accounting for all measured factors, the under-representation is specific to this one ethnic group and indicates that, all other things being equal, for every three white British pupils entered for the higher tiers, only two black Caribbean pupils are entered.'[3]

It's no surprise then that, according to the same study, black children are also the most concerned about how teachers view them and are less likely to feel their teachers would describe them as clever.[4]

Dr Maggie Aderin-Pocock MBE, space scientist and co-host of BBC2's astronomy show, *The Sky at Night*, can relate to these findings: 'At school I wasn't considered to be very bright, I suffer from dyslexia and so when you first go to school it's all about reading and writing. When I started the teachers said, "Oh yeah, okay, Maggie's not very bright," and they put me in the remedial class, and so I was in the back there with the safety scissors and the glue tucked out of the way and they didn't see me as having much potential at all. This is quite in contrast with what I was getting at home, because I was speaking with my father and he was saying, "Ah yes, you should go to university, you should study," and so the two were very much at odds. I didn't speak much at school about what I wanted to do because usually when I did I think the teachers would try to be kind, but they would look at me with little disappointed faces, like, "Oh Maggie, science is for clever people, you should consider something like nursing, nursing is good, and that's science, too." So I think they were trying to mitigate my expectations. I felt a bit disillusioned; I felt that school wasn't for me, so I would sit in remedial class. But things turned round at one specific moment for me, when I was sitting in a science class and a teacher asked a question. The question was "If one litre of water weighs 1kg, how much does one cubic centimetre of water weigh?" Now a cubic centimetre is one-1000th of a litre and I worked out, "Oh, that would be 1 gram." So I put my hand up to answer the question and I looked around the class and no one else had their hand up. Now knowing that I was the dumb one in the remedial class I put my hand back down, because I thought I couldn't be right. But then I decided to give it a go and I answered the question and got it right, and suddenly I thought, maybe I'm not as dumb as I thought. And science is a subject that gets people into space and so I thought "if I study science maybe I can go into space". That was a real turn-around for me, so I started paying more attention in science classes, and as my science grades started going up, my other grades went up, too. After that I got lots of encouragement at school, because that's when they saw I had an aptitude.'

Manifestations of unconscious bias in the classroom also extend to black girls being shown fewer leniencies than their white counterparts, and written off as problem children more quickly. The groundbreaking Swann Report in 1985 pointed out: 'Teachers' attitudes towards, and expectations of, West Indian pupils may be subconsciously influenced by stereotyped, negative or patronising views of their abilities and potential, which may prove a self-fulfilling prophecy, and can be seen as a form of unintentional racism.' In the UK, black children are almost four times more likely to be suspended from school than white children. In the 2013–2014 school year, 18 per cent of black boys and 10 per cent of black girls were suspended from school. This is compared to 5 per cent of white boys and 2 per cent of white girls.[5] In my school, I remember pupils being excluded because of their hair. Black kids were penalised for their hairstyles, whereas the white middle-class kids with floppy long hair were left alone. At the time I couldn't understand why one kind of hair was policed and the other not. If someone's hair doesn't affect their ability to learn, why should it matter?

I also remember thinking that there was often a double standard between the black girls and white girls in school. We were punished when they would be given second chances. Alarmingly, this is borne out in a study published in 2017 by Georgetown Law Center on Poverty and Inequality. It revealed that, starting as young as age five, young black girls are viewed by adults as being less innocent and more adult-like than white girls.

Heidi Mirza elaborates: 'If you just step out of line a little bit, if you're white and you laugh in the class they might laugh with you; it's kind of a joke. If *you* laugh, it's like, you're laughing at somebody, get up and go out of the room. So what they found was that there is a kind of stereotype of blacks being more aggressive, and it's like you said, this subconscious bias goes on, so any little thing is escalated much quicker.'

Dawn Butler explains how perceptions of teachers left her at odds aged 12: 'There was a girl, a white girl, called Andrea in my school, and she would always get As, no matter what she did she would always get As, so I decided I was going to buckle down and get an A. It was a history assignment and so I worked really hard on this history homework. It was a really good piece of work, and I remember going into school and I was really chuffed, and I brought it in, and then I got a D for it. And I compared it to Andrea's work, and we both compared it because we were actually in competition to see who could write the neatest and the smallest.

The teacher said that I had cheated. There was no way I could prove that I didn't cheat, that it was my bit of work and that I worked really hard at it. And I just thought, "things are never going to change" – I even had this discussion with Andrea. We decided one day we were going to swap work, because we knew that no matter what I put in I was never going to get an A and whatever she put in she was always going to get an A. Looking back I was so frustrated that I couldn't do anything to change this, but it was the first time, I suppose, that I realised that once somebody has an impression of you, it's very difficult for them to change that impression. So, you know, Andrea the white girl was always going to get an A, Dawn the black girl was never going to get an A. It was a hard thing to accept – I kind of didn't want to try my best anymore because it was just never going to be rewarded.'

Being an opinionated confident black girl was a no-no in my school, and as Jamelia, singer and TV presenter explains, her daughter's experience sounds similar: 'I've noticed it in their school, being in a private-school environment, they're still the minorities there, and I'm being called in and I've had a meeting where they've said, Oh, you know, she's just acting too confident. Yesterday, my eldest, she tested out a sociology class, because she wants to do it for A-level – she's finishing her GCSEs but they get a taster class – and the teacher said he showed her a statistic, a table, and at the bottom, it showed ethnicity and their success in exams, and he said black boys and black girls were at the bottom of the table. My daughter was like, I don't even know how he thinks that might have made me feel, and it shows that he just didn't even think, but, what I said to her is that at least he had a statistic. What he then went on to say was that the reason black boys are at the bottom is because they don't have father figures and my daughter called him out, and she got in trouble.'

There's evidence to suggest that if your teacher looks like you, you might do better in school. An American study revealed that when black students have black teachers, those students are more likely to graduate high school. 'The study found that when students had teachers of the same race as them, they reported feeling more cared for, more interested in their schoolwork and more confident in their teachers' abilities to communicate with them. These students also reported putting forth more effort in school and having higher college aspirations. When students had teachers who didn't look like them, the study found, they reported lower levels of these feelings and attitudes. These trends were most visible in black students, especially black girls.'[6] So it is particularly frustrating that in the UK, we don't have enough black teachers. According to the National College for Teaching and Leadership, only 12 per cent of trainee teachers in 2013–14 were from minority ethnic groups – a statistic that has not really changed in five years.[7] The lack of black teachers across the country means that there could be a lack of understanding as to how to motivate and work with black children. In 2007, Catherine Rothon argued that a lack of co-ethnic role models may explain poor performance from Black Caribbean boys,[8] and those teachers who *do* come from ethnic minorities report difficulties that include casual racism, lack of role models for black and minority ethnic (BAME) children, and being forced to deal with microaggressions from other staff. I go into more detail about the impact of casual racism in the 'Water Cooler Microaggressions' chapter.[9]

When I grow up . . .

What did you want to be when you grew up? Who were your role models? We can all remember what it felt like to be full of hopes, dreams and ambitions about what jobs we were going to have when we were old enough. But as the years passed, society – and school – often shut down those ambitions and set limitations before we had time to really know what it was we wanted to do. According to a BBC *Newsround*'s study, about one in five black children believe their skin colour could damage their job prospects. One child told *Newsround*'s reporter, 'This generation is still being judged and stereotyped, so it's going to be difficult for us to do what we want to do when we're older.'[10]

For black women, this is exacerbated by the fact that we tend only to be shown a narrow range of possibilities for ourselves, and are bombarded with the idea that there are only certain roles for certain people. Heidi understands this all too well from her research: 'There is so little representation of you, as a young black girl, in school, so you don't see your image in a positive way in the textbooks, in the history. A student of mine, she did her PhD on black history, and she said that when she interviewed black kids, boys and girls, and their parents, they said, "We don't want black history to be taught in schools because it's always about slavery and the enslaved, and then we get teased." She said it's the way that it's taught that is the problem. Not that it's taught as part of the horrors of the colonial and imperial system, no. Or how it fuelled the industrial revolution, no. It's taught as a separate thing, which is degrading, and so the only images that you do see are in chains, being lynched or something, and you'll never see positive images.'

One of the things we hope to achieve with *Slay In Your Lane* is to show young black girls that there is no limit to the roles they can carve for themselves in the world.

Malorie Blackman OBE is an award-winning children's author who held the position of Children's Laureate from 2013 to 2015. She believes it's incredibly important for black children to have these visible role models. 'When I was a child, even though I loved reading and I loved writing, it didn't occur to me that I could be a writer because I'd never seen any black writers, and in fact, the first time I read a book by a black author was *The Color Purple*, and that was when I was 21 or 22. Now, that's a ridiculous age to get to before you actually read about black characters written by a black author, and it was only reading that that led me to the black bookshop in Islington, when it was there, and that's where all my money went. I remember in one lesson, I said to my teacher, "How come you never talk about black achievers, and scientists, and inventors?" And she looked at me smugly and said, "'Cos there aren't any." And, I didn't know any better, I had never been taught about them, so I felt there was a huge gap in my knowledge about my own history: never been taught it, never come across any books about my own history, so when I found a black bookshop, it was non-fiction books, it was mostly African-American writers, but I devoured them.'

Sharing Malorie's views on the necessity of visible role models, Dr Maggie Aderin-Pocock has relentlessly pursued a schedule of school visits alongside her academic work: 'This is quite a multi-pronged challenge. My goal is to get more, especially black, girls into STEM [Science, Technology, Engineering and Maths], because it's the same across the board really, there are internal challenges and external challenges. Internally, I think many girls don't consider STEM, especially black girls, but it's the same with black boys really. When they see role models or black role models they see footballers, they see singers, they see people who are doing brilliant jobs, but they don't see many scientists. They see maybe a few more medical doctors now, but sort of within a limited catchment. And so it's trying to expose them to as many role models as possible in as many different disciplines as possible. It's funny, when I go to schools, I talk about science and I talk about space but I do not necessarily want them to become space scientists like me, I just want them to know that they have amazing opportunities and there are amazing careers out there that might be suited to them. Some of the children might be great as space scientists, but some of them might want to do something totally different. But it's showing them that as a black girl in a school, the sky's the limit, you can do anything you set your mind to, but you've got to actually know what the opportunities are. It's trying to get them exposure to opportunities. I think it doesn't happen quite so often, but I think in some places they still try to limit people's expectations. And that's especially true for girls and I think especially true for black girls. So it's sort of like the situation I was in – "Oh Maggie, don't aim too high" – almost know your place in life, and I find that quite frustrating. So I like to show my story as an example, you know, I started off exactly where you are sitting and now I'm up here and I'm doing really exciting things and I love my work. So it's showing them that there are amazing things that they can do, that they have the potential, and the thing is to believe in themselves. So it's trying to tackle away the external barriers and the internal barriers.'

And positive changes are happening. Natasha Codiroli finds that female students of mixed ethnicity and Black Caribbean origin are more likely to study STEM A-levels than white female students.[11] Indeed, black girls are the only ethnic group that outnumbers their male peers in STEM A-levels.[12] STEM is important in driving innovation and is the fastest-growing sector in the UK. There's never been a better time to encourage young girls into this industry. Role models like Dr Maggie Aderin-Pocock understand the need to be visible to school children, and outreach projects are becoming increasingly important in encouraging more black women into all sorts of industries.

Malorie agrees: 'So, as far as representation is concerned, I think it is absolutely vital, because if I hadn't read those books, it still wouldn't be in my head that I could be a writer because I'd never seen any! I remember, for example, when I first started writing, and I wrote a book called *Whizziwig*, and it was on CITV (Children's ITV) for a while. I remember going into a school – and this was really instructive to me in terms of representation, because I went into a school in Wandsworth – and I'd say about a third of the pupils were black, or children of colour, and two-thirds were white. I remember that I was talking about *Whizziwig*, and the idea, and it was on TV and a number of them had watched it, and a black boy put his hand up and he said, "Excuse me, so, *Whizziwig* was on the television and then you wrote it?" And I said, "No, I wrote it, and then it was on the television." He said, "But, it was someone else who did it, and then you did it?" And I said, "No, it was my idea and then I wrote the book and then it was made into a TV programme." And he asked me about five or six questions, all on the same theme, and I was like, "No, I wrote it." I know exactly what you're thinking, and I just thought, I loved it, because I was sitting with a sort of smile inside, thinking, I *want* you to look at me and think, hell, she ain't all that, so if she can do it, I can do it! And that's what it was, "You did it? You wrote it?"

And I thought, that's *exactly* the point! And so I just love that, and that's why, especially to begin with, sometimes it was two or three school visits a week, and I got out there, oh my God, and I was up and down the country and I made sure I got out there to show, not just children of colour, but all children, that writers can be diverse, that I was a writer. Here I was as a black woman and a writer!'

Similarly, in 2017, Yomi and I were invited by London's South-bank to mentor young girls between the ages of 11 and 16 for the International Day of the Girl festival. It took me back to my school years and the fear of not knowing what was ahead of me past GCSE results day. Unlike when I was growing up, these girls seemed more confident about what they wanted to do, and asked us interesting questions about our careers and why we made the decisions we did. They didn't seem lost like I did at their age and that filled me with great hope that things seem to be slowly but surely improving.

In summary, we've spoken about the need for an increase in black teachers, the need to tackle the bias held in some pockets of teaching staff through training and accountability, and that parents also need to better understand the school system so they can best support their children in the face of these obstacles. The general feeling of being lost that I experienced throughout school, and especially over that summer as I waited for my GCSEs, came from a lack of confidence in myself that originated in the school system. Changes are slowly happening, but we need to do more to raise the self-esteem of young black girls, so that they know that the sky is indeed the limit, and to actively give them the tools to help them realise their ambitions.

Black Faces in White Spaces

YOMI

'Lol my sisters oyinbo flatmates threw
her yam in the bin cause they thought it
was a tree log'
@ToluDk

When I learned I had got a place at Warwick University, I burst into tears. Not tears of joy, mind you: tears of fear. Aged 18, I had flat-out refused to apply to Oxford or Cambridge, my stomach churning at the stories of elitism, racism and all other kinds of 'isms' I wasn't sure I would be able to handle on top of a dissertation. I thought I would much rather learn about those things in a history course than opt into being on the receiving end of them, thank you very much. So instead I applied to SOAS, a very good London-based uni (which even taught Yoruba) as well as Warwick, to please my league-table-obsessed parents. Once I was offered my place, I was 'advised' (read 'ordered') to go to Warwick by them; it was a decision for which I'm now thankful, but at the time it felt like a form of punishment. I was absolutely petrified I would end up being the only black girl within a 400-mile radius. Even the term 'Russell Group' was offputting: it sounded to me like a band of 60-plus cigar-smoking 'Russells' for whom fox hunting and racial 'horseplay' was an enjoyable pastime. It didn't exactly scream 'inclusion'. Of course, when I got there, I realised I *wasn't* the only black girl. There weren't many of us by any measure, but there were enough of us to warrant a populous and popular annual African-Caribbean Society (ACS) ball – and even its Nigerian equivalent.

University was one of the greatest times of my life, but it wasn't without its challenges. If you are on your way to uni or are considering going there in the future, you will no doubt have already been given lots of advice from websites, teachers and those who have already graduated: don't leave your dissertation to the last minute; label your food in the shared fridge; rinse the Freshers' Fair for as many free highlighters and notebooks as you can; always accept the Domino's vouchers – you will need them. But often one very important topic is left off this generic list of well-meaning wisdom, and that's how to deal with racism. And when I say racism, I don't just mean blackface Bob Marley costumes at every conceivable event (there will always be one). As I'll come back to, statistics show that, like the police force, the health service and the workplace, university is a space where racism is embedded – beginning with the application process and continuing right up to graduation. From often alienating curricula to downright ignorance from flatmates, uni can be intimidating for any student, but this is especially so when you're black and female.

'We're not in Kansas anymore, Toto.'

For many black students, university will be their first time living away from home and also often their first time living in a predominantly white area or environment. The beauty of university is that it often thrusts you into the midst of people who are vastly different from yourself, broadening your mind in the process. But this can also sometimes leave you feeling seriously homesick, isolated and generally disconnected.

Little recognition is given to the culture shock experienced by many students coming from predominantly ethnic areas. Maggi cubes become as rare as precious minerals, and weaves often stay on far longer than you're used to, pretty much growing right off your head for want of a nearby hairdresser. People ask questions you may not be used to answering; for some students you'll be the very first, real-life, 3D black person they've ever met and they will have endless questions about your apparently baffling existence – which has been taking place just two hours down the M40 for the past 18 years – questions which, by the way, you are under no obligation to answer.

When I went to university, my fear that I would be the only black kid on campus wasn't quite realised, but on the other hand, Warwick wasn't exactly Croydon in terms of diversity. It is normal for freshers to struggle initially with making friends, but by the end of week one, when one of my first conversations had been with someone who told me he believed there was 'Me black' and 'Rihanna/Beyoncé black', I had already decided I wouldn't be spending much time at my halls or with my flatmates. Instead I found solace in the halls a stone's throw away from me, which housed about half of the uni's black female intake (again, this wasn't much). But in those halls I soon found myself a best friend, a boyfriend and a community. Together we searched for hair shops and discovered the clubs that played black music (as much of a banger as The Killers' 'Mr Brightside' was, we heard it more times during the entirety of our nights out than we did anything remotely 'ethnic'). 'Black music' was relegated to a Thursday night and primarily consisted of Sean Paul's discography.

We swapped eye-roll-worthy anecdotes on microaggressions and lamented the lack of available seasoning in our nearest supermarket. And the best friend I made? I could never have foreseen that eight years, several, several hours of phone calls and even more nights out later, we'd be co-writing a book together. Uni can really be the making of you, even if you don't always realise it at the time.

Dr Nicola Rollock went to university many years before me and it's interesting how similar her experience was:

'I think there were quite a lot of things I took for granted growing up in South-West London, even though I went to this mainly white and very middle-class school. Going to find a black hairdresser's or Black Caribbean food was normal. Brixton was down the road, Tooting . . . it was completely normal. I didn't have to go out of my way to find these things, yet going to Liverpool in the early 90s – and remember this was before it was the European Capital of Culture – was a real challenge, and at 18 I didn't actually know that I needed those things in my life. I didn't know they were important to me because I'd really taken them for granted. Even going out was a challenge, in terms of the kind of music I was listening to as a young woman. I had to go out of my way to find venues that would play music I was interested in; there was something called "Wild Life" that happened once a month that played R&B, soul and hip hop – this was once a month at university. So we – me and the few other black girls – ended up befriending black local Liverpudlians and going to "blues", as they were called, or "shebeens",[13] outside of the university context, because we were really hungry for and looking for places where our culture and identity was recognised and we could just relax.

'I remember with "Wild Life" we went to enjoy the music, and it felt like some of our counterparts went to drink, and again this was something I wasn't used to; I didn't grow up in a house where our parents would say "Go and have a drink," or, "Here's some money, go down to the pub." I didn't step into a pub until university, and even then I remember saying, "But I'm not thirsty!" Which completely misses the point of going to the pub, as it's not only about that, it's about connecting and sitting down and a place to meet, but for me it was just outside of my cultural frame of reference. So I found, in terms of food, music, hair – because my hair was relaxed and straightened at the time – finding a space in which I could be myself and be with others was a deep, deep challenge, so I felt very, very isolated. Then there were the things that many students experience, such as not having any money. I ended up needing to work as well as study . . . I just found it incredibly difficult and isolating. I would get the train back from Lime Street to London and I would come via Brixton (this was before Brixton was gentrified) and I would walk up the steps at Brixton station and literally, quite literally, exhale, because foods were there, black hair shops were there, my culture and identity was all around me. It was as if I had arrived home.'

> 'Ah, the racially insensitive party.
> A mainstay of primarily white institutions
> since time immemorial.'
> *Dear White People*

For me and my group at uni, our friendship was a wonderful buffer between us and a lot of things that didn't have nearly the effect on us as they might have done, had we not had each other. For instance, there was the time the cheerleading club decided to give its annual 'slave auction' (which in itself was a problem) a *Django Unchained* theme. Or when a Snapchat picture was uploaded to one of our university community pages on Facebook featuring a black man wrapped in a net with the caption, 'I caught me a nigger!' And let's not even start on the Stockholm syndrome of other black students who would tell the predominantly black women who kicked up a fuss to 'chill out'.

And the black face. My gosh, the black face.

Microaggressions (defined as a statement, action, or incident regarded as an instance of indirect, subtle or unintentional discrimination against members of a marginalised group) can range from a flatmate throwing out your plantain because they think they're rotten bananas, all the way to outright flagrant slurs. And in recent years, the racism that was once only whispered about among students has become a talking point on and off campus. Universities put to bed the dangerous myth that racism is the preserve of the 'uneducated' and 'ignorant' – in fact, it is often those in power who are the ones perpetuating it. Universities are, at times, so racist that they make headlines. The country gasped at the story of a black first-year student at my old university who had found the words 'monkey' and 'nigga' written on a bunch of bananas she had stored in her shared kitchen. Many black students tutted and sighed, not in surprise but in recognition.

Sometimes the racism is more subtle and underhand, as Afua

Hirsch, a barrister, award-winning journalist and author, experienced at Oxford:

'People always asked for weed, especially when I was with my friends, especially my male friends. They would just assume that they were local drug dealers. And it was always those really posh boys. In their brain, the only function of black men is to buy drugs from. That was one of the most infuriating and offensive things. Or you'd arrive at a party and they'd just assume that you were the local dealers showing up to supply. I hated that, I really hated that.'

A more 'in-your-black-face' form of racism is, well, black face. It was a costume staple at parties when I was a student, but at Cardiff University it actually made its way into a play written by medical students in 2016. A student actor blacked up and wore an oversized dildo to make fun of a black lecturer at the university, which unsurprisingly caused a feeling of 'segregation' between groups of different ethnic backgrounds.[14] Eight students of African heritage complained, and this, according to the independent report commissioned by the university as a result of the incident, led to a 'major backlash'. Some of the complainants were told by their fellow students they were being 'very and unduly sensitive' and that they should accept it as 'tradition', as the play was an annual occurrence. The students who had raised the objections felt they had been 'ostracised' and some decided to leave Cardiff.

Three years before, a couple of hundred miles away in York, four male students donned black face, too.[15] They were depicting the Jamaican bobsled team from the film *Cool Runnings*. Over in Edinburgh, law students painted their faces to dress as Somali pirates for an 'around the world' themed party.[16] Meanwhile, at the University of London, a student was actually rewarded with a bottle of wine for their racial insensitivity when they won a fancy dress competition at a union event by donning black face.[17] And in Loughborough last year, students organising freshers' events had to issue an apology after planning a 'slave auction' and 'slave night' as part of the entertainment for the university's new intake.[18] It is important to note that this kind of flippant racism is as common among those educated in the most elite of institutions as it is anywhere else. These are not isolated incidents but part of the very foundation of British society. They are being perpetrated by the bankers, lawyers and doctors of tomorrow: people who will become the managers who throw out CVs because they can't be bothered to pronounce 'Akua'.

A recent report[19] by race-equality think-tank the Runnymede Trust highlighted the feelings of exclusion and rejection felt by many black university students as they navigate alienating curricula, come up against lower expectations from professors, and experience brazen racism on campus. The report emphasised the importance of universities becoming 'actively anti-racist institutions' – something that, as bastions of 'progressive thought' and 'talented minds', shouldn't be such a big ask.

But very few universities have taken appropriate measures to prevent or punish racism, and students are often forced to take matters into their own hands. It was racist incidents such as those outlined above that led to the creation in 2013 of the Anti-Racism Society at my old university, run voluntarily by a group of undergraduates. It offers students advice or someone to talk to about race-related issues, and puts on events such as sleepovers, movie nights and panels offering often cathartic discussions about race and racism. Many students feel more comfortable reporting incidents to their peers, as opposed to their institution's reporting systems, but those who run societies like this are under the same pressures – in terms of racial tensions and university work – as those who come to them for help. The frequency of racial abuse on campus is something that universities, not students, should handle better, but even so, these spaces, groups and organisations are important. Anti-racist societies are different to an African-Caribbean Society, where the basis of meetings isn't always necessarily political; these societies exist specifically for tackling racism. Don't be afraid to be the person to create that space at your university if it doesn't already exist.

Sometimes the microaggressions can occur at the hands of the universities themselves. Femi Nylander was a recent graduate of Oxford when he found himself racially profiled. He was visiting a friend's office in Harris Manchester College and was locked out, so he went to the office's kitchen to do some writing, chatted briefly with staff and students he knew and then left. Later that day, a CCTV image of Nylander walking around the college was emailed to all of its staff and students, along with a message warning them to 'be vigilant' and to 'alert a member of staff [. . .] or call Oxford security services' if they saw him. His presence, it warned them, was a reminder that the college's 'wonderful and safe environment' can be taken advantage of, adding that its security officers 'do not know [his] intentions'. No one once asked Femi who he was or why he was there.

Afua remembers her visitors also being on the receiving end of similarly racist treatment at Oxford years before:

'I had this boyfriend in London who was black and I coped by running away a lot on the weekends and hanging out with him, and then he'd come and visit me and that was a big issue because he was a dark-skinned black man. One time when he came to my college, they wouldn't let him in and the porter rang me and said: "You should've warned us if you were expecting someone who looked like a criminal," and I'll never forget that. Even then, I was like, I cannot believe I'm having to put up with this. It was like there was no sense that . . . It was really bad and I was very conscious of being with him at Oxford because it kind of drew further attention to me as a black woman.'

These types of everyday microaggressions have sparked several conversations and motivated various campaigns, one of the most high-profile being the 'I, too, am Oxford' series, inspired by the 'I, too, am Harvard' initiative in America. In 2014, Oxford students organised a photoshoot consisting of 65 portraits of BAME attendees of the university, with the hopes of highlighting the ignorance they came across at Oxford – and confronting it. 'How did you get into Oxford? Jamaicans don't study', 'But wait, where are you really from?' and 'I was pleasantly surprised . . . you actually speak well!' were just some of the choice quotes written on the placards they held in front of them, forcing their peers to encounter the ugly face of university racism. It is hugely important that black students continue to have these conversations and to hold their universities to account, especially when white students so often centre racial discourse around themselves. During Afua's time at university, even the ACS wasn't a black safe space:

'I joined the African-Caribbean Society only to discover that it was run by a white boy from one of the elite private schools in the country because he loved going to Jamaica to his dad's villa in the summer holidays and he had fancied being a "DJ reggae man". At the time, I was just like, this is completely off, but I couldn't articulate it. It was classic white privilege, exoticisation.'

Perhaps as a result of the slowly increasing black student population, the voice of black students *is* beginning to be heard in universities in a way it hasn't been before, as Afua explains:

'For my book, I interviewed some black female students and it was interesting listening to them, because on one level they were describing the same microaggressions that we experienced, i.e. getting IDd when you were going to different colleges whereas white people weren't, or porters confusing you with the one other black person in the college even though you looked nothing alike, that kind of thing. But their attitudes were so different: they had names for it. We didn't have a word for microaggression and they had a confidence and ability to articulate their sense of oppression that I really admired. Even though on one level it was an acknowledgement that a lot of things hadn't changed, I found it really positive and uplifting speaking to these students because they were much more organised and assertive and they called things out when they saw them, whereas we just didn't feel able to. We would talk about it amongst ourselves but we just kind of had a defeatism about it.'

It may be that we now feel less apologetic about taking up space in a country that is rigged against us but which many of us still consider ours. But even with our newfound ability to speak up, some students still remain negatively affected by racism at university. In fact, the government was called on to take 'urgent' action after it emerged that black students are more than 50 per cent more likely to drop out of university than their white and Asian counterparts.

More than one in ten black students drop out of university in England, compared with 6.9 per cent of the whole student population, according to a report by the UPP and Social Market Foundations.[20] The government have made a whole heap of noise about increasing the numbers of black students enrolled at certain British universities, but the problem of how to keep them has been largely neglected. London universities are more likely to have a higher proportion of black students in attendance – and it's no coincidence that London has the highest drop-out rate of all the English regions, with nearly one in ten students dropping out during their first year of study.

'My best friend at Oxford, she dropped out in the third year,' Afua says. 'She was doing a four-year degree and she dropped out because she felt like she wasn't good enough. She just didn't believe in herself enough, she couldn't cope. It was literally just Imposter Syndrome, like, "Everyone else is better than me, cleverer than me and they deserve to be here." She went to a state school, she had a multiple sense of illegitimacy there and she took a year out, she came back and she got a first. I found that interesting because there was no question about her intelligence or her deserving to be there; it was just that sense of acceptance. I think it's really common – I was reading a report about how drop-out rates are higher for black students, and I've been mentoring a student, who, ironically, is from a very similar background to my friend and doing the same degree, and who just dropped out last year. It's so frustrating that you can't tell someone to stay somewhere that makes them feel unhappy but you do wonder, if this person had been supported, would this have happened?

'I think universities just assume that their jobs are to just get a few black people through the door. They have no sense of the extra emotional burden that we carry by being there, so they don't do anything proactive to support us. I nearly dropped out in my first year and it was basically like: if you're not up for it, then good riddance. There was no "How can we support you?", "What's going on here?", you know? There was just no intellectual curiosity as to what this phenomenon was, which ironically just confirmed why I wasn't supposed to be there anyway, because the possibility of me not being here doesn't remotely bother anyone.'

The reasons why black students' drop-out rate is higher than other groups are complicated and multifaceted. According to one report,[21] many universities struggle to respond to the 'complex' issues related to ethnicity, which tend to be 'structural, organisational, attitudinal, cultural and financial'. Other factors mentioned were a lack of cultural connection to the curriculum, difficulties making friends with students from other ethnic groups and difficulties forming relationships with academic staff, due to the differences in background and customs. The report also cited research showing that students from ethnic backgrounds are much more likely to live at home during their studies, perhaps making it less easy to immerse themselves in campus life. But Dr Nicola Rollock believes that not enough is being done to investigate the underlying causes of this:

'My concern is that these issues aren't looked at in any fundamental way: when they are, all black ethnic groups are amalgamated into one mass, and they shouldn't be. The data doesn't speak to distinct differences. And there's also a fear of talking about race. If they're talking about black and minority ethnic students, race needs to be a fundamental part of that conversation, but I would argue that as a society, and certainly within the academy and within education policy, race is a taboo subject. People are scared of talking about race and when they do, they do so in very limited terms. They believe that treating everybody exactly the same is the answer. Or particular tropes will come out for example: "These groups need mentoring," or "These groups lack confidence," or that "There are not enough groups coming through the education pipeline," and while I'm certainly not rejecting any of these points, I argue that to only focus on such issues is to miss the wider picture. Some people do have confidence but yet they are not progressing. How do you explain that? So I think there is a real limited and poor engagement with race both within the academy and education more broadly.'

'Sound so smart, like you graduated college.'

Going on to higher education, wherever it may be, and for whatever period of time, is an achievement. To choose to extend your full-time education, to opt in to taking more exams and willingly take on ever-increasing student debt, is deserving of a pat on the back. But it's notable that while black British youths are more likely to go to university than their white British peers,[22] they are also much less likely to attend the UK's most selective universities. This is not an indictment of the universities that aren't ranked at the top of the league tables, nor is it an endorsement of the frankly elitist system that sees some universities undervalued. Further education is just that: the furthering of education, and wherever that happens it should be valued. But it's important to interrogate why the under-representation of black people in these institutions occurs, especially when statistics show that there are more young men from black backgrounds in prison in the UK than there are undergraduate black male students attending Russell Group universities.[23] Black Britons of Caribbean heritage make up 1.1 per cent of all 15- to 29-year-olds in England and Wales and made up 1.5 per cent of all British students attending UK universities in 2012–13.[24] Yet just 0.5 per cent of UK students at Russell Group universities are from Black Caribbean backgrounds,[25] and there is little understanding of why this is the case.

One given reason is grades: black students are less likely to achieve the required results for entry to highly selective universities, which could help account for their lower rates of application.[26] The stumbling blocks that affect black students in school are outlined in the previous chapter, and help contextualise why this often happens. But the more pressing issue that many gloss over is that even when they *do* achieve the same results,[27] black applicants are less likely to be offered places than their white peers. In 2016, despite record numbers of applications and better predicted A-level grades (and the fact that UCAS predicted 73 per cent of black applications should have been successful),[28] only 70 per cent of black applicants received offers of places, compared to 78 per cent of white applicants.

In the same year, Oxford University's offer rate for black students fell to its lowest level since 2013, with just one in six being offered places, compared to one in four white students. In 2016 again, just 95 black students were offered Oxbridge places – 45 by Oxford and 50 by Cambridge. The 50 black students offered a place at Cambridge were chosen from just 220 applications, but the rate of offers to black students was far lower than that of white students: 22.2 per cent of black students who applied to Cambridge were offered a place, compared with 34.5 per cent of white students. Similarly, at Oxford University the offer rate for black students was just 16.7 per cent, while 26.3 per cent of white students were offered a place. The lack of black students at these institutions often leads to confusion, shock and at times outright disbelief from those both in and outside the uni on the rare occasions when they encounter them. Afua was on the receiving end of this many times during her student years:

'When I would go to the shops in Oxford and local people worked there, they would often try to be friendly, asking, "Are you a student?" and I'd be like, yes, and they'd say, "Brookes?" and I'd be like, no, Oxford, and they'd be like, yeah, "Oxford Brookes." It was just, why do you care anyway? It was local people. Sometimes when I went to Oxford student things, people would assume that I was from Brookes and not Oxford. I never really felt comfortable going to the Oxford Union and I think that this was part of the reason why. I was conscious that there was this other university that had many black people nearby. It was just a very common, frequent, casual interaction with local people and students, clubs and bars where that would happen. Sometimes I would show my student card for a discount or something and they would be like, "Oxford University?" in surprise. It was just the classic microaggression, often not meant to be offensive, and it makes you feel you have to explain yourself, where a white student would never have to explain themselves.'

Outside of Oxbridge, the success rate of black students applying to other highly selective universities – such as Russell Group institutions – also remains an issue, despite a sharp rise in applications from qualified students and the apparent 'commitment to diversity' we continue to hear about from just about every institution. In 2016, 61 per cent of black applicants were awarded places in these selective universities – an improvement on the year before. But according to UCAS's predictions, 64 per cent could have done so. Professor Vikki Boliver, a lecturer in sociology at Durham University who has carried out research on applications and acceptances of different ethnic groups at Russell Group universities, said this may also occur because BAME students' grades are more likely to be under-predicted. If this were true, she said, it would give backing to the argument for a post-qualifications application system for universities, with 'judgements based on fact, rather than predictions'.

She also suggested that name-blind applications could be the remedy for the current prevalent unconscious bias:

'Leaving people's names off UCAS forms would be an experiment to see if people are being influenced by names . . . If we don't have very clear procedures when selecting people for jobs or places on courses that mitigate against those stereotypes, there may be the danger that we unconsciously fall back on them . . . We may feel that certain people will "fit in" better.'[29]

The Universities of Exeter, Huddersfield, Liverpool and Winchester are currently piloting a system in which the names of applicants are hidden during admissions, in order to stop potential discrimination based on assumptions about students' names. But this is a mere drop in a tsunami of prejudice, bias and stereotyping in higher education.

The Russell Group responded to these findings with the argument that minority applicants have lower offer rates than their white peers with the same A-level results because they are less likely to have studied the specific A-level subjects required for entry to their chosen courses.[30] They also cited research[31] that suggests offer rates are lower because ethnic minorities are more likely to apply to heavily oversubscribed degree subjects such as medicine or law, perhaps as a result of the parental steering we discussed earlier. An in-house analysis of the data by UCAS also corroborated this, stating that a significant part of the reason for ethnic disparities in offer rates at Russell Group universities was down to subject choice.[32] Neither UCAS nor the Russell Group, however, have published detailed statistics to support their arguments.

Education, education, education

We may be under-represented in the Russell Group and other selective institutions but, interestingly, black students are over-represented and white and Asian students under-represented in other higher-education establishments. In these other institutions, there is a 14.3 per cent under-representation of Asian students and a 3.1 per cent under-representation of white students, compared to a 56.4 per cent over-representation of black students across the student body, at both undergraduate and postgraduate levels.

This over-representation of black students is especially apparent at newer, post-1992 universities, and institutions with highly diverse student bodies. While some universities are almost completely white (in 2014, Ulster only had a 3 per cent non-white student body),[33] at others minority students make up almost three-quarters of the student body with a corresponding under-representation of Asian and white students. Anecdotally, some think this imbalance may be due to a lack of information regarding university choices within the black community. Alexis Oladipo, founder of healthy food range Gym Bites, explains that for her, going to university was more about getting a degree, and not where it was from:

'I wanted to go to Kingston and Hertfordshire; Kingston because all of my friends were going there, and then Hertfordshire because there was a course that was interesting. Hertfordshire was my first choice, Kingston my second. I didn't get into Kingston and then for Hertfordshire, my grades weren't good enough so they transferred me to a foundation course, so that's why I had to go to clearing to get into Roehampton.

'Initially before choosing, my school helped with basic stuff – personal statements and the rest of it – but nothing substantial. Then [with] my mum, it was just a case of going to uni so, "sort yourself out" and all that kind of stuff. I just kind of got on with it really. I didn't have a great desire to go to university, I just knew that it was something [that] I had to do and something that was required of me and it's just furthering your education – you go to school, then you go to college and now you have to go to university.

'Me and education, we didn't really get along from young. I've always kind of struggled so I wasn't really excited to go. When I didn't get the grades, I was really upset and then I remember calling my mum and telling her that I didn't get into the uni that I wanted to get into and she was just like, "You need to find a uni, you not going to uni is not an option." I had to repeat a college year, so I had already done three years instead of two at college, there was no room for a gap year or anything like that, so I just went through clearing. My college helped me go through clearing – there was a list of unis that were taking people and I literally just went "ip dip doo" and picked a course at Roehampton because it was the closest university to Kingston. I thought about my friends again – we'd be like 20 minutes away from each other.

'I picked Media and Culture studies; I didn't really know what it was. I didn't enjoy it, I didn't understand it too well. I got a 2:2. But what I can say is that when my mum saw me in my graduation gown, she started crying straight away. So, I mean, it was not for me, it was for her, if that makes sense. It made her happy, she was proud . . . She was really, really proud and she was telling everyone, you know, "She's graduated now."

'So I did it more for her. I think if I took my time and really figured out what I wanted to do, maybe my journey would've been a lot more straightforward.'

A major reason why black students are less likely to be admitted to Russell Group universities is because they're less likely to *apply* to these universities, and there can be a number of factors at play here. Fear of alienation is often one, but also wanting to remain close to family, friends (shops that actually sell plantain . . .) can be another. Some students choose to apply to polytechnics simply because 'many prestigious universities . . . do not reflect the diversity of the cities in which they are located'.[34] There is also the fear of simply not being good enough. White and black students applied to Oxbridge with the same grades I had been predicted, but the niggling feeling that even if I did get in (which I was sure I wouldn't), I would still be the runt of a very smart and even posher litter kept me well away. I felt that although I might have been eligible for something 'on paper', between the lines of that paper it read: 'not for you.' And while I don't regret my choice at all, I do wish my motivation for not applying had been more about my wanting to go to my chosen uni and less about my hang-ups about other institutions.

A second reason, as Alexis's experience shows, is a lack of awareness from parents, who were often educated outside the UK and so are unfamiliar with the differences between certain educational establishments and courses. But having a parent in the know doesn't always mean they will be best placed to help you choose a university that is right for you: parents often simply assume that the higher up the league tables it is, the better it will be for you. Afua had a mother who knew all about the prestige of the university she was applying to, but this meant that Afua's reasons for choosing Oxford were based on her mother's preferences and not on how well suited she might be to it:

'Why did I decide to apply to Oxford? It's simple: African mum. It was "You are going to try to get into that university" and I have to say, I didn't fully get it. I just didn't get what the big deal was. I wanted to go to LSE. As far as I was concerned it was in the top five. I didn't really understand. I didn't really grow up in a proper establishment-type home so I just didn't get the extra advantage that came with Oxbridge. I kind of applied to humour my mum because she found it so important, and I got in. I just didn't see myself as an Oxford person, it didn't really occur to me that I would get in and that all links back to the stereotypes. When I thought of Oxford, when I pictured Oxford, I did not see myself; I saw posh white people so I didn't think I'd get in. I didn't take it seriously and then when I got in, I had a complete crisis because I went to a private school and it was very white and I'd been literally counting down the days until I could get away from it.

'I didn't get the academic advantages of it but I definitely got the social implications, which was that I'd be cut off from the community, that's what I felt. I'd be cut off from my whole scene, I was really into music journalism and I was in the new scene in London. I'd really worked hard to get away from the straightjacket of growing up in a very white area, so it was a big setback for me, that was my main concern. I just didn't have any positive things to counter it at the time.'

Perhaps the most important reason, as we've looked at in the previous chapter, is a lack of incentive to apply to these universities in the schools these students are coming from. Without this, very few pupils can believe that a Russell Group uni or Oxbridge is something within their reach – for many, the idea is nothing more than a pipe dream. While there are, of course, black children who attend private schools, the majority are state-educated. This becomes particularly meaningful when you consider that between 2007 and 2009 just five schools in England sent more pupils to Oxford and Cambridge (946 in all) than nearly 2,000 other schools combined. Four of those five schools were private.[35] The 2,000 lower-performing schools sent a total of 927 students between them to the two elite universities. Many of these schools sent no pupils at all, or on average fewer than one per year.

Afua, who mentored school children while she was at uni, describes the black pupils she met at state schools telling her that her university was a place they could never even dream of aspiring to:

'We all did mentoring talks in the summer. We would go to inner-city state schools and talk to kids and we were trying to say that whatever perspective you have of Oxford, it *is* like that but you *can* find yourself there. We would get them kind of motivated and interested and then at the end they'd ask, "What grades did you need to get in?" and I'd be like, "3 As" and they just looked completely deflated because no one at their school had ever got 3As, ever. It was unheard of. So then you just think, what's the point of going round to all these places when they're dealing with such a bigger structural unfairness? Oxford is very slow in recognising that a student at a really tough state school who gets Bs is possibly a better student and more talented than a student at a private school who gets 3 As, and I think other universities have been quicker to recognise that.'

Heidi Mirza also talks about the importance of these initiatives in raising the aspirations of young, black, largely working-class children:

'The universities in the States, like Cornell and Princeton, are going into primary schools in black communities and telling kids about universities from a very young age so that universities aren't seen as some kind of out-of-reach places; they're actually part of a mindset. And they've actually invested money in these programmes.'

Andrew Pilkington, Professor of Sociology at the University of Northampton, makes the important point that for the last few years 'the primary concern of widening participation strategies was social class'. Because of this, the important intersection of class *and* race has been ignored, and overlooked by policymakers. Therefore issues specifically affecting black members of the student body have been largely neglected.

The fact that there are more black students at university than any other ethnic group is largely as a result of how we view education. For many of us, as Elizabeth pointed out earlier, education is often posited as the antidote to racism. We believe we can educate ourselves out of inequality with the right qualifications and grades. But while education, especially higher education, can indeed do wonders for social mobility, it is unfortunately the case that inequality is still present on the way up. In order to get into university in the first place, black students must do better than their white peers, and they are still less likely to get into the more prestigious institutions, regardless of their A-level results.[36] As Dr Omar Khan, the Director of the Runnymede Trust, says: 'What message does that send to young people who have heard for decades now that "education, education, education" will ensure their equal opportunities in the labour market?'

Even more alarmingly, after they have jumped through the hoops to reach university, black students will, on average, leave with lower university grades than their white peers. These are students who have proved by their A-levels that they have the ability to thrive in the world's most elite institutions, but they fall short once they arrive. There has been little research into why this happens, but several of the issues discussed above – a lack of understanding surrounding the inevitable culture shock, multiple microaggressions at the hands of peers and staff – are likely to play a part. In 2010, 67.9 per cent of white students gained a first-class or upper-second-class degree at university compared to only 49.3 per cent of BAME students who entered with the same grades. Black students underperform compared to all other groups,[37] and this occurs regardless of the type of university they attend, while 72 per cent of white students who started university with A-levels of BBB in 2014 got a first or 2:1, compared with 53 per cent of black students.[38] Furthermore, despite an overall increase of BAME students in higher education,[39] they are still less likely to find jobs that match their education level once they leave, or to progress to professorships.[40] British ethnic minority graduates are between 5 and 15 per cent less likely to be employed than their white peers – and as if that wasn't enough of a blow, for ethnic minority female graduates in particular, there are large disparities between their wages and those of their white counterparts. The same study shows that three and a half years after they have left university, the difference in earnings between ethnic minorities – especially women – and their white peers actually increases.

Even if they are from similar socioeconomic backgrounds, grow up with similar opportunities and have similar qualifications, ethnic minority graduates are less likely to be employed than white British graduates. So at present, black female students are paying £9,000 – and rising – for a much poorer university experience than their peers. And then, post-uni, they are also being short-changed in their earnings, making it even more difficult for them to pay off those rising fees.

> 'I have written eleven books, but each time
> I think, "Uh oh, they're going to find out now.
> I've run a game on everybody, and they're
> going to find me out."'
> *Maya Angelou*

There is no one conclusive reason why black students are less likely to attend elite universities, just as there's no single reason why we get lower grades, but racists will assure us it's because we're undeserving, lazy or simply not smart enough. They complain that the places meant for equally talented white students are being 'taken up' by black students, despite the stats clearly stating otherwise. Imposter Syndrome often eats away at even the most talented of students, as they internalise these slurs and feel as though they're 'taking up space'.

Once you are at uni, it's important to remember you have earned your place – not at anyone else's expense but against odds that actually make it more difficult for you to be there in the first place. Afua Hirsch summarises this perfectly:

'My grandfather was a son of a cocoa farmer in the village in Ghana and he got a scholarship to Cambridge in the 1940s under the colonial system. In those days, they would pick who they saw as the brightest students in the country every year, it was part of the indirect rule. So, they would send them to Oxbridge so they could kind of condition them [to have] British values and then send them back to run the colonies for them. My grandfather benefited from that, he was really grateful for his experience and my cousin found all his letters from his time at Cambridge and it was so fascinating. I feel like, reading his letters, he was constantly apologising. If he didn't get the grades he wanted, he'd write and apologise and he'd say something like, "I hope in future, other students from Africa will come and redeem the good name of our continent," and he felt like he was the ambassador for the black race. Any failing on his part was a failing of the race – he just felt this great burden and I think that he felt like he had to constantly account for himself, and that really struck something in me. Even though my circumstance was so completely different, you do feel that sense of not quite belonging there, of having to explain yourself and having to account for yourself, as if, it's not your birthright to be there. That goes deep and it's an intergenerational thing about being a black person in a white institution where you don't feel you fit in. For years, I couldn't articulate it, I didn't have a name for it, but once I read my grandpa's letters something clicked and was like, "this is Imposter Syndrome." This is exactly what we all go through. My grandpa went to Cambridge in 1944 and so here I was, 65 years later. It's just crazy.

'We question whether we belong there and whether we have the right to be there, and I think that you've got to try and flip that on its head and think, I need to rinse this place for every drop I can get out of it. I'm going to use it before it uses me. I worked that out at some point and it really helped. I was like, you know what, whatever I can get from this place is going to give me what I need for my journey, I'm going to rinse it. It gave me a sense of control and it's hard when you're 19; you don't necessarily know what you want to do with your life and you don't feel in control, but the more you can tap into it and feel like you're running your own thing, that's really healthy.'

'Universities are not just complicit, they produce racism. They are no less institutionally racist than the police force.'
Dr Kehinde Andrews

Universities are predominantly white and middle class, not only in terms of attendance but also in terms of staff, which can often mean they also remain so in terms of syllabuses. More than 92 per cent of British professors are white; 0.49 per cent of professors are black; and a mere 17 of those are women.[41]

Only one black person is currently working in senior management in any British university. She is SOAS Director Valerie Amos, who is the first black female to lead a UK university and the country's first black vice chancellor (the chief executive of a university), full stop. Among the 535 senior officials who declared their ethnicity in 2015, 510 were white. The figures also show that universities employ more black staff as cleaners, receptionists or porters than as lecturers.[42]

Karen Blackett is listed as one of a handful of black university chancellors in the UK (a ceremonial non-resident head of the university) at Portsmouth, and out of 525 deputy vice chancellors or pro-vice chancellors, none are listed as black.[43] In 2011–12, there were no more than 85 black professors in the entire country, and for many of these, it isn't exactly plain sailing. According to a report by Professor Kalwant Bhopal, many ethnic minority academics often feel 'untrusted' and 'overly scrutinised' by colleagues and managers, as well as overlooked when it comes to opportunities for promotion.[44] Another report by the Equality Challenge Unit stated that BAME academics are also more tempted than their white counterparts to flee to overseas institutions to progress their careers.[45]

The issues regarding the retention of black staff are institutional, and have been the subject of many reports and papers that promise to bring about much-needed change through the reform of policies and programmes. But, as the Runnymede Trust noted in their report on race in higher education, it is all too easy for box-ticking and the filling out of required paperwork to become a substitute for real and substantial change. Many universities put their black students and staff front and centre on their prospectuses, but when it comes to actually ensuring they keep those members of the university body, they often fall far short of the mark.

For instance, the Race Relations (Amendment) Act 2000 initially required universities to develop and publish their race-equality policies, but many universities were reluctant to do so. Now, following the implementation of the Equality Act 2010, this requirement has been downgraded to mere 'guidance'. The lack of pressure on universities to retain their minority staff continues to affect the number of black lecturers visible to students. It's a pressing issue, as Akwugo Emejulu, a lecturer at my old university, points out:

'This under-representation of black women, not just as professors but throughout the academic staff in university, has lots of different effects. Firstly, it has a symbolic effect. Universities up and down the country, no matter whether they're the most prestigious, Russell Group universities or they're former polytechnics, they're sending a very similar message that black women are not wanted here. They're sending a very clear message that they do not value the research, interest and expertise of black women, they do not value black women as [being] authoritative, they do not value black women as scholars. I think there is this idea of "knowing agents", so there is this idea that black women, regardless of the discipline that they're in, simply cannot be seen as academic experts. I think that is the biggest issue and problem of black women: under-representation.'

Althea Efunshile agrees, adding that this dearth can impede the quality of education, too:

'We want black people everywhere, so of course it matters. If there are whole tranches of areas of public life where it's just white men that you see, then that means that there are whole tranches of parts of our community, our citizens, our people, who are likely to be thinking, "That might not be for me, so let me go over there instead," but your choice about "let me go over there, let me do that" is really just because you see that there are other people like you over there. That, to me, is not acceptable, it's not justice, it's not equality. So of course it matters. You want to be taught, or advised, or cured by experts, you want the best people, so obviously if it's a white man, it's a white man, but why would you want all the experts in your field to be white men? Diversity is important because it leads to different perspectives and different ways of looking at things.

'And not just in terms of race or gender, but also social class, or where you come from, or age and so on. In education, it matters, because education is about helping you learn how to think. It's not about the student as an empty vessel into which you pour a pot of knowledge. If it were, maybe it wouldn't matter who was pouring in the knowledge, you just pour it in. Education, especially at higher levels, is really about, "How do you think? What are the sorts of questions you're being taught to ask? What's the critique you're being taught to apply?" because we're thinking people, sentient beings. So it matters who's teaching you how to do that thinking and teaching you how to do that analysis. It matters.'

As with other professions, there remain barriers to progression within the university workforce for black academics. In the Runnymede report,[46] minority staff reported having little access to 'academic gatekeepers' and feeling locked out of the networks that would be able to provide them with the means to further their professional development – support networks they described as 'vital'. BAME academics and university staff remain 'outsiders' in higher education, and their place of work remains the preserve of those who are white, middle class and predominantly male, among the senior staff.

Stereotypes can plague university staff, too. Some academics noted that because of their race, it was not only assumed by their white peers that they were interested in or working on the topic of race and racism, but they were also expected by their colleagues to take on roles that were related to diversity and equality issues, simply because they were not white. Respondents said racism affected all aspects of their working lives, 'whether this was related to how they were treated by their white colleagues or students, the roles they were asked to perform or how they were judged in the academy'.[47] Alongside this, several spoke of a typically British kind of racism: passive aggressive and subtle, and difficult to provide evidence for. This leaves them reluctant to report inappropriate incidents to line managers because they are 'hard to prove'. For those who did bite the bullet and report it, they said their complaint was rarely taken seriously.

'The attitudes haven't changed,' Heidi Mirza says. 'And in higher education we have not actually done much in our training of lecturers, teachers, to improve it, for it to filter down into the system.

You just meet hardcore racist views. Now, we've got a culture of denial, so all you have to say is "I'm not racist!" – people will declare that. And, "Oh yes, I told them to become a hairdresser, it's not because I'm racist, it's because I care!" And so if you just declare yourself non-racist, you become non-racist. We call it performativity. You perform it. You hear people say the most horrible things – sexist, racist things – and they go, "Well, no I'm not racist, I'm just telling you like it is."'

Ethnic minority students who decide to take up roles within the student body also often encounter racism, and find themselves not only under scrutiny from other students, but also from the wider public. In 2017, Jason Okundaye, a student at Cambridge who headed the university's Black and Minority Ethnic Society, was targeted by mainstream right-wing press outlets for his tweets addressing institutional racism. A selection of those tweets were re-posted out of context, and the racist backlash went on for several days.

Esme Allman, who was elected to the position of the Black and Minority Ethnic Convenor at Edinburgh University, encountered a similar pattern of behaviour. A fellow student had commented on a Facebook post under the news of a US strike against ISIS; 'I'm glad we could bring these barbarians a step closer to collecting their 72 virgins.' It was reported that as a result of a complaint lodged by Allman about the post, the university began investigating the student in question. This caused uproar in the press. In fact, the University of Edinburgh confirmed that the student was actually being investigated for a breach of the student code of conduct rather than for mocking a terrorist group – Allman hadn't even mentioned ISIS in the transcript of her complaint. The university's overall handling of Allman's complaint and the subsequent media attention left much to be desired – they told her not to talk to journalists who had reached out to her, and, once the situation got out of hand as the story snowballed and online trolling from racists began, they simply assured her it would blow over.

For white students to make the news, they have to be actively racist and aggressive – black face, the N-word, the whole shebang

– before mainstream outlets show an interest. And when these students are written about, they often have readers springing to their defence decrying what they see as a witch hunt for 'a kid who doesn't know any better'. When was the last time you saw a white student make headlines for writing a string of tweets? And when was the last time you saw a black student extended the benefit of the doubt?

Each one, teach one

Until recently, not a single institution in the country offered a degree programme in Black British Studies. But in 2016 the first UK undergraduate Black Studies degree course was launched at Birmingham City University.[48] Given the vast number of degrees on offer in the UK, many of them very niche, it is a surprise that before then, no university had felt the need to offer a course exploring the history, experiences and background of a demographic that has been so key in shaping our country. With the black population in Britain being established more recently, we are a good 50-odd years behind our American counterparts, who began rolling out Black Studies courses in 1968, after their more diverse student body demanded that their history and experiences should be included in a curriculum that they too were learning from. Black Studies is now an integral part of US higher education, albeit only after several protests, boycotts and student occupations across the country.

But this isn't to say the black community does not make it onto the UK curriculum. Indeed, we often have our experiences explained to us from a far more anthropological standpoint, and find ourselves being the objects of detailed academic scrutiny by academics. In courses such as Politics, Sociology, Psychology and History, the black British experience is often analysed and examined, but it is usually from a distance and – considering the makeup of the teaching staff in most UK unis – usually by white academics. As William Ackah, a lecturer at Birkbeck, explained in an article: 'Black people are used to illustrate problems as diverse as educational underachievement, health inequality, and religious extremism.'[49]

The complex, diverse and nuanced stories of the black British population are sidelined by a narrative that only further adds to already existing narratives – backed up by research and through findings from the country's brightest minds. While white academics backpat each other for their commitment to inclusion, black students remain alienated, only seeing themselves reflected in their curriculum when it is part of a course on crime. This dearth of diversity within academic studies led to the creation of the 'Why is My Curriculum White?' campaign founded at University College London in 2014 as a response to the lack of diversity found on university reading lists and course content. Over the past four years, the campaign has continued to challenge the existing discourse, and it has since spread onto several campuses. This also prompted a public talk at UCL in 2014, led by Dr Nathaniel Adam Tobias Coleman and titled 'Why isn't my professor black?', seeking an answer to that very question.

Coleman is one of a handful of black philosophy lecturers in the UK. He claims to have been rejected for a full-time job at UCL because his proposed 'Critical White Studies' course did not find favour with colleagues wanting to offer a Black Studies programme that was less critical of the white establishment. Much of Coleman's work focused on university curricula being too white and excluding the writings of ethnic scholars in favour of 'dead white men'. After his fixed-term contract at UCL ended, he was informed there was no job for him (such precarious positions are more likely to be filled by those who are young, female and from black or ethnic minority groups, as opposed to them being offered permanent roles; for example, 83 per cent of white staff in higher education in 2012–2013 held permanent contracts compared to 74 per cent of BAME staff).[50] This was despite what he believed was an outstanding record in teaching and having been awarded Online Communicator of the Year by the university earlier in the year. His application to become a permanent member of staff was rejected, as it would require the creation of a new Black Studies MA, which was deemed unviable. Jonathan Wolff,

Executive Dean of UCL's Faculty of Arts and Humanities, said that the proposed MA was rejected because 'it became apparent that UCL [was] not yet ready to offer a strong programme in this area'.

But despite the lack of Black Studies courses in UK universities, whatever your degree, as a student, just being at university gives you access to a huge range of broad and engaging texts and resources. Despite my studying law, it was when I chose modules on race and feminism outside of my core curriculum that I fully engaged with learning during my final year, which essentially shaped the views that I have now. Afua did the same, and she speaks of the opportunities that were on offer to – to some degree – create your own curriculum:

'I started taking African papers and studying postcolonialism and engaging with subjects that were manifesting in my experience, and which gave me access to black professors and black writers and academics and thinkers, and so I had this intellectual community in my head as well.

'There is a lot of flexibility at Oxford. I was doing PPE; you can choose. There's such a range of options and I consistently chose options about decolonisation and political theories of equality and race and feminist theories and African studies. So those were the academics who gave me access, and the subjects that I was immersed in, and I think that helped. It helped me reconcile why I was in this place.'

The US is ahead of us in terms of curriculum, and Historically Black Colleges and Universities (HBCUs) provide a tailored educational space for black students that may well help in terms of engagement as well as attainment. Even US universities comparable to Oxbridge, such as Harvard, are much more forward-thinking than those in the UK in terms of diversity within the student body. The Harvard University incoming class of 2017 was reportedly the most diverse in its 380-year history – over half of the 2,056 students were non-white. But Professor Emejulu also believes that the US can learn a great deal from the UK.

'Historically Black Colleges and Universities are a solution in some ways but they were set up in the beginning to serve a so-called "talented tenth per cent". Those that were closest to whiteness, to be honest, to be quite frank. That history has been somewhat mitigated, but that still is a huge part, an underlying part of HBCUs. But they serve an important function. I think it's important not to valorise them completely. That's not to say that the existence of those institutions isn't important; being pioneers in Black Studies is absolutely crucial, but I guess, I always feel like, I don't know how much, in terms of the black diaspora, how helpful it is to always be looking to the United States. There were things that were in place here in Britain that have been dismantled that I think have been far more helpful, if we're looking at this from a black student's perspective.

'First, there's the issue of the maintenance grant. That in and of itself is essential for encouraging people into further and higher education. So I think that personally that has been far more consequential in terms of undermining people's access to further and higher education. The institution of fees? That's kind of the story that often doesn't get told about the American context, so even though there are fees here of £9,000, back when I was an undergraduate in the US, my tuition was $25,000 a year – plus housing and everything else, it was something closer to $30,000 a year. And so, you know, HBCUs are no different from that; they have to charge as well. Also in terms of what can be learned, I actually think, the lesson doesn't come from the US so much, it comes from South Africa and the movement for decolonisation. I think that has been something that is incredibly consequential in terms of thinking about dismantling the structures that we've been talking about; you know, those structural inequalities in terms of the pipeline from school to higher education, the dismantling of ideas of who gets to be a knowing agent, dismantling the idea that only some knowledge counts. Particularly, the knowledge of black women is somehow less valuable and less important. So these movements of decolonisation that began in South Africa have now spread across Europe and North America. For me, those are important models. In fact, the issue here in Britain was that there *were* key models that helped students in further and higher education that have now been dismantled, and so the thing is, how do we return to that? How do we take back control in that way?'

'Told 'em I finished school and I started my own business / They say, "Oh you graduated?" / No, I decided I was finished.'
Kanye West, School Spirit

Education is hugely valuable, and getting a place at university is a massive achievement. But too many ethnic minority students choose to apply because they feel they have to, or because they believe that if they don't, they will have in some way failed. This means that many end up on campuses they aren't quite suited to, studying subjects for the sake of it, unable to make university work for them. One of the biggest takeaways from this chapter should be that doing your research is crucial – not simply so that you learn what your potential uni can offer in the way of courses and facilities, but also that you know what its vibe and culture is. This way you will find out off the bat if it's somewhere that would suit you, or somewhere you can at least get the most out of. You should explore all your options: in terms of the choice of degrees on offer, the establishments themselves, when you should go, and indeed whether you have to go at all, as that, too, is of course an option. Increasingly, not all vocations require you to have continued into higher education, or at least not full-time. If she had known what she knows now about how her career has turned out, Alexis believes she would have taken a different route:

'I personally would've taken another year out. I would've tried to find myself, because when you come out of college, you still don't actually know what you want to do with your life, you're still quite young, you're 18. Coming from an African background, there is a lot of pressure to go on to university as soon as you come out of college.

'I would've done more work experience in that gap year and

explored my options and seen what I really wanted to do, then decided to go to university and kill it. I'm back in university now, I went back to do a masters, I'm doing it in business, which makes sense, and I'm excelling. I got a first in my first semester and I never thought that I could ever achieve a first-class – I've never ever got an A in my life! It showed me that there's too much pressure on students to go to university, get a load of debt for a course they have no interest in or that they might change their minds about later on in life. I didn't know what I wanted to do. It wasn't until my mid-twenties that I realised what I was really passionate about, and it makes sense that I'm excelling in it because it's what I want to do. I feel like people should just take their time, they shouldn't feel pressured by society or their parents, even though it's hard. Take your time and really explore what it is you really want to do. A lot of the time, you leave university after college and you still can't get a job anyway because they tell you that you don't have experience.

'University is always going to be there, it doesn't have to be done when you're 18 and fresh out of college, when you have no idea what life is. The world has told you, you go to college and then you go to university and then you get a lot of debt – at least get into debt for something that you're going to use!'

Sharmaine Lovegrove, publisher at the Little, Brown imprint, Dialogue Books, didn't go to university until she was 21, when she attended UCL to study Politics and Anthropology. Before then she had wanted to be a documentary filmmaker and had decided the best way of going about it was to get some work experience first, by working with production companies and becoming a runner. She had chosen her degree specifically, after three years *out of* education, and while she didn't end up taking the career path she had initially thought she wanted, her course led her right back to her first love: books.

'If I were doing it now, I would look at universities and colleges that offered part-time degrees to get the qualification,' Sharmaine says. 'More and more places are doing online degrees, and I would have done that in the evenings and at the weekends and then worked during the day. I just think that, you're paying so much money now, and most people I know, when I talk to them about coming out of university, they actually don't know what they want to do. I think higher education shouldn't be about buying more time until you work it out, it should be about actually attaining: in Germany, you only go to university if you're going to then do the job [which requires that specific degree], and your degree [trains you directly for] the job. Whereas here, you can go to university and study almost anything and then do something completely different. Idris Elba said that we as black people need to work ten times harder and we know that, so I always think, if you have something that stands out on your CV, people are going to raise an eyebrow and consider you over others if you take the same course as your white peers.'

> '**The minute black kids sit together in a cafeteria, white folks cry self-segregation. Never mind that white people have always sat together and always will.**'
> *Dear White People*

While uni goes some way towards preparing you for the real world and a number of the hurdles you may come across there, it is still very much *not* reality. My university was nicknamed 'the bubble' and it had a campus magazine of the same name. I spent the vast majority of my time at university on campus making memories and mates, but as I will talk about later in 'Black Girls Don't Cry', it was also quite an overwhelming time for me, as is it for many students. And like many students, especially black female students, I suffered in silence, hesitant to alert my faculty to 'mitigating circumstances' for fear of how I'd be viewed. When I eventually made the decision to take a year out, a bit of space and objectivity really helped me appreciate just how much I enjoyed university and how much I missed it. But it doesn't have to be that drastic – you'd be surprised what a drink with your friends back home or just some home cooking every few weeks can do for the soul. Getting off campus and getting out a bit more is often a much-welcomed and much-needed break, as Afua advises:

'I think, you need to get away, if only for your sanity, because there's a bubble. It's not the real world, a lot of people you encounter would never have met a black person in real life before and so you're on the front line of that experience of having to explain yourself or your hair texture and all these things. I have never lost the heightened appreciation I have for London having been in Oxford, because just the fact that I'm fairly anonymous is such a relief that I still value. I think I was impressed by the new generation of students who feel able, collectively, to own things, name them, call them out, and I think that the fact that they're a network helps them, so I think that's really important.

'I found doing mentoring work and helping other students really helpful because it gave me a sense of purpose. Even though I felt very ambivalent about being there, when I saw younger people coming through, it made me think, do I want it to be the same for them? Would I be happy with the conclusion that they don't belong here? And that would make me say no, we have every right to be here, so whatever I can do to normalise it, it's my duty. So, I think that sometimes it's good to step outside of your own self, your own sense of suffering and your own preoccupation of what you're going to do, and think about the bigger picture. You're not just there for yourself, you're there to try and stop other people from going through the same thing and I found that really helpful to pack into a sense of purpose.'

For many, the chance to make new friends is as much of a draw as the academic opportunities offered by university. Finding your tribe will not only help you to settle but it could also make the time you spend there more enjoyable. You might discover your friends on your course, in your halls and on general drunken university toilet run-ins. But if you find yourself feeling isolated culturally, there are increasing numbers of societies focused on identity – for example, my university had an African and Caribbean society, a Nigerian society and 'This Is Africa' – all of which held events that I attended with differing levels of enjoyment.

ACS and similar societies don't always work for everyone, and some students struggle to find their place at university at all. For others, the idea of trying to find your tribe at uni is not a priority. But if that's your choice, it's still important that you have a group of friends to turn to, even if it's off campus, to ensure you don't become socially isolated. Some students choose to hang out with other students from local, more diverse universities, as well as locals who aren't students. Others have friends from before university who they keep in touch with, or they travel back home often. You can choose to immerse yourself in campus life or to build or maintain a network outside of it – just make sure what you do works for you, and you don't underestimate the importance of support networks during your time spent there.

'I did make friends with other black people, and we sought each other out from other colleges and then we'd meet up and do stuff together,' Afua tells us. 'I felt like it created a bit of hostility with some of my college friends. They just couldn't understand why I had to have friends outside of the college, even though it was quite obvious that we were all black, and so, there was just this awkwardness because they didn't want to say, "Why are you hanging out with these black people?" They were like, "Why are you always doing stuff with other people?" I didn't want to explain to them why I had a need to create a social group of black peers, so, it was just that awkwardness.

'Having other friends – and they don't have to be black friends – obviously I had white friends from all backgrounds. When I look at the people I'm still friends with, they're not all people of colour, [but] what they all have in common is a slight sense of outsider-ness. So, whether it's because of their class background or their religious heritage or whatever . . . just [those] that have not come from what they felt was like, the conventional background and having gone through those same types of questions. So, they're not exclusive to race, I think obviously if you've got that visible difference, it's heightened because it constantly manifests in all your interactions. So, surround yourself with people who can relate to you for whatever reason, or who you can relate to and who are supportive.'

Alexis also speaks about the importance of her friendships at university – many of which have continued several years later:

'I didn't find it difficult socialising at all. I think the best thing I learnt about Roehampton was my social experience; it being an independent space from home, paying my own bills, just being an adult and starting to live an adult life and living myself. Even in the first year, I didn't live on campus, I lived with two guys in a house and everyone was like, "Aren't you scared to live with two guys?" And I was like, "No," and I thank God because the two guys, they were like my brothers. They literally were like brothers to me, it was a blessing . . . they looked after me and I looked after them. It was a really good experience, I met some really good people out there and most of the people I met are coming to my wedding; we kept our friendships.'

....

'The future's so bright, I gotta wear shades.'
Timbuk 3, The Future's So Bright

....

The long and short of it is that everyone's university experience will be different. Some people will end up going exactly where they wanted to go and then realise it's not what they had expected; others will go to their backup choice and find that it's the best thing that ever happened to them. The most important thing is to arm yourself with knowledge: before you make any life-changing decisions, make sure they are informed ones. That information may lead you to take a completely different route in itself: university is full of opportunity, but so is the world.

'To sum it up, don't think of higher education as simply the next step after A-levels, think of higher education as a pathway into a career,' says Sharmaine.

'When you think about higher education as the pathway to your career, you think about it in terms of its practicality. When you are at university, if you do decide to go to university straight away, then make sure that there is a lot of time in between writing essays; in your second year, make sure that you are getting those placements. Don't leave it to the university to do everything for you, actually think about it practically: what is it that I have to do to be better? Listen to your friends and then just think of ways that you can try to do things a little bit differently to stand out. Don't be afraid to not follow the crowd, but do it in your own, subtle, private way. Don't let people second-guess you, be like, "This is what I want to do," and go and speak to people in the industries and write to people and ask them to mentor you or ask people who do that job. Find the experts.

'My second thing is, *be* an expert. Be brilliant and bold and brave and know your industry inside out; know how it works and know the history and the culture, and just know it and breathe it and live it. I think that's just so important, when you get to university, it's not just about passing exams, it's actually about learning. Really learning a skill or a trade or having an understanding of a topic or a subject, and so really take it on board. See it as an opportunity to have the time. It is all part of the process. I think what's really important is that studying law or medicine to make your parents proud is a very different thing to *actually* studying it.'

Despite all the fuckeries and tomfoolery, university is still a brilliant place, where those who are lucky enough to go can find themselves, and so much more: lifelong friends, political views, endless knowledge and sometimes even a long-term partner. While there is still a long way to go in terms of diversity and inclusion, an increasingly self-assured and unapologetic student population is continuing to right wrongs at an unprecedented rate. I mentioned to a current Warwick student that there had been a slave auction during my time at uni and she told me 'they wouldn't dare' host one these days – let alone a *Django*-themed one. I only attended four years before her. And as Alexis mentioned, the newfound freedom is particularly wonderful, for all students, sure, but more often specifically for black freshers who are sometimes still under a form of curfew for way longer than their white peers. The transition from having to barter and bargain with parents regarding nights out to simply going out whenever you please is just one of the many priceless things about uni, and in itself it is almost worth all the deadlines and all-nighters.

A culture shock can be just that – shocking – but it can also give you the opportunity to meet people and have experiences you would never have had otherwise. Like most things in life, it's important to enter university aware, but also optimistic, as your future (as well as the future of these institutions) is set to get a great deal brighter.

WORK

'We don't need to get over a bar of excellence
we didn't create. Instead we have to create our
own lane and our own version of success,
our own version of good.'

Elizabeth

....

'We were bad, with very little of the boujee.'

Yomi

Work Twice as Hard to Get Half as Good

ELIZABETH

'I'm not just black, I'm a woman, so there
are two glass ceilings I have to break every
time I open my mouth. But if I wake up in the
morning and think, "Oh my God, I got two
ceilings I've got to smash today,"
that's no way to live.'[1]
Destiny Ekaragha

'Did the student who the teacher gave an A have two heads?' my
dad asked disappointedly as we were driving back from my Year 8
parents' evening. Growing up in a Nigerian household, I was accustomed to these rhetorical questions. This particular one was further
evidence that, one, my dad could exaggerate for England; and two,
yet again I had fallen short of meeting his expectations when it came
to my grades.

'You have to be twice as good as them' was something that was
implied in everything I did or – according to my dad – couldn't do.
As discussed earlier in the chapter 'Lawyer, Doctor, Engineer', the
importance of excelling at school knew no bounds. You could get 98
per cent in an exam and your parents would ask, 'What happened
to the other 2 per cent?' You would then get 100 per cent in the next
exam and you'd be asked why you weren't studying law like your
cousin; and eventually you would apply to university and they'd want
to know why you didn't apply to Oxford, as Warwick was good, but it
wasn't quite *the* most prestigious. Lessons on racism were intrinsic-
ally linked to work ethic. You work hard, you get good grades, so you
don't give *them* an excuse to treat you any differently.

Alongside feeling irritated and thinking they were overreacting half the time, I had some sympathy for my parents' attitude. They knew I would be judged more harshly than my white friends on certain occasions and that, whether I wanted to be a lawyer or run my own business, meeting the minimum standard would, at times, just not be enough. When former First Lady Michelle Obama gave her version of the 'Twice as good' speech in 2015 to Tuskegee University, a historically black university, she said a version of the thing all black parents say to remind you that life will be more difficult for you than for your white friends: 'The road ahead is not going to be easy. It never is, especially for folks like you and me. Because while we've come so far, the truth is that those age-old problems are stubborn and they haven't fully gone away . . . So there will be times when you feel like folks look right past you, or they see just a fraction of who you really are.'[2]

Unfortunately, those old-age problems *haven't* gone away, and discrimination rears its ugly head, both before we enter the workplace and then while we make strides to progress within it. It can often leave us feeling that we have to work twice as hard only to get half as good back. This can make for a tough existence as a black woman. When you enter white spaces you find yourself trying to figure out: will this qualification be enough? Will my South London twang give me away? Or are they simply plain old racists and I'll never get my just rewards no matter how 'twice as good' I am?

....

'Luck has nothing to do with it, because I have spent many, many hours, countless hours, on the court working for my one moment in time, not knowing when it would come.'
Serena Williams

....

I can't remember how many times in my career I have sat in meetings in which I am the only black woman or person of colour in the room. Yet without fail I've been surrounded by four Jamies or three

Chrises, all of whom are, of course, white men. I have no grievance with these particular names, but I've noticed how they tend to be over-represented in every place I've worked, whereas finding a black woman is like trying to find a black girl on TV's *Love Island*. And *that's* what I have a problem with. Where *are* we? In those meetings I find myself thinking, again and again, 'Why do I continue to be the only black girl in marketing in this office?' As Yomi pointed out in the previous chapter, we are proportionately the largest group of graduates in the UK, but we remain the most unemployed.

It's clear that Britain is a long way from being a level playing field of opportunity for all. Even after you've achieved the right grades in school, and you've gone above and beyond at extra-curricular activities, when it comes to the transition from education to employment something goes awry. In 2016 the Social Mobility Commission revealed that black and Asian children are less likely to get professional jobs, despite doing better than their white working-class counterparts at school.[3]

I always assumed that going above and beyond, and striving always to be exceptional, would be enough. I didn't think I had the privilege of just being 'okay': mediocrity wouldn't do. This resulted in an irrational fear of being left behind, the same fear that led me to try to get a job when I was 16, convinced that I was never going to get my GCSEs. You know the fear that wakes you up at 3am in the morning? You think it might just be pangs of hunger but it's actually a fear of failure that intensifies when exams loom, or on the night before a job interview.

An unintended consequence of my 'twice as good' mindset has been that slowly but surely over the years I have turned into an insufferable go-getter. Even though I didn't always have the right support in school, I knew I wanted to do well, so once I decided to commit to something, I was unstoppable, and I would always try to give myself a competitive edge in everything I did. So when most kids went to school only on weekdays, I attended Saturday school, too. When my friends had their lunch breaks, I assisted with the school's fairtrade stall, and when I had my first internship I was the first to put myself forward for the position of chairwoman of the corporate social-responsibility committee.

It instilled a work ethic in me that meant I never wanted to take anything for granted. Friends from Warwick tell me they suffered from the same overachieving addiction: from volunteering to be playground prefects to taking Duke of Edinburgh Awards, to attending after-school debating clubs. By the time they were teenagers they had assembled an impressive roster of extra-curricular activities. It is now more apparent to me than ever that we didn't just *end up* where we are out of luck: it is the result of a concerted effort over time. Some of us had challenges at school that we had to climb above, navigating the high expectations of our parents and sometimes the low expectations of our teachers.

ITV's Charlene White became the first black woman to present *News at Ten* in 2016: a seat predominantly occupied by white men since the show's inception in 1967. Despite, understandably, viewing it as a burden, the journalist and news anchorwoman credits having to work 'twice as hard' throughout her 20-year career in the industry as the reason she is where she is today.

'Well, I was always raised – as I'm sure everybody else that you've spoken to has been – to work twice as hard as your neighbour. So at school I had to work twice as hard as the kid next to me, I had to do the same thing when I was at university, and I've done the same thing within my working life. I don't know how to do any different, to be honest. So within my first few years of working, I did work placements from the age of 16 – not that anybody told me to do it. At 15, 16, I sent out 50 letters, because email wasn't a thing then, 50 letters to try to get work experience. I got the *Guardian* newspaper, and that sort of changed everything, because as a result of being able to get in there for a summer, it then became that much easier to get work placements elsewhere. Then when I was working at the BBC, I was working across six different networks at the BBC, so Radio 1 and 1Xtra as a staff member, but then freelancing having my own show on BBC London. I was presenting the 60 seconds news on BBC Three and I was presenting the entertainment news on the BBC News channel. I was presenting bulletins on 5 Live, and I was presenting the early morning half-hour news before *Wake Up to Money* on 5 Live as well – I was just essentially working seven days a week with double and triple shifts.

'I know for a fact that there's absolutely no way in the world that I'd have got to where I am now, at this age, had I not done all of those things. And yes, there'll be lots of people who haven't had to do any of that stuff, at all, and yes, that does annoy me. I hope that when I have kids and they're in the working environment, they don't have to go over quite so many different hurdles. I had no one in my family who worked in telly. And when you're working alongside people who, literally, it was their dad who insisted that their best mate give them a placement in a TV studio, and that's how they ended up working in telly, and it's like – do you know how hard I had to work in order to be able to get here? I didn't have that luxury. And it's also the understanding, and I don't think people always understand it, so I actually sat down with a friend of mine and tried to explain it to him, because he was like, "Yes, but just because, you know, I had a parent who worked in telly, yes, that was an introduction, but I have worked really hard in my career in order to be able to get to where I am," and I said, but what you don't understand is how hard it is to just walk through the door of a newspaper, or of a TV studio, or a news studio, when you know no one. That is the hard bit. So when you're able to do that, then I'm afraid we haven't come from the same part, or same perspective, or the same situation in any shape or form.'

A rose by any other name may leave you unemployed

Some may not accept this 'twice as good' notion as fact, but the statistics speak for themselves. You've probably heard the following: men apply for a job when they meet only 60 per cent of the qualifications, but women only apply if they meet 100 per cent of them.

As an ethnic minority, even when you do meet 100 per cent of the job description, you worry that it might not be enough and that you will still face discrimination. In 2012, an All-Party Parliamentary Groups report warned that ethnic minority women are discriminated against at 'every stage' of the recruitment process.[4] The report revealed discrimination against names and accents, which made it much harder for ethnic minority women to get responses to applications. Interestingly, some found markedly better results when they changed their names to 'disguise their ethnicity'.[5] People with 'white English' names were 74 per cent more likely to get called for an interview following a job application than candidates with an ethnic minority name, despite the two candidates having exactly the same qualifications.[6]

During a speech in 2015, the then Prime Minister David Cameron appeared shocked by a practice that is a shrug-worthy reality for most minorities. 'Do you know that in our country today,' he gasped, 'even if they have exactly the same qualifications, people with white-sounding names are nearly twice more likely to get callbacks for jobs than people with ethnic-sounding names?' Well, yes. We do.

'One young black girl had to change her name to Elizabeth before she got any calls to interviews. That, in twenty-first-century Britain, is disgraceful,' he continued.

Disgraceful indeed. Surprising? Not in the slightest. The young black girl Cameron referred to wasn't me, but it might as well have been. Trying twice as hard on my job applications is something I've become accustomed to. When I first graduated there was one particular marketing job at an ultra-posh investment management firm in Mayfair that I really wanted. Even though I was confident about my credentials and I felt I met the criteria, I knew it might not be enough. Before I clicked submit on my application I took one last look at their website. I went on the 'management team' section and saw a sea of white, mainly male faces staring back at me. This tipped me over the edge. These days you expect most companies to hide their lack of diversity and wheel out at least one person of colour, but this company were so unapologetically white. I read over my CV again and saw that I had proudly mentioned I was a 'Google Top Black Talent mentee' in 2012, a programme Google ran as part of their diversity initiatives. I looked back at the website, and then I did the unthinkable: I removed the 'Black' from 'Google Top Black Talent', so it read; 'Google Top Talent'. It's embarrassing now to think I did that, but I was so aware of my blackness and my femaleness and the sharp contrast between me and the management team that I felt I had to do what I could in order to secure an interview. Secure an interview I did.

My experience isn't unique; I have friends who have admitted to using their English names rather than their Nigerian names on applications, in order to get them past the first pitfalls of recruitment. Such is the insidious nature of the discrimination we encounter that even when black women exit the labour market and opt to set up their own businesses, we still have to get through arduous obstacles before we can emerge on the same playing field as our white counterparts. Dr Clare Anyiam-Osigwe BEM, a multi-award-winning entrepreneur who started her skincare brand, Premae, at the age of 26, resorted to creating an alter ego when she was trying to get her business off the ground:

'I've got my white alias, which is Nina Fredricks, and Nina is my alter ego – she gets me all the jobs, and all the gigs, and all the sales that I can't get. Being on LinkedIn I discovered that there's a little bit of a cartel. I would reach out to people – shopping channels. For instance, I'll give you this story, I was trying to get Premae onto shopping channels, I was inviting people to connect with me – they wouldn't connect. So I just went to page 100 on Google, found a white chick with blonde hair, ripped off a picture, created a fake profile that she'd only had two jobs, one of them was an unknown company and one of them was me – working at Premae as a wholesale manager – and her name was Nina Fredricks. And I got Nina to write to them. Within minutes they had accepted the friendship, "Yeah, Premae sounds amazing, we'd love to have you come on our show, let's arrange a buying meeting next week." So the day before the meeting comes, "Sorry, I'm not going to be able to come, but I'll send Clare, she's the founder, she knows everything." "Oh, no, no, no, let's postpone." "No, no, no, you don't understand, I'm going to be in Paris for three months launching Premae, so you need to see Clare." "Okay, okay."

'I go in there, I'm nervous, naturally, because I'm thinking, "There's so much resistance, what have I done to you lot? Why are you doing this to me? Why have I even had to create Nina? What is this all about?" I go there, and I think they just either forgot, or were just so ignorant, didn't care, but they were just like, "So . . . How long have you been working for the company?" and I was like, "Wow . . ." I remember I just leaned back and I said, "Well, I started baking these balms on my kitchen stove in Islington, North London, so I guess the beginning?" and they were like, faces flushed, going red, "Oh my God, I'm so sorry, you're Clare, Clare the founder . . . Right . . ." and then it becomes defensive: "So, where did you study? What do you know about beauty? Why are you here? How did you know this? How did YOU create the world's first anything? What makes you special?" – And I just said, you know, "I'm an allergy sufferer, it's my basic formulations," and at that point we'd gone out to over 200,000 homes through Glossybox and Birchbox, so we had got all these beautiful testimonials. "Hence the reason you want to see us, right? Because you've seen the brand. That's my work, that's what I do." So one of the buyers has a brother with eczema, so she said, "Well, you know, my brother could really do with this product, I think the UK needs to see this product. So I'm really in," and [she] was sort of looking at the other woman like, "We're in, aren't we?" and she was just like, "Still trying to process!" What? Because we could probably be the same age and she's looking at me thinking, "I've just got a desk job and here you are, an entrepreneur, creating a whole establishment, and I just can't, my brain won't allow me to accept that as real."'

Alter egos can be fun to create, the operative word being fun – just look at Beyoncé's Sasha Fierce, she kills it every time she hits the stage. However, they shouldn't be born out of frustration because of the blatant discrimination that black women come across when they try to progress in their careers.

Reviewing applications without the details of name and gender would be a positive step in broadening opportunities for people of ethnic minority backgrounds. But while David Cameron was able to persuade some companies – including the NHS, Deloitte, the BBC and the civil service – to allow job applicants to hide their names, only a handful of universities agreed to assess 2017 entry applications with the names of students blanked out. His plan for all university applications to be name-blind from 2017 was rejected by all the other academic institutions in the UK (see 'Black Faces in White Spaces').

....

**'The only thing that separates women
of colour from anyone else, is opportunity.'**
Viola Davis

....

One of the most common explanations for the gender gap in leadership positions is the notion that women aren't as ambitious as men. So despite the three waves of feminism, apparently the *real* reason why FTSE 100 companies are run by white men is that women don't have the same aspirations. Hilarious, right? Let's debunk that myth: black women want to succeed in their careers and they don't lack the ambition to do so. In fact, according to a report by an American-based think-tank,[7] while just 8 per cent of white American women aspire to a powerful position at work, 22 per cent of black American women (a similar percentage to that of white men) aspire to a powerful role and are significantly more ambitious. The study's authors found that 'Black women are more likely than white women to perceive a powerful position as the means to achieving their professional goals and are confident that they can succeed in the role.' Though there are no identical studies in the UK focusing solely on black women, and while our experiences vary somewhat over here, anecdotal evidence, as well as the 2015 Race at Work Report, suggests we have very similar attitudes towards our careers. It found that in the UK, black people in the workplace have greater ambition than their white colleagues: ambition to progress in their careers was at 72 per cent, in comparison to 41 per cent of white employees.[8] However, black people were also the most likely to report feeling stagnated in their careers and to say that their career has 'failed to meet their expectations'.[9] It's not hard to see why. The fact that black graduates are, on average, paid £4.30 an hour less than white graduates might also have something to do with this.

After President Trump beat Hillary Clinton to the US Presidency, I remember reading a tweet that said, 'For the first time in history, Hillary Clinton knows what it feels like to be a black woman. You can have 30 years' experience on a job you are over-qualified for and yet they still pick a white MAN with NO job experience over you.' Isn't that the truth?

It is safe to say then that it is not a lack of ambition, or their attitude, that holds back black women in the workplace. So what is the barrier that thwarts their ambition to a point where they feel less valued and inspired after only a few years at work? The concrete ceiling, that's what.

Whereas white women experience career anxiety about the glass ceiling – the informal yet impermeable barriers that keep women from getting promotions or moving on to the next stage of their careers – for black women this ceiling can sometimes feel like it's made of concrete. While glass may be tough, at least you can smash it. If you've ever dropped your iPhone you can relate to the painful sound of glass shattering against the concrete floor. However, the concrete ceiling faced by black women is even tougher to break down, and practically impossible to break through by yourself.

With glass, you can see through it to the level above and you know that there is something there to aspire to. If you can see it, you can achieve it, right? Concrete, on the other hand, is impossible to see through. There is no visible destination, just what seems like a dead end. You can't see a black woman partner because, most likely, there isn't one. So it's like looking at nothing – the next level isn't visible.

Just as Malorie Blackman and Dr Maggie Aderin-Pocock spoke of the need for role models for school children to aspire to, so this need continues into the workplace.

Don't get me wrong. There isn't *always* a concrete ceiling. There are some black women in leadership roles who have brilliantly navigated the complexities of being both black and a woman in the workplace. Look at the sheer number of black women we have interviewed who have not only smashed the glass – and concrete – ceilings but who now dominate in their fields. But for many of us, when we first enter a workplace we often discover unwritten rules for getting ahead that we struggle to understand, let alone follow, and therefore, unlike our white male or female counterparts, we can't hit the ground running, even with all the enthusiasm and ambition in the world. We often find ourselves shut out of the informal networks that help white men and women find jobs, mentors and sponsors, and through no fault of our own, we then fail to navigate these spaces successfully – which explains the feelings of career stagnation and frustration as evidenced in the Race at Work Report.

But surely the recent attention that has been given to issues of diversity in the workplace is helping to bring down this ceiling? Well, not exactly. Despite all the talk of diversity that has been happening over the last couple of years, it looks like black women have been sidelined yet again. Noticeably, when there is a drive to get women into prominent positions in business, it tends to end up being just one kind of woman. If I had a pound for every time I went to a diversity panel only to find it made up of white men and women talking about how to increase diversity, but really actually only meaning that the door should be widened to let *white* women in, I would be a millionaire.

It can be all too easy to hold up gender as the symbol for diversity in an organisation, and we have centred white women on the diversity agenda in the same way we have centred white working-class boys in the educational attainment debate. But diversity is about much more than just gender, and we shouldn't be amalgamated into the same monolithic talent pool. For far too long, black women's aspirations in the UK have not been part of the conversation. The sooner we realise this the sooner we can have richer conversations about it and work together to come up with practical solutions to the problem.

Research in 2014 revealed that the gap at management level between BAME people and white people is not only disproportionate to their representation but also still widening.[10] It therefore came as a big surprise when the Tesco chairman John Allan warned that white men are becoming 'endangered species' on UK boards: 'For a thousand years, men have got most of these jobs; the pendulum has swung very significantly the other way now and will do for the foreseeable future, I think. If you are a white male – tough – you are an endangered species and you are going to have to work twice as hard.'[11] This, from a white man who sits alongside eight other white men and three white women on Tesco's board . . . It came as no surprise that research in 2017, conducted by the *Guardian* and Operation Black Vote, found that Britain's most powerful elite is 97 per cent white. Proportionally, there should be 136 BAMEs in The 1,000 power list. There are just 36. It gets worse when divided along gender lines, as less than a quarter of those BAME positions of power are occupied by women.[12]

Ultimately, helping black women progress in their careers at the same rate as their white counterparts is both the right thing to do and the profitable thing to do. It could add £2 billion to the UK economy each year, according to a government review.[13] The author of the report, businesswoman Ruby McGregor-Smith, said, 'The time for talk on race in the workplace is over, it's time to act. No one should feel unable to reach the top of any organisation because of their race.' When you feel things aren't fair you are more likely to feel resentful and therefore disengaged at work. Treating all women in the workplace as if we face the same challenges within this diversity agenda is ineffective. Organisations need to take bold and crucial steps to remove the systematic discrimination that has been allowed to run rife.

The invisibility vs. visibility problem:
Now you see me, now you don't

In order to ensure that black women don't regard their careers as concrete dead ends, we need to understand the subtle, and at times concealed, challenges we face upon entering the professional environment: challenges that can stop us from progressing and breaking through the glass (and concrete) ceiling.

Firstly, there is the invisibility/visibility problem. This is two-fold. By virtue of being a double minority you are very visible: you stick out like a unicorn, and this is reinforced by microaggressions that frequently remind you you're the 'other'. But 'being seen' isn't as straightforward as you might think, because with this visibility comes more scrutiny. Dawn Butler explains how the double-edged sword comes into play: 'As black women, you are both visible and invisible. If you ever do anything wrong, people will always see you as the person who did something wrong. You do something right it's like, oh well, what do you expect? And so you are both invisible and visible. You can be invisible, looked over for promotion, and you can be visible when they want to blame you for something.' Simply, if something goes wrong, you become the rule and are judged more harshly, but if you do something well, you're seen as the exception.

In order to progress in your career, you *need* to be visible, to do good work and be seen as leadership material. Yet studies have found that black women are being overlooked and are less likely to be rated in the top two performance-ratings categories, or to be identified as 'high potential' at work, compared to white employees. Black women are at an immediate disadvantage in the workplace, because we do not look or sound like the people who overwhelmingly make up the majority of today's business leaders – white men.[14] I've been incredibly conscious as I progress in my career, of how white and male it is, and increasingly aware that I look nothing like my boss, his boss or his boss. Some might say that doesn't matter, but I'm inclined to say it does.

I remember one occasion at work when I asked a colleague to send me a new picture for our business-banking brochure: the licence on the one we had was running out so it was time to replace it. The current photo was a stock image of a white man in a suit, looking at his iPad, with a backdrop of a glass office – very clichéd, but it gets the message across, right? My brief to him this time was, 'Please send me something a little more diverse than this?' An hour later he sent me an image of another white man, a younger millennial guy this time, wearing business casual wear. Again, I replied, 'Not what I was thinking, are there any more options?' I had made up my mind not to specify, and I was intrigued to see what he would come up with. An hour later, he sent me three images: one of a white man looking powerful in a suit (this time he was giving a presentation), one of a black man in a suit in another glass office and one of a white woman in a suit. I went over to his desk and asked, 'Are these the only stock images available?' By this point he was obviously irritated, but I was standing over his shoulder and I could see lots of stock images of black women he could have chosen, but he hadn't.

According to Valerie Purdie-Vaughns, a psychology professor at Columbia University, the same unconscious bias my colleague demonstrated is at play when the average person thinks of a woman leader: 'the image that comes to their mind is of a white woman – like Sheryl Sandberg. However, If you picture a black leader, you're more likely to think of a black man than a black woman.' She continues, 'Because black women are not seen as typical of the categories "black" or "woman", people's brains fail to include them in both categories. Black women suffer from a "Now you see them, now you don't" effect in the workplace.'[15]

Black women are already leaning in; they want leadership positions but they are being overlooked. When you go to work you just want to do your job to the best of your ability, be appreciated and recognised fairly for it, rather than having to show the world that you're perfect. We shouldn't have to be invisible or visible at the whim of other people's prejudices, but we need to stop fighting that visibility; instead we should try to take advantage of it. 'Putting our heads down', hoping our hard work alone will pay off and 'covering', downplaying what makes us different, as Yomi discusses in the '***Flawless' chapter, won't do much for our career progression.

Dr Maggie Aderin-Pocock says we can turn this visibility into positivity: 'I'm working in a very white-male-dominated arena, I always think, no matter what I do they're going to remember me, because there's only one black female in the room and it's me. So when I'm in meetings I try to be as positive as possible, I try to make an impact, I want my voice to be heard and I want them to remember me for something positive.'

Vanessa Kingori MBE, Publishing Director of British *Vogue*, explains why we should embrace visibility rather than fight it.

'If I'm in a situation where I'm sat around a room, there's no point pretending that I'm less visible; I have to be aware of that and then I have to make good of it. But I think it's such an advantage, because if you think about it, there are many business books written about trying to be noticed, trying to get cut through, trying to get your bosses' attention, trying to whatever. We celebrate that in our work and our output, right? So it's like, "I want to be noticed." We have that in our physicality, rightly or wrongly, there's no point fighting it. It just is what it is, but use it as an advantage. There are lots of people who look the same, who will not get the opportunity you have to have that cut through, so you use that platform.

'Be prepared for that meeting, go there with a few things you're already ready to say, that will challenge opinions and make people think "That's a smart cookie." So it's all about the prep and being present in that room and not shrinking. You can't try to do something that just physically isn't possible. You can't be less black and less female, right? So just make it count. Don't fight something that is a given, I think it's a massive advantage.'

But how do we go about making it count? Performance ratings are key; they are an opportunity to illustrate to your manager what you've achieved that year. Ratings affect promotions and pay rises, so it is important that your manager takes note of you and is exposed to the work you have done throughout the year. But how do we come

across as driven and ambitious without rubbin[...]
way?

Multi-award-winning senior lawyer and di[...]
UK, Funke Abimbola MBE, explains how she be[...]
ent pool and made sure she was identified as h[...]
law firm.

'I went about ensuring that my work was visibl[...]
off way, and you have to be very clear not to be seen as being out for
yourself, either. So, I did it through my team, showcasing what we
are doing as a team, individually and collectively, and that can only
happen if someone is an effective leader. So, the way I showcase the
visibility is: we've got all sorts of internal communication channels
here that want stories about what different teams are doing, we've
got a magazine, we've got a Google community, we've got a weekly
email that goes out, we've got all sorts of channels for communication. So, as a team, we drip-feed positive stories about all aspects of
what we're doing – the announcements don't always come out from
me; individual team members will sometimes put out announcements about others, so quite often others put out announcements
about me winning awards and I do the same for them, to try to avoid
anyone thinking that you're just doing it to promote yourself as an
individual. In many ways, the stories can get out there. It is about
showcasing what you're doing and the impact, communicating that
and really driving that narrative, so that there are so many examples
of what you've done, that when it comes to the end of year, you've
got a long list of examples of what you've done. The evidence is
always overwhelming; really, it's like, here it all is, and this was the
impact.'

However, there may be some instances when you're doing all of
the above, already working twice as hard and trying to take advantage of that visibility, but it isn't reflected in your progressing to the
next level in your career. This can be really frustrating, and it may
then be that it is time to look elsewhere. Dr Anne-Marie Im[...]
MBE agrees, 'If those people don't recognise it[...]
things. That door may be closed; another will be o[...]

knock on those doors, and you might think it's because ...ack, you might think it's because you're young, you might ...it's because you're a woman, but none of that matters; there's door that'll be open for you somewhere else because you are those things, but you have to go and find that door; don't be knocking on a door that's not going to value you.'

Mentoring and sponsoring

On my first day of Year 7, every girl in my year was assigned a 'Big Sister', a girl from one of the older years whose role it was to guide you through your first year at secondary school. I found it reassuring that there was someone who would watch my back, look out for me and tell me how to get by. She showed me that I wasn't alone, and also what a 'good student' looked like in person.

We cannot underestimate the positive impact that having a mentor and sponsor can bring to your career. Studies have shown that ethnic minorities who advance the furthest in their careers all share one asset: a strong network of mentors and sponsors who nurture their professional development.[16] However, there is currently a lack of mentors or sponsors for black women in the workplace, and this often can be a problem when it comes to our development.

I always thought that mentors and sponsors were the same thing, and I would use the words interchangeably, but they aren't, and knowing the difference and taking advantage of it could really make an impact on your career progression. Funke Abimbola explains how it works:

'I call this the triumvirate: sponsorship, mentoring and coaching are the three things that are essential to career progression, and they're all very different. Mentoring is guidance and advice. Sponsoring is someone actively looking for opportunities for you and putting you forward for them. Coaching is actually teaching you the skills: how to influence; how to communicate; how to get by; this is how you should run the meeting and so on. All three have been absolutely essential for my career progression.'

Black women who want to advance in their chosen fields can benefit hugely from the added visibility and support that a sponsor brings to their careers. This is because within every company there are a few people who are part of the decision-making process, who steer the more plummy projects. These are the people who have the access to talk you up behind closed doors and also to defend you against detractors. This matters, in particular, because it is on the more high-profile projects and assignments that you will have your chance to prove yourself to your peers and to this cohort of decision-makers.

If you can find a sponsor who is impressed by you and wants to support you, your chances of promotion and pay rise increase tenfold, as Sandra Kerr OBE explains: 'These processes are often that of advocacy, where senior leaders recommend known individuals for consideration – a form of active sponsorship, whether it is formalised or not. If these conversations do not include either BAME leaders or senior leaders who are being exposed to BAME talent, the diversity of the pipeline is unlikely to change.'[17]

CEO of Stemettes, Dr Anne-Marie Imafidon understands first-hand the benefits of sponsorship: in 2017 she received an MBE, and having a sponsor who advocated on her behalf was essential. Interestingly, to this day she still doesn't know who sponsored her application, but the person in question really understood Anne-Marie's personal brand as a STEM leader.

'I didn't apply for the MBE; you don't nominate yourself for an MBE. Someone else has to do a whole load of work, on your behalf, without you knowing, puts their name on the line, or puts their neck on the line, and says this person needs to get an honour, "Because what they're doing is a lot." That's how honours work. That person didn't mentor me to have an MBE. That person sponsored it.'

How do you get a sponsor? Karen Blackett says it has to come organically: 'I find it weird when people at events, who I've never met before, ask me to be their mentor, because you've got to have some sort of chemistry with the individual and know a bit about them to be able to help. So I think getting a sponsor needs someone you have to have a relationship with first, and I think if black women are finding it difficult to get a sponsor, it's because they haven't worked out their own personal brand to have somebody be able to advocate for them. So once you've worked that out – and it takes time, it takes rewriting and rewriting, sitting there, saying it out loud, writing it down once you write that down to be able to articulate it, you've then got to stress-test it to see what somebody else thinks. Once you're able to do that, I think it's easier to find a sponsor.

'Having cheerleaders is incredibly important – some of the women that you're interviewing are my cheerleaders and I'm theirs, because I think it's really important to have people that are objective, who aren't necessarily in your workplace, who know the real you, the authentic you, who can basically give you a verbal slap when you have those moments, those crises of self-confidence, those moments of lack of self-belief – and we all have them – and you need somebody that's basically going to say "Why not?" and counsel you through it. And drink lots of wine, if need be, when something's gone wrong.

'But you all need someone that's "Team Karen"; everybody needs that. And so I definitely think you need somebody as a sponsor because you need to be in the room, and not just in the room, you need to be at the table. If you're not, you need somebody who is going to talk on your behalf, because that's where your next career move comes from. That means you have to have a personal brand, and that person needs to be able to articulate it. And if they can't, that's why it's difficult to get a sponsor.'

Karen is right; having a sponsor comes more easily once you know what your personal brand is and you're able to articulate it to others. Again, Yomi goes into this in '***Flawless', and it isn't something that necessarily comes easily. For me, it started with building up my confidence and self-belief, and it also meant I had to shut out the voices, inside and out, that would tell me I wasn't good enough and shouldn't be there and that I had to work harder – the voices that had been so loud that summer of my GCSE results. An unintentional consequence of growing up with a 'twice as hard' mindset was constantly experiencing Imposter Syndrome. As I explained in the 'Lawyer, Doctor, Engineer' section, I was raised with mixed messages: with parents who would boast about my achievements to family members in one breath and then criticise me in the other for not getting straight As. As a result I was not able to internalise my achievements properly and would instead attribute my accomplishments to luck, as opposed to the fact that I had worked hard for them. Confidence building is a big thing, and understanding I have a right to be in the room, that I have a contribution to make, I have value to add, has been key in my career development. Don't let Imposter Syndrome stop *you* realising your potential.

Malorie Blackman talks about her experiences of feeling like an imposter: 'I was at the Black Powerlist dinner last year, and I was sitting there, and I was at a table and I had a CEO to the left of me and an Admiral to the right, and I was thinking, "Why am I here?" I was thinking, "Oh my God!" and everyone sitting at the table was the great and the good, and someone else was managing a portfolio of millions and millions, and I'm thinking, "Why am I here?" So I just kind of thought, "No, you've been invited! You have a right to be here just as much as anybody else." But the fact that I was still thinking that, just said to me I still have a way to go, I still suffer from Imposter Syndrome.

'The one person who blocks me most is myself. When people say, "Can you do this?" or, "Could you do that?" and I think, "Oh, I can't do that!" And I look back now and there have been some opportunities where I think, "Oh, you *should* have done that." And it was me thinking, "Oh, I'm not sure that's for me," or, "I can't do that."

'I really don't mind failing because I think I learn a lot from my mistakes and my failures, but for me, the worst thing would be to be on my deathbed and to think, "I wish I had tried and I wish I'd had the guts to try, and it was the fear holding me back and I should never have let it do that." And that would be worse.

'And I think for me as well, it is about appreciating that your comfort zone is very nice, but it's called a comfort zone for a reason, and I think the way you grow is to move outside the comfort zone, and to take risks and so on. And I think it's been instructive to me, especially in my writing career, that the books that have done the best for me are the books I've taken risks on and the books where I've thought, "I'm going to get a kicking for this one!" but I'm going to do it anyway.

'And even if you don't believe in yourself, it's kind of like what they say about "Fake it till you make it." So, fake it until you absolutely believe it and don't have to fake it anymore, because you can do it! And you've proven to yourself that you can do it.

'There are certain times when I'm asked to do stuff and I think, "I don't think that's for me!" you know, but now I kind of think, "Okay, why is it not for you? Is it really not for you, or are you just shying away from something?" And then just go out there and grasp these opportunities, because sometimes it's true: they will only come once.'

A seat at the table

For those of us who do try twice as hard as our neighbours at school, then our colleagues at work, and eventually succeed in breaking through the concrete ceiling, being a trailblazer can bring pressures of its own. Shonda Rhimes, in her book *Year of Yes*, spoke about being the 'First Only Different': taking a seat at the table as the only black woman and the pressure that comes with it. In her decision to cast Kerry Washington in *Scandal* as the ABC network's first lead, black, female character in 37 years, she was aware of the consequences if this move didn't pay off and the show didn't find an audience. How long would it take for another opportunity to come along for another black female director? She said, 'When you are a First Only Different, you are saddled with that burden of extra responsibility – whether you want it or not. I was not about to make a mistake now. You don't get second chances. Not when you're an FOD. Failure meant two generations of female actors might have to wait for another chance to be seen as more than a sidekick.'[18] As black women, we are not strangers to striving for success, but as we go through our careers we realise that getting that promotion and a seat at the table is bigger than our own personal victories, and we begin to fear that there is no room for failure because it runs the risk of *them* not letting in more girls who look like you.

BAFTA award-winning director Amma Asante knows all too well the weight of this responsibility.

'I think the hardest thing is knowing that the world outside, even your own community, doesn't necessarily always have the opportunity to see or know what you go through as that "one and only" with a seat at the table. That seat at the table comes at a price.

'Oftentimes you're invited to the table to sit, but you're being asked to speak in the same voice as those that you're occupying the table with, as opposed to being invited to the table to reflect and represent the voice that is uniquely yours and might in some way represent something of your community.'

Trying twice as hard and smashing the concrete ceiling can often mean you become a role model for others. This can be intentional or unintentional, but being one of the few black female faces in a certain space can bring its own challenges. Karen Blackett, who became the first woman to top the *Powerlist 100* of most influential black Britons, acknowledges this.

'I think there is pressure in being a role model. Of course there is, because any person who is good and has got a good heart wants to pull other people through. So that you're not the first all the time and so that you're not always the pioneer, and to make it easier for other people to get through. But you would hope that if you're sitting at a table, you're sitting there because of what you're good at and what you've achieved, not because of your gender or because of your race, but because you're good at what you've achieved.

'You're there because of something that you can do, which complements everyone else around the table, or what everyone else around the table can't do. And then it's about pulling other people through, until it becomes the norm, rather than the exception. And that's the thing, I'll never rest until it's the norm that there's a multitude of faces around the table, rather than just one or two.

'So yes, there's pressure, yes you feel like being a role model. You need to make sure that you're really good and you make things easy for the people around the table to have more like you come in, and that you're around the table because of what you can do, not because of your gender or your race.'

#BlackExcellence

From one role model to another: if there's anyone who embodies the twice-as-hard mentality, it is Serena Williams. Navigating and dominating the whitest-of-white sports, she rose above racism and sexism to win 23 Grand Slams. She isn't just a great female athlete or even the best black athlete: she is undisputedly one of the greatest athletes ever. When I was growing up, I would support her as if she were British: her blackness and femaleness were central to both our identities and she made me so proud to be a black girl. Why? Because I realised that my desire for her to win was because she is a shining example of black excellence. In a society that often makes us feel, as dark-skinned women, that we are at the bottom of the pecking order, her success on the court made me feel better about my existence as a black girl in the world. It gave me the confidence to believe that I too could achieve great things if I also worked twice as hard.

Yet in spite of this, Maria Sharapova, Williams's blonde, white 'non-rival' rival, was for a very long time the highest-paid female athlete in the world, despite only winning five Grand Slams. What Maria lacks on court she makes up for in her financial advantage off it, because corporate sponsors prefer a certain type of 'look' to be the face of their products.

When this was brought up in a *New York Times* interview with Serena in 2015, her response was diplomatic: 'If they want to market someone who is white and blonde, that's their choice – I have a lot of partners who are very happy to work with me. I can't sit here and say I should be higher on the list because I have won more. I'm happy for her, because she worked hard, too. There is enough at the table for everyone.'[19] I respect Serena for her humility, but working twice as hard and sometimes getting half as good back has sometimes left a bad taste in my mouth.

Oprah Winfrey once said, 'I was raised to believe that excellence is the best deterrent to racism or sexism. And that's how I operate my life.' I grew up believing this was true, but now I think that while excellence is great and all, it doesn't deter racism. Don't get me wrong, I'm happy when I see the #BlackExcellence on a picture of a black person doing amazing things on social media. Damn, I'll be the first to retweet it. However, it is the pursuit of excellence to *counter* white privilege and racism that I can find demoralising. This pursuit can often feel like having both my hands tied behind my back while trying to swim upstream against waves of unconscious bias and discrimination. Black women are, of course, resilient and we have broken, and will continue to break down, the glass and concrete ceilings in order to take a seat at the table and ultimately continue to emerge as leaders in our fields. But our resilience shouldn't be taken for granted.

Always trying to be excellent can put an unnecessary level of pressure on us. I see it in myself and I can see it in my friends' experiences, too. Mediocrity is real: I witness it every day. White men are allowed to be mediocre, and they walk into every room entitled as shit and will still be successful. Some days I would love to be okay with being mediocre too, and not always having to, exhaustingly, go above and beyond to be seen as just as good. Yet, 'Did the student who the teacher gave an A have two heads?' always echoes in my thoughts.

Although there is no silver bullet that magically solves the issues I've raised in this chapter with progressing in our careers, what I do know is that we shouldn't constantly have to reach a bar of excellence that we didn't create: a bar that is built by the expectations of other people, family included. Sometimes trying twice as hard can leave you twice as self-conscious and half as confident in your own ability. And this is damaging to our self-esteem. Sometimes I haven't even wanted to try to do new things because I have been paralysed by my fear of failure – just as Yomi's self-doubts held her back from applying to Oxbridge. When you're just as good as everybody else, but still treated differently, it can really knock your confidence, and we have to learn that when we push ourselves to be the best we can be; that should be enough. We don't need to get over a bar of excellence we didn't create. Instead, we have to create our *own* lane and our *own* version of success, our *own* version of good.

Having a strong sense of identity is central to this. It should be about knowing at all times what you are bringing to the table, and, just like Karen and Serena, not apologising for your femaleness and blackness. So when you encounter challenges you should still remember to chase *your* version of good, not one that is tied to white privilege and that leaves you feeling inadequate when you've not hit the target of what it is to be both black and 'excellent'.

The quest of black excellence can't be to the detriment of our self-esteem and confidence, because we're getting half as good back. Our idea of success should not just be linked to external measurements but also to how we feel inside when we are achieving these markers of 'excellence'. If you are going to be twice as good, make sure you're not neglecting your sense of self as you progress in your career.

To answer my dad's question, everyone in my class obviously had one head and therefore one brain. But not getting an A turned out to be not quite the end of the world that the 13-year-old me had believed. Growing up, I wish I had been allowed to make a few more mistakes so that I could have learned from them and built up my confidence and resilience in the process. Instead, I have learned to come up with my own definition of success, and of 'good', and I now know that the quest for *good* is a marathon and not a sprint; it is measured over years, not fleeting moments; over failures and mis-steps and, of course, successes. As black women we understand this journey more than most, and our continued motivation and our ambition for the future is testament to that.

Water Cooler Microaggressions

ELIZABETH

> 'I'm a *strong* black woman. And I cannot
> be intimidated. I cannot be undermined.
> I cannot be thought to be afraid of
> Bill O'Reilly or anybody. '
> *Maxine Waters*

You walk into your office building after a long weekend; annoyingly you've left your pass at home so you go to the security desk and ask for a temporary pass for the day. The man at the desk skims his eyes over you, and then he says, 'No, you're not a manager, you'll have to call a colleague from upstairs to sign you in.'

'Okay,' you reply. 'But I am a manager.'

He looks you up in the system and reluctantly gives you a pass. You're irritated but you smile politely. Strike one.

As you walk into your department you begin to mentally prepare yourself for the onslaught of comments about your new hairdo. It takes all of three minutes, and it begins. One of your colleagues looks up at you and starts singing Bob Marley's 'One Love' because he says your braids give him *'that vibe'*. Several colleagues gather around: 'Oh wow, your hair has grown over the weekend,' says one sarcastically. 'Your hair makes such a statement, is it political? Can I touch it?' pipes up another. You grope for the right thing to say. But what's the point? Your desk area is now an exhibition, your hair is the main attraction and the excitement is palpable. You smile, this time awkwardly. Strike two.

Then while you're waiting for a meeting to begin, someone announces while looking in your direction, 'hip hop is an art form,' and asks which side you were on during the 'east-coast west-coast hip hop feud', and how did it all begin? Because, like *obviously*, you're black, you should know. You don't know. Strike three.

Chances are, as a black woman working in what is likely to be a predominantly white space you will have experienced someone making a comment about your hair, questioning your authority or assuming you're the spokesperson for all black people, black slang and black cultural trends. Wave after wave of casually racist remarks head our way each day, and it can sometimes feel like we're facing down a tsunami.

While structural racism leaves black women feeling they have to work twice as hard – and ensures that our pockets are hit the hardest – we shouldn't underestimate the less-obvious ways in which people can inflict harm on us. Racism is fluid. It has changed over time, but it hasn't disappeared. Instead it has assumed a more casual, implicit form which is often more covert, indirect and ambiguous. Because of this it can be hard to identify and confront it and we often find ourselves asking, 'Am I overreacting? Did that just happen? Did he *really* say that?' As a consequence, simply existing as a black woman in these white spaces can be hard to navigate, a constant negotiation of who you are, and therefore exhausting on a daily basis. Sure, these comments don't carry the same weight as explicit racism, and of course the insults aren't always intentional, but we shouldn't have to accustom ourselves to strategically smile at and step around the racial slights that litter our days.

I hadn't really thought about how words and actions that seem banal at first can sometimes mask appalling attitudes until I saw this pushed to the extreme in cinematic form in *Get Out*, a horror film about a black man who meets his white girlfriend's parents for the first time on a weekend trip to their secluded estate in the woods. Drawing on the visceral experience of being black in a predominantly white space, what begins as a friendly encounter quickly turns into a social nightmare. Unfortunately, in real life, the horror of casual racism (deliberate or unintentional) is something that, for black people, lingers long after the credits roll and the last bit of overpriced popcorn has been eaten.

> '#BlackWomenAtWork are paid less, asked to
> do more, are constantly antagonised, and then
> called angry/abrasive for setting boundaries.'
> *Tora Shae*

It was my first interview after graduating and I had arrived, ultra-keen, at reception 30 minutes early. I walked towards the receptionist and she asked me my name and who I was there to see. I gave her my first name and the full name of the hiring manager I had been told would interview me. She asked for my surname and I said '*Uviebinené*'. She looked back at me with a cheeky grin and said, 'So it's *Uvveee blah blah* . . . I'll just call you Elizabeth,' and she started to laugh. I stared back at her, astonished that she would make fun of my name so audaciously. Granted, my surname has never been one that rolls off the tongue for the average person. For me, this was part and parcel of being an African kid in school. When Skepta rapped: 'When I was in school, being African was a diss, sounds like you need help saying my surname, Miss?' I felt vindicated. I was used to teachers butchering my surname, which was one reason why I hated end-of-term assemblies. I would mentally prepare for my name to be called out and briskly walk up to collect my certificate while my classmates sniggered in the background. I would brace myself, trying not to look embarrassed, whispering, 'Shut up, man,' as I returned to my seat. Looking back, it was kind of a rite of passage; character-building, you might say.

But this receptionist wasn't one of my immature classmates. She didn't need help saying my name: she didn't even bother. Yet if I'd asked her who was her favourite Italian designer, I bet she would have made more of an effort in the pronunciation department. Her idea of a joke immediately made me feel unwelcome in that space. Needless to say, it bothered me. However, I smiled at her and sat back down, suppressing my annoyance. Confrontation wouldn't do. I was trying to get hired, not escorted out of the building!

There is a name for these offensive, inappropriate and insensitive comments that can leave you feeling violated. We've talked about them in earlier chapters; they're called *microaggressions*, and Dr Derald Wing Sue, a professor of psychology at Columbia University and author of the book *Microaggressions in Everyday Life*, defines them as 'brief and commonplace daily verbal, behavioural, or environmental indignities, whether intentional or unintentional, that communicate hostile, derogatory, or negative racial slights and insults toward people of colour'.[20]

There are three types of racial microaggressions that Dr Sue has identified. *Microassaults* are the most explicit intentional form – 'old-fashioned racism' – i.e. deliberately serving a white person first rather than a black person at a restaurant, or clutching your handbag when you see a black person in the street. Then there are *Microinsults*, the more unconscious, subtle form, which are usually wrapped up as a compliment – 'Wow, you're so articulate, you're the whitest black person I know' – in which the *microinsulter* associates the qualities they like in you with whiteness. And finally, *Microinvalidations*: comments that subtly exclude or nullify the thoughts, feelings or experienced reality of a person – the 'No, where are you *really* from?' jibes. According to Dr Sue, the microinsults and microinvalidations are potentially more harmful because of their insidiousness and the difficulty when trying to confront the perpetrator about them.[21]

Microaggressions tend to happen in seemingly insignificant, private situations, but their impact on us can be substantial and they occur more often than we might like to think, something that was revealed in 2017 by the viral hashtag #BlackWomenAtWork. Right-wing commentator Bill O'Reilly had mocked Congresswoman Maxine Waters while she was delivering an important speech on policy issues by saying he was too distracted by her 'James Brown' wig to listen to anything she had to say about President Donald Trump. 'I didn't hear a word she said,' he said on-air. 'I was looking at the James Brown wig.' On the same day, White House secretary Sean Spicer reprimanded respected journalist April D. Ryan by cutting her off mid-question and asking her to 'Stop shaking your head'.

This belittling of a grown woman – the scolding of her as though she were a child – happened in a room full of journalists and was broadcast on national TV. It is hard to imagine Spicer speaking to a white, male reporter in the same manner. Both incidents occurred very publicly with women who are veterans in their respective fields, and both involved white men criticising black women in a way that seemed designed to embarrass and mock them at their places of work.

Frustrated by the fact that this kind of thing happens every day to black women at work, activist Brittany Packnett decided enough was enough and encouraged other black women to share their own experiences using the hashtag #BlackWomenAtWork on Twitter. She said: 'I wanted the hashtag to make the invisible visible, to challenge non-black people to stand with black women, not just when this happens on television, but in the cube right next to them.'

It wouldn't be an overstatement to say #BlackWomenAtWork became a public venting board where black women gathered online from across the world to share their experiences. Their stories ranged from feeling isolated at work, to experiencing blatant disrespect and having their confidence lowered as a result of being on the receiving end of countless microaggressions. #BlackWomenAtWork felt like a much-overdue therapy session, as black women found solidarity amongst each other's stories.

It can be so frustrating to stare into the face of the microaggressor and know that the only response you're allowed right at that moment is a complicit smile or a laugh. Why should this be the case? For two reasons: one, for politeness' sake, in order to protect their feelings (maybe they didn't mean it like *that?*); two, as black women we're aware that if we express rightful annoyance, we run the risk of being stereotyped yet again as 'angry', and we don't want to look overly sensitive. So instead of saying, 'Are you fucking kidding me?' – as I had wanted to say to that receptionist – we are tactful with our responses, we keep our cool and we learn to brush it off. And so they read our silence as compliance, and the cycle continues.

However, sometimes taking the high road isn't an option.

Sometimes your boundaries are crossed and someone has violated you with their words and they have really hit a nerve. You have the internal debate: do you stay calm and let it go because you don't want to cause a scene? But, maybe because you've had a long day at work, you've missed your train, you're tired, you decide then and there that not only will you cause a scene, you will deliver an Oscar-worthy performance and call that person out.

Other times it can happen so fast that you don't even have the time to comprehend what's been done or said and you're effectively stunned into silence. Radio presenter Clara Amfo has experienced this: 'There's been times when I've had my picture taken with someone and it's happened so quickly you can't react, they've grabbed hold of my hair and I'm like "Oh, oh" and I *smiled*. "Okay!" You know sometimes you can't always be on it. Sometimes people will come in and go straight for the fist bump rather than shake my hand like an adult. I'm just thinking "No, you don't know me like that, so don't, it's nice to meet you – shake my hand."'

Even though Bill O'Reilly later apologised for his comments and said it was all in 'jest', the incident reignited an important conversation around the harsh reality of being a minority in the workplace. Microaggressions create hostile and invalidating work environments, and these seemingly innocuous comments have a way of sapping our confidence and energy. In a study by the Center for Generational Kinetics and Ultimate Software, it was noted that a lack of emotional safety at work is the reason why six out of ten employees leave their job, and it's not hard to see why.[22] A toxic culture of harassment, offensive comments and microaggressions breeds negative working conditions, and, alarmingly, 28 per cent of BAME employees have experienced or witnessed racial harassment from their managers in the last five years.[23]

One black woman reported: 'I worked with a colleague who would constantly have loud discussions about "black on black crime" and why black people shouldn't complain about police harassment, as "black on black gun and knife crime" is so prevalent. I complained to a manager who witnessed the conversation, but nothing was done about it and I was made to feel like I was creating a fuss about nothing.'[24]

The 2015 Race at Work Report revealed that racism is often a daily, if not a constant, feature of working life for ethnic minority employees, and that racist 'banter' was among the most common type. If you push back on these 'jokes' to try to set boundaries, you are accused of playing the race card: it's not as if your colleague is calling you the N word, right? And it's not as if there's a sign at the door saying 'No blacks, no Irish, no dogs'. You're not made to feel unwelcome in explicit ways, but through covert ways that make it harder to explain. Although they can make us want to scream, 'I do have feelings like you,' the corrosive power of microaggressions is that they are often framed as ignorance, and over time we have been conditioned to question ourselves and not the person making the microaggression. Sadly, it's so easy to wonder whether your own feelings are legitimate. But it *is* legitimate, as a TUC poll in 2017 discovered that 'one in three British BAME workers have been bullied, abused or singled out for unfair treatment' and of this two in five (41 per cent) women wanted to leave their jobs because of bullying and harassment, but could not afford to.[25]

In 2013, Oprah Winfrey revealed that she had been the victim of a racial microaggression in a Zurich fashion store when a shop assistant refused to show her a bag, claiming it was 'too expensive'. *Hello?* I don't think they got the memo that they were serving one of the *world's richest women*. Oprah observed, 'Racists these days don't come right up and call you something horrible to your face, it doesn't happen like that anymore. Instead, you get the kind of thing I suffered in that Swiss shop. White people like that shop assistant – they make an assessment based upon my appearance.'

Even though she decided not to have the 'big blow-up thing', Oprah was dismissed by the owner as 'oversensitive' and the media alluded to her having 'diva tendencies'. In the end, it was Oprah who felt compelled to apologise: 'I'm really sorry that it got blown up. I think that incident in Switzerland was just an incident in

Switzerland, I purposefully did not mention the name of the store,' she said. 'I was just referencing it as an example of being in a place where people don't expect that you would be able to be and rather than there be some accountability there.'

But that's the thing. There *should* be accountability. Rather than the perpetrator taking responsibility for how their microaggression has made you feel, they often immediately go on the defensive and react badly, which can make confrontation a perilous option. They respond with comments like, 'I'm not a racist, I don't see colour – see, I have black friends!' or 'You have no sense of humour.' In my case, I've had, 'Why do you have such a chip on your shoulder about race?' Granted, no one likes to be pulled up for their behaviour, but when a person's first priority is to put up a wall of defence, they don't take the time to question and review their own actions. One of the worst things about microaggressions is that they can come from all types of people: from open-minded, forward-thinking liberals who see themselves as guardians of multiculturalism to the unapologetic right-wing Bill O'Reilly types. They are not limited to roaring racists; they are woven into the fabric of society, and this is what makes them so insidious.

Being a victim of this racism or even witnessing it has a direct and adverse impact on ethnic minorities' emotional and mental health. It was cathartic yet depressing to see the amount of #BlackWomenAtWork tweets that spoke about how microaggressions over time had resulted in depression, loss of self-esteem and anxiety. We spend a lot of time at work, and this experience of constantly feeling like the 'other' can take a physiological and physical toll on your health.

It's normal once in a while to second-guess yourself. But when you're constantly questioning your own instincts and feelings it has a big impact on your mental health. This sophisticated form of emotional abuse is called gaslighting.[26] Dr Nicola Rollock explains how there is a high price to pay if we don't confront the issue.

'I think that the costs are quite clear. There are serious costs in terms of well-being, health and mental health. So being in a space where you are isolated and you're experiencing racial micro-aggressions is only going to induce more stress in you. And we also know the data around hypertension, high blood pressure and so on that disproportionately affects the black community and black women. It's something we really need to take quite seriously. Research in the States shows there are health consequences to being subject to constant racial microaggressions. It is a very important issue and an area that really deserves much more attention in the UK. We still operate in an environment where we believe being tolerant is a sufficient label to override and or excuse the very evident racial problems we have within mainstream society.'

Talk that talk

If we are to speak out as black women, we need to do so without fear of repercussion. In 2017, England striker Eniola Aluko was dropped from the women's England football team after speaking out about the racism and victimisation she experienced from the England women's team manager, Mark Sampson. He is alleged to have told one of his black players to make sure their Nigerian relatives did not bring Ebola to a game at Wembley. Eniola noted that for months, one member of staff used to talk to her in a fake Caribbean accent. Due to the nature of that toxic environment, he was empowered by the culture to do this and thought it was funny. In an interview in the *Guardian*, Eniola said, 'Race, for some reason, is this taboo subject that everyone avoids talking about. The minute you are brave enough to talk about race, you are in a difficult situation. That in itself is discrimination: the mere fact I am in this position. I probably can't play for England again. I've lost my England career despite being the leading scorer in the league last season.'[27] Eniola was painted as a 'troublemaker', a 'know-it-all' and 'a pain in the arse', just for speaking up. Companies need to take more seriously the duty of care they have to their employees and to have a zero-tolerance approach to all types of racism in the workplace. How will they learn if we are unable to speak out and tell our truth?

One black woman who did speak out was Member of Parliament Dawn Butler when she revealed that a fellow MP had mistaken her for a cleaner. Another is Britain's first black female MP, Diane Abbott – one of the most visible black women in our country – who, dishearteningly, has been continuously subjected to racist abuse throughout her 30-year career. Diane and Dawn, just by virtue of turning up to their place of work every day, challenge the status quo. After all, they work in one of the whitest institutions in the western world. During the 2017 General Election Abbott wrote a poignant piece in the *Guardian* entitled 'I fought racism and misogyny to become an MP. The fight is getting harder' to address how the politics of personal destruction is silencing minorities. 'Suppose that someone had told me back then that 30 years on I would be receiving stuff like this: "Pathetic useless fat black piece of shit Abbott. Just a piece of pig shit pond slime who should be fucking hung (if they could find a tree big enough to take the fat bitch's weight)". I think that even the young, fearless Diane Abbott might have paused for thought.'[28]

Like the young Diane, many of us feel similarly fearless and enthusiastic when we start work. We are ready to take on the world, to prove ourselves – even in the face of overt and covert racism. But what is the cost to our self-esteem, our confidence, our well-being? Diane herself stepped down from the shadow cabinet mid-campaign because of the toll it was taking on her health.

So how does one navigate these situations? How do we speak out against microaggressions without paying too high a price? Dawn's advice is that it depends on the circumstances:

'So you have to tailor it to whatever the situation allows, unless you want to go into full destructive mode. One of the best bits of advice I was given is to choose your battles, because when you're young you fight everything. I fought everything when I was young and that's all good, you've got the energy. When you get older you realise that you're tired and you can't always fight everything, so you have to choose your battles.

'I've done it in various ways. Firstly, disrupting – I've challenged, straight up, in your face, "Who do you think you are? What makes you think you can address me in that manner?" Secondly, I've tackled it discreetly by challenging someone about their racism, about their unconscious bias, about them maybe not realising that what they did, or said, or have done was racist. Finally, I've also challenged it through the media. I let the media take care of it, and maybe have the shock factor of, yes, this is what has happened.'

However, as Eniola experienced, there can be consequences to challenging the status quo. Dawn explains:

'Disrupt when it's going to give you the most advantage. Because they will always use it as an excuse to bring you down. So sometimes disrupt, sometimes challenge, sometimes discreetly have a word, because sometimes that person that you've discreetly had a word with will be more enlightened to be your best advocate because they realise you could've exposed them and you didn't. Like I've given you a chance, I haven't exposed you. I've given you a chance and an opportunity. And sometimes that empowers. So sometimes use that to have all of these tools in your arsenal to be ready to be used. But it does mean that in that split second you've got to analyse that situation and analyse your mood. Because there have been times in Parliament when I just want to flip out and say, "You don't know me, so don't mess with me."

'I mean, there are situations where I haven't done any of those things. I haven't challenged, I haven't disrupted, and I haven't gone to the media. Some days it burns me that I've done nothing to challenge something that's happened. But I hold faith in the fact that at some stage I will expose the situation. So there have been people who maybe will think that they've got away with something with me. They haven't. And I will wait for the right time, at the right moment, to expose them.'

Butler's choice of tactic when her fellow MP confronted her in the lift was to disrupt and challenge. 'When the MP said, "This really isn't for cleaners," it didn't even occur to me that he was talking to me and it was only when the lift went up and I said to the man, there's only me and a couple of you in the lift, so you're talking about me! So I asked him, "Are you talking about me?" and there was no sort of response. And I said, "Look, even if I was the cleaner, that's rude and disrespectful. You need to think about and examine your behaviour and your attitude."'

In my case, I have learned to go with my gut: if it 'stings' and feels 'off', then most likely my feelings are valid. Depending on my mood and the severity of the comment, I ask myself 'What do you want to gain from the situation?' Sometimes my sole desire is to disrupt and communicate how much they have offended me, and on some occasions this will be enough. There is a variety of ways to deal with it and it's at your discretion if you prefer to engage and educate. I'm more likely to do this if they are a colleague, less so if it's a random person on the train.

Dr Maggie Aderin-Pocock takes the educative approach:

'In my everyday life, I have dealings with the public, but usually I'm going to give a lecture or something, so they are pre-warned as to who I am. But as I say, I hop into a taxi and they say, "You what, you're a space scientist, really?" They are surprised and I think it's because I'm female and I'm black.

'In the past I think it was more so; when I was younger. I remember when I was studying for my PhD, I was having lunch, a guy had come over from Holland, he was studying his PhD there. And we'd had a nice lunch and just at the end of the lunch he turned to me and said, "Whose secretary are you?" Everybody else on the table was studying for the PhD, but he assumed that I was somebody's secretary. And the guys that we were having lunch with, because I was in the engineering department, so they were all guys there, they all took a sharp intake of breath, like, oh no, what is she going to do?

'I remember thinking, why on earth does he think that? And it was sort of a flash of anger, that's terrible, why did he make that assumption? And I thought, well, hold it, there's nothing wrong with being a secretary, the problem here is his assumption, that because I'm black and female I must be a secretary. So for me the key is education. So I could have blasted him across the table and been, "How dare you!", had a rant at him. But I think it's much better if I say, "Oh no, you're mistaken, I'm not a secretary at all, I got my degree at Imperial and now I'm doing my PhD." And to try to educate, so that he goes off and says "Hey, I met this really cool woman the other day and she's black and she's doing her PhD." And it's a much more positive message to send than, "I was at lunch and made a simple mistake and then she shouted at me." So, to me, it's all education. It's the same with the guy who thought I was the cleaner, I didn't shout at him, I just said, "No no, you're mistaken." I'm trying to re-educate. And there's lots of ways to do it, you can do it on an individual basis, but that takes an awfully long time. So that's why going on TV and appearing as a role model and training other role models, we can get the message out there much quicker. That's the aim: not to tell people off for making these judgements, but to show them that they are mistaken and that there are lots of black women doing this sort of thing. We are the movers and shakers. So that's my goal and that's why it's great to be an ambassador for Terrific Scientific – it can showcase to a lot of people what we are doing.'

If there's an opportunity to challenge and affect that person's behaviour in a positive way then I'll be more likely to pull them aside and shine a spotlight on their actions and words. I might say, 'What do you mean?' or, 'That question makes a lot of assumptions because . . .' and bring the microaggression to light, hoping for the best but usually expecting intense denial. When you choose to challenge, it doesn't always need to be in a severe telling-off kind of way, or by saying something accusatory like 'You're racist'. Instead, just let them know that what they said was offensive. It can be awkward to watch them scramble for an explanation, but so very worth it. However, it is a challenge to prove intention when it's implicit and not articulated. If you find that microaggressions are a continuous problem in your workplace, book in some time with your manager, go prepared and list the occasions, time and dates and people involved in these incidents so you have evidence.

By law there are processes in place at any workplace that should safeguard you from racial harassment. But it is also – according to research published by the TUC in 2017 – unfortunately the case that 42 per cent of those bullied or harassed because of their race said their direct manager was the main perpetrator. That's a really high number and it points to the fact that all workplaces need to have a zero-tolerance policy and a clear process of reporting such behaviour that protects the well-being of workers. TUC General Secretary Frances O'Grady said: 'Racism still haunts the British workplace. Racist bullying, harassment and victimisation should have no place anywhere, least of all at work. And it's clear that people are being denied opportunities because of their race. Employers must take a zero-tolerance attitude and treat every complaint seriously. It's a scandal that so few black and Asian workers feel their bosses are dealing with racism properly.'[29]

Whatever you decide to do, though your heart may be racing, your fists clenched in anger, face fixed in annoyance, first pause, then calm down. Although encountering these situations can at times leave you despondent, it's important to have an understanding of the options available to you – the price you're paying is too high to do nothing about it.

....

'MediaCom were actually quite good, but there's no way we would ever have had a female business director, let alone a black one.'
Unnamed white male

....

When the Oscars had their most diverse year in 2017, we cheered: We're getting somewhere! However, the inclusion of more black people in a white-dominated space inevitably has repercussions. As the saying goes, 'nothing is certain but death and taxes,' but black people can safely include 'microaggressions' in this list, and the awards night didn't disappoint. *Hidden Figures* and *Fences*, films in which the leads were played by black actors, were mistaken for each other multiple times and efficiently reduced to unidentifiable versions of the same film. While social media had a field day with creating 'Hidden Fences' memes to highlight the gaffe, there was one particular faux pas that *really* nagged at me. TV host and seasoned interviewer Ryan Seacrest asked actor Viola Davis how she 'managed' to memorise all of her lines in *Fences*, a ridiculous question to ask an actor of her stature. Would he have asked Meryl Streep the same question? This questioning of her accomplishment and credibility as an actor really floored me.

Seacrest's question left a particular sting because, in the workplace, black women's overall competence and capabilities are often challenged and undermined by their white colleagues.[30] From having people speak over them at meetings, to sharing an idea and being ignored – only to find that idea suddenly becoming the best thing since sliced bread when someone else says it – black women can often feel invisible in both their value and worth at work.

So what's the point in working twice as hard when no one notices? In a study called 'Double Jeopardy? Gender Bias Against Women of Color in Science', published by WorkLife Law, sixty female scientists of colour were surveyed, and it was found that black women have to 'provide more evidence of competence than others to prove themselves to colleagues'.[31] I remember when I was recently promoted to Marketing Manager and a colleague deliberately called me a *junior* Marketing Manager in front of everyone, in what I felt was a dig to undermine my contribution to a task. I had to pull him to one side, challenge his words, explain to him why it was a problem.

I've also had to be hyper-aware of the choice of words I use when talking in meetings and double checking when sending emails, and of my tone when I am putting forward a point of view that differs from the rest of my team. When my white colleagues have been commended for holding their ground and being assertive, I've been met with accusations of being argumentative. 'I don't want to argue with you,' a colleague once said, and I sat there in disbelief and thought, 'What do you mean you don't want to argue with me? I am calm. I have not raised my voice once. How is the onus on me now as the aggressor?'

Therefore it is no surprise that in a survey of over 300 BAME women leaders, it was found that over three-quarters felt the leadership style of white women was more positively perceived in the workplace and 80 per cent felt that the communication style of white women was more positively regarded.[32] It can feel incredibly frustrating to be passed up for promotion based not on your work and what you've produced but on people's perception of who they think you are.

The reality is, I want to progress in my career and the work I produce should be enough, but I have had to learn to be more tactful and accommodating with my communication style in the workplace in order to build relationships with people and offer them a version of me that is more palatable. Why? Because, let's be honest, not having a positive professional relationship with key stakeholders is a one-way ticket to career stagnation. Friends tell me that they too have strategically tried to find common interests with their white colleagues, by de-emphasising racial and ethnic differences to assimilate seamlessly into their work environment. They shift their body, speech and attire to counter perceived images of inferiority and stereotypes. Black women are pros in accommodating everyone else (see '***Flawless'), and code-switching is a coping tool used by many of us to fit into white work spaces.

However, I have also accepted that there is only so much I can do without morphing into a shadow of myself at work. The fact is, there are ingrained negative attitudes towards black women and if I completely modify myself to suit other people's unconscious biases, it will only enable them to remain as ignorant towards the next young black girl who follows me.

Take, for example, a friend of mine who works in a company where she is the only black woman. She was asked to give an office tour to a potential new recruit who was there for an interview: a young black girl. It was clear that the girl was bubbly, full of personality, 'had life in her', but my friend said that, as she was showing her around, she remembered thinking, 'They're not going to give her the job, she has too much life for this place.' Knowing that my friend is someone who is also full of personality, I asked what was the difference between the two of them, and she replied, 'They'll definitely say she's a little intense. White people are allowed to have big personalities and be kooky in these environments, but as a black woman you have to tone yourself down. As the only black girl in the office I've given them the most toned-down version of myself.' She did, in fairness, say that she wasn't present at the other woman's interview, so she didn't know how she performed. But, long story short, she remains the only black woman in the firm.

In *Get Out*, there is a scene where a policeman asks to see Chris's driving licence even though he knows that Rose, his white girlfriend, was the one driving. The policeman's tone changes as soon as Rose steps in to offer validation. This is an example of the white co-sign, where the endorsement of a white colleague can often be how some black women gain credibility in the workplace. Anne-Marie Imafidon is someone who has always been a high achiever, at school and at work, which has meant she has been in environments where her input is regarded highly and she is respected by those who are aware of her knowledge and skills. However, for those who are on the outside looking in, her prowess can often be met with confusion and challenges. Anne-Marie says: 'This person was questioning my knowledge of the system that I worked on at Deutsche, and I was probably the only person on the team who understood it on a technical level, and so that meant that when I said something, and that person said, no, that's not true, he then took half an hour to find what I'd said was true.' Her manager had to step in and support her, saying, 'Anne-Marie really knows what she's talking about,' thus providing her with the 'white co-sign'.

Anne-Marie maintains, speaking about the man who did this to her, 'If I was older than Felix, whiter than Felix, maler than Felix, he would have found a different way to say it; he would have gone and written an email two weeks later. He wouldn't then, in a room, go, "Nah, I don't think you know what you're talking about," but, you know, that's more Felix's problem than it is my problem.' True, it is his problem, but it can be extremely frustrating and exhausting to feel that you constantly have to prove yourself, or find a white person to back you up. Anne-Marie contends, 'If I was someone else he wouldn't have said that to me, but even in that scenario, because of the value that I have for myself but also that my team had for me, it was one of those things where immediately that person was slapped down and there were repercussions for that person, which I think is another thing that doesn't always happen.'

When you've done a great piece of work and someone finds it hard to see past the colour of your skin and give you the credit you deserve it can be hurtful to experience microassaults in return – the 'old-fashioned' kind of racism. In 2002, Karen Blackett led a pitch for a well-known breakfast cereal brand and found herself on the receiving end of this.

'We didn't win it, but in such a small industry, you sort of know who your opposition is. The media agency that did win took the client out for dinner and asked them, as you would do (and I'd do exactly the same thing), "What did the other agencies do?" so you get a little bit of competitive insight. And they asked about MediaCom.

'Rather than offering constructive feedback, the client said "MediaCom were actually quite good, but there's no way we would ever have had a female business director, let alone a black one." I would be lying if I didn't say that that was incredibly hurtful. That was personal. It wasn't about the work that we had created as an agency. It was about me. I'm resilient, but not *that* resilient. So that was really personal, but I know the work was good so I know it is their loss. And that's hard to get your head around initially, when you first hear that feedback. And I felt so responsible because I felt as though I'd lost the agency a pitch, because I'm a woman, because I'm black. It was awful and I thought that if they'd fielded somebody else we would have won it.

'But then you talk to your cheerleaders, you talk to your sponsors at the agency, who were like, "Well, do you really want to work with anybody like that? Because they're vile human beings, so do we really want to work with anyone like that? No, we don't."

'Then thinking about it rationally, if we had won that account and

I'd been forced to work with those two people, day in, day out, I would have been miserable because I would have been trying to cover and not be me. And I don't want to do anything about my gender. I don't want to do anything about my ethnicity. I'm actually very happy.

'They just didn't like me, not because of the work, or what I was saying, or the advice I was giving, but just because of what I looked like; they didn't like me. I really do believe in karma, and there's that Buddhist saying that, "Holding on to anger is like holding on to a hot coal with the intention of throwing it at somebody." So you let it go, and then because I am incredibly competitive, you go out and win a load of other business and let them regret the fact that they didn't appoint you.'

As black women in the workplace we need to have an awareness of the stereotypes so that we're not totally in the dark about them, but Funke Abimbola says we also have to stop being apologetic, and having a strong sense of identity is key.

'People are more likely to have a negative impression of you because of the colour of your skin, and you could be the most well-spoken person ever – I've had people assuming I'm the secretary in law firms, the admin assistant, the photocopyist, purely because of the colour of my skin. If I were a white woman dressed in a suit, they wouldn't make that assumption – you really need to know who you are first and foremost, and make no apologies for the fact that you are a black woman, because I think we almost bend over backwards and almost apologise in all sorts of ridiculous ways for being black. I mean, trying not to be too assertive because we're concerned that people will see us as an "angry black woman". Well, actually, you can express your anger effectively without being seen as the volatile, angry, black woman. But learning who you are and owning that is very important.'

Also, as Karen has highlighted, it's so important to have a net-work of people you can seek advice and support from in the face of constant microaggressions – whether it's your squad of girlfriends or family members, as long as it's someone who gets it. There have been so many occasions when I've called Yomi to rant about a situation, to seek advice or just to offload. Simply having someone who can validate your own feelings, and offer what I call 'sanity checks' about the existence of said discrimination, can make a world of difference in diminishing the potential adverse impact these situations can have on one's self-esteem. The idea of this book was created from one of those 'sanity checks' when I called Yomi in a huff and a puff, and *The Black Girl Bible* was born.

'When they go low, we go high.'
Michelle Obama

If there's anyone qualified to know what it feels like to endure personal vicious racist and sexist attacks it is former First Lady Michelle Obama. Making history and breaking the glass ceiling as the first black First Lady came at a price. When she was asked about her time as FLOTUS and how she was treated, she said, 'The shards that cut me the deepest were the ones that intended to cut – knowing that after eight years of working really hard for this country, there are still people who won't see me for what I am because of my skin colour.' Obama's surprisingly candid comments were an effort to remind people that they are accountable for how they treat others and how they make them feel. She could not pretend those remarks had not hurt because that would effectively be giving the people who made them a pass.

What really shook me was when she said, 'Women, we endure those cuts in so many ways that we don't even notice we're cut, we are living with small, tiny cuts, and we are bleeding every single day.'[33] Preach. Explicit or implicit biases have serious consequences beyond hurt feelings. As black women we really do know how to get on with things in the face of adversity, it's in our DNA. We get up every day and face the world, aware that some people will take one look at us and make comments and treat us not on the merit of who we are but on the basis of pure prejudice. These slights can and do cut deep. Inappropriate and offensive comments matter because they are symptoms of a larger underlying problem in society, and to play it down it is to underestimate how these tiny cuts can, over time, develop into larger wounds that make you feel a shadow of your actual self.

We tend to make a lot of excuses for the perpetrators of these microaggressions and want to believe that their comments are not underpinned by intent or malice. However, these 'jokes' and banter are one of the ways in which racist stereotypes are reinforced and reproduced. By being so focused on the intent, it can amount to letting microaggressors off the hook and unintentionally allowing racism to remain part of our culture. This matters even more in the context of Brexit and the rise of nationalism. Karen Blackett agrees:

'Up until last June [when Britain voted to leave the EU] and, sort of, up until last November [when President Trump was elected], with what happened in the UK and what happened in America, I would have said "yeah, things have changed". My slight concern about the result of Brexit and the result of President Trump and his values and views, is that people might feel vindicated to have those views again. Because if there were a set of people who did still have those views, they had been sensible enough to hide them, and not vocalise them. Whereas now there's been a 57 per cent increase in hate crime, after the vote to leave Europe. I just feel that some people with those sorts of attitudes feel vindicated again, that's all. And whether or not they'd actually gone away, I don't know, and maybe they were always there but they were just hidden.'

Asking me to teach you the latest hip hop dance craze can be annoying as fuck, but other slights cut deeper. As Michelle Obama defiantly said amidst the ugliness of President Trump's campaign, 'When someone is cruel or acts like a bully, you don't stoop to their level. Our motto is, when they go low, we go high.' But going high can mean different things in different situations, and always taking the high road and being the bigger person can be tough. As black women we're expected to travel down this road more times than others.

Depending on the situation, there's nothing wrong with disrupting and challenging microaggressions: standing firm in your convictions rather than bottling it up in an effort to rise above. Yes, you may provoke a defensive reaction, but when it really comes down to it, the intention behind sexist and racist behaviour is irrelevant. By only focusing on the intention of the person who is responsible for the microaggression, we end up prioritising their feelings over our own. There needs to be a balance between the impact and intent.

Above all, it's about being honest with yourself and acknowledging when someone has crossed the line, however you choose to react to it. Seek support and a sanity check from your best friend, your friends, family and cheerleaders, because a cut is still a cut, no matter how small. Not all biases are unconscious and that can be a hard pill to swallow. Ultimately, only you can determine what the best course of action is for you, because 99 per cent of the time you'll probably be right.

***Flawless

YOMI

'Girl, you know how these white people are.
If you want to be successful here, you've got to
know when to switch it up a little bit.'
Molly Carter, Insecure

When we were at university, Liz and I shout-spoke and laugh-howled like we were still 14-year-old 'back of the bus girls' in 2007. We hung around in a group comprised of young black women who were largely similar – many were from South London, most had attended state school and the majority would do gun fingers by reflex if 'Talkin' The Hardest' came on. We were very black faces in the very white space of Warwick University campus – unintentionally exasperating our white flatmates by crowding the kitchen, filling the halls with the smells of jollof rice and plantain and the sounds of Wizkid and D'banj. In a space more overwhelmingly white than many of us were used to, we were doubly homesick – for family and friends as well as for the familiarity of 'ends'. So we tried to bring home to us. Our group found comfort in each other and the way that, though we'd just met, it was like we'd all somehow lived the same childhoods and teenage years, just on different streets. But sometimes our cackling laughter, boom-voiced anecdotes and 'bruckin out' at clubs was met with head shaking, tutting and eye-rolling from our peers that befitted church aunties. On one day in particular, a friend from the year above informed us that the gaggle of black girls we hung out with were referred to as the 'too loud, too black freshers' – by *other* black people.

At the time, I remember us fuming. I, in particular, was the kind of girl who climbed on tables at raves, danced on them and later toppled off them because I'd had a tad too much to drink. We drunkenly grinded on guys, girls, each other while some of our black peers watched on, appalled. We were bad, with very little of the boujee, yes, but we were also 19-year-olds experiencing the freedom of a night out away from parents who hadn't even permitted sleepovers when we were growing up (see 'Black Faces in White Spaces'). Before going to Warwick I had fretted at the thought that I would be the only black person there, but instead, when I arrived I found an entire ACS – an Afro-Caribbean Society – but, to my shock, I wasn't much of a fan of it. I soon realised my behaviour was almost even more policed there than it was on the rest of the campus. It was as though if you weren't prim, proper and pursuing a career in the City, you were penalised by white *and* black people alike. I couldn't comprehend why, at university, the one time you're allowed to have the time of your life, there were people who were jarred by the sight of first years getting drunk and sloppy and dancing outrageously. We knew how our behaviour would be read by white students, but black students considering us 'too black' was mind-boggling.

But now, after several years have passed, I have begun to understand the hostility. We had been accepted into a top-ten, majority-white and middle-class institution because of our grades, but that didn't mean *we* were accepted. We didn't give much thought about what other people thought or how we came across – and we didn't particularly care either. In fact, though it was before the coining of the popular term, we truly were the walking, loudly talking definition of 'carefree black girls'. And that meant we were often uninhibited, messy, loud, emotional and, at times, ratchet. That freedom meant sometimes occupying the very stereotypes that black people are so rightfully afraid of being tarred with. And that meant rubbing some people up the wrong way: people who felt we were 'letting the side down' – a side they were trying to prove was just as worthy of their places in these spaces, too.

R-E-S-P-E-C-TABILITY

By definition, respectability politics is an attempt by 'marginalised groups to police their own members and show their social values as being continuous, and compatible, with mainstream values rather than challenging the mainstream for what they see as its failure to accept difference'.[34] It is a seed sown by white society and watered within our own communities. Taking cues from the rest of the world, many of us internalise the idea there is a 'right way' of being a black person, and that the 'right kind' of black person is rewarded with slightly more access because of their rejection of things that are considered 'black'. This idea is why elder female relatives can sometimes see me rock my hair natural and ask me why it's 'not done'. It's why fellow black people can place limitations on how 'black' you should appear in certain places. It leads to punishment twice over – from inside and outside of the black community – for certain things that are not considered 'acceptable' by the white masses.

Our loudness and 'blackness' at university was seen as exacerbating already existing damaging tropes that many were trying to distance themselves from. Behaviours are referred to as 'ghetto' and 'ratchet' because we're holding each other to the same standards of acceptability that wider society has set upon black women, instead of questioning their legitimacy. But it's a difficult mindset to shake, when blackness is pitted as the opposite of 'professionalism' and success – and when the behaviour of some is made representative of the behaviour of all. The sad truth of being a black face in a white place is that you find your actions being not only held to a different standard to those of your white peers, but somehow linked to every other black woman in the country. A foot out of line sets our joint, big, black, communal foot one step back. This is why, whenever a heinous crime is reported in the news, we pray fervently that it hasn't been committed by one of 'us'. White people across the country can commit crimes without the white population somehow feeling responsible for it. Black people, on the other hand, read or watch with a sinking feeling, knowing that they'll indirectly pay for the indiscretions of others. A mouthy black girl on a reality TV show elicits mass shame because she is seen as adding to and worsening one predominant narrative – a narrative that even the meekest of black women cannot escape. We aren't permitted the luxury of individualism. In spaces where we're outnumbered, it can be easy to feel as though you're responsible not just for how you are perceived by others, but for how black women as a whole are perceived.

Many have commented on the otherworldly perfection of Michelle Obama as though it were God-given instead of something she has had to master through sheer necessity. Had she been caught plagiarising a speech, as Melania Trump was, she'd have never made it to the point of making the speech that Melania would eventually steal. She simply couldn't afford to ever be anything *but* Michelle Obama – perfection personified. A real class act. A model minority.

Blackness is rarely afforded the room for mistakes, the benefit of the doubt and the benevolence of a second chance. For many, a first impression is the only impression, and so it becomes about 'outdoing' your skin. The pursuit of respectability ensures that on casual Fridays you're never too casual, because you don't want to be 'that black girl'. There's an unspoken, unwritten pressure to speak more softly, dress more formally, smile more broadly than everyone else. Life at work becomes a constant battle to counteract stereotypes that say black women are angry, sassy, lazy and 'ghetto'. The room for error is marginal and the pressure palpable – something that Melanie Eusebe, the co-founder of the BBB Awards (Black British Business Awards) knows all too well. Having worked in one of the more restrictive sectors – the corporate world – for several years, the first time she ever broached the topic of race to her boss was when she saw someone make a mistake she knew she simply couldn't afford to as a black woman: -

'My boss and I were talking about an instance of white privilege – someone who'd messed up in leadership. I went off on this person, "Can you imagine if Sophie [Chandauka, co-founder of BBB Awards] and I had done the exact same things as this person, our businesses would be done, the awards would be done. I cannot believe that a person could mess up so bad, appropriate, misappropriate, all kinds of business and they can just waltz back in and all their little friends can help them. See? That won't happen, that doesn't happen to us. That's what I'm talking about – that's privilege."'

In the cult classic animated sitcom *Daria*, black character Jodie Landon is president of the French Club, vice president of Student Council, editor of the yearbook, on the tennis team and valedictorian of the graduating class of Lawndale High. She is everything at school, except herself, as she says in one of the show's most memorable moments. 'At home, I'm Jodie. I can say or do whatever feels right,' Landon laments. 'But at school, I'm the Queen of the Negroes. The perfect African-American teen. The role model for all of the other African-American teens at Lawndale.' Most black women have at one time felt like Jodie. It's hard not to when there is so little room for mistakes. But as the rest of this chapter shows, there is more than one way to be a role model. For Amma Asante, she wants to be a role model to young black women by reaching her goals as herself, and no one else. 'For little black girls that are growing up today, I want them to be able to look at me and go – obviously respecting my journey and respecting my path, but go – "You know what? If she can do it, I can, too." I don't want them to look at me and go, "Wow, she's so polished and she's so perfect, and she's so stoosh that it's unattainable."'

The truth is, the British work environment, whether it's the creative industry or the corporate world, wasn't built with us in mind. Work culture takes its cues from a wider, white culture, which can be hard enough in itself to navigate. With the added stipulation of 'professionalism' that is required in a work environment, and the false dichotomy that puts blackness at the opposing end of 'polished', many black women can be left feeling as though elements of who they are must be left at home in a drawer. But even when we lower the music from our headphones and come to work with the most convincing and flattest of weaves, our skin can't be discarded in the same way. We cannot truly 'behave' our way out of the perceptions placed upon us. As Jay Z summarises on 'The Story of O.J.' – 'faux nigga, real nigga / Rich nigga, poor nigga . . . Still nigga'.

Warning: Working while black

Though no one brings their entire selves to work, as Liz has talked about in the previous chapter, at times for black women the realms of respectability mean almost leading a double life of sorts – speaking differently at home, speaking about different things, wearing our hair differently, eating different food. Everyone shows a particular and specific side to themselves at work, but what if you feel unable to show any?

Though there isn't equivalent data available in the UK, according to the research done by the Center for Women Policy Studies, in the US, 21 per cent of women of colour do not feel free to be 'themselves at work'. The same study found more than one-third of women of colour believed that in order to be successful, they had to 'play down' their race or ethnicity. Standards of professionalism are built around the default person expected within that space, which in most positions of power is white men. The work environment ought to require you to be the best version of yourself, not a version of someone else entirely, and that's what navigating a predominantly white workplace can often feel like. In the UK, the best version of a black woman is essentially a white man or, at the very least, a white woman. It can feel as though you are playing dress up, as opposed to putting your best foot forward. For example, a white woman and a black woman coming to work with straight hair simply isn't comparable. While white people may see relaxing and flat-ironing afro hair as another simple hair change ('What's the problem? You guys change your hair all the time!'), these can be often irreversible, permanently damaging 'solutions' begrudgingly adhered to in the pursuit of professionalism.

A parliamentary committee in 2017 heard that a black woman applying for work at Harrods was told she would not get the role unless she chemically straightened her hair, because her natural style was considered too 'unprofessional'. She is by no means the only one: there was the case of Simone Powderly, who applied to get on the books of 'a respected leader in the luxury recruitment industry' and was informed after the first round of group assessment that she had been successful, but that she had to take out her braids. Another woman, Lara Odoffin, was emailed by her employer in very straight terms: 'Unfortunately we cannot accept braids – it is simply part of the uniform and grooming requirements we get from our clients,' the email stated. 'If you are unable to take them out, I unfortunately won't be able to offer you any work.' And these are just the stories that make the papers.

The idea that braids or natural hair is in some way unkempt isn't a new one or one that exists solely in the workplace: as we saw in 'Lawyer, Doctor, Engineer', our hair is often policed in schools, too. A 14-year-old student at Fulston Manor School, in Kent, came in with braids and was told to return her hair to a 'normal' style on the first day of the new school term, as it was in breach of school rules. These standards are even imposed on those in television: despite her fame, singer-turned-presenter Jamelia wasn't immune from criticism about her hair during her time on a popular weekly television show.

'I was on a show and every single week, without fail, I was asked to straighten my hair, I was asked to relax my hair. I was crying every week. And I was explaining to them, relaxing my hair is a permanent chemical process, I don't want to do it to my hair. At that point I'd been growing it for about a year and I was saying I've just gone natural and I don't want to perm my hair. And they were like, we just don't think it looks good, we don't think it looks professional, we don't think it can look elegant. They would come into my dressing room, and I would sit down and we'd have to discuss hair and make-up looks every week, and they were like – ooh, could you wear a wig this week? And I was like, but I don't want to! And then I'm talking to my management, and I'm saying "do you understand how offensive this is to me? And do you understand what you're saying to my children, and to every other child, or woman, who has hair like mine?

That's so wrong!" And I remember they were just like, "Well, don't you think you could straighten it just for this week?" And I said, "No, it doesn't work like that, fam!" It just got to the point where I knew that we were going to have that conversation every week, and I was gonna have to fight my corner.'

There was much-needed nationwide uproar in 2016 when Nicola Thorp, a white female secretary, was sent home from work for refusing to wear high-heel shoes. Many could not believe that such blatant sexism was permitted in the workplace. What many still don't realise is that for black women, the combination of sexism *and* racism ensures the policing of not just our shoe choices but our hair, too.

'You tried to change, didn't you? Closed your mouth more. Tried to be softer.'
Warsan Shire, for women who are 'difficult' to love

As we've touched on already, one of the biggest challenges at work and in wider life can be navigating the 'angry black woman' stereotype – especially when so much of your progression at work relies on being able to put your foot down and put yourself out there. Black women have to be able to prove that they are more competent than anyone else in the room, but are often fenced in because one of the primary ways to do so is through assertiveness, which can too often be misread. The downside of this, then, is not being able to prove ourselves, for fear of coming across as aggressive. As many noted when Sheryl Sandberg released her famous *Lean In* book, most black women have been 'leaning in' for years, but it has been at the cost of being stereotyped as 'too assertive' or 'angry'. White women often, rightfully, say that they are read as being angry in the workplace when in fact they're being assertive. It is a shame that despite this, many white women, like white men, also align black women's assertiveness with the damaging 'angry black woman' stereotype.

Emotion is a natural part of life and everyone gets angry sometimes. The expectation that it is something we have to compartmentalise and save for later when we're home is not only unrealistic, but damaging. Of course no one should be flying off the handle, arms flailing and mouth frothing, but as Funke says in the previous chapter, we also shouldn't be held to a higher, different standard because of stereotypes that are out of our control. Keisha Buchanan, a founding member of one of the country's most successful girl groups, the Sugababes, recalls being held to a different standard by the press and subsequently depicted as 'aggressive' with very little evidence. Despite all the girls being working class, she noticed Heidi Range was spoken about differently to Buchanan and bandmate Mutya Buena, both women of colour. With them, she says, it was clear 'they were the ethnic ones'.

'When I look back now I see that there were a lot of articles written that suggested [I was] the feisty one. And it wasn't just me, Mutya got it, too – Mutya was Filipino and Irish, but she is still ethnic. I don't mind being the edgy one because the edginess is, whatever, but I feel like it came with a negative vibe a lot of the time. And now, when I see people like Megan McKenna [reality TV star famous for her temper tantrums], no one has ever, ever seen me react in that way, and I've had way more criticism about my demeanour, and no one's ever seen me kick off . . . I think, "Oh my gosh, you've never even seen me act like that, but you have a perception of me and you can write articles."'

Sometimes the angry black woman stereotype can be dished out simply because one is devoid of positive emotions and trying to remain neutral – when a black woman doesn't laugh at a joke, asks someone not to touch their hair, shares their opinion or is anything other than a super-sweet, saccharine 'yes woman'. As a result, in order to offset existing stereotypes, many black women's work life becomes an extended exercise in proving, not their ability, but that they're a 'different sort' of black person. For example, feeling obliged to stay behind just a little bit longer to show that the lazy stereotype doesn't apply to you. But this can backfire; instead, staying behind may lead colleagues to assume you're simply unable to complete your tasks in the allocated time. Just because you change, unconscious biases don't necessarily change with you.

Because of these biases, many of us in the workplace just try to put our heads down, in the hope that hard work alone will pay off. However, the outcome is often a lack of sponsorship, and the further invisibilisation of black women (see 'Work Twice as Hard'). Other colleagues may take the opportunity to lay claim to our work and ideas, with the result that although we avoid the angry stereotype we also avoid any promotion. So, half of us are leaning in and being read as aggressive, while the other half are so frightened of that outcome that we don't lean in at all. Both groups suffer in different ways. Ironically, black women often have the most to prove but the least means to prove it.

At work, no one wants to be a 'too loud, too black' fresher. Downplaying blackness becomes a means of survival – you may be black but you don't want to 'rub it in anyone's face'. A black female candidate with straight hair, a posh accent, living in a mainly white area is still a black woman, but is more of a 'fit' than an equally qualified black woman candidate who wears a 'fro, is vocal about racial injustice and lives in the last non-gentrified parts of Peckham. Dr Nicola Rollock details how 'fit' is prioritised by UK employers:

'Colleagues working at UCLA have talked about the ways in which institutions support and promote people of colour as seen as having the most "fit", and "fit" is one of those terms that prospective employers use with free abandon, which I really think needs interrogating further. Colleagues at UCLA argue that we can think of "fit" in terms of those who are *racially palatable* or *racially salient*. That is, institutions regard people of colour who minimise or downplay their racial identity – that is they are seen as *racially palatable* – as more likely to fit in with organisational culture and norms. Conversely, institutions are less likely to see those who embrace their racial identity or who foreground issues of race – who are therefore seen as *racially salient* – as complementing their organisational culture and norms.'

Funke Abimbola MBE speaks of something similar but from the perspective of the employee: the idea of 'covering'.

'Showing the best professional self is important, though without feeling that you have to cover for what you are. There's this huge thing around inclusion theory, inclusion in all ways, called "covering" and it's where you feel you're having to spend a disproportionate amount of energy covering an aspect of who you are, which really you shouldn't have to cover at all. And it can be anything: where you went to university, the fact that you didn't go to a private school – you have to toe the line between being your best professional self, while remembering that you shouldn't have to cover something that's core to who you are in terms of your identity.'

When we repress our blackness by avoiding certain topics, hiding our hair and whatever else, we can seem to be rewarded with 'you're so articulate' exclamations, back pats and pub invites, but the price we have paid is usually greater than any potential pay increase. In the second series of *Insecure*, high-performing Molly accidentally finds out she is being paid less than her white, male colleague. The solution in her mind is simple: to be paid as much as a white man, she must become a white man, and she spends a great deal of the season attempting to assimilate with her bosses, suddenly popping up at their football games and practically choking at all of their jokes. She was rewarded for her efforts with the offer of a 'rising star' award, her picture on their website and a piece of paper, but no more money. She also lost a great deal of her sense of worth. The mental toll of essentially wearing 'white face' to work, suppressing cultural identity and shrinking oneself is inevitable – and things get even more difficult when the subject of race itself is brought up.

Let's (not) talk about race

While talk about sexism is likely to get people's backs up, talking about race has people backing towards the nearest exit as they contemplate how to make the case that the term 'cracker' is actually a reverse-racist equivalent to 'nigger'. The combination of the two usually just leaves people silent. Studies show that employees in UK workplaces are less comfortable talking about race than they are about age and gender: 37 per cent believe their colleagues are comfortable talking about race, compared with 44 per cent who say they are comfortable talking about age and 42 per cent about gender.

Speaking about race can be difficult anywhere; a study into the *Guardian* comments showed that of the ten most abused writers, eight were women (four white, four non-white) and two were black men.[35] They received this abuse no doubt because of what they were writing, combined with who they are. And while racist and sexist trolling won't take place as easily in a work environment, broaching these topics when you're not a writer being paid to do so and are being paid to do something else entirely, can be difficult. Discussions regarding race are central to Dr Rollock's work, and despite this she, like so many others, has been faced with defensiveness and fragility when attempting to discuss it with colleagues:

'There are white colleagues – not just within my sector, but across other sectors – who will say absolutely, "I don't know this area, and I'm also a white person, so I have a limited and can only have a limited understanding." If someone comes to me from that perspective the conversation can be productive, but quite often what I find is that there is a sense of lack of humility and reflexivity or just a belief because someone says they're committed to social justice, they believe [they have] sufficient knowledge with which to enter a conversation about race. I would like to see more humility amongst white colleagues, across all sectors, when it comes to engaging in these issues. How do I manage it? I'm not sure I always do, sometimes I can see a learnt pattern of responses whenever one's race is raised. One of the things I experience is defensiveness, sometimes anger, sometimes upset, and that can be quite draining, that can be quite challenging. And what it has served to do is take away the attention from the wider structural issues that we're talking about, and then it becomes a personal issue, it becomes about them individually and while I do believe, and evidence does show, that there is everyday racism, there is everyday sexism, I'm mainly and also talking about the way we have policies and the way we organise institutions and how that impacts on people of colour. So quite often the sensitiveness, the anger and the upset, serves to detract attention away from the key issues or it seeks to reposition white people to the centre of the conversation, which is not the point. The point is to attend to the way in which racial inequality is purveyed in every step of British society today, and in the past.'

Repeated attempts to explain phenomena invisible to those not experiencing them can be physically and mentally exhausting. This can often lead to black people keeping quiet about racism, even when racism permeates the work being created. For instance, if you work in an industry where representation is at the forefront, an inability to articulate problematic portrayals of minorities can be bad not just for you, but for the company. If only someone had stepped in at an early stage to explain why an advert featuring a black child in a monkey costume (a 2014 faux pas made by clothes shop Matalan) might not have been the best idea, it could have avoided its inevitable dragging on Twitter.

Black professionals often feel obliged to show feelings of serenity generally, but specifically in response to racial issues. This usually applies not just to racism within the work environment but also in response to continually growing racial tensions in post-Brexit Britain. Emotions of anger and annoyance are often subtly discouraged in favour of a kumbaya, colourblind rhetoric which is far more comforting – not for the black employee, of course, but for the white fragility of the office. Several friends of mine have experienced this walking on ever-present eggshells, but one story in particular comes to mind. A close friend (we'll call her "Tasha", in case her employer comes across this anecdote and is feeling fragile as usual) was sitting among staff, chit-chatting, when a co-worker turned conversation to the only other black member of staff. She said she 'looked scary', describing her as wearing a 'messy head dress, like a bandana, with all her hair coming out'. What she'd been describing was a popular headwrap style commonly worn by black women, where the fabric is tied up on the top of the wearer's head, mimicking a bun. 'She looks like she's come straight out of the ghetto!' the co-worker said in hysterics. Tasha said nothing. She was silent because she feared chastising the woman for her comments would lead to Tasha being penalised, instead of her. 'I got angry at myself because I thought, "Tasha, you actually like this look, this is something you would wear." But I couldn't bring myself to say anything. How could I even broach the fact that this isn't okay?' The woman made her comments without fear of repercussion – Tasha couldn't respond without worrying about backlash.

Many people feel they have to suppress their opinions, not just on social injustice and general racism, but about personal instances of mistreatment, too. In 2015, the Race at Work Report found that 32 per cent of black employees in the UK who have witnessed or experienced racial harassment in the workplace have done so in that year alone, an increase of 7 per cent on previous years.[36] Opportunity Now's Project 28–40 also found that 69 per cent of black women have experienced bullying and harassment at work in the last three years, compared to 52 per cent of women overall.[37] In the same way that sexist jokes can be written off as banter, this is often the case with racialised humour, too. Black women are on the receiving end of both.

When people do overstep the line, it's now become even more difficult for those who find the courage to speak out, and for us to hold to account employers who fail to protect minority people from racist bullying. Since 2013, when prohibitive fees were introduced, employment tribunal claims have fallen by 67 per cent. It is issues such as this that lead minority groups to feel more isolated in the business world, with only 55 per cent of BAME employees feeling they are a valued member of their team, compared to 71 per cent of white employees. Suffering in silence is not only permitted, but seemingly encouraged. Brits are well known for stiff upper lips, and if there is one thing we are taught to keep our lips slammed together about, it is race and racism.

> 'Every black American is bilingual.
> All of them. We speak street vernacular
> and we speak "job interview".'
> *Dave Chappelle, Inside the Actors Studio, 2006*

I don't know what my real voice sounds like, or if I even have one. I never consciously put one on, but in the same way people have different sides that they show to different individuals, I, like many black women, definitely have bespoke 'voices' that surface depending on who I'm talking to. When I'm speaking on a panel or on the radio, the voice I honed in my years at university bursts to the forefront. When I'm joking, I'm a mirror of my parents, with a Nigerian twang that I use for emphasis and laughs. When I'm angry, I sound like what can only accurately be described as a 'roadwoman'. At work, when my phone rings, the change in my tone, accent and words is audible and seamless. If I step out of the office and into the foyer, a 'wagwan G' might slip to the friend on the other end, who would barely blink at the sudden seismic accent change, they too are accustomed to having to 'code-switch'.

The term 'code-switching' initially came about in linguistics and referred to mixing languages and speech patterns in conversation. But now its meaning is more aligned with this definition provided by journalist Gene Demby at NPR: 'Many of us subtly, reflexively, change the way we express ourselves all the time. We're hop-scotching between different cultural and linguistic spaces and different parts of our own identities – sometimes within a single interaction.'

Code-switching is a survival tool that's second nature to most black people. But the 'right' voice is at times valued over competence. A study found that 82 per cent of industry leaders in finance felt presentation held back candidates from poorer backgrounds – more so even than poor exam results. Finance-industry executives outlined having the 'wrong' accent and mistakenly breaching dress codes as two prevalent factors. Almost two-thirds of them believed they may be turned down because they just wouldn't 'fit in' with the office culture.[38] And like most issues around race, this isn't something that only takes place in the workplace – an academy school in South London banned its students from using slang words and phrases like 'bare' and 'innit' in an attempt to specifically clamp down on the use of 'urban slang'. School seems a strange place to forbid the use of slang – they're kids, for goodness sake, and if they don't use it, who will? But what really sticks out is the targeting of so-called 'urban' slang, as popularised by predominantly black, working-class, inner-city children, as 'unfit' for a place of learning and development. Does the term 'fam' illicit the same derision as 'mate'? Or 'feds' as 'old bill'?

Because of this demonisation of a specific accent and slang usually attributed to black working-class people, many black women have perfected their 'work voice' or, to put it another way, they have learnt how to 'play Becky'. While there is no such thing as a 'white voice' literally – a white person raised in Nigeria will talk just like the locals – many people will be familiar with changing their voice on the telephone in order to try to convince the person on the other end that they're speaking with Kate instead of Kemi. Or in Clare Anyiam-Osigwe's case, 'Nina Fredricks'. In the same way that ethnic names can 'out' a candidate, accent and word choice can sideline a potential employee before you can say 'bruv'. Even those who aren't attempting to obscure their identity can sometimes find themselves in an awkward situation where people are surprised upon meeting them that their 'well-spoken' accent is coming out of a black mouth. Then there is the challenge of code-switching creating an identity crisis within your own community, when it is perceived as 'putting on airs'. Moving between what can seem like two completely opposed worlds can be confusing, especially when you can start to feel as though you belong to neither.

'It's weird, because when manoeuvring yourself within those industries, you do kinda feel like you're stuck in this weird parallel because sometimes you feel like you've outgrown your friends from the ends,' says Irene Agbontaen, founder of flourishing clothes brand TTYA (Taller Than Your Average). 'Because how they perceive you is, "Oh, you're in this creative industry, you're going to all these events, you travel so much, you're around all these people," but then it's like you're trying to fit into this world that isn't really catered for someone like you. You're in this weird kind of parallel universe, stuck in between two worlds. Don't get me wrong, I can still relate, I can catch up with my friends from ends. When you're in freelance employment you kind of have this spiritual freedom, but at the same time you're still fighting for a voice, you're still fighting to be heard, you're still fighting to be acknowledged. It's a tricky one. I don't really feel like you ever have to leave your personality at home, but I do feel you need to adapt – there's an adaptation into fitting into somewhere that isn't really built for you.'

It can be difficult constantly flitting between faces (and voices), but at work in particular people – and arguably black women more than anyone – are forced to be inauthentic due to the prioritising of white-created protocols. Learning to read rooms and code-switch are often key factors to navigating different worlds, but you need to ensure that you don't lose who you are altogether. What must be truly prioritised is authenticity.

....

Express yourself

....

Work consists of several structural and cultural problems, so many of us aim to simply survive, let alone thrive. In terms of diversity, many places of work are committed to doing the bare minimum, if that – by 'diversifying' through box-ticking and recruitment campaigns, but rarely challenging a work culture that leaves some members of staff feeling alienated and targeted. The issues may seem insurmountable, and they are pervasive. The systems are in need of the sort of change that our ancestors hoped would by now have been achieved. But we can acknowledge this while also recognising that there are ways to make our existence within these structures easier, and that would mean we could even flourish within them, as our interviewees for this book have. For in spite of the hurdles, black women continue to ascend to the top against all odds by making good of what we're given. So while changing the entirety of white working culture may seem impossible, what *is* possible is ensuring our ideas are heard, going to where our contributions are appreciated and ensuring we take stock of what we have to offer.

An important and often overlooked tip for getting on in the workplace is simple assessment of your soon-to-be surroundings beforehand. One thing interviewees forget to do is to *interview* their interviewer: try to find out as much as you can about what it's like to work at wherever it is you hope to go. 'Culture' is becoming more and more important in working spaces, offices and organisations as a whole – a job may look all you dreamed of on paper, but try to figure out what the 'vibe' is going to be before taking a role, and *then* make a decision on whether it's for you. In interviews, when you're asked if you have any questions, you do. Your question is: 'What's the working culture like here?' If their answer to this question fills you with dread – it's too rigid, too conservative, perhaps – think about the toll that is likely to take on your day-to-day life. For some, adhering to certain 'rules' isn't as difficult as it is for others, but this should be an equally important part of your decision-making process as the salary you are being offered.

When you do first start a job, it is useful to listen more than speak. First, understand the place and the people who occupy the space, then react accordingly. Most of us don't jump into a job already knowing who we're going to be, and as black women, at the outset of a new job or when we first step into a space it's a luxury that not many of us have. It's important to be realistic – and in some roles, this may mean playing the game to survive. But it also means being realistic about what you can and are willing to take.

Respectability politics can take its toll on you mentally, but it is important that you don't let it also take a toll on your ideas. If you work within a predominantly white workplace, seeing your perspective as a help instead of a hindrance is key. It is certainly easier to say than do, but you have a perspective that the vast majority of the people at your desk do not, and that is valuable, especially as brands increasingly appropriate and borrow from elements of the culture they continue to undervalue and sideline. This quote from American corporation Hyatt, outlining their approach to diversity, puts it perfectly: 'Diversity without inclusion leads to conflict. Inclusion without diversity may create harmony, but since everyone is alike, the organisation will not be able to reach its full creative or innovative potential.'[39] Ethnic minorities are under-represented in almost all professions – in the City, the media and FTSE 100 companies, and across the board at every management level – in comparison to white counterparts with the same level of education and attainment. The last thing many boardrooms need is another middle-class white man, even if they don't yet know it.

So wherever you work, a black female perspective always matters because you're likely to be one of the few people with one. Besides, black women have transformed and continue to dominate all areas of pop culture, which informs so much else – you have an important edge, so use it. Karen Blackett OBE reached her current position by not only being aware of and faithful to her personal brand, but also choosing to leave companies where she was not valued for who she was:

'Once you know your own personal brand and feel comfortable in your own skin, you don't have to try and morph into something else to succeed. And there's this study, carried out by Deloitte University, that talks about covering. It was 61 per cent of people interviewed, and they interviewed in ten different industry sectors – over three and a half thousand people; 61 per cent of people suppressed some aspect of their natural personality in order to try and succeed at work. When you're constantly trying to be something you're not, you're gonna be bloody unhappy. So I think that makes for an unhappy working population and an unhappy life, because you can't keep up that pretence forever. If you are in an organisation where you fear you have to morph into something else, or be something that you're not, leave. And I've had that in my life, where I've gone into an organisation and there's a sort of cookie-cutter mould of what you should be like, and that's not me. I think finding a place where you can be yourself and bring your whole self to work is important. I think that most people, black or white, moderate their behaviour and present a certain version of themselves at work – speaking the right language, for example. But we shouldn't have to become someone completely different, someone inauthentic, just because our difference scares people. It's their issue, not yours. I wouldn't know how to be someone else. And I couldn't keep it up, either, I'm not that good an actor – I wouldn't be able to do it.'

In an ideal world, people would give less of a shit about what you look like, listen to, speak like and eat like at work and more about, you know, your work. But for now, learning how to move between different audiences, styles and approaches when at work should also mean keeping your true self and sanity intact. 'Flexing your style' shouldn't mean a hairstyle change or accent transplant, but rather being yourself while having conversations and presenting ideas and remaining aware of what you bring to the table – even if that table has to be in a pub for the sake of your boss.

Being inauthentic at work is commonplace and in many ways rewarded, granted. If you play politics it may well help your personal arc, in the short term, but the women we have spoken to are real movers and shakers – game changers – who refused to play the game and found huge long-term success by sticking to their guns. Despite the challenges, many have cited being their authentic selves as integral to their success, but it must be noted, this is something that has become easier with time and status, as Althea Efunshile points out. 'I think that as I've got older, as I've got more successful, as I've got more confident in the sense that other people respect me for what I do, that I've been more and more comfortable with just being me.'

And though I haven't yet reached the heights of Efunshile, it is something that I've learnt, too. Being 'too loud, too black' freshers, employees and women has come with hurdles, but it's who Liz and I are, and have always been. And it if wasn't for being who and how we are, I can honestly say I don't think this book would exist. Sure, we 'flex our style' when need be, but we still shout-talk and laugh-howl too, and the more our belief in our abilities has been validated, the less reason we have ever had to be anything other than who we are.

GETTING AHEAD

'Your particular story and your individual perspective on life is an invaluable asset: one that many of us fail to recognise. The opportunities for black women to make money from what we know have never been more abundant.'

Elizabeth

Independent Women

ELIZABETH

....

'I was standing in the middle of Richmond, and
I burst into tears. I was trying to explain it to my
dad, the reason why, and he was like, "It's bricks
and mortar, I don't understand why you're
getting so emotional," and I'm like, "It's about
more than that, it's my independence, it's the
biggest thing I have ever done all by myself."'
Charlene White

....

When I was a kid I was never given pocket money, it wasn't something my parents saw the value in doing. After all, they provided well
for me, clothed me, put food on the table, and even though I would
beg for a cheeky pound so I could join my friends on a sugar-rush
bender at the local shop, they refused. The only time I encountered
money was the 30 precious seconds when family members would gift
me ten pounds and my parents would swoop in from behind like an
Arsenal defender at a cup final and wrestle it away from me, promising to look after it. And, surprise surprise, I'd never see that crisp
tenner again.

However, this changed one day when I was entrusted with the
responsibility of buying my week's bus pass. Twelve-year-old me
didn't go to the newsagents to buy it, as I was supposed to. Instead, I
swaggered straight to school feeling like Charlie with his golden ticket,
but rather than a chocolate river and giant candy canes, I had South
London's finest chicken shops to tuck into. Three pick 'n' mix trips,
boneless wing meals for my friends and an arcade trip later, I had
spent all of my bus money. It was only the third day of the week and
it was finished, finito, fini. Miss Moneybags had lost control and I had

to admit defeat. I didn't have enough left to get home. I sat anxiously at the bus stop knowing I'd get the punishment of my life once my parents found out. Feeling helpless, as the last of my mates boarded the bus and the first wave of workers fled the city, tears began to fill my eyes. Fortunately for me, my teacher Miss Rodriguez spotted me on her way home. After a confession and a telling-off, she bailed me out, bought me a bus pass and sent me on my way. This was the first time in my life I realised the importance of being responsible with money and the consequences of money mismanagement.

They say it's often an unexpected situation that inspires us to really take a closer look at our finances. The second time the spotlight glared on my bank account was when I became estranged from my family. This left me exposed financially, with no one to bail me out this time, not even Miss Rodriguez. I suddenly had to find a place to live, put down a hefty deposit and hope for the best. Like most black girls I knew growing up, I hadn't been taught the importance of a long-term financial plan, at home or in school – money just wasn't something we spoke about openly. But this wasn't just about having enough for a bus home: I was worried about my whole future.

Though the pay gap between men and women is well documented, what's less publicised is how the double whammy of race and gender impacts negatively on the pockets of black women, which in turn can prevent them from supporting their families, building up savings and creating a long-term financial plan.

'Who runs the world?' Beyoncé asked – it's not who, it's what. Money does. It plays a powerful role in the way the world runs, and, frustratingly, black women are still playing catch up.

Please mind the gap

The gender pay gap is real and pervasive, and it affects all women. By definition, the gender pay gap is the earning difference, based on hourly rate, between men and women in paid employment within the labour market, and we use it as one of the many indicators of gender inequality in society. Crazily, the current median gap between women and men in the UK is 18.4 per cent, which means women, in effect, work for free for two months of the year. Although the pay discrepancy is narrowing, at the current rate of progress it will take over 60 years to close this gap. Eeek!

Equal Payday was created to highlight this injustice, marking the day when women essentially stop earning relative to an average man's salary. On this day you can spot your favourite celebrities sporting 'this is what a feminist looks like' T-shirts, and frantic politicians jumping on the bandwagon following suit. Nevertheless, it really should be called *white women's unequal* payday, because behind the T-shirts, slogans and social media campaigns, it has become clear that ethnic minority women are invisible within the gender pay-gap debate. A study by the Fawcett Society in 2017 revealed that despite the progress we have made as a society, the pay gap between women from almost every minority ethnic group and white British men is growing, while black women experience the largest full-time gender pay gap, at 19.6 per cent.[1]

In America, Black Women's Equal Pay Day is on 31 July. For them to earn the same as a white man does in 12 months, black women would have to work 19 months – seven whole months of extra work. Let that sink in.

This grave inequality in pay stems from a variety of reasons, including the fact that black women are more likely to be employed in low-paid, insecure work. And then, of course, there's the elephant in the room: discrimination. This occurs at two points, which we talked about in the previous chapter: entry to the job market, then in the workplace itself, where black women encounter barriers that can stop them progressing as quickly as their white counterparts.

Remember when I said that it would take 60 years for the pay gap to close? Horrifically, for ethnic minority women, this increases to 158 years: 158 years of lower wages when we are hired, promoted and rewarded bonuses. Shocking, right? The reality is that right now we are losing out financially, and it looks like we may continue to do so. According to a recent report, it is low-income black women who will pay the highest price for austerity, and by 2020 they will have lost nearly double the amount of money that poor white men will have lost in the same period.[2]

This all makes for uncomfortable reading, but it is an inconvenient truth that black women in the UK are increasingly facing economic disadvantage. But you wouldn't be able to guess this from the dearth of conversation around intersectionality within the equal-pay campaigns that come around every year.

While a good deal of attention is focused on the pay gap affecting women in general, less is known about how those with more than one 'disadvantaged' identity suffer a significantly greater pay penalty than those with a single disadvantage.[3] This is called the 'Snowballing Penalty Effect'. Professor Carol Woodhams, who produced a report explaining how factors such as race, disability, sexuality, age and class intersect with gender to create multiple layers of disadvantage for women, explains: 'A woman who is black has a qualitatively different experience. And it should be acknowledged in legislation that a person in this experience should have more legal protection. I would encourage the government to look at the implications of having more than one protected characteristic – to be a woman and black, or a woman and disabled, or all of the above – because that combination has a snowball effect in our pay gap, of them all working together, against individuals.'[4]

A key recommendation put forward by the Fawcett Society is for UK law to finally formally acknowledge cases of multiple discrimination through legislation. Section 14 of the Equality Act 2010, 'The Ethnicity Pay Gap', was never implemented due to an apparent 'lack of evidence', with the result that the current law 'does not respond to the reality of people's lives and identities'.[5] Yet it's clear that some black women are discriminated against at every stage of the recruitment process[6] and the number of black women on temporary contracts has risen to 82 per cent in the past five years.[7] Dual discrimination of race and gender cannot continue to be overlooked, and discrimination law should reflect a person's true intersectional identity. The lack of urgency to address this issue by legislation is lazy at best and disgraceful at worst.

The ethnic gender pay gap is complex, and the current single-minded approach is insufficient. It is a gap that has lifelong financial effects and, as low income and insecure employment are all recognised contributors to poverty, it directly impacts on the standard of living of black women. More than a third of black women and 40 per cent of ethnic minority women live in poverty[8] – twice the proportion of white women. This has an obvious negative consequence on the wealth and well-being of their families and the communities in which they live. Notably, in 2017, a study by the Resolution Foundation think-tank found that minority ethnic families in the UK earn as much as £8,900 a year less than their white British counterparts.[9]

We must combat the explicit and implicit bias in the labour marketplace that is penalising black women. But how?

First, we must strengthen our laws to promote pay transparency and to confront and address unfairness in the current system. In 2017, a government-commissioned review recommended that companies should publish data on how ethnically diverse they are by pay band. Ruby McGregor-Smith, who led the independent review, revealed that she was 'shocked' when only 74 FTSE 100 companies responded to her call for anonymised data on ethnicity by pay band – and just half of them supplied meaningful information. The cynic in me wasn't shocked at this figure; just look at the outrage caused when the BBC published the salaries of their top stars. You could practically hear white men across boardrooms in Britain shuffling uncomfortably in their three-piece suits, dreading the looming calls for more transparency around pay.

The outrage was warranted: the BBC had had two years to get their act together, yet social media was up in arms that the highest-paid white man still took home roughly the same as all of his BAME colleagues together. Though we're told repeatedly that 'angry black women' don't get promoted, we *need* to be angry at this injustice. Melanie Eusebe agrees.

'Anger is such a passionate, driving force, and again, on the other

hand I encourage people to be angry – I encourage them to acknowledge and recognise the anger, but it's more about the manifestation
of that anger and how that happens. There was an article, I remember a magazine interviewing me and they were saying, "Advice for
young women?" and I was saying, "I want them to get angry!" We're
disabused of our notion of anger – anger is a beautiful, healthy emotion that says to us, "Our boundaries have been crossed." Either our
boundaries are messed up, or someone has crossed our boundaries,
but something happened. Do not take away that anger, because
there are some things that women should be angry about. I think we
should be angry about equal pay.

'I don't understand why you can make it law to charge 5p for
bags, so you can say that we value bags, and you put a law in for
that and you make sure that Tesco charges me for a 5p bag, but you
can't make sure that Tesco pays me the same amount as my male colleague if I'm doing the same job? That's anger for me.'

Despite there being current legislation to force large employers to
publish data on their gender pay gaps, McGregor-Smith's recommendation to use the law to enforce transparency around the ethnicity
gap was rejected. The government at the time preferred a 'business-
led, voluntary approach, and not legislation, as a way of bringing
about lasting change'.[10] I disagree; the business-led approach isn't
working and it's about time businesses put their money where their
mouth is and took meaningful action towards closing the ethnicity
pay gap.

....

**'We have to learn about stocks and shares, in the
way that we know about lipstick, hair and makeup.
We need to make sure we know about this stuff.'**
June Sarpong

....

The 1990s was a decade of girl-power anthems. It was the golden
age of girl bands, and there was a girl group to suit your every mood.

Destiny's Child were the older, cooler black girls you wished were your sisters. Out of all their anthems, the one that struck a chord with me most was 'Independent Women'. The lyrics declared that women shouldn't rely 'on a man to give you what you want'; instead we should stand on our own two feet in order to achieve financial liberation. The music video showed them in coordinated outfits, in boss mode sitting at the head of the table, giving out orders. The 13-year-old me was hooked. I made a mental note because I was determined to become the independent woman they championed.

This was easier said than done. As I made the transition from my teens to my early twenties, I realised I hadn't acquired the knowledge that would equip me to be in the driving seat of my financial future. Let's be honest, the complexity of the financial system doesn't make things easier: it effectively excludes those who don't have the tools to understand it. Financial literacy refers to the set of skills and know-ledge that allows a person to make informed and effective decisions, and I had little of these. I didn't understand the basics of savings accounts, how to use a credit card properly and the impact of credit scores. So I made a lot of mistakes – costly ones. If I wasn't stumbling about in the dark I was two-stepping around it. I was comfortably uncomfortable with being bad with money and would constantly procrastinate when it came to financial tasks.

I wasn't taught about practical money-management skills at school or at home; my understanding of money started and stopped at what it could buy you. Jamelia's relationship with money was similar; she had her introduction to it when she signed her first record deal at 15. Essentially you could say her first job was being 'Jamelia', the singer. 'One day you're in a council house and the next day they're giving you a cheque that's more than your mum's annual salary. At 15, the first thing I did, I went out and I bought trainers for my whole class at school. I didn't have any financial advice, I was a child being given stupid amounts of money.'

For me, money only came up in my household when it was brought up in arguments, or when a household appliance incon-veniently broke down. Having spoken to my friends, we all had similar experiences: we were taught that talking about money is somehow uncouth, unladylike and bad-mannered. In Fidelity Investments' Money FIT Women Study in 2015,[11] they found that eight in ten women would refrain from discussing money with family and friends, feeling too uncomfortable about it or thinking it was too personal. The awkward truth is, money is often linked to status, and status is linked to power. If you don't have a lot of the former, talking about it can often make people feel like they're powerless, which results in a dearth of meaningful conversations around it. But money is a form of power, and full equality for women is financial equality. The same study also found that 92 per cent of women were keen to learn about money and finances and only 7 per cent of women would currently give themselves an 'A' for their knowledge of investing.

We live in a society that is happy for people, especially the most disadvantaged, to feel powerless about financial matters. Financial education does not exist in our most disadvantaged communities and schools, yet this is where it's needed the most. Economics professor Annamaria Lusardi's studies have documented the gaps in financial knowledge among different demographic groups. She explains, 'What the data on financial literacy shows is that financial knowledge is unequally distributed. Those with the least knowledge are also the most vulnerable groups in economic terms. As a result, the lack of financial literacy exacerbates economic inequality.'[12]

Actor Susan Wokoma recalls how this unequal distribution of knowledge negatively affected her childhood: 'We did not have money, and sometimes people make it into a little Cinderella story because it's cute. But we had no money. We were poor. All I remember is bailiffs coming to our house. Now as an adult, as I look back, I don't think my parents managed whatever little money they had, because they would constantly borrow money, and then as soon as they got money coming into the house it'd have to go back out again, so there were all sorts of sacrifices made. I realised it was to do with the bad management of money. But things got better as we got older, and I realised the thing that you needed to avoid was debt. I'm so scared of debt. It took me ages to finally agree to have an overdraft account, because

I needed it when I got kicked out of my home. So I needed to have an overdraft account, a student account, and I *really* didn't want one; I do not want to owe anyone anything. I think one of the things that we should be taught in schools is the management of money.'

In contrast, Vanessa Kingori was given pocket money and taught very early on about managing her own finances, which has set her up well for adulthood: 'I had a bank account from quite young, I was given pocket money but I was never given pocket money "just coz": I had to do chores to get it. So even in the winter I was out washing the car, and no one does that anymore, but I had to do that. I had to do silly things – from tidying, to organising my mum's files or her dressing table. I think if you are raising children now, the idea of hard work, gain and reward is really important to instil.'

If financial literacy is what you need to understand how the financial system works (including understanding things like tax and credit scores), wealth literacy is how you put your knowledge to use so that you can create and work towards your financial goals. Studies show that, compared to white people, black people in the UK have a lower participation across the range of financial products, including ISAs, premium bonds and stocks and shares.[13] In my case, investing was never something I was interested in, or for a long time, I thought it didn't apply to me. I saw it as something white men in suits like Lord Alan Sugar did on *The Apprentice*. My mentality was, 'I don't have millions so what am I investing?' However, the reality is, investors don't have to fit this stereotype and you don't need to know chapter and verse of the London stock exchange to be an investor.

June Sarpong insists it should be about getting the balance right: 'I think, in general anyway, we have to learn about stocks and shares, in the way that we know about lipstick, hair and makeup. We need to make sure we know about this stuff. It's really important, because that's what gives you independence and freedom, when you don't need to take a job to pay the bills. I would say my first thing would be *save*. Save, just get used to having at least 10 per cent of what you earn that you don't spend. Just put it away. And then have a long-term plan as far as what you are going to do with that money and how you're going to make it grow, having a proper sort of investment portfolio. There are loads of things that the rich know about creating wealth and making their money grow, and I think it's really important that we learn them, too, so that we have options.' June is right. This stuff is important and we need to know it.

When it comes to managing finances, I always notice that some of my friends seem to have it more together than others. They use financial language confidently and are knowledgeable about their financial situation. However, wherever you are in your financial journey, if you're focused on getting out of your student debt, want to save for a house deposit, or just want to know what's available, I've highlighted some key steps that can help you take control and be in the driving seat of your financial future, because there is no time better than the present to come up with a plan.

Firstly, what's your credit score? I know it's not something people walk around saying, but your credit score plays a key role in your financial journey. It is a number that evaluates your credit-worthiness to lenders such as banks and businesses and is based on your credit history. They use credit scores to evaluate the probability that you will repay them back, thus it is a deciding factor in whether you'll be approved for a mortgage, credit card or loan. You've probably already willingly or unwillingly contributed to your credit score rating, negatively or positively. But, if you don't know it, find out. Without good credit you can't even get a phone contract. There are companies like Clear Score, Experian and Noddle that can help you have a good idea about what shape your score is in. Once you know this, you should look into ways to build this up positively, through things as simple as registering to be on the electoral roll and setting up a direct debit to make sure you pay your bills on time.

Then, it's important to keep track of your outgoings and, it goes without saying, you should be spending less than what you earn.

Take some time to understand your spending patterns; if you don't have a budget already, create one – compare your expenses to your income and then establish 'SMART' (which stands for 'specific, measurable, ambitious, relevant and time-sensitive') long-term financial goals. These goals are unique to everyone and they could be a house deposit, a holiday or a car, or simply getting out of your overdraft.

If you don't have a savings account, look into opening one. Like June said, if you start by saving at least 10 per cent of what you earn, you can begin to earn interest on your income. If you're anything like me, who looks at my phone at least 100 times a day, consider managing your finances via the new range of personal budgeting apps. They are a great way to keep track of your spending: they show you how much you spend on little things, such as coffee, and text you when you're closing in on your budget. They can even save money on your behalf. I get a text message at the start of every week about how much money I have in my current account, it's forced me to understand my spending habits – for better or for worse.

Also, simple things like having all your direct debits come out of your account on the same day can make money management so much easier. Or even having a separate account for your spending and another for your bills. This all sounds basic but it still surprises me what little knowledge my friends and I had, and how much better off we were once we got into the habit of managing our finances.

Don't forget pensions, too. Most employers have a scheme that you can sign up to where they contribute to your pension plan. If in doubt, get in touch with your HR department to find out details. Why do pensions matter? You're not going to be able to work forever, so it's never too early to start planning for your retirement.

And finally, buying a house isn't the only form of investment opportunity out there – there are also stocks, bonds and investment funds that you can put your money into. Speak to your bank about this and they can let you know how to make the most of your money. But whatever you choose to invest in, do your research – don't commit to an investment or financial product if you don't understand it. Ask questions. Yes, it comes with a lot of investment jargon, but don't be put off by this, there's a useful site called Boringmoney. co.uk that explains financial products in plain English – jargon-free.

When you take your first steps, it can seem overwhelming and there might be a lot of information to process. However, getting a head start will benefit you in the future. It takes time to build good habits, and you do not have to implement them all at once, but the sooner you begin learning and evolving, the sooner you can start taking care of your financial well-being.

> 'And I had to decide then, "Do I rent with some of my friends? And be in the thick of it and just enjoy this moment? Or do I trade it off?" And I decided to trade it off.'
> *Vanessa Kingori*

As a result of the ethnic minority pay gap, black women are less likely to have the opportunity to build up significant savings for a rainy day. And living in England, if there's one thing we understand, it's that when it rains, boy can it pour. We all know that life doesn't always go to plan, but you're more financially vulnerable to emergencies if you have found it difficult to save.

Savings are vital, providing a safety net against dips in income and unplanned situations. Even in relatively small amounts, savings can help people avoid debt or severe hardship.[14] A Fawcett report reveals that ethnic minority women have low levels of savings and high levels of debt, which makes them particularly vulnerable. Three-quarters of black women have less than £1,500 in savings, compared to half of all white women. Moreover, 24 per cent of black women are in arrears, compared to 9 per cent of Asian and white women. This debt will in turn be incurring more debt, particularly when low-income women have no access to collateral and are forced to turn to loan sharks.[15]

Debt is a very scary thing, and it is something that singer VV Brown experienced when she was 21. 'I got signed to Universal at 18 and moved to LA. I made an album, bought a house, lived like a rock star, got ill-advised and lost everything. I got shelved and at 21 I was in debt to over £100,000. It was one of the worst times in my life. I still look back on it and I can't believe that I got through it. To be honest, I can handle anything now. It was really, really hard and it was a massive test of character and strength, especially being 21. Obviously, when I paid it back and then started to make money again, there were so many things I learned – from opening up a tax account specifically for your tax so you're always organised financially; get yourself the right accountant; open up several accounts and distribute your money across different accounts; categorise your accounts specifically. Now I have an account for my personal life, which is where I pay myself a salary, I have a limited company, but I also have separate accounts for things like childcare, car and cleaner. And so actually categorising my accounts specifically to my lifestyle has actually helped me budget.'

Many do not have the luxury to build up an emergency fund, or what writer Paulette Perhach calls a 'fuck-off fund', that gives you the freedom to live the life you want, or just financial freedom to fuck off from a toxic relationship, job or household situation. Even though I was never really a saver – because I didn't know what I would have been saving for – when I became estranged from my family I was lucky enough to have an emergency fund that I used to put up a first month's rent and deposit. This meant I could find somewhere to live within hours of leaving home.

Because I no longer had the financial fall-back of my family, I had to make sure I accounted for every single penny coming into my bank account. Even though I had a full-time job, I was still very nervous about having the means to look after myself. How much money would I need if something happened? If I lost my job would I have enough to tide me over until I found a new one? In the space of 12 months, I had to move three times due to substantial increases in rent, and each time I moved I was required to pay a new deposit and the first month's rent in advance. It was tough. At the time, the housing charity Shelter were warning that more than a million households living in private rental accommodation are at risk of becoming homeless by 2020 because of rising rents, benefit freezes and a lack of social housing.[16] With this harsh reality at the back of my head, this ultimately meant that I had to make what Vanessa Kingori calls a 'trade-off'.

'It's understanding that every single thing in life is a trade-off. Everyone that you see living large, they've traded something off, right? And everything that you own is a trade-off for something else. If you want the small thing, and you're like, "I just want it," you have to have in your mind that at the time you're getting the small thing, this is going to mean that it's going to take you longer to get that other thing. So I literally am thinking about what am I trading off if I'm . . . ?, and this is not just a money or possessions thing – it is money and possessions as well – but it's also in my time, which is hands-down, I think, our most valuable, my most valuable, asset now.

'I remember when I was saving to buy my property now, I just was living slightly out, and all of my friends were moving to East London. I was still in West London and I had quite a good setup, in that I was paying really low rent where I was and it worked with getting to work and everything. And it was a really defining moment for me, because I was young, I was single; I wanted to be there on the Friday night with everyone. I wanted to have those, the thing where someone phones you and they're like, "Can you make it in 10 minutes?" and to be like, "Yeah, I can!" But I also wanted to own my own property, and I wanted to not be pouring my money away in rent. And I had to decide then, "Do I rent with some of my friends? And be in the thick of it and just enjoy this moment? Or do I trade it off?" And I decided to trade it off and stay in West London, which I now absolutely love. And I still live in West London, and own my own property. Now both had value to them, it's just what was important for me. But you have to know what you're trading at the time and you have to think that through. That's literally how I think about every-thing – from career opportunities, to time, to purchases, to extra jobs and work that I take on. In a way, everybody is doing this, they just don't always know that they are.'

Trade-offs are difficult, especially when you work hard, and of course social media doesn't help. Biggie Smalls didn't tell a lie in 'Mo Money Mo Problems'; even when you make money and things start looking up financially it can be easy to fall into a trap of overspending and living beyond your means. It is hard to avoid peer pressure and the fear of missing out, particularly in these times, when social media comparisons can be just a click and a like away. Now it only takes an hour of perusing your favourite apps to know what you need to own in order to keep up with the world. The truth is, of course, that social media is just a highlights reel, a snapshot of people's lives, and we have to remember that it deliberately captures only the most glamorous aspects of them.

Melanie Eusebe understands all too well the burdens of consumerism fuelled by social media.

'You have all these things, and then you don't use them or you don't need them. I think there was a point where I was decluttering, and then you just realise when you start actually budgeting, how much money you spent on things that you no longer use or want or desire.

'I wish I had known a bit more about myself in terms of what made me really, really happy, so I could invest in it. And what would've made me really happy is having my own business and having freedom to do whatever I wanted on projects and stuff – not work for a little bit, to travel for a little bit, rather than be beholden to bills. I've learned that the things I purchase don't make me happy.'

Of course, there is a middle ground. Vanessa Kingori says take a 'Gains, rewards, hard work' approach.

'I was taught to, every time I was paid, have a mini celebration, because if you try to – this was my mother's, in particular, point of view – if you try to be too frugal, you get to a point where you just want to splurge, right? And then you blow it all. Or if you're just splurging all the time, splurge, splurge, splurge, then you're like, "Oh, I've got nothing in the pot."

'So try and find a sense of a middle, so if you're constantly thinking, "I remember when I got these earrings and what for," think:

a) it gives a sense of meaning to the things that you own – like every milestone I buy myself a little something and when I wear that bag, I think, "That's my promotion bag!" And b) It feels better when you wear it, it's not just, "Oh I got that at some point, when I was splurging continuously." And it just gives a sort of quality to how you live, the experiences you have, they mean something.'

....

'Be unapologetic about asking for how much money you deserve.'
Nicki Minaj

....

As mentioned earlier, the racial pay gap took centre stage on TV's *Insecure*, when Molly, a high-powered lawyer, mistakenly receives the paycheck of her white male colleague and discovers that he has earned more than her despite him not working nearly as hard. It reveals the classic adage we've already spoken about at length: black women are putting in twice the effort for half the reward. Talking about money on a good day is hard enough, but negotiating your salary can be a whole other beast in itself.

As we've already noted, black employees are more likely to say that their careers have failed to meet their expectations, and it's easy to see why, when on average they are obtaining a lower return financially for their education.[17] The increase in qualifications for young black employees has yet to make a dent in the persistent wage disparity that they experience, which in turn stunts their chances of achieving more economic security.

One of the most important things to be aware of as you progress in your career is your earning potential. How do you make sure you are maximising your qualifications and work experience so you can work towards a career that's going to pay you enough to live the life you want to live?

Rapper Nicki Minaj does not shy away from asking for what she is worth: 'At a very early stage in my rap career, I was making six figures for shows. If I heard there was another rapper making that, I thought, "You know what? I get out there and demand or command a crowd. I get out there and make my fans happy. I get out there and give a real show. I want that, too." And I pushed myself to be better with my showmanship, but I also decided, you know what? I want to be compensated well. If you know you're great at what you do, don't ever be ashamed to ask for the top dollar in your field.'

When Jennifer Lawrence expressed anger about Hollywood's gender pay gap in 2015, fellow actor Kate Winslet was dismissive. She was quoted as saying, 'I understand why they are coming up . . . I don't like talking about money; it's a bit vulgar, isn't it? I don't think that's a very nice conversation to have publicly at all . . . I am a very lucky woman and I'm quite happy with how things are ticking along.' That's nice for you, Kate, but what if you're not happy with the way things are 'ticking along'? We don't have the luxury of waiting 158 years for the playing field to level out. In Rihanna's words, 'Pay me what you owe me.'

So we must negotiate our salaries at every opportunity to make sure we are asking for what we deserve.

However, as black women we may face unique challenges in negotiating, in comparison to our white female colleagues. While they fear being labelled as 'pushy' when asking for a promotion and subsequent pay rise, my black female friends don't want to come across as the 'angry black woman'. As we've seen, black women can often be held to a higher standard than their white counterparts. As a black woman, if you are too nonchalant, you may be seen as not caring enough – 'too cool for school'. If you're too passionate, you're perceived as angry. Joan C. Williams, co-author of the book *What Works for Women at Work*, says that those asking for pay rises may face discrimination on the basis of race as well as gender, 'To the extent that white men kind of get a pass on swagger that's denied to other people.'[18]

So how do you go about this? It is not usually the done thing to talk about pay at work, but yet again, you have to do your research. When I felt ready for my first promotion, one of the first things I did was research my market rate. I updated my CV, got in touch with recruiters and searched online for the salary range that a person with similar experience to me could expect to earn. Arming yourself with this information will give you perspective on and confidence about what it is realistic to ask for and what you should be expecting to receive.

Next, book a meeting with your manager and let him know in advance what the meeting is about: no one likes being caught off guard. When you approach your manager, don't get personal, discuss the facts. Rather than saying 'I'm worth X,' be as objective as possible and instead approach it by saying, 'After researching it, I can see that someone of my experience is paid in the range of X amount.' Then go on to highlight specific examples of how you have demonstrated your experience and expertise in the work you have done. This is no time to be modest. We've looked at how black women have to provide more evidence of competence than others to prove themselves to their colleagues, while the opposite is true for white men. If you're a white male, the world is pretty much your oyster; you can ask for what you want. In fact, Joan C. Williams says, 'White men are punished for being "too modest".' But for women of any race and for black men, 'that doesn't seem to be the case.'[19]

Actor Yvonne Orji, aka *Insecure*'s Molly, says, 'Yes, your work should speak for itself, and should be recognised, but I also think that you should advocate for yourself. Women aren't the best at advocating for ourselves, but anytime you're working on a project, and you know you're killing it or your contributions impacted the outcome, you've got to keep notes and records of that, so when there is talk about a raise or a promotion, you have the facts. It's not just built on emotions. You have facts. Like, hey, this is what I've done to impact the bottom line. It may sound like you're tooting your own horn, but if you don't do it, who will?'[20]

You should outline your accomplishments in a factual manner. In my particular job, I always find it easier to do this by using numbers to demonstrate how effective I have been on a particular campaign. It's all too easy to get emotional and assume your manager already knows how hard you've been working. However, even those with the best intentions may not remember all the great things you have accomplished, and therefore you should come prepared with specific examples of how you have contributed to the business objectives.[21]

Secondly, as Anne-Marie says, practice is key: 'Always practise your negotiation – with a friend, with a mentor, with your mum, with your dad. If you've said it out loud, and you've practised that thing, then it's a lot easier for you to go into negotiation, because you kind of already know what could happen or not, so it's not a new thing for you. So you've got the confidence, the other thing that's come from actually practising, and doing it and going through the motions of so many different things. I speak a lot at events and people always say, are you nervous? And I'm like, no, I'm not nervous. Why? Because I've done it before. Nothing's going to happen, my clothes are not going to simultaneously combust and fall off, right? So what's the worst that's going to happen?'[22]

And finally: go into it knowing how much you want and what is the lowest amount you will accept. When I was negotiating, in what felt like an arduous process of back and forth, I didn't want to come across as pushy and ungrateful, yet I was determined not to settle just because it would be easier. The worst thing you can do is settle for an amount you're really not comfortable with, because it will only store up resentment down the line.

....

'I felt like it was time to set up my future, so I set a goal. My goal was independence.'
Beyoncé

....

Ultimately, pay rises, promotions and equal pay matter because money matters. Not only just because of its functional benefits – paying bills and buying the things we need – but because the value we place on money is inseparable from the opportunity it gives us to be independent.

Charlene White recalls buying her first house and the independence it gave her.

'Yes, I'm proud of doing the stuff with *News at Ten*, of course I am, but I bought my house at 24, and all by myself with no help. I don't come from money or anything, so it's not like Dad could find a spare tens of thousands to give to me as a deposit! I had to do that myself. I've just completed on selling it about ten days ago, and during the whole process of going through it I was completely fine, completely fine, not emotional about it whatsoever, and putting all of my stuff into the storage container, I was fine with all of that, until the day that it completed and the solicitor called me to say that it was done, and I was standing in the middle of Richmond, and I burst into tears. I was trying to explain it to my dad, the reason why, and he was like, "It's bricks and mortar, I don't understand why you're getting so emotional, it's just bricks and mortar!" and I'm like, "It's about more than that, it's, it's my independence, it's the biggest thing I have ever done all by myself. It doesn't require a mentor, it doesn't require any of those things, it was me, only me, no family or financial input or anything, it was all me."

'That was a physical representation of my hard work, of my tenacity, of my parents raising me to be this person who was able to buy somewhere at 24. That's what that house means to me. I realised, when I burst into tears, I suddenly realised the importance of it. I absolutely love my other half to bits, but it's that feeling of that's the last thing that I'll ever have had that was just me working for. Because now we're working on stuff together and we're buying a house together, and that's a wonderful thing to do, but also it's saying goodbye to that level of independence.'

Encouraging us to learn better financial and wealth literacy isn't enough to put the ball firmly in our court. If we are to have a chance to reach the level of independence that Charlene speaks of, the ethnicity pay gap must be addressed. Visibility is key. Policy should not take a generic approach in addressing the experiences of minority women. There are particular challenges facing ethnic minority women and a one-size-fits-all approach does not work. We shouldn't have to wait 158 years for things to magically fall into place. But we need our personal financial behaviour and public policy to work together.

Building personal financial knowledge is helpful and something that will help you in the long term. Money management is something we should all strive to be better at: arming ourselves with the knowledge to make informed decisions about our futures is key. Everyone's circumstances are different: personal finance is exactly that – *personal*. However, we can all agree that money should give you choices and that real freedom comes from being able to use it to live life the way you want to. So getting closer to your finances allows you to create a life with experiences that are tailored to you. It's never too late to get started, or to get better at it. So what does financial independence look like for you?

When Life Gives You Lemons, Make Lemonade

ELIZABETH

'For a long time I defined myself by what I wasn't. My life changed when I focused on what I was good at, what I liked most about myself and what made me stand out.'

Issa Rae

One of my favourite computer games as a teen was *Diner Dash*. It was about a young entrepreneur called Flo who decides to leave her dreary city job, follow her dreams and open up a restaurant. Rising through 40 challenging levels in the fast-paced game, I would stay up until the early hours of the morning, taking Flo from a greasy spoon café to her five-star, fine-dining, dream restaurant. Fictional though she was, I admired her hustle and was devoted to helping Flo reach her entrepreneurial goal.

Just like Flo, more of us in recent years are starting side hustles alongside our nine to fives, before eventually stepping out on our own. This burgeoning cultural trend has been driven by the digital era: when you can create a logo and website and register your company within the hour, getting your hustle on is really only a few clicks away. A Millennials Deconstructed study reveals that black millennials are the group who feel most optimistic about their futures, even in the face of discrimination.[23] We are more open to breaking down boundaries; we see barriers as opportunities and we imagine new ways to solve problems and add value to the world – all characteristics required to be a successful entrepreneur. It's perhaps no coincidence then that Babson College's Global Entrepreneurship

Monitor revealed that black people are establishing businesses at a higher rate than white people and other minority groups.[24]

Many of us have ideas for potential side hustles or businesses, but taking that leap of faith and transforming it into a product or service is where the real challenge lies. Because life gets in the way, right? But if you have a good idea, there are more opportunities than ever to create your own lane and build something great from the ground up. This chapter isn't designed to be a step-by-step guide on how to start a business: there isn't the space for us to give you a true picture of how much is really involved in starting and running a successful venture, and – contrary to what the media tells us – not everyone comes up with an app idea overnight in their bedrooms and then sells it for millions a year later. What this chapter aims to do, though, is explore *why* so many of us are starting businesses and advise you on *how* to take those first steps when you have that killer idea. It can be difficult to stand out from the crowd, especially in the digital age, but we will also recommend helpful resources so that you too can turn that lemon into lemonade.

The road to entrepreneurship is a challenging yet rewarding one. There is no blueprint for success, but as the great Maya Angelou once said, 'Success is liking yourself, liking what you do, and liking how you do it.' Stepping out on your own, creating something from nothing, gives you the opportunity to do just that.

....

**'I always wanted to be an entrepreneur.
If I was afforded more success in the corporate
world, would I have stayed a bit longer?
Probably, if I wasn't working twice as hard.'**
Melanie Eusebe

....

Ethnic minority businesses play a significant role in the UK economy, with an estimated annual contribution of £25–32 billion.[25] According to the Ethnic Minority Businesses and Access to Finance report, ethnic minority groups have significant aspirations to launch businesses, especially Black African (35 per cent) and Black Caribbean (28 per cent) groups. This is compared to a figure of just 10 per cent among white British people.[26] Within this group, black women are the most likely to start their own businesses.[27]

The motivation to create a business can spring from the most interesting of places, and for a variety of reasons. For many black women, however, there are some common trends that help to explain why so many of us are venturing into the world of self-employment.

Firstly, more of us are achieving additional qualifications and gaining work experience. As we will see in 'Fifty Shades of Beige', Florence Adepoju began working on the Benefit makeup counter when she was 17, where she found herself becoming frustrated at the lack of makeup available for darker skin tones. When she was invited for a training day in the Benefit lab she became fascinated by how the different pigments and textures were made and subsequently learned the process of mixing makeup. Florence fell in love with the industry, was inspired to pursue a career in science and went on to do a degree in cosmetic science. She started her degree knowing that by the end of it she wanted to create a beauty brand that was inclusive for all women: 'In my personal statement to apply, I was talking about the fact that I wanted to create my own thing. The idea and the feeling of me wanting to create a beauty brand was from something that I think definitely all women of colour experience: loving beauty but then kind of, it not being for you – I just wanted black women to feel good. So I definitely went into my degree thinking I want to create something. And even if I don't do it from my own brand, I want to change how the industry works.'

Secondly, there is the insidious effect of the concrete ceiling, which, as we explored in the 'Twice as Hard' chapter, can lead to a lack of opportunity for black women to progress in the workplace. This has resulted in some women feeling dissatisfied with the status quo, and deciding to seek fulfilment outside the culture of micro-aggressions and white privilege that dominates their workplace; a culture that makes it difficult for them to reach their potential. Often employed beneath their skill set, they have become exhausted trying to be promoted or recognised for their worth. Melanie Eusebe talks about the feeling of trying twice as hard but not progressing as fast as her white colleagues. Even though she had a very successful career at EY, where she specialised in designing and delivering business transformation programmes, she says: 'I always wanted to be an entrepreneur. If I was afforded more success in the corporate world, would I have stayed a bit longer? Probably, if I wasn't working twice as hard. I knew I was smarter and better, but I still wasn't getting ahead like my other colleagues. Some of these guys couldn't talk to rocks, they had the social skills of gnats, and on top of that I knew that I was not only well-read, reading the *FT*, I was teaching the course on consulting and I wasn't doing as well as them.' So, taking her knowledge and her experience, Melanie decided to start her own consultancy business. In addition, in 2013, after seeing the surge in black people starting their own businesses, she co-founded the Black British Business Awards, which celebrate the outstanding achievements and contributions of black business people to the UK's economy.

Finally, the lack of representation in mainstream brands (see 'Fifty Shades of Beige') has presented an opportunity for young black entrepreneurs to take matters into their own hands and create products and services that actively solve the problems that they, and two million others, face. Florence knows this all too well: 'I think when it comes to black entrepreneurship and women, and especially black women, I think our entrepreneurship almost comes out of necessity. And I think a lot of people don't realise that entrepreneurship is a lot more about providing solutions and bridges, and building platforms and providing answers, than it is about just making money.'

It's true, our skin tones, hair types and experiences aren't 'limited' editions (as the mainstream brands would have us think), so until we find ourselves in a perfect world where we can walk into a high-street store and see a wealth of products that accurately cater to black women's needs, there is still a real opportunity for us to address this lack of representation from brands. After all, we have the inside knowledge: no one knows us better than ourselves, right?

Lack of representation comes in many forms, and it isn't always based on racial identity. From an early age, Dr Clare Anyiam-Osigwe BEM suffered from severe acne and eczema. She was unable to find a product on the high street to help combat this without the use of steroids, petroleum or lanolin. She had been working for The Body Shop for six years when she decided to make her own products at home. Her knowledge of the industry meant she was able to identify her potential customers pretty easily and could understand the business from the inside out.

'I was suffering with allergies and I would say to them, "You're losing people." I treated every customer like a friend, I would have intimate discussions with them or I'd notice people – I'd see a chick with rice crackers in her hand and we all know no one's eating rice crackers out of choice, because they don't taste good, and they didn't taste good ten years ago. So I'd ask, "Are you coeliac?" "Yeah, are you?" "Yeah! Oh my God, what are your allergies?" "Wheat, dairy, gluten, yeast." So we would talk, and they'd be saying, "I'm looking at these ingredients in these products, I can't use them," and I'm like, "I feel so fraudulent, I'm here selling these products but I don't use them, I make my own."

'It was really just taking that leap of faith and leaving the industry. I had been a makeup artist at that time for years – built my own portfolio, left Body Shop, started mixing and making these products. My acne and eczema were gone, I became a vegan, started making products out of the ingredients that I was eating, and took small batches every Sunday to Spitalfields Market in East London, and started selling my products.

'The light-bulb moment came from people telling me they had been using the product for a month or two, and they would come back saying, "Clare, these products work, where can we find you apart from here?" and I'd say, "I don't know . . ." How am I going to take it to the next level? I'm not a celebrity, nobody knows me. You know, friends and family and the odd tourist at Spitalfields is okay, but making it a proper brand . . . I sort of took a leap of faith, got a bank loan for the first time ever and switched on the website on 1 December.'

With eight million eczema sufferers in the UK alone, Clare's products soon gained recognition from Allergy UK and since then she has launched Premae UK, now selling her award-winning products into millions of homes through Shopping Nation.

Whatever your own personal reason as to why you want to start working for yourself, being your own boss can give you flexibility, greater job satisfaction and the opportunity to make a difference to other people's lives.

> 'I felt there was a girl like me, who was always excluded and I wanted to make that excluded girl feel included.'
> *Irene Agbontaen*

So, you have what you believe to be a great idea to fill a gap in the market, the next big thing. After your initial excitement, the next stage should be the idea validation process – testing and validating your idea before launch. You need to find out whether your business idea has any legs and whether it offers any real value. It's harsh but true – you don't want to waste time coming up with an idea that nobody wants. This process will also help you create the best product or service for your potential customers, finding out what they want and whether your business idea meets this demand. It will answer the central question – *should I even be starting this business?* Validating your idea involves doing market research to identify what problem, want or need your business solves, and exactly how it solves it. It exposes your idea to your target audience before you build and release the final product.

There are a variety of research methods available for you to use. The internet is a cheap and simple way of doing market research.

Using survey tools such as Typeform and SurveyMonkey®, you can create and send out surveys to your contacts, allowing you to gauge if people are attracted to your idea. This is what Irene Agbontaen did before she started her clothing brand TTYA (Taller Than Your Average) in 2013. Using social media she was able to find out in a pretty short space of time whether her business idea met a need, and whether there was a clear demand for her potential product. 'With TTYA I went travelling. I went to Asia and I realised during that trip that people could pack so light, and because of my height it was really inconvenient for me because I had to pack layers or things to make my outfits work. And I was just like, "It's so annoying that I can't get staples, I don't have tall staples," and I thought, "I work in fashion, I know loads of models, there must be loads of girls like me." So I put out a post on Facebook, just using SurveyMonkey®, asking, "Can people fill out this survey for me and let me know what your feeling is on fashion for tall women?" I got over 1,000 responses just from Facebook, and then I thought, "Do you know what? This could actually be a good idea." Then I started doing all my market research; I looked at my competitors and saw that there wasn't actually a cool, jersey, staple apparel for tall girls – everything associated with tall fashion was kind of always frumpy, not really on trend, you know? So it was really important to me to make the girl who's always felt excluded, included.'

Similarly for Yomi and I, when we came up with the idea of *Slay In Your Lane* in 2015, although we really believed in it from the jump and knew that there was an obvious need and market for it, we still made sure we did our market research. We wanted feedback, so we set up a focus group to better understand our demographic and what their interests were. Between Yomi and I, we reached out to a variety of black girls, from different backgrounds and age groups – some we knew well and some we knew from social media. We reserved a section of a restaurant so we could have a relaxed environment where they could share their views, and it was great to see such a diversity of women come along and talk about their experiences of being a black girl in modern Britain. We discussed the various themes and topics we wanted to tackle in the book and explored some ideas we hadn't thought of originally. Even though we were all different, we were able to find common ground and experiences. How could we claim it was going to be the 'Black Girl Bible' if we couldn't represent a cross-section of black women's experiences?

While we took a field-based approach with our market research, and Irene took a desk-based one, we both did competitor research, which was key to understanding our unique selling point. You need to ask yourself, what else is out there? What is going to be unique, compelling or different about my idea? Does it meet an under-served group, or fill a real gap in the market? Can I make something a little better, cheaper and faster? Your unique selling point is the heart of your business idea: the point of differentiation that will help you to stand out from the crowd. It is the reason why your potential customer will choose you over anyone else. You should spend time working on this and really understanding the strengths of your business idea. It's what will give you a competitive advantage in a crowded marketplace. As Steve Jobs famously said, 'You don't have to be the first, but you've got to be the best.'

Understanding her USP and competitive advantage was central to the success of WAH, a business founded by Sharmadean Reid. The hip hop and fashion magazine that started out as a passion project when Sharmadean was 22, has since grown into a world-leading nail brand. When she first started WAH, standing out from the crowd by being at the forefront of technology was key for Sharmadean.

'The internet's completely responsible for why we dominated in nail art, because a handful of other people were experimenting with nail art that we were doing, but they just weren't as prolific with their output as we were. I constantly blogged and posted on Facebook – because there was no Instagram then – so we had a WAH blog, we had a WAH page on Facebook, and I would just always be posting all the work we did, but also all the activities around the salon.

'A brand isn't literally about their output, it's about all the things that happen pre, during and post the output – so it's about the girls who come into the salon, it's about the nails being done, it's about the end result of the nails happening, and I think I just shared every bit of the journey online, whereas other people were maybe just showing the nails. Instead, I built a story around it.

'So we grew really fast early on, I'm a natural early adopter for any new technology that comes out, so the minute Tumblr came out, we were on Tumblr, the minute that Instagram came out, we were on Instagram – which just gives us a head start against anybody else. So the fact that we were one of the first nail salons on Tumblr, one of the first nail salons on Instagram, meant that if people were looking for nails on that platform, they were always going to follow us because we were there. So that helped massively.'

Once you've identified your USP, you need to make it part of your brand vision. This vision should encapsulate your end goal: an aspirational statement that paints a picture of what you want to achieve with your brand in the future. Because Sharmadean had a strong brand vision she was able to take advantage of the social media channels in showing WAH's personality when creating content online. Yes, that's right, your business should have a distinctive personality. One of your greatest challenges as an entrepreneur will be to create a unique vision that sets your business apart from the rest. For example, Bill Gates wanted to put 'a computer on every desk and in every home'. Sharmadean Reid wanted to have the 'coolest salon ever', and with *Slay In Your Lane* our vision was to create 'a guide to life for a generation of black British women: *The Black Girl Bible*'. The best ideas are simple and clear to communicate, which is why you need to perfect your elevator pitch – a short, pre-prepared statement that includes why your brand is here, what it stands for and what it aims to achieve. Designed to be pitched to anybody, regardless of whether they have an understanding of the industry or not, the ideal elevator pitch should be interesting and memorable; it should spark interest.

'My signature fade with the Bevel blade.
That's a major key.'
Nas

But what if you have the drive and want to start a business, but you haven't had that light-bulb moment yet? You're not alone, and if this is you, and you are just missing a killer idea, you should begin by exploring your passions and interests – spend time discovering what it is that you truly care about. Think about your hobbies, what are you good at? What do you love doing? How could you mould this into a business idea? Starting a business is challenging and inevitably your commitment will be tested, so you're more likely to commit and be motivated to stick it out if it has its roots in something you're passionate about.

In the case of Alexis Oladipo, her quest to be an entrepreneur started when she became frustrated with her journey as a freelance fashion stylist. She then took a job as a cleaner, but it gave her no real job satisfaction.

With the help of The Prince's Trust – a youth charity – who gave her a £3,000 grant and assigned her a mentor, Alexis was able to create Gym Bites, a food product for people with a hectic work and social life who are struggling to maintain a healthy diet on the go. Alexis found that at that time the options for takeaway salads were limited, and in her view, boring, so her light-bulb idea was to put the 'fun back into healthy eating'. Through hard work and determination, in 2017 she won 'Best Health Food Provider 2017' at the UK Enterprise Awards.

However, creating an award-winning brand hasn't been easy or straightforward. Alexis changed her business plan four times and explored various business ideas before finding her true passion. Simultaneously, in her personal life, Alexis was going through a break-up and also recovering from a medical procedure. In one of her sessions with her mentor she reached her breaking point.

'I just started crying in front of him. I told him I was looking to stop doing cleaning and I wanted to create something that fills a gap in the market: "I want to do something, the drive is there, I'm in pain right now, my heart's broken, I haven't got money, but I need to do something." I cried in front of him and I broke down. I said, "I just don't know what to do, I don't know how to narrow it down."

'He was like, "Okay, calm down." The question he asked me, I'll never forget, he said, "What are you good at?" and I was just like, "Fashion, food, I like to cook" – that was something I've always done but I'd always looked at it as, I like to eat nice food so I just cook nice food. "I've always been a food fanatic and people have always told me to be a chef."

'At university I was always that go-to girl, the guys would come with their bag of chicken, "Lex, can you please help me out?" I was just always that "person who could cook". So my mentor was like, "Okay, you've done the fashion thing, let's leave that alone now. Let's focus on the cooking part – your passion for food." I said to him, "Okay, I actually do have an idea, but I told a friend a year before, and because I didn't get the reception I thought I should've got, I kind of just didn't bother with it" – it was sort of indirect discouragement. I'm sure he was very much unaware of it, but it didn't motivate me to pursue it any further. So when I told my mentor, he was like, "That's an amazing idea. You need to go off and do that," I was like, "What, really?" and he said, "Yeah, go and do that."'

'Do that' she did.

From the beginning, Alexis knew that she not only needed to make great food, but also great design and branding. In an interview she later told BuzzFeed: 'I wanted to make a product that when people Google it, they'll be like, "What? This is a black Nigerian girl from Hackney?"[28]

'I was using our social media, and I was just tagging everyone – tagging Tesco, tagging Co-op, tagging Nike – I was just tagging everyone related to food and fitness, and Selfridges was part of that, so I tagged them.' The Selfridges food-buying team pored over Alexis's Gym Bites Instagram page and were impressed by its strong brand identity and its creator's vision.

'So a lot of people might think I got to Selfridges because I worked there [as a brand specialist and sales consultant], but that wasn't the case at all. I don't even think they knew I worked there when I got in there. One day I was in Barking Market, in the car, waiting for my mum, she had to go and buy hair cream. So I opened my Instagram and I just saw loads of notifications. It was the restaurant director of Selfridges, the food buyer of Selfridges, the Selfridges page, and just everyone having their own conversation underneath one of our pictures. And I thought, "Okay, what's going on?" So I opened it to see what's being said, and they were like, "This is amazing, we need this. This is amazing. This is fantastic, look," tagging this other person to come and look. I was like, "Nah, I'm dreaming, this is not for real. This is Selfridges really loving my page right now."

'It was: "Hi Gym Bites, we've seen your products on social media, we're really interested and we want to discuss it further – what are your prices? Is it available? Can we get exclusivity?" And I just started crying, literally, tears of joy. My mum started crying.'

Three months after the first Gym Bites salad was launched it was available in the prestigious Selfridges foodhall. With little in the way of funding for her business idea, Alexis had nonetheless been able to grab the attention of one of the biggest retailers in the world. The power of social media had struck again.

Once you have a clearer sense of what your passion might be, you should think about what could be improved in that particular industry. Do some research, swot up. Look at business and consumer trends, ask yourself what might be next? What might you be able to bring that might not yet exist? This is exactly what entrepreneur and CEO of Walker and Company, Tristan Walker, did in 2013 when he left Wall Street to launch Bevel, a technologically advanced shaving system for black men. He saw an opportunity in the billion-dollar personal-care market and decided to start a business he was already an expert in. Armed with his education (a graduate from Stanford Business School) and an intimate knowledge of the problem – people of colour tend to have curly hair and when they shave with multi-blade razors they're more likely to get razor bumps, skin irritation and ingrown hairs – Tristan created the single-blade shaving system, Bevel. He leveraged his contacts from his previous work experience in Silicon Valley to raise $9.3 million in start-up funding – even attracting investment from celebrities such as rapper Nas – and built his product from the ground up.[29]

His entrepreneurial mission was to 'make health and beauty simple for people of colour'. To date, Bevel has been successful in gaining a presence in retail stores, and in 2017 he launched FORM Beauty, a technology driven women's hair-care line, designed to meet the specific needs of women of colour.

Whether, like Alexis, you find a way to turn your passion into profit, or, like Tristan, you are driven to solve a problem you face directly, or whether you're simply motivated by financial gain or creative growth, as an entrepreneur you will have the unique and satisfying opportunity to create something impactful. But this opportunity will only come if, like them, you are prepared to put in a great deal of hard work and effort. Like they say, the dream is free, but the hustle is sold separately. The fact that it's so easy to set up profiles on social media and create a website can sometimes give the illusion of productivity when you may not actually have produced anything worthwhile. Melanie Eusebe advises: 'In terms of working hard, I honestly don't think people are taught how to work: just work, as in a concerted effort over time to produce something. There's a lot of stuff going on . . . But it's just like, "What's the product? At the end of an hour, what have you done?" I don't think people know how to work, and that's across the board – black people suffer from it, white people suffer from it, it doesn't really matter, men, women, I honestly don't think that we're trained to just be kind of product-oriented. When I say product I don't mean product, like, a microphone, I'm talking about actual productivity.'

Because the barriers to entry with regard to website creation, acquiring a Twitter handle and registering a business on Companies House are low, it's easy for people to give themselves the glamorous title of 'entrepreneur' without actually having any of the substance or dedication required to build something worthwhile, which might be successful in the long run. When it comes to making your idea into reality, it can be easy to get distracted and spend time on the wrong thing. So you must plan your time effectively, focus on one task and learn to be productive rather than simply looking busy.

....

'We should each be CEO of our own board of directors.'
Vanessa Kingori

....

We've all heard the saying 'your network is your net worth', and this is even more relevant when you're an entrepreneur. This is not limited to money, but includes skills, knowledge and access to opportunities. You will need to draw upon your own network of people to help you at different points in your journey. This book would not have been possible without a network of people to whom Yomi and I were able to reach out and ask for help in the initial stages. The fact is, you have to network and potentially collaborate with people in order to build a successful business. A lot of the time in business, people buy into people first, and building strong and positive relationships is key. But it does take time, commitment and authenticity. A great way to get your entrepreneurial juices flowing is to get out there and network with like-minded people. It will require you to step out of your comfort zone, engage in new activities, attend events and meet new people, but it will bring many opportunities and potential rewards.

But simply attending events is only half the battle. There is an art to networking and your approach to it will determine how successful you will be in creating new contacts and clients. Not many of us naturally know how to network effectively. Vanessa Kingori explains how to put your best foot forward.

'When they hear "networking", lots of people think it's about going to events and handing out a business card. That isn't networking. What it *is* about is putting yourself in a position where you're more likely to meet the right people. And when you meet people, creating a connection. That's not simply giving out a business card, that's not necessarily saying "I want to do this, can you help me!?" Everyone is so busy. It's about saying, "I really admire you because X", "I read that that you did", "I saw this that you did", "I loved this … " and flattering that person. It could be the manager you had who was a little bit more helpful. Even if you want to move on from that career or what have you, it's about just staying in touch with them and every once in a while saying, "Do you know what, that thing that you said back in the day has really helped me." It's about feeding back to those people as well as taking from them. And what I find now that I'm in the position that I'm in, lots of people that I meet, they say, "I want to do this, can you help me? You've got a responsibility to help me! I'm black, you have to help me, too!" That's not how it works. Because why would I help you over and above – it's not that I don't want to help, but I need to choose who to help within the parameters of the time that I have available.

'On an individual level, I want to feel fulfilled by the person I'm helping, and if I can only help three people, who are the people who are going to be most likely to take my advice forward? And those are the people who say thank you. Those are the people who acknowledge that my time is short. This is what I did for the people who helped me. Those are the people who are helpful and say, "Can I do something that helps you? I'm doing x, y, z, I've got spare hours here that I could come and help with that event," or what have you. Most of the time, the people that you're trying to network with probably won't take you up on that, but it sets in their mind that you are different. And that's how I networked; everyone who I counted, who I felt had been helpful to me, I kept saying thank you, I kept feeding back to say "this is what I'm doing now and I'm doing this because you gave me this advice, I don't know if you remember, etc." It then meant that when they came to the point when someone said "I'm looking for someone to do x, y, z," I would still come to mind, and they would go "I know this girl, you should speak to her." That's what networking is, it's not handing over the card, it's not saying "follow me on Twitter or on Instagram" or whatever.

'It's about making connections.

'Someone once said to me, which was the best advice I was given about networking, that we should each be CEO of our own board of directors. You guys are your own board of directors. You [Elizabeth] had a great idea, you told your best friend [Yomi], she said "let's do it", and you will draw in around you a group of different people, who you might call up for different problems, or different things that you're excited about, you're buzzing about. That's like a board of directors, right? Those are the people to whom you say, "Oh my God, I had this idea; I'm buzzing about it, etc. What do you think? What should I do? Etc." So building your board of directors is about you building people you're happy to confide in. They don't have to be like you, they just have to empathise with your position and your point of view.'

So, yes, go to events with a business card and be ready with your elevator pitch introducing who you are and what your idea is about, but also make sure you have an opinion on trends affecting your industry and ideally some background knowledge of the people you might be meeting. This can spark interest and develop a richer conversation, thus making a connection.

However, while it is important to go out and meet people, young entrepreneurs are increasingly using non-traditional ways of networking and are going online to establish business relationships. Social media has become an important tool to facilitate these interactions. With just a few clicks you can send a tweet to people in your network requesting the need for services from 'graphic designers' to 'videographers', or even just connecting offline to collaborate with like-minded people, which can enable better leads and access to richer resources. Irene Agbontaen explains: 'Social media's a nice entry-level platform, but then you need to actually go and meet people, and say, "Can we have a coffee? We have similar ideas, let's connect." I can't even explain how great it is to just meet people and vibe with them, and they're like, "Okay, I'm into this, cool, we should do this," or, "Are you into this kind of art gallery? Let's go see some galleries together." People are so open to you.'

But authenticity here is key. Irene says: 'I feel like now with the new generation sometimes it gets lost in translation – people always assume, "Oh, can you do this for me?" "Oh, I need a contact for this." "Oh, I need a hook-up for this," you know? There's no authenticity in it anymore. It's not like people who genuinely share similar interests and are interested in the same things. It has to be authentic, it doesn't work out when it's not authentic. When you have ulterior motives of, "Oh, I'm only going to be friends with this person because they're going to get me into here," or, "They're seen as this," it's not authentic, it doesn't work out. So work on building authentic relationships.'

Networking is important, but according to Adam Grant, a professor at the Wharton School, 'It's true that networking can help you accomplish great things. But this obscures the opposite truth: Accomplishing great things helps you develop a network.

'My students often believe that if they simply meet more important people, their work will improve. But it's remarkably hard to engage with those people unless you've already put something valuable out into the world. That's what piques the curiosity of advisers and sponsors. Achievements show you have something to give, not just something to take.'

I couldn't agree more. The best networking events I've attended are when people are there because the event is based on our specific interests. So it is not about networking just for the sake of networking, but having something meaningful to say and learning from one another or helping each other out. As Grant argues: 'In life, it certainly helps to know the right people. But how hard they go to bat for you, how far they stick their necks out for you, depends on what you have to offer. Building a powerful network doesn't require you to be an expert at networking. It just requires you to be an expert at something.'[30]

So remember, networking alone won't lead to anything more fruitful than just empty transactions: what you want to create are rich relationships that can hopefully turn into opportunities.

> 'I'm trying to set myself up to create a big business. Not because I want to line my pockets, but because the industry I'm in needs a transformation at that scale.'
>
> *Florence Adepoju*

After Yomi and I had developed the initial idea for *Slay In Your Lane* – building on our focus group research – we began to draft a book proposal. Neither of us had written a book before or knew anyone who had. We just had an idea we believed in that had been validated through research. So, for the first five minutes we were a bit like, what's next? Thank God for the World Wide Web, where within minutes we found a guide on how to write a book proposal. This is when shit became real and we had to come up with detailed answers to questions about our idea. We spent a great deal of time on this, but looking back, we believe this was the reason behind the nine-publisher bidding war that kicked off when the proposal was sent out. Even months later, we would meet people in the industry who were still talking about our pitch. It was clear it had been memorable and thorough – notably *Elle* UK called us 'the queens of pitches'.

Similarly, in the business world, once you have established your USP and your brand vision, you need to come up with a comprehensive business plan: a written document that describes your objectives and strategies, helps you understand the type of business you want to build, the action plan you will need to follow, and which includes sales, marketing and financial forecasts. This plan is essential if you want to be successful; it's a valuable roadmap for launching and growing your business – after all, failing to plan is planning to fail. Your business plan should be strategic. However, not everyone understands this, as Melanie has found out: 'I would say about 5 per cent of the young people who approach me on a regular basis for their business – on average I get about 5–10 a month – 5 per cent of them in the history of me doing these awards have a business plan.' Ideas are plentiful; if you're really serious about making yours a reality, make sure you come prepared when you approach people about your business, especially when you're asking for investment. It's a no-brainer, really: a business plan will help you identify potential weakness and opportunities that will help you make informed decisions before you – and your investors – commit financially and legally.

You need money to make money, as the saying goes, and financial capital is key when it comes to growing a business. Raising money is always challenging, but there is evidence to suggest that, when it comes to getting outside investment, the challenges for black women entrepreneurs are particularly tough. Businesses launched by women of colour tend to grow more slowly than those started by white men, and this is in part because they're less likely to get outside funding.[31] Entrepreneurs who don't already have significant savings typically tap into their family and friends networks at the earliest stages of their business, when an injection of investment can help launch and accelerate it. However, this remains beyond the reach of some black women, who may struggle to gain equal access to capital.

Dawn Butler MP recognises that there is a funding gap and believes the government should play a greater role in closing it. 'Black people in particular find it difficult to get loans from banks, because they seem to deem them as a high risk, which isn't always fair or correct or just. So what the government can do is look at how banks operate, because at the end of the day banks have been operating irresponsibly for a number of years. That's why the country had to bail out the banks. Now, in all the time that they were acting irresponsibly it was never, it was never favourably towards people of colour. They were always treated more harshly and had to jump through more hoops and prove more that they were able to repay the loan or go and make a profit in their business. And so banks were risk averse to lending to black businesses, which stifles a lot of black businesses. So, the government has a role to play in that, and public services do, too.'

Nick Clegg, former Deputy Prime Minister, once addressed the issue. He said: 'We know that 35 per cent of individuals from black African origin say they want to start a business, but only 6 per cent actually do. Are they having problems accessing the loans they need?'

Past evidence shows that firms owned by individuals of Black African origin have been four times more likely than 'white firms' to be denied loans outright. And that Bangladeshi-, Pakistani-, Black Caribbean- and Black African-owned businesses have been subject to higher interest rates than white- and Indian-owned enterprises.

While in office, an inquiry was launched by Clegg. However, the subsequent report, *Ethnic Minority Businesses and Access to Finance*, indicated that there was no direct evidence of racial discrimination, but it did acknowledge that ethnic minority businesses do disproportionately face challenges that make access to finance more difficult. Again, unconscious bias prevails as banks are inclined to focus more attention on prospects with higher income and savings as they can prove to be more profitable. As already mentioned in the 'Independent Women' chapter, the UK's Department of Work and Pensions found that 60 per cent of black households have no savings at all, compared to 33 per cent of white households. Black wealth has further taken a hit following the recessions, and post-recession lending is tighter and credit scores play a bigger role. Therefore, some banks taking this approach is unintentionally leading to institutional bias against ethnic minorities who might not typically fit into the criteria that they actively look for as being 'investable'.[32]

Florence started her hip hop-inspired makeup line in 2013, straight after graduating from the London College of Fashion. She had to put together a business plan as part of her dissertation; however, this provisional plan turned into reality when she applied for a business grant of £10,000 from her university, which she then used to buy equipment and set up a lab in her parents' garden shed. 'I think that as a woman, as a black woman, when you decide to go into business you take this completely unknown path, and you really task yourself with building something from nothing and doing the impossible, without ever really knowing if you will get the gratifi-

but there's nothing more satisfying than knowing you've got your own thing, whatever it is – whether it's a big thing that works out really well, or it's just a tiny thing, it doesn't matter as long as it's yours, because it's so satisfying.'

Once you do manage to take that first step towards turning your idea into a business, keeping up momentum can be difficult, especially if you are already working full-time or have other responsibilities. But believe it or not, having a nine-to-five job can be a help, and it also offers security in the early stages of your new business. Being an entrepreneur doesn't have to mean leaving your current job immediately, and there are ways to build upon your entrepreneurial skills while you are still in the world of work. For instance, there might be a particular project or campaign that may not necessarily fit into your typical day job, but through reaching out to the person in charge of it, putting yourself forward and taking up the opportunity, it could help you in the long run when you start out on your business path.

If your business idea is in the same industry as your job, that's even better – you can be building your skill set, making connections and gaining relevant experience. I work in marketing and I have been able to draw upon this experience at every stage in *Slay In Your Lane*, from working on the pitch, to social media, to the events. I have also benefited from access to resources and to so many talented individuals. Sometimes, experience that might not seem related to your business idea can also prove useful when you least expect it: that random Excel course you were forced to attend all those years ago can make a world of difference when it comes to tackling the finance side of your business.

Above all, making the transition from your day job into your own business *gradually* will provide you with a solid backup plan as well as a steady income. YouTuber Patricia Bright worked in the City for years while she was also making content for YouTube. What started out as a hobby quickly grew until she had over a million subscribers to her channel and had attracted advertising from major brands. Eventually she felt able to make a calculated decision: 'I am an Excel kind of person; I did a calculation and I assumed how much I could potentially make in a certain amount of time versus how much I could potentially make if I continued working my job. I counted for inflation and percentage of salary. I was very black-and-white about it and calculated that I could make more, enjoy myself more and have more flexibility to create something than if I was to stay in my career. So that was my decision-making process.

'Obviously I spent four to five years making videos as well as working and I never just quit my job. I thought that work experience was extremely useful and I believe that's why I'm actually as good as I am. I feel that it's important for people to develop some kind of knowledge and experience outside of just social media. Because, realistically, if you run a business you really need to know how to speak to an accountant or a manager or a solicitor, or read the contracts, and all these things that are extremely important. So it's important to have a little bit more.'

<hr>

'Good things come to those who hustle.'
Anaïs Nin

<hr>

Your particular story and your individual perspective on life is an invaluable asset: one that many of us fail to recognise. The opportunities for black women to make money from what we know have never been more abundant: more and more of us are taking advantage of technology to create podcasts, online platforms and e-commerce sites. Now could be a great time to start something. Irene agrees:

'I think at this time, black women are at a point where they are super empowered, we have that drive, and I think it goes back to a lot of us being first generation, so we've seen our parents struggle, we've seen them come here and fight to make a better life for us. I feel this work ethic has been instilled in us as well. We saw their hustle, now we're ready to put in the work. We know that things are not going to come easy.

'So I feel at this time the platforms are open – everything in terms

Elizabeth Uviebinené   Yomi Adegoke

Florence Adepoju

Funke Abimbola MBE

Irene Agbontaen

Amma Asante MBE

Vannessa Amadi　　　　　Vanessa Kingori MBE

Jamelia　　　　　Dr Clare Anyiam-Osigwe BEM

Ade Hassan MBE

Althea Efunshile CBE

Dr Anne-Marie Imafidon MBE

Charlene White

Dr Karen Blackett OBE

Clara Amfo

Malorie Blackman OBE

Melanie Eusebe

Lakwena

Sharmaine Lovegrove

Susan Wokoma

Dr Maggie Aderin-Pocock MBE

AJ Odudu   Alexis Oladipo

Margaret Busby OBE   Dr Nicola Rollock

of society, social media, culture, music, arts, fashion, everything's kind of just aligned now. So this is the time for us to really just grasp it and move forward.'

Entrepreneurship is all about embracing challenges, having the courage to commit and persevere, and always being aware of the bigger picture and the difference that your product or service can make, big or small. It requires creative thinking, determination, the capacity to take risks, leadership, and, of course, passion. The stakes tend to be high, the bumps in the road frequent. Remaining focused, regardless of the obstacles, is paramount. But the reward could be the chance to be in full control of your life.

If you decide this is the path you want to take, then all of the challenges associated with striking out on your own could be a small price to pay. It will require you to step outside your comfort zone, both personally and professionally, but as the saying goes, 'a comfort zone is a beautiful place, but nothing ever grows there'. Outside this zone the opportunities to grow and learn are limitless.

....

List of resources to help you get started

....

www.virginstartup.org
www.startups.co.uk
www.princes-trust.org.uk
www.fastcompany.com
www.bteg.co.uk
www.squarespace.com
www.wordpress.com
www.typeform.com
www.surveymonkey.co.uk

www.startupbritain.org
www.generalassemb.ly
www.campus.co/london/en
www.startuploans.co.uk
www.enterprisenation.com
www.greatbusiness.gov.uk/
     women-in-enterprise
www.bl.uk/business-and-ip-centre

REPRESENTATION

'The issue isn't black British actors stealing
roles from African Americans. It's a film industry
that has black actors scrambling for parts,
in both countries.'

Yomi

Being Susan Storm

YOMI

'It's not trailblazing to write the world as it
actually is . . . believe me, people of colour are
never anybody's sidekick in real life.'
Shonda Rhimes

When I was in Year 6, my primary school put on a production of
Grease. For many kids, including me, the prospect of missing lessons to wear a pink satin jacket and to hand-jive was as exciting as
if the fake cigarettes we were fake-smoking had been real. I leapt at
the opportunity and went for the joint largest role – the archetypal
white girl next door, Sandy.

When auditions came around, I was confident. I knew I was
unlikely to be scouted by Disney and carted onto their conveyor
belt of terrifyingly precocious child stars, but I could dance, carry
a tune and show off a great deal – which, aged ten, is essentially
indistinguishable from acting. I learnt my lines, hit some notes and
strutted away convinced that my performance had been enough for
me to be crowned with the blonde wig of Miss Olsson.

But I wasn't. I didn't get the part of Sandy – a blow supposedly
softened by the silver lining of being given the role of resident bad
gyal, Rizzo. While anyone in their right mind knows that Rizzo is the
true star of *Grease* (Sandy was just a land-Ariel, giving up her legs
for a bloke, but in her case legs were a cardigan and good grades),
she wasn't the biggest part and the biggest part was meant to go to
the person who had given the best audition. And I knew that person had been me. You might think that this is simply my embittered,
self-aggrandising interpretation, but it's not. You see, while talent is
often subjective, the teacher's decision to cast a blonde-haired, blue-

eyed schoolmate of mine and then rewrite the script so *I* had to sing Sandy's songs because she couldn't sing at all, pretty much cemented my suspicion that the decision had been an aesthetic one. The girl who was chosen didn't have a single solo in the school musical, but boy did she have a killer set of baby blues.

This reverse Milli Vanilli routine was the first time I realised something that now barely raises an eyebrow from me: black women's voices are wanted, but not if they come from our own mouths. If you look at the music charts, blue-eyed soul artists dominate simply because they sound like their black peers, who can't seem to catch a commercial break in the UK themselves. White artists are given award nods for sounds that not only came from black women, but also often relegate those women to outside of the top 40. Similarly, white actors are able to flourish in their own countries first, while black actors must often achieve success overseas before they are championed at home. Thankfully, my singing and dancing dreams pretty much began and ended aged ten, but for those who go on to follow them, the problems persist even when they do come true.

'BAFTA stands for black actors fuck off to America.'
Gina Yashere, Black is the New Black

Over the years, the same inability to think outside of the box has seen our favourite actors up sticks to America in their droves, in the hopes of a more welcoming reception in Hollywood. And while America is hardly known for its racial cohesion, in terms of diversity within acting, they're a great deal better off. Lenora Crichlow, Nathalie Emmanuel, Freema Agyeman, Carmen Ejogo, Gugu Mbatha-Raw and Ashley Madekwe are some of the actors that have followed the trail left by Idris Elba, David Oyelowo, Naomie Harris, Marianne Jean-Baptiste and so many others, who jumped ship long before and found success abroad. America still has a long way to go in terms of diversity, but Britain has further. America's black population is around four times bigger than the UK's – 3 per cent vs 13 per cent – which explains the increased visibility for black actors in America. But in both countries representation remains below the national average.

One of the UK's largest exports to the US is arguably our actors, but what's interesting is how different the journey is for the various actors who decide to head across the pond. The plummy-voiced, pale-skinned British men, before they attempt to crack the US, are firstly championed over here as national treasures – they have already conquered the hearts of their own nation, and now simply hope to do it all over again in America. Black actors and musicians, however, often leave out of sheer necessity. Idris Elba has long been one of the US's biggest stars, while back in the UK we continue to argue over whether our British icon Elba can portray another of our British icons, James Bond. These artists leave the country relatively unnoticed and underrated, only to return to a hero's welcome once the Americans have given them the nod of approval. The situation is so brazenly bad that even politicians have commented on it: Labour politician Chuka Umunna has called it 'unacceptable' that black British actors cannot achieve mainstream success in the UK without having to break the US first.

Actor and singer Cynthia Erivo is something of a poster child for the black British entertainers' American dream. After being spotted by an American producer while performing in a show, she moved from South London to the US and has since won the 2016 Tony Award for Best Actress in a Musical performance for her role as Celie in the Broadway revival of *The Color Purple*, as well as the 2017 Grammy Award for Best Musical Theater Album. She has now landed a starring role in Steve McQueen's *Widows* and has been cast in the lead for an upcoming Harriet Tubman biopic.

'I feel like it takes a while here [in the UK], it really does, and I can understand why black female actors have gone over [to America] and found more things there, because I think people are able to take more of a risk over there,' she says. 'And I'm not saying it's perfect,

I'm not saying they have it all together completely, but I definitely think they're more open to trying new things and putting different faces in, working with different writers, working with different stories, so that you can see it happening and you can see more faces like mine on TV, in theatre.

'Whereas here I think we're still slightly behind, really. I think I was lucky in that I was able to do a show that was really brought here by an American producer who saw me and thought, "She's really great, I'm going to take her to Broadway." In essence, I feel that America was brought here for me and I went back with it.'

Sarah-Jane Crawford, who has a successful career in the UK as a TV presenter, agrees that America's attitude towards diversity within the media is miles ahead of Britain's. Not only was she quick to secure a gig hosting for E! news, but she has also found the country to be incredibly receptive to her as an actor.

'Over the last few years I've been up for some massive roles – as a new actor I'd never be put up for these roles if it wasn't for the fact that they are so enthusiastic about seeing fresh black talent. And casting directors are looking for black people more than ever before because of the success of black shows like Empire, How to Get Away with Murder, Scandal, etc. I've had about eight or nine auditions in the last six months for major shows, whereas here [in the UK] I wouldn't necessarily be considered for British drama.

'Another important thing to remember is that when you are black over there, there are a lot of other sub-genres that are successful. Tyler Perry is a massively successful director. Think about the Spike Lees of this world. Black cinema is huge in America – much bigger than it is here in the UK. Don't get me wrong, I've worked on urban films with people like Femi Oyeniran – he put me in the first proper film I ever did, It's a Lot. So there is a lot of black and urban talent in the UK doing majorly well, but over there, black cinema is huge and we've all grown up watching films like Boyz n The Hood and all those rom-coms, and Love & Basketball and people like Gabrielle Union, who have come through the ranks of that and now are huge, because she's doing things like Being Mary Jane, as well as Kerry Washington.

So all of those beautiful, really talented, successful black actors have all probably done their fair share of "white cinema". But that's amazing, because even if I went over there and had a career in black cinema, that's still cool because it's more successful over there.'

Black British actors and entertainers continue to make huge waves across the waves. Their success has been so great, in fact, that it has attracted its own controversy. In an interview with radio station Hot 97, Hollywood veteran Samuel L. Jackson suggested that Jordan Peele's satirical horror film *Get Out*, which starred British actor Daniel Kaluuya, would have been better off with an African-American in its lead.

'There are a lot of black British actors in these movies,' Jackson said. 'I tend to wonder what that movie [*Get Out*] would have been with an American brother who really feels that. Daniel grew up in a country where they've been interracial dating for a hundred years. What would a brother from America have made of that role? Some things are universal, but [not everything].'

He also pointed to Ava DuVernay's historical drama *Selma*, which cast David Oyelowo in the role of Martin Luther King, as another example. 'There are some brothers in America who could have been in that movie who would have had a different idea about how King thinks,' he said.

Similar logic hasn't stopped African-American actors from playing black British parts (Don Cheadle's accent in *Ocean's Eleven, Twelve* and *Thirteen* is infamously awful), but what really irks is the fact that the likes of Michael Fassbender, Emily Blunt, Ewan McGregor, Kate Winslet, James McAvoy, Emma Watson, Rachel Weisz – white British actors who have dominated US cinema for years – are not under the same scrutiny by their white American counterparts. The issue isn't black British actors stealing roles from African-Americans, it's a film industry that has black actors scrambling for parts, in both countries.

Perhaps the lack of options for actors of colour in the UK has something to do with the stories we're willing to tell. A British staple like *EastEnders* should be brimming with roles for black British women: though Walford is fictional, it's made even more unbeliev-able with its utter lack of Jamaican hairdressers and cloth-selling African aunties. But that's not the Britain we're trying to export. That's not the Britain that sells. As Riz Ahmed writes in his essay 'Airports and Auditions' in *The Good Immigrant*, 'The reality of Britain is vibrant multiculturalism, but the myth we export is an all-white world of lords and ladies. Conversely, American society is pretty seg-regated, but the myth it exports is of a racial melting pot, everyone solving crimes and fighting aliens side by side.'

'Black' and 'British' are often presented as oxymoronic identities. The concept of labouring, hard, cool blackness is perceived as dia-metrically opposed to the widely exported notion of polite, coddled, flustered, bumbling Britishness. For many audiences across the world, even now, the idea that someone can be black and British – from the bad-weather-ridden, chronic tea-drinking, red bus-riding, whitest of white countries – is truly mindboggling. British identity is contingent for minorities. Our claim to Britishness often depends on how well we're behaving. It's often said that if you're compet-ing for the country in the Olympics, the papers will refer to you as British, but if you've just been done for petty theft, you are suddenly described as being from the place of your parents' birth.

Denise Lewis OBE is one of the country's most successful Olym-pians, winning the gold medal in the heptathlon at the Sydney 2000 Olympic Games. Though it hasn't happened to her personally, she has seen 'Britishness' awarded to individuals based on the kind of story being told about them:

'I recall a couple of instances when sportsmen have been described as "Jamaican-born" or "Somali-born" in the tabloid press when to me it would be appropriate to just refer to them as British, as they hold British passports and have represented the country at the highest levels possible in sport. It appears that your "Britishness" comes under scrutiny when the media story is not a positive one.'

So, black Brits are considered British when it suits. During the 2012 Olympics, the Britain we celebrated was multicultural and multifaceted, but the recent rise in the popularity of period drama has seen British TV at its whitest. I used to joke that if you rode a time machine back to Georgian England, every woman you would encounter was Keira Knightley in a bonnet. And for years this has been the Britain we have exported – the Britain of *Downton Abbey* and *The Crown*, of royals and debutante balls, where black people apparently cease to exist for a hundred-odd years. When asked about a lack of roles for black Brits in an interview, black British actor Sophie Okonedo responded, 'I think a lot of it is [due to] costume and period drama, which must be, what, at least 40 per cent of what we do here? Which means that 40 per cent of opportunities are closed to me already.' I'd bump that 40 per cent to 60 per cent: we do love a good period drama in the UK and we especially love to leave all the slavery, colonialism and racism off-screen, even in our most historic-ally accurate depictions. No one wants to acknowledge the thieving from the African continent while they are swooning over Lord Perky-Bottom, with his hands down the knickers of a virginal chamber maid. It's not sexy. It kills the mood. But the 'counting out' of actors like Okonedo in period dramas must be taken for what it is: an active decision. Black period dramas addressing the realities of the past can have commercial success – Amma Asante's critically acclaimed *Belle* being a recent and relevant example. In America there were the 2013 films *12 Years a Slave* and *The Retrieval*, both of which were hugely successful internationally. This country can make period dramas fea-turing black actors, too, but it would also mean coming to terms with a past that is far less pretty than the one with the elegant frocks in it.

Stereotype gripes

While things are bleak for black actors, full stop, black female actors have it particularly hard. The lack of worthwhile roles for women, multiplied by the lack of worthwhile roles for black actors, equals very few worthwhile roles for black female actors. Black British actor David Harewood received acclaim for his portrayal of Nelson

Mandela in BBC drama *Mrs Mandela*, and Martin Luther King in the London play *The Mountaintop*. 'Nelson Mandela and Martin Luther King are great roles, but they are very few and far between for us,' he lamented.

Few and far between they may be, but they are certainly recurring ones: Idris Elba played Mandela in *Mandela: Long Walk to Freedom* in 2013 and David Oyelowo played King in Ava DuVernay's *Selma* a year later. There was only one Nelson Mandela and only one Martin Luther King, however, so despite the seemingly endless adaptations, the number of reincarnations is finite. But at least the stories of great black men are told, albeit rarely.

Hollywood is only just starting to tell the stories of great black women. *Hidden Figures*, the true story of three African-American women at NASA who helped launch astronaut John Glenn into orbit, was a box office success but still remains an exception to the rule. And while there may be some roles for black British female actors over in the US, there are still far fewer than those for their white female counterparts – white female counterparts who also lament the lack of good roles for women. If that's the case in America, the 'land of opportunity', you can imagine how much worse things are over here. A study by the British Film Institute (BFI) analysed the representation of black actors in more than 1,000 UK films over the last decade and found that despite the black British population growing, the number of UK films with roles for black actors had plateaued. It's worth reiterating that the black British population is only 3 per cent, compared to 13 per cent of the US African-American population, but even in dramas and films set in London, where some boroughs can be up to 50 per cent non-white, representation is distinctly lacking.

The same study also found that 59 per cent of British films did not feature any black actors in either lead or named roles. Only 13 per cent of UK films have a black actor in a leading role. According to the BFI, a small number of films will feature a high number of black actors in lead roles in what they call 'clustering'. More than half of all the leading roles for black actors were in just 47 of the 1,000 films analysed, meaning that less than 5 per cent of the 1,000 had cast a black actor in a named role at all. So, as British society becomes more diverse and integrated, our films are depicting an era that is long gone.

Roles for black female actors in Britain are few – and even fewer if they refuse to partake in the usual one-dimensional and damaging stereotypes. The faces of black womanhood are frequently presented as one of the following: the welfare queen (the modern equivalent being the golddigger), Sapphire (now depicted as the angry black woman), the Jezebel (the hypersexualised 'hoochie mama' or 'video vixen'), or the best friend of the multifaceted, more complex white counterpart (there's a running joke that if you were to visit the apartment of a black best-friend character, it wouldn't be furnished, as their lives have no value outside of the white, main character). But other than stereotypes and limited character development, the rule seems to be that black people must only be depicted in pain, suffering or surviving, as opposed to thriving. And while hardship is part of the black experience, it certainly isn't it in its entirety, though many would be forgiven for thinking this is the case given its depiction on screen.

'The broadcast and film media have a tendency to stereotype black people,' Chuka Umunna said in a 2013 speech, 'to present an image of black British people that suggests we can succeed in sport, entertainment and music, but not necessarily in other fields.' When you look at the films that feature in the BFI's study of 1,000 films, the idea of singular black narratives is definitely present. *Selma* is a film about civil rights, and *Mandela: Long Walk to Freedom*, apartheid. *12 Years a Slave* does what it says on the tin, and *Half of a Yellow Sun* documents the Nigerian civil war. *Honeytrap*, *Brotherhood* and *Adulthood* all centre around crime, and *Fast Girls*, on athletics. These films provide much-needed visibility, but they also show that there isn't an appetite from the British film industry to financially back films showing facets of the black experience they are unfamiliar with. There is a reluctance to fund 'black films' in the first place, but if they are made, they almost always focus on themes widely considered the only stories that black people have to tell – war, slavery, crime and sports.

Bola Agbaje's first play *Gone Too Far!* won the Laurence Olivier Award for Outstanding Achievement in an Affiliated Theatre in 2008 and was adapted into a film that was released in 2014. Her priority when writing was to illustrate a world she recognised, which was very different to the one that she saw portrayed in film and theatre.

'When I first started writing, the thing that was really important to me was a truthful portrayal of what our experience was. People would often ask, "Oh, but how come it's [*Gone Too Far*] so funny, are you just a comedy writer?" And I'm like, "no!" I think just black people in general – you see it online as well – we find the funny in everything. And I think that's what I felt was missing at a particular point in London, in England in particular, in terms of the representation of black characters. I felt that we were portrayed in such stereotypical ways that there were never any grey areas to us. I felt that the only thing I could do to change that was just to write characters that people could relate to, that I felt were truthful. And you can't always please everybody – there are people out there that'll go, "I don't believe that character," or, "I don't think that character would exist." But I know those characters exist and I've experienced some of the things that I write about and I know people that have experienced some of the things that I write about. And I think sometimes when other people are writing about our cultures and about characters that they don't know, sometimes they miss the nuances. It's not that they can't do it, because it's not like I can't write white characters. It's just that sometimes the nuances of those characters or of those lives are missed. The things that we should be sensitive about, those are the things that are missed. And even now, when I write black characters, I'm always trying to find the grey area, the in-between that people can relate to. I'm always trying to kind of look for the truth within those characters. Because that's what people will relate to the most.

'My end goal is that I'm trying to change that perception by showing the world that there are so many different shades to our blackness and there are so many different experiences that we've gone through. The same as our white counterparts – there's people that like *East-Enders*, and there's people that like *Downton Abbey*. And sometimes they're the same groups of people and sometimes they're not. For the black experience, there's one thing that represents us all and I'm trying to change that. So that's where I don't compromise, when I go into a meeting and I'm coming up with an idea for a story and someone goes "This is a bit niche because you're talking about the Nigerian experience," or, "This is a bit niche because the lead is a black woman or a black man." I don't compromise on that, because I don't want to add to what already exists.'

Bola started as an actor and only turned to writing because she was frustrated with the lack of roles available for black women. 'I decided that I was gonna write my own play and put myself in it,' she remembers. This is indicative of another important element of the BFI study, which lists the actors with the most leading roles in UK films since 2006. *Kidulthood* star Noel Clarke tops the list with eight roles, but only 15 black actors have played two or more lead roles in UK films since 2006. Five of the 15 are black women. We have spoken of building new doors if existing ones remain shut, and a second glance at the list shows just how crucial this is – Noel Clarke's roles in films such as *Adulthood*, *The Anomaly* and *Brotherhood*, all of which he directed, is what puts him at the top of the rankings. It says a great deal that the person with the most lead roles over the past decade has only managed this feat by casting himself.

Michaela Coel also stars in her hugely successful TV show *Chewing Gum*, a role one could argue may have been difficult for her to secure had she been just as talented but less in charge of the sitcom. Shows like *Chewing Gum* depict black women in ways we're not accustomed to seeing them: silly, shy, caring, sexually inexperienced. For some of the British population, Tracey, the lead in the E4 comedy, is among the few depictions of black women they are seeing. The importance of shutting down stereotypes is all-encompassing – from obliterating the idea that successful black women are an exception rather than the rule, to freeing black women from the rigid boxing-in that so often plagues us in reality. Stereotypes don't stay on screen – the frequency with which black women are depicted as aggressive, angry and unreasonable, as well as lazy, ignorant and incompetent, cannot be disassociated from the fact that people often think black women are all of the above.

I grew up in the *Ker-Ching, Comin' Atcha* generation, when kids' television was somehow more diverse than it is nearly 20 years later. Looking back at those two shows it's hard to believe they ever existed. *Ker-Ching*'s protagonist, Taj, reminded me of the black boys I knew in real life – savvy, budding entrepreneurs fixed on getting rich, selling sweets in the playground. He lived with his sister and mum, who was a nurse, and he had created the online company Rudeboy with the goal to make a million for her. *Cleopatra* hit home even more; when I first watched their music video, as the second of three sisters who spent the best parts of our weekends lip-syncing to Brandy in front of the television, seeing girls who looked just like us – same skin tone, same hair, who shared a bedroom between three, too, whose mum scolded them for making too much noise – was magical. It was even more magical when I realised they were British and they had a TV show. Sometimes I can hardly believe CITV ever took a chance on three black, Mancunian sisters living with their single mother, then I remember the girls were already in a successful band whose first single had entered the charts at number three. This level of wholesomeness – the portrayal of black kids as black kids, has never been seen on British televisions since.

As the numbers of black Brits continue to grow, so conversely does the demand for television and films that depict a country we haven't lived in for some time. Perhaps the more we continue to grow, the stronger the desire to reclaim an increasingly distant Britain is becoming – not just from those who consume our nation as an export, but those who live in it, too. The Brexit vote can attest to that.

....

Black voices, white faces

....

As with black female actors, black female musicians in the UK often seek success elsewhere, namely the United States. Singer Estelle found commercial success in the US, winning a Grammy. Unsurprisingly, once she had cracked the US, her status in the UK began to rise. Floetry, a Grammy-nominated soul duo many don't realise were British, dominated the charts in the mid-noughties. The group recorded two studio albums and sold over 1,500,000 records worldwide, their success undoubtedly owing much to the fact they were embraced abroad. Eighties pop star Sade Adu is cited as a huge inspiration by many musicians, black and white, but she is also a star who shone brighter after gaining icon status in the US.

Although it is still present, stereotyping in the music industry works differently to the way it does in film and TV. A big part of the problem for black British singers in the UK is the stereotype that black women are naturally gifted soul singers – a stereotype that, for once, white people actively seek to turn on its head – leaving them considered to be 'standard' and unremarkable. When a black woman can sing it's often regarded as uninteresting, compared to white men and women whose take on R&B, no matter how traditional, is seen as a marketable novelty or a more palatable face for a much-beloved sound. Beverley Knight explains the phenomenon in an interview with the *Independent*:[1] 'There are two general assumptions: that most black female singers can seriously sing as a rule, and they generally sing R&B/soul. Therefore, a great voice does not make her exceptional. The other side of this situation is that a female of any other ethnicity who has a great soul/R&B voice stands out immediately. We have all heard the phrase, "She sings like a black girl." That singer is already a marketing dream, and stands more of a chance of success.'

Britain often doesn't know what to do with black female singers, choosing to box them off as 'divas' from a bygone era rather than positioning them at the cutting edge. This has resulted in standout performances in theatre musicals and Broadway (Alexandra Burke in *Sister Act*, Beverley Knight in *The Bodyguard* and Leona Lewis in *Cats*), but it's a popularity that doesn't necessarily translate into the mainstream. Divisive American rapper Azealia Banks signed to British label Polydor Records in 2011, and explained in an interview with *XXL* magazine that problems persisted with how she was marketed: 'It's ironic because the US side wanted to do all of the non-contemporary songs,' she told the publication. 'And then the UK side was like, "Oh no, we need another '212'. You need to talk about pussy." The UK side was trying to make me into some stereotypical, black thing.'

Banks has a point: marketing black female artists in the UK relies heavily on stereotypes. Even in hindsight, 'Scary Spice' – with her relentless leopard print, sass and tendency to be photographed fake-shouting in every press shot – was a far more problematic depiction of a black womanhood than I was aware of as a child.

MOBO award-winning musician Laura Mvula has also grappled with being a black musician in Britain who sits outside of indus-try expectations, and she has been both rewarded and penalised for it. Mvula won an Ivor Novello for best album last year, but just before that, she was dropped by Sony via an email. The problem, she notes, was an inability to find a 'fit' for her within the main-stream:

'The thing that became most apparent to me starting out was that the whole world, or certainly the Western world – were far more ready to accept me as Laura Mvula the soulstress, the black female singer/diva in the making: "the black Adele" or whatever. That's how it started out. I think it got harder for eyes and the ears to digest that, "Oh, I'm this composer, I'm a producer, someone that nurtures the music from the moment it's conceived." So I'm in the studio, I'm there with the pencil and the manuscript paper, and it was astound-ing to me that even after quite a bit of profiling, people, particularly men, would ask if I'd written songs myself or they would presume that there was a male presence somewhere in the process. It's rare in the eyes of modern society that a black woman would basically run, write and perform her own shit. And more so over here in the UK than in the US. I think we're a little bit behind.

'Most of the rooms that I enter are male, white male, and whether that's a recording studio, a boardroom, other projects, you know, people with the resources – the gatekeepers, the merchants, people with the money. I think that's been a wake-up call for me, because I've always been making music, in my family and with my siblings – we only saw our immediate community, which was diverse and black a lot of the time.

'It's frustrating that I never got to face the middle-aged white man who decided that Laura Mvula doesn't belong at RCA anymore – I don't know who the dude is [laughs], but I know that him and the dude above him call the shots. Just like in most other major-label set-ups. It's how the commercial industry works.'

British music is renowned worldwide. According to the stats, one in six albums sold worldwide is by a UK singer and the UK music industry accounted for 17.1 per cent of the global music market in 2016 – its highest ever share. In 2015, Adele had the top global album, Ed Sheeran was second and Sam Smith fifth. But what about black British musicians who make the same music? Over the past few years, white singers influenced by soul have managed to clean up at the Brit Awards and then done it all over again several months later at the MOBOs. If we believed the charts, most of Britain's biggest soul exports over the past decade are all white – Jessie J, Adele, Amy Winehouse, Jess Glynne to name just a few, who've managed to be consistently successful in the UK charts.

'I think Adele's great, I think Sam Smith is great, but I know a million black Sam Smiths, and I know a million black Adeles doing backup singing,' Jamelia says.

'And I'm sorry, but when you look at people like Adele and Sam Smith, look at their surroundings, look at where they grew up, look at who influenced them – it was us.'

By their own admission, many successful white singers owe a great deal to the likes of Aretha Franklin, Etta James, James Brown and Whitney Houston – to the black pioneers of soul, the blues and R&B. But considering they're making music of black origin and subsequently raking it in by doing so, many show an unbelievable amount of contempt for the issues faced by those they emulate.

In 2016, when a number of black artists were snubbed for Brit Award nominations, musician Lily Allen raised the issue and had her comments immediately shot down by blues crooner and nominee James Bay, who didn't understand why she 'had to go down that route' and assured us it was 'about music'.

Similarly in 2014, controversy surrounding several white MOBO nominations was immediately written off as 'annoying' by songstress Jess Glynne. 'It's not about the colour of your skin, it's about your music,' she echoed, not realising that's the exact point people critical of the almost entirely white shortlists are trying to make. 'I think people read into things too much and jump on the whole "it's not equal" thing.'

Around the same time, Ed Sheeran was nominated the 'most important person in black music' by the BBC 1Xtra power list and he swiftly implored sceptics to 'listen with their ears, not their eyes'. Maybe he misses the problem that some people do 'listen with their eyes', and that this saw him top the list in the first place. Sadly not everyone sees the world as he does – at least not in the music industry, where a doe-eyed white boy certainly paints a prettier picture than a black one and makes a prettier penny.

This does not mean that the nominated artists aren't talented. It's simply that black artists, whether they are more, less or equally as exceptional are not equally rewarded – even within a predominantly black genre. White artists do not thrive within a predominantly black genre in spite of being white, they thrive because of it. Artists are continually nominated for making music pioneered by black artists – usually at the expense of black artists. And any acknowledgement of this is met with huffing and puffing of epic proportions. The fallout from the 2016 Brits meant the lead up to 2017 awards focused heavily on trying to repair the diversity crisis with several nominations of young black talent. But the only non-white winner from the UK was Emeli Sandé. And while black representation at the MOBOs has greatly improved, gender diversity remains a big problem. Last year, only one female act won an award at the MOBOs out of fifteen categories – Stefflon Don, for best female artist (which had to be awarded to a woman, anyway). Not a single woman made the best album shortlist either.

However, it's not all bleak. With the rise of male-dominated music genres grime and UK rap, the tide has turned for young black musicians – ones who aren't singing, at least. And the popularity of young female rappers and grime artists such Little Simz, Lady Leshurr and Nadia Rose, who are finding fame both here and overseas, suggests the issue might be slightly worse when it comes to R&B singers. Being relatively new genres, it should at least be some years before white artists start dominating them.

Estelle weighs in: 'If I were to give you an example of people who were doing what I've done and who've done it and who are really doing it, living it, Little Simz and Leshurr – they're known overseas.

'They said, "Cool, cool, cool, I'm still going to be me, I'ma do this anyway." That's the stuff you have to celebrate.

'If we sit and we worry about every black artist that doesn't get the shot and take that and rolls with that and says, "Well, I can't do nothing," we're not going to have an industry, we're not going to have careers, we're not going to have music. You have to celebrate and support the ones that say, "Alright, cool, I'm just going to run around this and do what I have to do." They're doing it and they're doing it on their terms. They're working and they're living and they're proving. All of that stuff's wonderful, living that reality, that's the thing you should support and big up.

'It's been going on since the 50s – a white artist comes along, does our music and blows up. What do we do, stop? Stop being artists? Stop creating? Stop being who you're born to be as an artist? No, you do what you're supposed to do – if you're a singer, you sing, if you're a rapper, you rap, if you're an artist or producer, that's what you do. You do music, you do creative, you create . . . It happened before me, it happened generations before me, it happened while I was doing my music, and it's going to happen for the next generations. We cannot focus on that, we [just have to] do what we've got to do.'

'Across cultures, darker people suffer most. Why?'
André 3000

Another issue affecting black entertainers – albeit not all – is colourism. A legacy from slavery, when white slave-owners had dominion over mixed-race and lighter-skinned slaves, but by allowing them to work in the house, placed them above the dark-skinned slaves, who were forced to work outside in the cotton fields. It still haunts the black community today: in dating, in our day-to-day lives and, most visibly, in the media.

It must be noted that of the black British female actors I listed earlier who have made it in America, the vast majority are either light-skinned or biracial. *Essence* magazine last year did a feature entitled 'The Brit Pack', outlining black British male actors making waves in the US, and featuring dark-skinned actors Ashley Thomas, Daniel Kaluuya, John Boyega, Damson Idris and David Ajala. A similar listicle by the same publication listed black British female actors, too, but it looked very different – 13 out of the 19 profiled were mixed race and light-skinned, not by the publication's choice but owing to the fact that this is simply the reality. There are limited strong roles for white women, fewer for light-skinned women, and for dark-skinned, broad-nosed, 4c-haired black women there are even fewer.

When the film *Straight Outta Compton*'s casting call hit the internet, it proved this was a problem that permeated not just the main roles but the parts for extras, too. The posting was broken into categories: A Girls, B Girls, C Girls and D Girls. 'A Girls' were described as 'Models. MUST have real hair – no extensions, very classy looking, great bodies. You can be black, white, Asian, hispanic, mid eastern or mixed race, too.' The 'D Girls', whose ranking was clearly an indication of their worth and desirability, were described as the following: 'These are African-American girls. Poor, not in good shape. Medium to dark skin tone.' A similar request was made by Kanye West, whose

Yeezy Season 4 fashion show casting call requested 'multi-racial models only'. Even when this is deviated from, the attitudes stay put. American journalist Alessandra Stanley infamously described dark-skinned actor Viola Davis as 'less classically beautiful than [Kerry Washington], or for that matter Halle Berry', who are both fairer.

Hollywood colourism goes hand in hand with Hollywood racism, and while racism affects all black actors, colourism affects only dark-skinned ones – and benefits lighter actors. The careers of many legendary black actors and singers, such as Dorothy Dandridge, Josephine Baker, Eartha Kitt and Lena Horne were jump-started owing to their perceived proximity to whiteness. Their dark-skinned counterparts remain even further down the pecking order. Even in biopics portraying individuals who were dark-skinned in real life, actors with fairer skin win out. Look at the Nina Simone biopic, which cast Zoe Saldana as the passionately pro-black Simone, and *Half of a Yellow Sun*, in which mixed-race Thandie Newton played Igbo character Olanna. In music, three of the most visible and successful female artists in America are black: Rihanna, Beyoncé and Nicki Minaj. It hardly needs saying that their skin tone plays a part in their mainstream success.

The media seeks, at best, that black women should conform to a beauty standard that the mass considers the 'ideal': a white woman. At worst, it promotes the erasure of the black woman. Unless a particular stereotype is being reinforced, black women are usually kept out of the picture, especially if wealth, aspiration or beauty are being promoted. And yet, despite this, there is still an awareness that we are consumers/viewers who need to see ourselves reflected, which means our complete exclusion from the media isn't quite possible. So often black women are presented in a form more palatable to the masses. If there is a character of high desirability who is black, she will in most cases be fair-skinned with western features, regardless of whether it is in mainstream or black media, because colourism also remains rife within the black community.

In the past, in 'black shows', dark-skinned characters have been recast as light-skinned. When dark-skinned actor Janet Hubert

Whitten left the sitcom *The Fresh Prince of Bel-Air*, she was replaced by light-skinned actor Daphne Maxwell Reid. In *My Wife and Kids*, Jennifer Freeman took Jazz Raycole's place. But it doesn't stop at individual roles. When characters cast are dark-skinned in 'black' film and TV, they tend to be in roles that exacerbate problematic stereotypes surrounding darker black women.

Darker-skinned black women are rarely the lead or love interest in black films or TV shows. The role of the 'black bestie' in white films exists in black films, too, but this time the main character is light and the 'sidekick' dark. As noted by blogger Justin 'King of Reads' J, the light protagonist is often 'prettier, nicer, "classier", more reserved, and/or overall more likeable and desirable', while the dark-skinned character is 'shady, mean, loud, desperate, abrasive, aggressive, and/or overall less attractive (many would say "ghetto")', as exemplified in many films and shows, such as *Coming to America* (shy, sweet, light-skinned Lisa McDowell versus her abrasive sister who goes after Prince Hakeem, Simi and even her sister's ex-fiancé. Three guesses who is the rightful queen of Zamunda?) and even children's cartoon, *The Proud Family* (Pretty Penny, who is the star of the show and the object of Sticky's desires, versus neck-rolling Dijonay, who is not, despite her continued efforts). Many of these films and shows were released a while ago, but even in the 2014 film *Dear White People* – a satirical comedy following a diverse group of students in attendance at a predominantly white Ivy League university – biracial character Samantha White was given a complexity and nuance denied to the dark-skinned female supporting character, Coco Conners. Conners was instead portrayed as vain, pretentious and jealous, and no mention was made of how navigating campus life as a dark black woman would have given her less room to be as radical as non-conformist Samantha and more susceptible to respectability. These damning depictions have real-life ramifications; according to research in the US, black girls with the darkest skin tones are three times more likely to be suspended from school than black girls with lighter skin.[2] In family sitcoms, dark-skinned father and son characters never seemed to be an issue, but the requirement for women to be attractive has meant that mothers and daughters are almost always lighter (see *One on One*, *All of Us* and several other of your favourite childhood shows).

While many feel that the black community serves as a buffer to black women from the mainstream media, a study conducted by Maya A. Poran indicates that black women are not immune to prevailing cultural preferences, as well as being subject to intraracial preferences (i.e. preferences within the black community itself; lighter skin, hair with looser curls, light-coloured eyes and a big pair of thighs accompanied by a bigger bum), and that they believe these are standards they are expected to embody. The subjects of the study explained the strange phenomenon of not seeing themselves reflected in images intended to reflect 'all black women' and instead seeing what they were meant to be 'trying to live up to'. As the American feminist writer bell hooks puts it, black people 'can on one hand oppose racism, and then on the other hand passively absorb ways of thinking about beauty that are rooted in white supremacist thought'. Even user-generated natural hair blogs regularly come under fire for their over-representation of 3a hair – curls that are looser and more common in biracial women. Here in the UK, two black magazines made the mistake of using models who were not black as models for a double-page feature and on a front cover. In one case, the model was later caught making racist comments on Twitter, some specifically denigrating black hair. While both of the women could easily have passed for biracial, the over-representation of ethnically ambiguous women in black media might have you believing that dark-skinned, kinky-haired black women were the minority. The number of mixed-race people with white and black heritage is less than the number of people who identify as black, but casting preferences make it all too easy to assume that the latter are the smaller group.

In the media's reluctance to portray black women with overtly African features, they begrudgingly 'make do' with biracial and light-skinned women. Diversity is presented, but western beauty standards are still to some degree upheld in what sociology professor Margaret Hunter refers to as 'the illusion of inclusion'. Furthermore, black women who already somewhat adhere to western beauty standards are often brought further in line with these standards, through makeup techniques or virtual skin lightening, and are almost peddled as white women via magazines, film posters and album covers.

Retouching of photographs is an immediate way to 'fix' a celebrity of a darker hue, too. Whether it is a dark-skinned actor like Gabourey Sidibe, whose 2010 *Elle* cover sparked controversy when she appeared as noticeably lighter, or Beyoncé who, despite already being fair-skinned with blonde hair, was significantly lightened for a L'Oréal advert in 2008, the whitewashing of women of colour is rife. For a handful of women (particularly in fashion, where the 'offbeat' is welcomed, within limits) their dark skin is embraced, but it is subsequently othered – commodified as alien and exotic. Dark skin is made novel, not the norm: the darker the berry, the more quaint the fruit. Susan Wokoma summarises this perfectly:

'Basically, for women – for all women – we are judged by the way that we look. It doesn't matter whether you're a doctor, it doesn't matter whether you work in Sainsbury's, it doesn't matter whether you are an actor. Your worth is measured against how attractive you are. And one of the reasons colour comes into play is because the socially accepted version of being attractive is being light, having European features, or if you're not that, you are model-looking. You're Lupita Nyong'o, you're Grace Jones-looking. You look like a model. You are dark-skinned but you're interesting and exotic, and that comes with its own bullshit as well. "Omg, you have these really weird features, omg, you're so strange, I want to put you in a museum."'

June Sarpong, arguably one of the most visible black women in the country, has remained a comforting reflection for many young black girls for several years. But she recognises there is a lack of nuance in the representation of black women in the media, too.

'We often don't see positive role models. We don't see positive examples of ourselves. We are more or less invisible in the magazines, if you're buying mainstream magazines,' Sarpong says. 'So I think there's a certain extra level of strength and confidence black women have to have. But when we have it, it's undeniable. So when you see a

Michelle Obama or Oprah it's so extreme, because it is the essence of true self-acceptance. Because it doesn't come from outside, so it has to come from inside. Don't be a black girl trying to look for outside validation, you're going to be real upset there. You better figure out how to like yourself. Every day, look in the mirror and say, "Yes, I love you," because you're not getting it from the outside in the same way, you're just not.'

The problem persists behind the camera, too

According to figures produced by Creative Skillset, just 24 per cent of those in senior roles in cable or satellite firms are female and only 4 per cent of employees in positions in senior terrestrial broadcast are BAME.[3] There are apparently no BAME people at all working on the senior production side of independent film companies. Similarly, a report by the Creative Industries Federation and the MOBO organisation reveals that BAME people occupy just 11 per cent of jobs in the UK creative sector,[4] though the figure should be around 17.8 per cent because nearly a third of creative jobs are in London, where 40 per cent of people are non-white – a figure that continues to grow.

There are moves to address these issues, with the BBC appointing Tunde Ogungbesan as its new head of 'diversity, inclusion and succession', and in April 2016 they announced new targets: gender parity across every part of the corporation; 8 per cent of staff hired would be disabled; 8 per cent of staff would be LBGT; 15 per cent of staff from BAME backgrounds. These numbers will be replicated on screen, lead roles included, and are roughly equivalent to averages for the overall population of Britain. At the moment, though, change is still slow, with broadcasting regulator Ofcom criticising British broadcasters for a 'woeful' lack of diversity amongst their staff and accusing the BBC in particular of failing to lead the way. National treasure Sir Lenny Henry, on the other hand, came for the neck of Ofcom, saying they promote 'fake diversity' by refusing to set targets for those who work behind the scenes. Speaking in parliament, Henry said: 'It's all very well to say: "Look, this person has an Asian antagonist or a gay second lead." That's great, but who was the producer, who was the commissioner, who was the script editor, the head of casting, the photographer, the director, the First AD? If the deciders remain the same then nothing has really changed.'

Improvement cannot come quickly enough. So far, only four black women have directed a feature-length film that has been released theatrically in the UK – ever. Ngozi Onwurah became the first in 1995, with her film *Welcome II the Terrordome*. Debbie Tucker Green released *Second Coming* in 2014. A year before, there was the release of Destiny Ekaragha's *Gone Too Far*, adapted from Bola Agbaje's screenplay.

Amma Asante makes up one of the four, with her 2004 BAFTA award-winning debut, *A Way of Life*. Nine years after her first film, she directed the critically acclaimed *Belle*, and her third feature followed soon after, *A United Kingdom*, with which she became the first black female director to open this year's BFI London Festival. However, despite her huge success and seniority, Asante says that even now the situation is still difficult for black female directors, owing to pressures from both the black community and white gatekeepers to make 'the perfect film'.

'The one thing that no writer can do is please all of the people all of the time. It's not like you can go down to the movie theatre on a Saturday night – let's just say there are 15 movies on, you won't even get three that have got female black leads, right? So when you've got that one, *Belle* or whatever it might be, it is expected to be all things to all black peoples – and I mean peoples – all of the time, and it can't be.

'Whereas if you went to the movie theatre on a Saturday night and there were three to five movies with black female leads, you would say, "Well, that one's not for me and I'm not really keen on that filmmaker because I don't really like the perspective she comes from. I don't really want to see that film because it's set in the eighteenth century and I'm not down for that. I know I want to see a contemporary film tonight and I know I want to see a film with a black female in it," and that's the one I can choose. When you only have that one option, you're more critical of it.

'We as the first, or some of the earlier ones, to get a seat at the table are fighting a fight all day every day. We sleep it, we wake up to it, we eat it, we drink it, it's there all of the time. And there is never a movie that I work on that I am not constantly trying to school the people around me in why the direction they want me to go in is not going to work for the audience that I want to nurture. And even if I don't get an audience for that movie, the only real legacy that I leave behind is my body of work. So regardless of whether it pleases all of the peoples all of the time, I want to leave behind a body of work that I think honestly represents what I have to say.

'Now, there are times, for instance, when I will take on a project because if I don't I have to think about who the alternative is that will tell that story. When I think about what that alternative is, what I know is that I, as a black female, will not have a voice. I have taken projects on that I have not written in order to put them in a place where we can actually feel more than just about okay with what I'm seeing on the screen. And what is never questioned is, "My goodness, what were those projects like before?" People are always, of course, judging the end product – they're not necessarily judging the struggle that you went through to get it to that end product and what it was in the beginning. I'm sure there would be more than a few gasps if they looked at what has been presented to me in the first place.'

The work produced by black women in media isn't created within a vacuum and the same strictures and structures that are present in any other sector remain, too. The same people tend to have the money – white men – many of whom still remain sceptical of the value of portraying black women as they are, or indeed at all.

Novelist Malorie Blackman has also experienced her ideas being affected by commerciality:

'My second book was turned into a film. So I'd sold the film rights, and I took the money and ran basically! My book was about two black girls and a white girl, and when the film came out it was about three white boys. And I thought, excuse me? I was watching this thinking

– is this my book? And I thought, oh God, it is! And then I thought, oh my God! They've made them three white boys! And not one of them is a girl, for God's sake, never mind black! And I thought, that's not going to happen again. Then I applied to the National Film and Television School and I did my MA in scriptwriting there, because afterwards when people said they wanted to adapt my books, I would say – and I'd like to write the script! And they'd say, do you have a particular take on the characters? And I'd say, "yes – they're black."'

Her critically and popularly acclaimed *Noughts and Crosses* series uses the setting of a fictional dystopia to explore racism, and yet it was very nearly adapted to be very different:

'I got taken out to lunch when *Noughts and Crosses* first came out, and somebody was interested in buying the dramatic rights. One of the guys at the lunch from this production company said, "We were thinking about making the crosses Asian, rather than black." And I said, "Why?" And he said, "We just feel we'd reach a bigger audience that way." And I sat there thinking, hmm . . . interesting, thank you for the lunch!'

Funnily enough, we were asked if we'd consider making *Slay In Your Lane* about women of colour instead of black women during a pitch meeting with a publisher. Thankfully, we had enough interest from other parties to ensure we could write the book we wanted, but it's easy to forget that this isn't always the case. Sometimes, these books, films and TV shows risk not being made at all.

....

'You can take the girl out the hood but you can't take the bits out the bitch.'
Nadia Rose, Mufasa

....

The arts are often exclusionary culturally, but also literally. Financial security and economic advancement is often a priority within the black community, with parents understandably putting great emphasis on social mobility when advising young people in their career choices, to ensure a more comfortable life than the generation before.

While fewer than one in 12 of white British people live in a 'deprived neighbourhood', the statistic for black people is one in five. Black people in the UK also have worse wage and employment rates regardless of whether they live in better-off or deprived neighbourhoods, and though, when it comes to the transition from education to employment, white boys fare much better than other ethnic groups; despite trailing at school they are less likely to be unemployed and to face social immobility.[5] These statistics may seem irrelevant, but they matter when you take into account that a career in the arts is hardly known as being a financially viable choice. Only 16 per cent of actors are from a working-class background, whereas nearly half of all BAFTA winners went to private secondary schools. The same also goes for nearly half of the country's leading journalists, 94 per cent of whom are white.[6] Only 7 per cent of the country attend these schools, but they remain massively over-represented in the arts. Eddie Redmayne, Damian Lewis, Tom Hiddleston, Benedict Cumberbatch and Dominic West are some of the country's most successful actors at the moment and they all attended private schools. Hiddleston and Redmayne both went on to study at Cambridge University. Less than 1 per cent of all British undergraduates attend Oxford or Cambridge University and only 1 per cent of that figure are black.

This means there is a lack of black people in the creative industries both behind and in front of the camera. As black people are more likely to be from working-class backgrounds, the fiercely competitive low-paid, unpaid or underpaid roles are often only a luxury of the privileged. Charities such as Creative Access, which provides paid internships to BAME youth, have been the target of government cuts, which means many of us will have even less access to an already inaccessible industry. From the outset, believing something isn't for you because there are no signs that it is, is enough to stop many from even trying to find a place within an industry. Right now, all the signs suggest that Britain's creative industry is not for black people – especially black women.

'Over there [in America], I think that it's less about class,' says Sarah-Jane Crawford. 'And racism and classism often go hand in hand with each other – they're like the cousins of one another – so what you find there is that people are more willing to take a punt on you no matter your background. Over there I am seen as posh, whereas here I'm like a South-East London girl done good. My dad was a bus driver, my mum never really had a massive career, I'm a proper working-class girl from Lambeth who has managed to work with Simon Cowell and do Radio 1Xtra for seven years. But when I go over there, suddenly I'm this really well-spoken black girl. The irony is that when I'm over there, I'm this really middle-class British girl, but over here I'm not seen as that. I'm almost seen as more British over there than I am on home turf, because I'm black here.'

The show must go on

It cannot be denied that, in Hollywood at least, change is coming and it is constant. A 2017 study by the Creative Artists Agency found films with more diverse casts perform better at the box office than less diverse ones, confirming what minorities have consistently argued for years. For this study, 413 films released between January 2014 and December 2016 were included – those with at least a 30 per cent non-white cast have tended to financially outperform films that don't. It was also found that minorities made up around half of the ticket buyers who attended screenings during the opening weekends of many of the most successful films released – 45 per cent in 2015 and 49 per cent in 2016: an increase that perhaps occurred because of more diverse castings in recent years.

An excellent example of this was last year's dark horse, *Girls Trip*, which became the first black-led movie to earn over $100 million at the box office. Shows and films are not only being rewarded financially but critically, too – *Dear White People*, *Atlanta* and *Insecure* all have 100 per cent ratings on Rotten Tomatoes. Off the back of these successes, 2018 looks set to be an incredibly black year for film, with *Proud Mary*, starring Taraji P. Henson, and *A Wrinkle in Time*, directed by Ava DuVernay, who has assembled one of the most diverse casts ever to appear in a Disney film, with Storm Reid as lead alongside Gugu Mbatha-Raw and Oprah Winfrey. Then, of course, there's *Black Panther*, featuring a stellar all-black cast of just about everyone in black Hollywood, ever. Netflix has also bought the worldwide rights to *Been So Long*, a musical movie starring Michaela Coel and Arinzé Kene, which is set in Camden. The value in the diversity of stories is slowly being seen.

Conversely, whitewashed media is consistently being panned. *Ghost in the Shell*, a film adaptation of a popular Japanese manga, earned just $19 million at the box office compared to the film's $110 million budget. A Paramount executive agreed this was likely caused by the choice of casting white actor Scarlett Johansson over a Japanese one, which spawned a frankly justified backlash. *Guerrilla*, the 2017 Showtime series about the 1970s British Black Power Movement, looked as though it might offer a chance for black British female actors to be given centre stage, but black women still somehow remained bit parts in the depiction. It featured performances from mixed-race actor Zawe Ashton and black actor Wunmi Mosaku, but Asian actor Freida Pinto was the only female lead. Only 182,000 viewers tuned in to the first of six episodes. In comparison, Issa Rae's black-led comedy series *Insecure* drew over 410,000 live TV viewers per episode and at the competing Starz network, *Power* drew close to two million viewers per episode.

While this is all encouraging, there is of course the creeping fear that diversity is simply currently 'trending', as opposed to a real structural change occurring. That comes with its own problems: all things that come into fashion are destined to tumble out of it at some point. If the backing of inclusion is purely economical, it is only a matter of time before it falls out of favour. Take Marvel comics, for instance, who made a concerted commitment to diversity with a female Thor, Pakistani-American superhero Kamala Khan, a biracial Spider-man and many more multicultural, all-American superheroes. But when the company's sales started to flag, an executive linked these two phenomena and concluded that readers were rejecting the company's push for diversity.

Malorie Blackman has seen diversity in vogue before – and seen it fall right back to the bottom of the agenda:

'I've been writing now 26 years, and I kind of feel we were here 10/12 years ago, and then we went backwards. I feel that when I started I'd go to literary events and so on, and I'd be the only black face, or maybe one of two, and in the first iteration of *Roots*, I remember there was a bit in it where they were at some function – there were two black people, African-Americans at a function – and one turned to the other and said, "Are you the token or the obligatory second?" And every time I would go to these places, I would think, am I the token or the obligatory second? Then, after about ten years, it got better, and suddenly you think, okay, there's *more* faces of colour – this is brilliant! And then about four/five years ago, I went back to being the token and the obligatory second and I thought, what the bollocks? What's going on? We've gone backwards!'

The huge success of Oscar-winning *Moonlight* and the critically acclaimed *Get Out* in America (and worldwide) will hopefully reverberate into UK cinema, in the same way the success of series such as *Black-ish* and *Insecure* will do the same for British television. But even then, the changes taking place in the US are still slow to manifest entirely – a recent report found that the representation of women, minorities, LGBT people and disabled characters in Hollywood films remained largely unchanged from 2016 to 2017.[7]

TV shows like *Chewing Gum* and the BBC's *Undercover* were welcomed in the UK for their multifaceted depictions of black characters, but both remained the few examples of such types of programming here – and only one has been renewed for another series. While things continue to change at the bottom, middle and top, the very, very top of the media remains whiter and maler than ever, and that's where the money and therefore power lies, as Amma Asante points out:

'I'm doing well, I'm battling a lot, but I'm not totally there yet. It's a journey. I see my endgame in the distance, it's not, "I made *Belle* and that's it, that's enough", "I made *A United Kingdom* and that's it, that's enough." No, I'm working within a confine – the confines of a world that still owns the finance, that still owns the distribution, that still owns the TV stations and commissions, controls who is the controller of each channel and each network. I'm still working within the confines and as Scorsese says: "You have to learn to smuggle your ideas." And for me, that's what I'm doing right now.

'People have no concept that with each film I've made, financing has become harder, not easier. Financing became harder after I won a BAFTA, not easier. So the concept that it becomes easier is crazy. There is a racism that also exists in terms of the fact that our work is also judged more harshly outside of our community, totally separately. There's a separate thing called racism. That still doesn't go away just because you might make a hit. Within the context of that, I know that the subject matters of my films are judged more harshly than even when a white female wants to tell that story.'

It's easy for an outsider to assume there is more agency than there is once a certain level is reached within the media. But restrictions remain even right at the top. Shonda Rhimes, who is now one of the most powerful people in television, comes to mind when Amma mentions 'smuggling ideas'. She debuted with the hugely popular *Grey's Anatomy* in 2005, starring blonde-haired, green-eyed Ellen Pompeo as Meredith Grey. Her next hit was *Scandal* in 2012, with black but 'classically beautiful' Kerry Washington as Olivia Pope, the lead. By the time she created *How to Get Away with Murder* two years later, Rhimes had created some of the most popular shows on television, and the casting of a dark-skinned, 48-year-old Viola Davis as main character Annalise Keating was not only game-changing, but a move she probably couldn't have made at the start of her career. Her new show, *Still Star-Crossed*, features two black leads stepping into one of the world's most precious to white society – Shakespeare's.

Change is coming to the mainstream, yes, but only because it remains financially viable. So how do we secure it in the long term? For change to actually last, inclusion needs to go further than being something trendy and #trending. While it's great that the media is responding to what is wanted by the masses, this could change at any given moment. We need to see changes that create access at every single level of the process, because it's something that will always be worthwhile.

It's unlikely that a role like Annalise Keating would have been created and given such prominence if it weren't for a black woman behind the camera. It's also unlikely that game changers such as last year's 'Brit-Hop' shoot in British *Vogue* – showcasing a variety of black British musicians such as Nadia Rose, Stefflon Don, Section Boyz and J Hus – would have occurred without the magazine's first black editor, Edward Enninful, at the helm. This diversity of thought of those in charge is what must continue to be pushed for in all avenues, as a dearth of difference affects every sphere – from magazines, to books to presenting. TV presenter AJ Odudu explains:

'I don't feel like they're being any more diverse than previous years. Pretty much the same amount of black people are on TV as there were on when I was young. It's not like there's a new generation. They're still bringing [people] back. "Oh we need a black person on TV, let's get Andi Peters!" who was presenting children's BBC *20 years ago*. They're absolutely fine, but you've got some fresh, amazing talent out there who should be celebrated not just because they're black, but just because they're good and they deserve opportunities just like everybody else. I don't like the sort of statement that they're changing it, really, because it's the same as ever, I think.'

It's a similar story when it comes to music, as Gemma Cairney, BBC Radio alumna and TV presenter says:

'People feel like things are being represented in their own spheres. So, you know, one of our main TV channels won't necessarily commission a spot for urban music in the same way that in the 90s it might have done. They might have taken SBTV, had a meeting with Jamal, and say, "I really like what you're doing; here's some money, go and develop this, because it's needed in the mainstream culture." The head of the channel is just looking at what is ticking boxes for the mainstream, and it feels like all the sectors of our society are being represented online, on YouTube.'

The changes required at the top are ones that few of us are in a position to implement. What we can and do continue to use, however, are our voices. Had it not been for social media, I'm sure diversity would have been dropped by several outlets and brands years ago. But platforms such as Twitter can make or break a film. Another white-washed film, *Gods of Egypt*, didn't resuscitate after Twitter dragged it to death for its casting choices. In the same breath, Twitter created a buddy film starring Grammy winner Rihanna with Oscar winner Lupita Nyong'o that will be produced by Netflix, directed by Ava DuVernay and written by Issa Rae. The project began as an online meme when a shot that was taken in 2014 of the two women in the front row of a Miu Miu fashion show went viral, prompting calls to turn it into a movie. Since its conception it has been confirmed that 'the original Twitter users who imagined the concept for this film will be credited and included in some form'. Now *that* is power.

Power is also being part of the demographic that is arguably in charge of the internet and everything within it that is 'popping' (see '#RepresentationMatters'). There is no doubt about it, black women are light years ahead, tastemakers by nature, and the pioneers of so much – just ask the Kardashians. Our true potential is constantly being realised via the internet, so much so that many black women don't actually want to go mainstream, owing to the aforementioned restrictions. The internet has democratised the media in a way that has never been seen before. We have the chance to make the films we want and cast them the way we want. There are platforms to showcase them to the masses, and unlimited investors in the form of crowdfunding. In 2012, American director Justin Simien crowd-funded *Dear White People* and nearly doubled what he had asked for in donations. The film has now been adapted into a television series by Netflix. Issa Rae's HBO series *Insecure* spawned from her massively popular YouTube series, *Awkward Black Girl*, and its success led to HBO purchasing and developing another black web series, *Brown Girls*. Over here, writer Cecile Emeke's hit YouTube series *Ackee & Salt-*

fish was later commissioned by BBC Three as well as Kayode Ewumi's *Hood Documentary*. *Brothers With No Game*, an urban comedy, was aired on London Live in 2014; *Venus vs Mars*, a black British drama, was purchased by Sky the year after, and *All About the Mckenzies*, a family sitcom, was launched on ITV2 in 2016. Last year, Channel 4 also gave Elijah Quashie, also known as 'the Chicken Connoisseur', his own show off the back of his YouTube channel reviewing Britain's chicken shops. The undeniable desire for diverse programming has also reverberated directly into offline spaces, leading to the one-off black sketch show on BBC Two, *Famalam*, and *Timewasters*, a series focused on a group of black, South London time travellers, broadcast on ITV2.

Through the popularity of their work online, these writers bypassed the people who would have said no to it, and since numbers don't lie, they were later given backing by the mainstream after clearly proving the 'diversity alienates' arguments to be wrong. And though in the UK some of these series were only aired for a short period, the internet ensures that they are still able to garner support and views, regardless.

Music has been similarly democratised by the internet. Rapper Cardi B entered our consciousness as a loveable Vine star and quotable Insta-comedian – by 2017, she was the Grammy-nominated newcomer who became the first female rapper with a Billboard number one in 19 years. Croydon-based comedian Michael Dapaah found international fame after he appeared on Charlie Sloth's BBC Radio 1Xtra show *Fire In The Booth*. His comedic tongue-in-cheek rap 'Man's Not Hot' became a meme and charted at number six in the UK. At 23, Chance the Rapper won a 2017 Grammy for best new artist with his album *Coloring Book*, and for best rap performance. That year, the Grammys made streaming-only albums available for awards consideration for the first time, and Chance made history as the first artist to win a Grammy based on a streaming-only album. He was not and is still not, signed to a record label, just like several grime artists in the UK. Laura Mvula was snubbed in the Brit nominations in 2015, and in hindsight she believes that industry nods mean increasingly less in a world where music is validated more and more by fans.

'I'm becoming more sure that the way that things are going to change is through being committed to your own thing without being reliant upon whether it's a major thing like the Brits, or whatever it is. I almost regret making a big deal of not going to the awards, because ultimately the Brits don't represent anything to do with who I am. That doesn't take away from me. I don't become less successful or less valuable because they don't value me.

'Somebody said to me the other day, "So much of it is about longevity." I think a lot of the cats that get the chart positions now, who over and over again clean up at the Brits or whenever, it's hard to see how in time to come that stuff's going to last, because I think formulaic music – with pop acts that are just constructs – they have a sell-by date. So it almost doesn't make sense for any artist that has real depth to give much attention to what's happening in the com-mercial industry.

'And also it's a mess today. No one's selling records anymore, so people are doing crazy things in order to top the charts. I'm just realising more and more culturally how it has nothing to do with me! It's about money and it's about the same old stuff that the last decade's been struggling with. So I see my responsibility as focusing on what I'm doing and my craft. I'm 120 per cent confident that I'll be making music in the next five to ten years, just because that's who I am. I think that's what's important. I don't know when it became so important for me to be Brit-nominated. It's not.'

At last year's Grammys, Beyoncé was passed over for Song of the Year, Record of the Year and Album of the Year in favour of Adele. Adele herself then praised Beyoncé in her album-of-the-year acceptance speech. Solange Knowles soon after took to Twitter and implored readers to 'create your own committees, build your own institutions, give your friends awards, award yourself and be the gold you wanna hold my gs'. External validation may or may not come, but as Solange tweeted, 'Black girls/women ARE grammys mothafuckaaaa,' regardless of what the mainstream says.

Specifically, we must continue to champion and support the black women who are doing it for us, whether they are overseas or over here. Black British actors not only go to America to work but black British audiences often engage more with content from overseas, owing to constant and consistent marginalisation within the UK. While there is still a deficit of visible black female role models, individuals such as Beyoncé, Rihanna, Nicki Minaj, Shonda Rhimes – and even Michelle Obama – remain so integral to popular culture it's no surprise that black women here often decorate mood boards with them. But there are many black British women within the media, several of whom have been interviewed for and appear in this book, who are equally as important and pioneering and who should be championed in the same way.

Not everyone has a self-generated belief that they can do anything they put their mind to, or a support network of others who generate that belief for them. White people (especially rich white people) are far more used to seeing people who look like them in all kinds of roles. Whether they are actors, bankers or teachers, success in the white eye of the beholder can come in many different forms. But for many of us black women, in a world where everything seems to point to you not being able to do something, sometimes we want to semi-see it to believe it, as Karen Blackett says at the very beginning of this book. Seeing someone else doing what you want to do is often the closest you can get to visualising yourself doing it. Jamelia told us this is primarily why she doesn't want to leave the UK. As a black British music and TV veteran, she knows her presence is not only appreciated, but needed. 'I don't want my daughters – and it's not just my daughters, it's anyone's daughters – to feel less-than. My daughter has said to me in the past, "My mum is the only person I see on TV and see myself," and to me that breaks my heart.'

We can't underestimate how much visibility matters, for a number of reasons. Coming from a family of show offs, I had actually been galvanised into auditioning for *Grease* as a kid because of my older sister's own school-play debut. She had been cast as the very male, very middle-eastern character Joseph in a school adaptation of

Joseph and the Amazing Technicolor Dreamcoat. I don't remember ever thinking she could have been considered 'miscast' or not fit for the role owing to either her sex or her skin, but I do remember our family's pride and excitement at Yem being chosen out of all those other children. Though I'm sure the choice of her as Joseph wasn't meant to make a statement, it did for me.

It should be common sense that actual ability is prioritised over other people's preconceptions, but as in the workplace, unconscious bias often clouds judgement when it comes to casting. Some would rather ensure that a fictional character looks a particular way, rather than being portrayed in the best way. Or that certain voices should come from particular singers. While Yem's school was able to think outside the box six years before my audition for *Grease*, mine couldn't conceive of the idea of me playing an all-American sweetheart. Imaginations had been stretched already in me being cast at all – had we been in 1950s America, I wouldn't have been a Pink Lady, I wouldn't have even been able to drink out of the same tap as them. But I suppose Sandy was too much of a stretch. Yem being chosen to play what was supposed to be the role of a white boy signalled to me that I could play anything I wanted to, whereas my casting as Rizzo showed me I would be billed a 'bad girl' whatever I did. Both castings affected me more than I'm sure either of our Year 6 drama teachers could have ever imagined.

Fifty Shades of Beige

YOMI

....

'Black women aren't ugly – they're invisible.'
Mary Jane Paul, Being Mary Jane

....

When I was a kid, I used to buy a magazine called *Sabrina's Secrets* – a 90s tween mag based on the *Sabrina the Teenage Witch* series. In my Pentecostal Nigerian household it was contraband, featuring the forbidden trifecta: boys, witchcraft and makeup.

I loved that stupid magazine, with its cheap nail-art pens and 'lipgloss', which was pretty much just petroleum jelly with glitter glue mixed in. Every fortnight each issue came with a free hair or beauty gift that went into a super-camp, spangly, purple box that accompanied the inaugural edition. It was the perfect, cheesy pre-teen bible; backpage 'Does your crush like you back?' quizzes were my Psalms, aged ten.

That stupid magazine was probably my first ever experience of unrequited love.

Because while I loved that stupid magazine, it certainly didn't love me back. To be honest, it didn't even know that girls who looked like me existed. Week after week I'd solemnly put aside the freebies – butterfly clips that my hair would break, hair wax that sat atop my plaits like a sneeze – with the hope that next week something neutral would come through the post: 'Yes! Clear mascara! Toe separators!' But although nail files and aqua-coloured nail polish may have been colour-blind, I almost tore out the entire hair tutorial mid-section on a weekly basis.

You see, Becky with the good hair was my nemesis long before she was Beyoncé's. Each week without fail a grinning blonde model, almost-definitely-probably called Becky, would use scrunchies and

Kirby grips and crimpers to recreate whatever hairdo our Sabrina God ordained. But I, the most loyal of Sabrina's subjects, couldn't join in: my hair didn't grow down, it grew out; it wasn't long, it was wide. The French braids they did with such ease looked nothing like they were supposed to on me.

It was my first real realisation that black women were a fleeting afterthought when it came to beauty – if we were thought of at all. I have no idea why Sabrina's sidelining surprised me, as her one black sidekick, Dreama, only lasted one season. I learned to live with it.

And I learned to live with it when I switched from *Sabrina's Secrets* to *Bliss* magazine, and from that to *Sugar*. Along with snogging tips and the definition of toxic-shock syndrome, there's one thing black girls quickly absorbed from teen magazines: the makeup freebies were not for us – not unless 'dusty, ashen corpse' was actually the look you were going for when applying foundation. After our first brush with a way-too-pink blusher and the inaugural spritz of a defrizz spray that only worked on certain types of 'frizz', we soon learned to stick to the middle-page perfume samples instead. Fast-forward a few years and, frankly, fuck all has changed.

Nude is in – just not yours

There are several coming-of-age milestones that mark a young girl's life: starting your period, buying your first bra, and, for most black girls across the UK, your first kiss . . . of death, at the hands of a clerk at a department-store makeup counter who is clearly trying to drive you into a stress-induced faint.

It's a shared mass memory; the names of the shops and the assistants may differ, but the setup is always the same. Cast your mind back to the well-meaning, messy-bunned brunette excitedly ushering you into a makeup chair. Her smile slightly dips when she looks at your face, and then at her foundation shades, then back to your face again. The selection she has ranges from Lily Cole to Katie Price in shade, and you're not getting any lighter. She's not a quitter, however. They never are. She proceeds to dab you with the very darkest foundation she has – a light almond, if you're lucky – and you both grimace through small talk, ignoring the fact that you now look like you're wearing a brown polo neck made of your own flesh. You thank her, and as soon as she's out of eyeshot, snap a selfie – not because you like it, mind, but because if any good can come of this makeup monstrosity, it's banter for the groupchat.

While high-street shelves are brimming with makeup options if you are white, black women are usually meant to make do with a lone 'one-shade-suits-all' offering, which is somehow supposed to work for hues ranging from Lupita Nyong'o's deep chocolate tones to Rihanna's latte-like complexion. Personally, what is often the single 'black' option in stores either makes me look like my face has just come back from a week-long stint in Barbados (in which my much lighter body was left behind) or as though I've been hitting the bleach bottle, and hard. Yes, all the shades that black comes in are beautiful, but it'd be really, really cool if the makeup I'm buying remotely resembled my skin colour.

Finding good beauty products as a black woman is like searching for a needle in a particularly pale haystack. Black women are big spenders on beauty despite a shocking lack of options available to us, probably because the media spends so much bloody time telling us we're ugly. We spend over £4.8 billion on skincare products and services each year, worldwide – twice as much as consumers of other races. Black British women specifically shell out a massive six times more on hair products than white women, which quite frankly justifies our mass disdain for people touching our hair. It's expensive!

Nevertheless, we're still poorly catered to, usually having to turn to high-end brands just to buy the very basics. The high street is like a scrub we just can't quit – we know it doesn't care about us and spends its time catering to all its other women, but somehow we wind up digging around in our wallets each time they promise to 'do better'. And like TLC wisely warned, they never do.

Let's be real, when magazine headlines shout 'Nude is in!' at us, they're talking about skin that we don't have. In a dark way it's comical, the idea of us being earnestly encouraged by magazine editors to slip into 'second skin' tights that weren't even created with our first skin in mind. It was even more darkly comical when, in 2010, Associated Press were so blinded by the ubiquity of whiteness that they saw fit to describe a champagne-coloured dress worn by a very non-champagne-coloured Michelle Obama as 'flesh-coloured'. One sceptical fashion editor was all of us when he responded, 'Whose flesh? Not hers!'

I remember my shock in primary school when someone explained to me that plasters were intended to blend seamlessly with the colour of 'our' skin.[8] When I pointed out they didn't, it dawned on me that the world had a very specific 'our' in mind. By the time I was 14, I was thoroughly conditioned – I didn't even flinch at only peach-coloured undies being described as 'skin-coloured'. Nor at the fact that the bras that matched my tone were sold among the reds, blue and polka-dot designs, as though the concept of brown skin had never crossed marketers' minds.

Some (baby) steps forward

Despite all this doom and gloom there are some subtle silver linings. Sleek MakeUP is the brand with which many of us made our crucial Vaseline-to-lipstick transition. It has faithfully served women of colour for over 25 years, despite initially only providing products for Afro-Caribbean and Asian skin tones. Although this meant the products were relegated to independent afro hair and beauty shops, it was eventually permitted a seat among its white makeup peers in Superdrug and Boots, ending an ongoing cosmetics apartheid. With Sleek MakeUP's wider reach came the inevitable broadening of their collection, which now caters to all races.

It makes one wonder why other brands have not been as quick to cater to different skin tones. Sleek illustrated just how easy it is for brands to expand their ranges. It isn't half as big as some of the companies that have stubbornly refused to cater to black women, yet they are more than willing to be inclusive, so why has it been so hard for the same to happen across larger brands? Somehow, despite its unyielding whiteness, the high street still continues to look around at the makeup aisle and say 'needs more white-people makeup'.

As well as these wobbly, baby steps sideways, a strident step *back* for the British high street was the failure of 'K by Beverley Knight', a makeup line for black skin which came out in September 2009 and was discontinued only two years later. Despite a well-known founder and some high-profile coverage, it didn't take off. Some blamed the demise of the brand on the most common problems faced by black-specific brands: limited availability and not enough advertising. With increased product choice must come increased coverage, although it rarely does. Think about it: when was the last time you saw an advert for an afro hair product on television, if ever? The sheer shock of see-ing a Dark 'n' Lovely poster on the underground was once enough to make me nearly cause an accident on the escalators, God knows what the British population would make of seeing a texturiser kit on TV. Florence Adepoju outlines the issue around the visibility of black products in Britain, explaining that lacklustre marketing often sees products that work for dark skin pulled from shelves:

'It's a problem that needs to be dealt with on so many different levels. When people do provide solutions, when brands say "actually, yeah, a bunch of our customers have moaned and we're gonna put something out for them, for women of darker skin tones", because it's not celebrated on every level and at every stage, the product doesn't get out there. So a brand will produce a line or add more colours to their line and put it in stores. The sales will not pick up because people literally don't know it exists or is available, because marketing didn't put a big enough budget on it or the buyers only brought it into their stores in certain areas. Then it's like, "Oh, welp, we're gonna pull this project out," or, "This was just only limited edition." I started wear-ing Armani Face Fabric, and was like, "This foundation is changing my life." And then I went into Selfridges to try and buy that same foundation and they were like, "Oh no, it was limited edition, we don't sell it anymore." I was like, "I'm not even like the darkest black woman out there, I'm light-skinned, what do you mean!? If I'm limited edition then what about my mum, who's five shades darker than me?" That's crazy! The salesperson said it in a flippant way, "Yeah, here today, gone tomorrow" kinda thing, but if you're not the person experiencing that issue, you'll never really understand how it is to be told so flippantly that a product that is suitable for your skin tone is not necessarily something that needs to be made available. And there's the aggravation of being pushed to other places – "well, it's in America, or online" – even that is stressful enough, but okay I really want it, so I'm gonna go and order it. But just to be told it doesn't exist anymore is insane, it's completely insane.'

Marketing has recently and rapidly changed in terms of representation, however. Pressure applied to brands, from social media especially (see '#RepresentationMatters') has certainly seen diversity sky-rocket over the past few years and has led to campaigns such as the award-winning author and celebrated feminist speaker Chimamanda Ngozi Adichie becoming the new face of Boots. But problems remain in terms of actual inclusion, as the impact of the diversity trend on the high street is still questionable. When we *are* seemingly included, it is usually in campaigns that commence with a lot of fanfare and conclude with very little having changed. The 'dark skin is winning' poster child, Lupita Nyong'o, was announced as the face of Lancôme in 2014, and many saw it as a turning point in makeup marketing. After she was appointed ambassador, many black women said that they hadn't even realised Lancôme offered much darker skin foundations. It was an easy error to make: a visit to the average department store reveals that the darker Lancôme shades are usually left off the display counter and only made available upon request. So, while Lupita was front and centre, the very shade she was actually wearing was still given the Harry Potter treatment: black girl magic bundled under some department store stairs.

Similarly, in 2016 Maybelline launched its Dream Velvet foundation with Jourdan Dunn as the face of the campaign, but only six of the 12 total shades were available in UK stores – and all six were colours for fair skin. Ironically, Jourdan couldn't have walked into a shop on the British high street and bought a shade that matched her own skin. Fortunately, a year later, Maybelline extended their line of foundations for women with darker skin on its bestselling ranges. Hot on their heels, Topshop Beauty recently extended their foundation range to cater for darker skin tones, adding two darker shades.

But many campaigns simply pay lip service to inclusion in order to shift lippy, meaning their commitment to it is feeble and fleeting. L'Oréal's 2017 'All Worth It Campaign' for its newly extended foundation range was intended to celebrate diversity, but they sacked their first transgender model, who was of Caribbean heritage, for calling out systemic racism in a Facebook post. Munroe Bergdorf was dropped after writing a response to the events in Charlottesville in 2017, where protesters carrying Nazi flags clashed with anti-racism demonstrators and a woman was killed in the process. She posted: 'I don't have energy to talk about the racial violence of white people any more. Yes, all white people. Because most of ya'll don't even realise or refuse to acknowledge that your existence, privilege and success as a race is built on the backs, blood and death of people of colour. Your entire existence is drenched in racism.'

The cosmetics company issued a statement saying that her comments were at odds with their values and they ended their partnership with her. Clara Amfo criticised the decision soon after, stating 'A trans woman of colour who L'Oréal hired to sell makeup because of who she is. Who she is, a woman who wrote a nuanced post on institutional racism and white supremacy in relation to Charlottesville and how the foundations of those heinous ideals trickle into every facet of our society . . . She has now been dropped from the campaign because L'Oréal feel that she is "at odds with our values". If she's not "worth it" anymore, I guess I'm not either.'[9]

Questions of durability aside, while several brands *have* rolled out diverse campaigns over the last few years – L'Oréal, Estée Lauder

– the problem of distribution still persists. Lines might be extending but this doesn't mean they are being stocked, and many stores don't feel the need to do so without prompts from members of the public.

I remember when Elizabeth and I used to live together: she would often run out of foundation and would be unable to find her shade in Croydon – an area where less than 50 per cent of the population is white and which has the highest Black Caribbean population in the country. So while the wilfully obtuse may put the lack of buying options down to the fact that there are a fair few more white people than black people in the UK, distribution is a problem that still persists in even the blackest boroughs of London.

Elizabeth explains:

'Most marketing roles include the distribution element. This means, you do the fun part, the artwork, but you also have to do the distribution side – so actually figuring out the logistics of getting it into stores, and the quantity they require. In my role, I work with designers in terms of making sure it looks good, but then I also manage the distribution side, so from working out what it looks like on the computer screen to getting it printed in a factory and walking into a high-street store and seeing it in person. The problem with diversity being a trend is when it only filters from design, they're wrapped up in it as a trend, only focusing on making the product look good on a computer screen. Thus they make it look as if change is happening. I'm not saying it's not, but this approach isn't long term, it's not embedded in the fabric of the company and it's all about the numbers. Some stores may be like, "Well, I don't actually want to stock this many dark foundations." It sounds crazy, but because it's in terms of stock, they may think of their clientele and not see it as a priority. Marketing is only one part of the campaign. If you don't have a business that sees catering for a diverse range of women as a priority, you're always going to fall short if you don't have a long-term strategy.'

Marketing and distribution work hand in hand. Marketing creates awareness but distribution actually gets the product into the stores.

Many brands have focused on the former but forgotten the latter. Darker shades are being created, but when stocks run out are they reordered for darker-skinned consumers? Diversity can't simply be a trend or ploy to shift products. It has to be embedded into 'business as usual' – there's not much point making darker shades available online if black women can't go in-store to try them out in person. When you consider the vast amounts we actually spend on makeup, this lack of distribution doesn't even make *economic* sense.

And speaking of economics, an independent survey conducted by Superdrug found that 70 per cent of black and Asian women felt the high street did not cater to their beauty needs and they were forced to spend £137.52 more on their beauty products per year than anyone else. The cost of a foundation well-suited to darker skin was found to be at least £15–£25 more than a foundation for lighter skin from the established high-street brands. Superdrug's Shades of Beauty campaign, aimed at making affordable shopping more accessible for black and Asian women, has helped make strides by making a diverse range of products more readily available. The store is also working directly with brands to open up shelf space to carry their full foundation range, but as far as the rest of the high street is concerned, there is still a long way to go.

High-end brands, such as Bobbi Brown, have also made a commitment to diversity in recent years, broadening their shade ranges to offer more than 30 different tones. But while it is encouraging that the more costly cosmetic companies are becoming better represented in terms of in-store inclusivity, it still means that diversity remains a largely luxury proposition. Slaying comes at a price, and it's certainly not cheap. And even if you do have the ability to fork out, it doesn't necessarily mean you're going to be catered to. Outside of the beauty market, Christian Louboutin introduced a range of shoes with the primary aim of matching most skin tones. So far, they are the only major luxe label to take the matter of diversity seriously by extending their offerings in response to the fact that women come in all colours and that many have the means to afford designer clothes and shoes.

The marketplace assumes it knows what we want, what we'll buy, how much we'll pay, but it appears to have got its information through a game of Chinese whispers with no black female players. Simply put, we're not privy to conversations about ourselves: our wants may be being discussed, but it's behind our backs and by individuals who simply don't know us.

'Aut viam inveniam aut faciam'
(I'll either find a way or make one)

It's been established: black women are currently making do with very little. Despite the fact that as individuals we spend considerably more on beauty products than our white counterparts, as a whole the market for black or Asian beauty products in the UK is a niche one, valued at £70m – just 2 per cent of the total market for women's haircare, skincare and makeup, and well below the percentage of the country's BAME population. Unsurprisingly, the resulting lack of choice can make even an impromptu shoe-shopping trip or makeup splurge frustrating.

But out of that frustration can come great things. If there's one thing black women have a knack for (see 'When Life Gives you Lemons'), it is making lemonade from a whole lot of lemons, à la King Bey. Take lingerie and hosiery brand Nubian Skin, which was created after its founder failed to find any wardrobe staples in her skin tone and launched her now-flourishing line out of sheer exasperation.

'I don't like settling and was annoyed I couldn't find things that worked for me,' Ade Hassan explains. Despite a job in finance and no first-hand experience in the fashion industry, Ade decided to stop waiting for the mainstream to create the products she needed and did it herself. She took a year off from her job to study fashion design in Paris, before going back to London to launch Nubian Skin.

It was an instant hit with the media, receiving masses of coverage and finding favour with black girl magic muses Beyoncé and Kerry

Washington. But most importantly, it was a Godsend to thousands of previously invisible black women who suddenly felt they could be seen – as opposed to our Godforsaken white bras poking through our shirts.

Aside from the continent-sized gap in the market, it was the attention to detail that saw public interest in Nubian Skin products soar. Hassan took her lingerie brand a step further by doing what so many others refuse to within the beauty business: acknowledging the diversity of the black community:

'The colours took me over a year. There was no precedent. I couldn't walk into a shop and say, this is the colour I want. I started off visiting makeup counters and going around them with a Pantone swatch trying to match them with popular foundation colours, sending it off to the factory, having them come back and realising that it didn't work, adding some red, adding some yellow until I got the colours for the bras sorted.

'The tights were trickier because they're sheer, so I couldn't simply say "these are the colours I've picked for the bras, now make it in the tights." It was again lots and lots of back and forth. Finally, I got incredibly frustrated because the colours weren't quite there and ended up in my kitchen with a bunch of pots that had black tea in one, Rooibos tea in another and coffee in the other, all so I could achieve the undertone. I took to boiling these tights in the teas, letting them dry and getting people to try them on to see what worked and then, finally, sending that off to the factory. It was quite a process.'

In the end, Ade perfected four shades for her range – Cinnamon, Café Au Lait, Berry and Caramel – all with matching foundation guidelines giving buyers a better idea of which shade best matches their skin tone.

It's a testament to Ade that more attention has been paid to the needs of black consumers by Nubian Skin than by the entire lingerie industry. What is true for beauty products is even more true for lingerie. Despite it being abundantly clear that there is a market for inclusive products, mainstream stockists still appear hesitant to house brands they consider 'niche', upholding the harmful notion that white is the default:

'When you tell someone about it, they say "that makes perfect sense," but when you're trying to talk to a department store about carrying the brand, it's "that's maybe not for us."' Ade says. 'People still see it as high risk, not realising that maybe if they gave it a chance and catered to their customers, their customers would be grateful for that. It's still an uphill battle.'

We yearn for a future in which the high street no longer regards the needs of our white peers as a priority and ours as peripheral, and where diversity is no longer a trend but the unspoken norm.

'A diva is the female version of a hustler.'
Beyoncé, Diva

It's crucial that established companies understand that beauty doesn't simply come in one shade, but in several. Until they do, however, like Ade we must fill the gaping gaps in the market whenever we can. We need to continue to take up space that was not intended for us – there are only so many times you can ask for a seat at the table before you simply pull up a chair yourself.

This is what Florence Adepoju did when she began making her products in her parents' garden shed in Rainham, Essex. Three years later, Florence's MDMflow makeup is stocked in Topshop. Like Ade's, her idea was born out of a lack of high-street options. Having worked on a Benefit makeup counter during college, she had experience of women coming into the store and struggling to find products that worked with their skin tone amongst the brightly coloured shades on the shelves. She decided to make a product with black women's skin specifically in mind:

'A lot of black women have had the feeling of going in, seeing an amazing colour – whether it be an eye-shadow, whether it be a lipstick – and thinking "Okay, I swatch this, why does it look ashy? Why does it look grey? Why does the colour not show up on my skin like it does on someone of a fairer complexion?" And I think that a lot of those issues that women have, because they don't understand how things are made, internalise it. And it's like, the amount of people who say "red doesn't suit me, I can't wear a lipstick. Purple doesn't suit me, I can only wear brown." You reply, "But think about it, why can you only wear brown?" It's because this is something that's been formulated to look a certain way, and why can you never wear red, but somebody else can wear red? It's not you, it's the formula. As a formulator and as a cosmetic scientist, having that on-the-job experience of women coming in and saying "I can't wear red" and then me showing them like 50 of the red lipsticks in store and two that are formulated well enough to suit them and them saying, "Oh, okay, I like this red," that complete change. I meet a lot of black women who are like, "I don't wear makeup, it does not look good on me, I don't wear it." And they're just completely removed from this experience just because they don't have that selection. For me, it was really about looking at that emotional response that people have to colour, and also colours that aren't necessarily within beauty standards. So, people who want to wear blue lipsticks, who want to wear black lipsticks, who want to express themselves in a way that is away from what is being dictated as the norm. Because a lot of western beauty ideals come from beauty influences that aren't diverse and aren't from women of colour. A lot of brands play up to the Marilyn Monroe and the Greta Garbo ideals. And it's like "How can I ever be relative to Marilyn Monroe?" It's just not gonna happen. So for me, initially, I put a lot of emphasis on creating a brand that not only was formulated correctly, but looked at diversity, not only from a point of darker skin or different skin tones, but also a point of beauty influences. Alicia Keys has influenced me more than Marilyn Monroe ever could.'

But alongside individual efforts like Nubian Skin and MDMflow, VV Brown, who left a lucrative record deal with Island records to set up her own label, believes collaboration within the black community is the key to unlocking diversity in any industry.

'We need to start collaborating. We need to start featuring on each other's business plans, music, art projects – we need to create collectives. Someone wants to start a makeup brand? Start a makeup brand and get in touch with a black model to model it.

'That black model should be excited about supporting an up-and-coming business. And then that black model goes to a black designer and wears her clothes. And that designer goes to a black musician to get the music for their show. It's more than just starting a business. It's about us coming together *within* business.'

She's right. Collaboration is crucial and it is what has seen several of these brands go from strength to strength. It's the antidote to industries that sideline products and ideas aimed at black women. Whether through sponsorship or a simple plug on Twitter, the sisterhood is currently in supportive overdrive to make up for years of being shut out. Black women embrace each other's projects not only because they are often great, but because they are created by and for black women – and who knows better than us how much this stuff is needed?

Ladies, let's get in formation

But what about those of us who don't have the means, ability or even interest in creating our own brands? What about those of us who would like an affordable high-street option of a great concealer, without having to make a pilgrimage to pitch at *Dragons' Den*? At the end of the day, an inability to create something for yourself does not mean you don't want more shades of foundation, or that you can't make a difference.

Aside from diversifying the market ourselves through creation and collaboration, canvassing companies to acknowledge us as consumers is something anyone can do. Ade is clear on this, 'If you are entrepreneurial, then go for it. If you're not? Write to brands. Say, "I want makeup in my colour" or, "I want plasters in my colour," because they should know that demand is out there. Companies are driven by their bottom line – if they know there is demand for a product, they'll make it.'

Years ago, while I was crying hot-snot tears over not being able to wrap white-girl beads around a dainty dangling plait, a friend of mine, Rochelle, wrote an impassioned letter to the editors of a now-defunct teen magazine, interrogating them on why they never featured any black girls on their front covers. In the next issue a beaming biracial prepubescent adorned the cover, and while they then defaulted back to a white child for the next issue and were still some way from committing to a dark-skinned covergirl, my friend recalls future issues being somewhat more diverse. She certainly left more of a mark than my tears did.

Pressure can be applied indirectly through the visible success of competing companies that cater to different groups, too. Take Rihanna's makeup line Fenty Beauty, which launched with a bang last year and has already changed the game in the process. As a new company, diversity and distribution was considered from the jump, and became not just part of the brand, but its priority. Unlike other lines that considered these points an afterthought, Fenty Beauty launched with 40 highly varied shades. Diversity had not been central to the brands of Fenty's competitors (in some cases, it was almost a decorative add-on), but when it began being reported that the darkest shades of Fenty Beauty were selling out across stores, other beauty companies began to take to social media to showcase their own range of shades for darker complexions.

It's as important for us to get a foot in the door of the mainstream as it is to create an entirely new one altogether – one without the exclusionary entrance policy. By both applying pressure to already existing companies and creating our own, we can get a great deal done.

'I'm rooting for everybody black.'
Issa Rae

But as well as making sure our voices are heard by the mainstream, it is crucial that we support those who are able to create what the mainstream won't and who are actively doing so.

As Ade Hassan succinctly puts it, 'If there is something you like or appreciate, support the brand. If you don't, they're not going to be here and you can't really complain people aren't catering to you.'

The same is said by Sandra Brown-Pinnock, a businesswoman who launched her own high-street beauty supply store, XSandy's, in 2015 after realising that all the afro hair shops in her area were run by people who were neither women, nor black. Hers is the only black-owned hair shop in the whole of South-East London, a statistic that should shock. Like Sandra, most of us have found ourselves in the surreal situation of asking Pakistani men for advice on lace closures, and have too often wondered why black women aren't advising black women on something we know a great deal about: our own hair.

While XSandy's stocks many of the same products found in any similar store, Brown-Pinnock and her team pride themselves on offering clear advice and sound knowledge of the products they sell. She also fervently supports other black-owned products and brands and believes it's crucial the UK's black population does the same: 'We've grown up in this country with the idea that buying from a black person is more expensive or that they don't have the things you need that maybe a bigger chain might have,' she said in an interview with the *Voice* newspaper.

'When consumers tell me that a black-owned shop is more expensive, I'll reply, "Have you been in there lately?"

'Often the answer is no. And when they check it out, it's often not the case. If enough of us are not buying from black-owned shops in the first place, they will not survive, so we will be forced to go elsewhere.'

The quality of information and products on offer to us, when doled out by those without direct experience or personal interest in them, is almost always compromised. And the outcome of this can be far more grave than just bad weave advice. According to a recent five-year study, the seemingly innocuous goops, spritzes and glues we put in our hair can have serious health consequences. Black hair products have been found to be some of the most toxic beauty products on the market, as we will see in 'TLC'.

The sleek, shiny-haired black girls on the front of my childhood conditioner and detangler bottles sold a wholesome, healthy image of haircare of which I was envious – at that time no one was aware that those products could result in early puberty for their users.[10] Products that are both marketed at and used by black women are rarely researched for toxic health consequences. And though the conspiracy theorist in me wouldn't be surprised if this was part of a much bigger plan to snuff out the world's black female population by cunningly poisoning us through spiked edge control, most put the lack of regulation and care down to the fact that black women are rarely involved in the process.

'Sadly, those who gain financially from filling shelves with cheap chemicals promising beautiful, shiny hair are unconcerned with the health risks. They are not made by the black women who use such products themselves,' says Rachael Corson, CEO and co-founding director of ethically-sourced haircare brand Afrocenchix.

'We started Afrocenchix in part because of my allergic reactions to black hair "care" products. I'm now very glad that I suffered from burns, rashes and other problems, as the need to make our own natural and organic products in collaboration with scientists has likely helped us to avoid a whole host of other health problems.

'We've had emails from two different African-American women who work with cadavers and found that black women would frequently have chemical damage to the skull, and in some cases scarring on the brain, which were believed to be linked to relaxer use. The fact that our families use our products gives us an extra incentive to ensure they are only full of goodness.'

Relaxers now account for only 21 per cent of black haircare sales, and purchases have declined by 26 per cent since 2008. This is primarily because of a natural hair movement led entirely by black women and the subsequent creation of natural hair ranges such as Afrocenchix, offering healthy hair alternatives that the mainstream didn't provide until very recently. Despite this, if you do manage to stumble across black haircare products in a non-black outlet, they are, more often than not, the kind of products that have been fast falling out of fashion for years.

White-owned beauty brands have told us we're ugly all our lives, then lined their pockets by offering us solutions to the problems they told us we had. It's no wonder we often struggle to find darker skin foundations, when other products are not-so-subtly suggesting we lighten it. These brands cost us our self-esteem, our health and our money, which is why the entry of black-owned beauty brands such as MDMflow into the market are important. The fact that black women are attempting to undo these white supremacist beauty regimes by offering products that celebrate and not eradicate our blackness is crucial; the fact it is the black community who profit from them economically, matters, too.

Not too long ago, the idea of black women intentionally getting darker would have blown our collective minds. Yet 2012 saw the launch of Karamel & Brown, a sunless tanning solution specifically formulated for brown and dark skin tones. Ask yourself, in a world more than happy to see us remain within our rigid binary of dark vs light beauty, is this a product you could envisage anyone else but a black woman pitching? When I was growing up, most beauty treatments were designed to burn away all traces of blackness and involved us dipping ourselves in a vat of harsh chemicals. Now, as more and more black women enter the market, it's about enhancing the features we once were taught to sear off.

These black-owned companies matter for another reason, too: longevity. Black businesses have a vested interest in catering to black consumers that is unlikely to wane when the diversity trend inevitably loses the interest of larger, mainstream companies.

It's not rocket science: black women need to be involved when making things for black women. Whether it is makeup, knickers or hair products, without our involvement they either get made very badly or won't get made at all. To ensure this doesn't happen, we must be proactive in whatever ways we can be. This means creating our own products and spaces, but also pushing companies to recognise us as consumers and supporting those who are doing what they can to change things. The answer to our gripes with the black beauty industry in the UK definitely does not lie with old, white men in boardrooms who have never seen an afro outside of a powerpoint.

It lies with us.

A shit wig isn't the end of the world. Ashy foundation won't kill you. But right now we're essentially putting our hard-earned money on the line to be asked if Diet Pepsi will do while everyone else in the restaurant is being given exactly what they ordered. And in the case of haircare, the wrong products can be a matter of life or death. So however small or large our actions are, we need to act.

We owe it to each other, and ultimately to ourselves.

#RepresentationMatters

YOMI

**'Black women run the internet
and it is sooooo fascinating.'**
Kimberly N. Foster, editor of 'For Harriet'

I suspect the reason behind the cliché of millennial navel-gazing and our fervent need to constantly self-identify, is that the internet has robbed us of our unique sense of self. Our generation is perhaps the first to have had our bubble well and truly burst about how individual we actually are, because the internet has shown us undeniably that there are far more of us than we realised. Think you're the best artist out there? Go online. Think you're the only person who puts milk in the bowl before cereal? There's a forum dedicated to it. But for black women, instead of the internet bringing our individuality into question, it has allowed us to *be* individuals. In a predominantly white country like the UK, it has allowed our stories and ourselves to be entirely visible to each other for the first time.

Before the internet, I'd internalised the singularity of the black story so aggressively that I was truly shocked when I met other black girls who spoke like me, liked the same things as me, and had been called both a Bounty and ghetto by completely different groups of people for completely different reasons. I used to think my love of comic books and cartoons as a black woman was in some way unique, but the website Black Girl Nerds connected to me to thousands of black women who also loved all things neeky – from gaming to cosplay and everything in between: everything I had been taught to believe was the preserve of white men. I saw my awkward humour played out by Issa Rae in the *Awkward Black Girl* YouTube series.

Forums sat me down between their virtual thighs, as so many aunts have done over the years, and did my hair. They provided the visibility and advice I couldn't find in magazines. I saw black beauty in fashion blogs like Black Girls Killing It and Tumblr, where blackness was represented in ways I had never seen. I read, laughed and cried about the black, albeit American, experience on sites such as *Clutch* magazine and *For Harriet*. The UK eventually followed suit, with platforms and sites outlining the black British female experience popping up in their multitudes. I joined in in 2012, creating a physical magazine and website aimed at young black girls in Britain, something I would never have had the means to do without the web. Before the internet I thought I was special, and after its arrival I realised I wasn't – and there was nothing more special than that.

But the net was also where I realised how far we still had to go in terms of racism. I knew racism existed, but in the heavily mixed borough of Croydon where I grew up, it hadn't been something I was forced to think about daily. In my early teens, however, when I came home from school and turned on the computer, a world seething with racist sexism and sexist racism flourished in the same space that had made me realise I wasn't alone. I can still feel the burning sensation I experienced when I typed in 'Why are black girls . . .' and the Google autofill answered me: '. . . ugly, angry, dumb'. I still remember the first time I stumbled on the forums dedicated to diminishing our existence. They actively reinforced the stereotypes the web series were trying to shatter; they would spend pages and pages tearing back down the hair that bloggers had taught us to love. Back then, the internet was both black women's greatest love and our biggest enemy – and very little has changed.

(Un)Learning online

As a teenager, I was (much to my dismay) the only one of my friends who wasn't allowed to relax their hair. Not being able to have my hair straight was a very different problem to that of a white girl whose mum wouldn't let her have highlights. Having an afro wasn't simply 'off-trend', it was ugly. It was 'undone'. For generations, physical traits prevalent among black women have been negatively juxtaposed against European features (see 'Fifty Shades' and 'Does He Like Black Girls?'). And for generations we've been encouraged to move as far away from our 'undesirable' end of the spectrum as we can. Since the prevailing beauty standard is one that even the majority of white women sit outside of, the lengths black women can go to in order to conform are often extreme and, sometimes, harmful. Relaxing was once all the rage, now I cannot think of a single friend who still does it. Thanks to blogs, YouTubers and Instagram accounts, black women are now basking in the blackness we've been encouraged to escape since birth.

But this is about much more than simply building self-esteem.

Affirming online images of black women with natural hair saves lives: not in the intangible way that campaigns for Dove and other beauty products lay claim to, but literally. Uplifting user-generated images have helped curb trends that have cost black women their health for years. The reclamation of yet another N word – nappy – has seen black women learn to love the hair we have been taught to hate. The natural hair movement on the internet has galvanised women to ditch painful practices IRL, swapping toxic products for organic oils.

There have been several iterations of the natural hair movement – famously in the 60s and 70s as part of the civil rights and Black Panther movements in the US – but even further back, the famous quote: 'Do not remove the kinks from your hair – remove them from your brain' was said by Marcus Garvey, who died in 1940. It has spread several times before, but in 2007, cultural anthropologists noted the beginnings of the natural hair movement as we now know it – perhaps the biggest one yet. The new wave had no outward political agenda and it was not an organised effort, but women, predominantly across America first, and then, thanks to the internet, the world, began transitioning for their own personal reasons. For some, those reasons were to do with self-acceptance, for others it was for health, but the majority were spurred on by the journeys and stories of other women who were now visible to them online, and the wealth of information about afro hair that had become readily accessible. Like many others, street artist Lakwena was inspired by the natural hair community online:

'I grew up in a predominantly white area and school, so hair obviously comes up as a real point of difference. So I used to look a lot on black hair blogs, back in the day when they were starting. Yes, the internet existed back then! I remember my friend setting up an email for me on Hotmail back in the day – I was so isolated culturally, and it was like, "Where do I look to?" There were people [transitioning] in America. They're often doing stuff. I got a lot of power from that – just a lot of encouragement.'

Like Lakwena, Susan Wokoma found strength and encouragement online, specifically through visuals we had so long been starved of. She speaks of the implicit permission the internet has given black women to be themselves, unapologetically, and to take up space as ourselves entirely: 'I started following lots of different accounts, whether they were magazines or makeup tutorials or hair tutorials or, you know, charities. I literally splurged. And it's been fantastic, because what you see is black women especially being visible as fuck. And it means you don't have to wait for anyone, no one gives you the red light, nobody has to say, okay, alright, we're gonna allow you.'

The internet has enabled the movement to spread globally at such a pace and so aggressively that even the mainstream has had to acknowledge the shift and diversify their offerings to cater to it. In a bid to compete with the ever-increasing, usually black-owned smaller organic brands, companies once primarily known for selling relaxers have added natural hair lines to their range, or are attempting to highlight the natural, 'organic' elements of chemical-based products, as opposed to majoring on their strength, as they had done in the past. ORS, for example, launched a new range of HAIRepair products in 2014, focusing more on hair health than on sleekness, and brands such as Dark and Lovely have also shifted their range to reflect the wants of largely natural consumers.

Although there is no data available for the UK, according to a report in the US, relaxers were the only category of black haircare not to see growth since 2008,[11] suggesting that natural hair is the 'new normal'. The report also states that the 'natural hair trend' has increased the sales of styling products for natural hair and that in 2013, 70 per cent of black women in the US wore or had worn their hair natural. Online educational tools helped black women learn not only to love ourselves as we are, but also about the consequences of putting certain products on our hair. Most importantly, we have learnt how to actually *take care* of hair that has been historically described as a 'problem' in need of 'fixing'. Previously, if not braided or in a weave, the only way a black woman's hair would have been considered 'done' was if it had been straightened, slicked or relaxed; the natural hair movement has helped reveal to many that nice hair doesn't simply mean Caucasian hair.

In primary school, I distinctly remember desperately trying to get a day off because I had removed my hair from my plaits only to find out that my hairdresser had cancelled at the last minute. The idea of attending school with my hair in an afro was totally foreign to me – and embarrassing. Even my mother, who was born and raised in majority-black Nigeria, felt that the only 'solution' was to take a super-hot hot comb to it, like a wand of fire, quite literally burning my hair into submission. Countless other times I would be getting my hair braided in a hair shop and a man would come in – black, white, young, old, sexy, not – it didn't matter. Immediately I would feel as though I'd been seen at my very worst, as though I had been caught undressed somehow and I would throw my arms around my head to try to conceal it. In my teens, I was surprised when peers said they couldn't leave the house without wearing makeup, not realising it was the same anxiety that left me terrified of anyone seeing my hair in its natural state. At no point did I think that me having my natural hair out would be an option, and even now, sometimes I still find myself surprised at how normal something so 'normal' now is to me.

Black women's presence on the internet undid 22 years of conditioning with a handful of deep-conditioning tutorials. Within a year of watching various vloggers, I understood my hair texture, its porosity, what products it needed and, above all, that there was absolutely nothing wrong with how it looked. Like me, Bola Agbaje also feels how important this has been for us as a community, who were initially offered such limited options of haircare: 'The internet has allowed us, as black people in general, to talk about our experiences and to find solutions to problems. Especially with people and natural hair, and how to maintain your natural hair. For the generations before us, if you didn't know how to braid hair and you didn't perm your hair, what were the other solutions for having your hair out? Whereas now the internet provides solutions – all of our hair is different, so we all have different textures, we all have different ways of managing our hair, so you can go on to the internet and Google "my hair is this texture and these are the best products to use to help my hair grow and to help me maintain my hair on a day-to-day basis". Before we didn't have that, that didn't exist. And that's what I think is amazing about the internet for black people, is just having that, our experiences are shared, and so our experiences become valid.'

Like relaxing, the dangers of skin bleaching are also well documented (see 'TLC'). But seismic shifts can be felt here as well, and while bleaching is still prevalent, it is rapidly losing favour among black women. The internet has seen stocks of melanin soar as amazing images of dark-skinned women have been normalised in a way never previously seen. Women now proudly share sunbathing holiday snaps under the increasingly popular hashtags #TanOnFleek and #SunKissedMelanin.

Self-esteem, self-love and self-acceptance are important by-products of black beauty movements. But the rejection of white beauty standards by black women has been crucial to our physical as well as to our mental health – and that is almost entirely down to the World Wide Web.

But the lessons learned do not simply stop at beauty. For many, the black history we have so often craved in schools has been taught via Tumblr pages and Twitter threads. As American schools have often whitewashed black history, the little black history we have been taught in British schools has been usually whitewashed black American history. Topics such as colonialism are rarely even touched upon, but these stories are now being told on every social media site imaginable. Projects such as 'Crimes of Britain' taught me about our nation's colonial history and blogs such as 'Gradient Lair' taught me terms I now use daily, such as misogynoir, intersectionality and microaggression. The word 'woke' may have had its day (after being thoroughly co-opted by mainstream media outlets who, in their usual eagerness to 'borrow' from black Twitter, have completely changed the meaning in the process: centring on themselves and their white readership) but after so many years of being 'asleep' to so many of our own stories, it truly feels like an awakening.

From the internet I learned that what I had thought was historical fact was often sanitised or watered down. For instance, on 2 March 1955, a 15-year-old girl boarded a bus in Montgomery and sat down. When told to surrender her seat to a white passenger she refused – nine months before Rosa Parks did. Despite us being taught for years that Rosa Parks had been the sole pioneer, Claudette Colvin was actually one of the first women arrested for refusing to comply with the state's segregation laws and social codes of racial deference. I learnt this from a Twitter thread that also outlined how fair-skinned, married and committed civil-rights activist Parks was seen as the 'right' kind of agitator to spark the much-needed movement. Colvin, who was dark-skinned, from a poor black family and was a teen mother to the child of a much older and married man, was not.

The internet also taught me about things I'd simply never come across. While searching for hair inspo on Tumblr, I found the story of King Leopold II of Belgium, who massacred ten million people in the Congo. Leopold would order the Congolese to have their hands and feet cut off as a form of punishment, and he did this without ever setting foot in the country. The same platform showed me Sarah Baartman – the 'Hottentot Venus' – who was brought to England from South Africa in 1810 and spent four years being paraded on

British stages as a human zoo attraction because of her large posterior. She was later sold to an animal trainer in Paris, where she died in poverty, aged 26. After her death, her body was dissected and her remains displayed for more than a century and a half. Visitors to the Museum of Man in Paris could view her brain, skeleton and genitalia as well as a plaster cast of her body. Her remains were only returned to South Africa in 2002.

Just a bus journey away from me is Brixton, one of the key bases of the Black Power Movement in the UK. But it was only online that I learned Britain had had its own vastly different iteration of the Black Panthers. While they adopted the same name, the two groups had distinct aims and approaches and had no official links. And to this day it fascinates me that I learned about the American group at school, but found out about the British Black Panthers through my own online research. While in an ideal world curricula would be far more broad and there would be more IRL spaces for black women to share ideas, the internet at least ensures we have the access and ability to self-educate on an unprecedented scale.

'The internet reveals things like, how the Africa that appears on the map is a lot smaller than it really is in real life,' Bola says. 'It has woken people up to the fact that there are so many more people like us around the world. And so it's made a global community feel closer to home than in previous generations, because before, you [would] have an experience and you would go through a situation, and again, there's not that many people you could speak with about it, or reflect on a situation. Whereas now the internet gives you that opportunity to go, "Wait a minute, as a black woman, I think . . ."'

Power to the people

Black women across the globe are the chief executive officers of online culture. Who runs the world? White men, sure. But who runs the World Wide Web is a very different story indeed. A report[12] last year showed black women in the US to be trendsetters who play a key role in influencing mainstream culture in fashion, beauty, television, music and civic engagement for women of all races. Black women's use of social media in particular played a crucial part in this influence, and the study even recommended that companies, brands and marketers should be particularly aware of black women's influence when creating products and content.

One of the most groundbreaking changes the internet has brought about is the ability for black women's experiences, voices and various identities to be centred on and highlighted on the world's biggest platform. This has allowed black women to control our narratives for the first time and to truly take some form of control over not only how others view us but how we view ourselves. It has also meant that the voices of those who used to dominate without audible dissent are finally hearing much-needed clapbacks.

The power of the Twitter drag is well known. While to some, Twitter activists may look like little more than overzealous keyboard warriors, cracking their fingers for meaningless virtual battles, the last few years have shown that they are more than capable of creating real change. Take the Oscars, for instance. As mentioned in 'Being Susan Storm', while the film industry is diversifying, it's taking its sweet time. But black Twitter has and continues to be the rocket up the ass that Hollywood needs. African-American activist and writer April Reign created the hashtag #OscarsSoWhite in January 2015 after the nominations for the 87th Academy Awards featured no actors of colour, for the second year running. By 2017, after several thousand tweets were sent under the hashtag decrying the lack of diversity, Academy president Cheryl Boone Isaacs pledged to create a more inclusive membership. That year, seven of the 20 acting nominees came from ethnic minority backgrounds, topping the previous record of five. Of the nine films nominated for best picture, three told stories of black people and featured mostly black casts. Barry Jenkins became the fourth-ever black nominee for best director, and his film *Moonlight* won the award for Best Picture.

Spurred on by the changes in the US, the hashtag #BAFTAsSo-

White was spawned in 2016, after only one black star – Idris Elba – was included in the nominees for the four major acting categories. Soon afterwards, protesters gathered outside the BAFTA awards ceremony and, as with the Oscars, BAFTA's chief executive, Amanda Berry, acknowledged that the Academy needed to address the issue. Now, from 2019, filmmakers will 'need to demonstrate that they have worked to increase the representation of under-represented groups' to be nominated for the Outstanding British Film and Outstanding British Debut Filmmaker awards. BAFTA also announced that it would add 375 new members, a group that will include 43 per cent women and 18 per cent members of 'minority-ethnic' groups.

As well as affecting change in film, online activism has brought about changes in other forms of media, too. Magazine covers, for example, are far more diverse than they once were – and this is undeniably down to mounting pressure from those who previously did not have the proximity to take these publications to task (I'm sure an adult Rochelle is somewhere fist-pumping at these developments). For years, black women have lamented over all-white magazine covers, but we have only had access to each other to air our grievances. *Vanity Fair* magazine had always had a bad habit of relegating black and ethnic minority actors to the inside fold of their March pull-out cover – an annual showcase for Hollywood's best and brightest. But by 2013, the backlash to their all-white cover was so severe, the internet quite literally forced the magazine into being more diverse. In the 2014 edition, among the performers featured were six actors of colour: Chiwetel Ejiofor and Idris Elba, who featured on the front with Julia Roberts and George Clooney, as well as Michael B. Jordan, Lupita Nyong'o, Naomie Harris and Chadwick Boseman.

Conversations we used to have with each other behind closed doors have moved into the public sphere and are increasingly harder to drown out. 2015 was the year that grime truly found its place within the mainstream, and yet, as we saw in 'Being Susan Storm', when the nominees for the 36th annual Brit Awards were announced in 2016, in categories for which only British artists were eligible, only five out of the 53 spots available were filled by acts featuring black artists (this five includes counting Little Mix – twice). Meanwhile, Adele, James Bay and Years & Years managed to secure four nominations each. The resulting #BritsSoWhite hashtag and a petition with over 2,000 signatures saw organisers performing a major shakeup of the 1,000 people who sat on the voting academy and setting up a panel to help bring in 700 new members who better reflect the music industry, including 48 per cent women and 17 per cent BAME. Last year, Brit nominations included Skepta, Kano, Craig David, Michael Kiwanuka, Stormzy, Lianne La Havas, Emeli Sandé and Nao – a drastic change from zero black nominees the year before.

Twitter hashtags, primarily created by black women, have completely changed the face of the virtual and the real world. The now ubiquitous #BlackLivesMatter movement was created by three black women: Alicia Garza, Opal Tometi and Patrisse Cullors, after Mike Brown was shot and killed in Ferguson, Missouri, by a white police officer. Activist Brittany Packnett kicked off the hashtag #BlackWomenAtWork (see 'Water Cooler Microaggressions'), which enabled black women to congregate online and discuss the stereotypes and microaggressions so prevalent in workplaces in the US, the UK and across the world. CaShawn Thompson started the campaign #BlackGirlMagic in late 2013 to celebrate black women, and the same year Zeba Blay created #CarefreeBlackGirl to counteract the overbearing strong-black-woman narrative thrust on the black female population. Divisive hashtags such as #TeamDarkSkin and #TeamLightSkin were all the rage a few years ago, but they have recently been taken over by unifying hashtags such as #BlackOutDay, #UnfairandLovely, #FlexinMyComplexion and #MelaninOnFleek – all of which create an online catalogue of sublime selfies, featuring beautiful skin of all shades.

Outside of representation, moves have been made in other spaces thanks to campaigns and petitions that have gone viral. Last year, as we will see in 'Does He Like Black Girls?' the Mayor of London, Sadiq Khan, said he would look into accusations of racism at central London nightclub, DSTRKT after the #DoILookDSTRKT hashtag and subsequent protest garnered national attention. Although the club had been under scrutiny for several years prior to this, nothing had ever been done about it. The Oxford University #RhodesMust-Fall campaign to take down the statue of the British imperialist was inspired by the 2015 hashtag of the same name, originally directed against a statue at the University of Cape Town commemorating him. Neither campaign was successful, despite garnering thousands of petition signatures each, but in Oxford the furore led to the removal of a plaque dedicated to Rhodes. Off the back of the campaign, following calls from students and many people online, Cambridge University agreed to repatriate a bronze cockerel that had been looted from Benin in the nineteenth century. This has been mirrored in the US, where the rise of Trump and the far right has seen a corresponding rise in protests demanding the removal of Confederate statues in various states – some of which have agreed to take them down.

Online, many black people rage in unison as structural inequalities play out across the globe, reminding us that our skin is often not the only thing that links us. The hashtags continue to pile up after the death of yet another unarmed black person in the US by police brutality – #TamirRice, #EricGarner, #SandraBland, #AltonSterling – but the same rage is felt in the UK, as we use hashtags in remembrance and to highlight the many black people who continue to die in police custody. These instances – the successful changes as well as the ongoing battles – are more visible than ever. They go global and they go viral, making many of us more engaged than we ever have been.

As the black diasporic identity is continually strengthened online, for black Brits who have, for many years, had to turn to the US to see ourselves reflected, the internet is now reinforcing our own sense of self. American podcasts and platforms are being overtaken in popularity in the UK by our own iterations, outlining our specific experiences. Series documenting the black British experience have also moved from the online space onto television screens (see 'Being Susan Storm'). Their large numbers of fans and views have set the agenda in terms of diversity on TV, revealing exactly where the several thousands of lost television viewers have gone, and in part why.

Even in reality TV, where black women often have the rawest deal and are cast only to exacerbate existing stereotypes, if at all, an antidote has been found on the web. American reality TV has a subset of shows with predominantly black casts, as they do with TV dramas, comedies and films. Many of these shows may be controversial – they too are known for peddling dangerous myths about black women – but the sheer number of them means there are often several different narratives to choose from. In the UK, there is clearly an appetite for black reality TV cast members, too, as a similarly divisive YouTube debate show, *BKChat London*, has made undeniable waves across black Britain. The popular and controversial series dominates Twitter on a weekly basis and the team behind it signed a development deal with VICELAND in 2016.

The internet continues to connect black people to each other, to an audience and to resources we have never had access to before, without needing to ask prior permission. As a result, the gatekeepers within the mainstream are finding themselves with little choice but to unbolt those gates. But with or without their approval, black content and creators continue to thrive, networking on their own terms and forging their own connections, as Susan Wokoma explains:

'It means that you don't have to wait for other people to shout about your work; that's what's been difficult about acting, you'd do the work, but in terms of the publications who would want to cover your work or whatever, they would never come for you. But with those platforms, you can shout about the work that you're doing. You can collaborate. The amount of people that I've got who've sent me a message going: "Hey, would you like to come in for an interview, would you like to do this, could you come to this function, can you talk about, can you just tweet about this survey that we're doing for college, and like, I want people to talk about this study that I'm doing?" It means that people can collaborate. And you can feel less lonely, ultimately. There are bad sides with the world getting smaller, I think, but I think for minorities, for black women, it's been the making of us, I really, really believe.'

In the case of music, grime and UK rap, both of which had been relegated to pirate radio stations, mobile phones and the iconic, albeit underground, TV station Channel U, have found wider audiences on online platforms such as SBTV, Link Up TV and GRM Daily, which have had an undeniable impact on the genres' rise within the mainstream in recent years. Florence Adepoju explains how the internet has helped black UK culture make its mark, not just across the world but at home, where it matters most:

'I was saying to someone recently – we were listening to the radio, I think it was Capital Xtra – and artist after artist after artist was British. And I was like, this shouldn't even be a thing, but for the first time in my life, I feel like British culture, and the diversity of British culture and different elements of British culture – grime, British rap music, British soul artists – are really being celebrated on a mainstream platform. And I think for a long time that didn't happen. There's always been incredible black British women. You are going to speak to women who've been doing what they're doing for years and years and years. But I feel like the internet democratised everything. And accessibility to information online meant that someone who is looking for those role models can find them, whereas prior to this it was just whatever the media served you. And I think now because the media sees certain pockets growing and developing, they're like, "We need to stay in the know, and we need to celebrate black British women." Marsha Ambrosius from Floetry, I used to be inspired by them, but I thought of them as American, and of Marsha as American. I didn't know when I first heard Jamelia that she was British, because so much of the media growing up was American media.'

Girls online

One of the most revolutionary aspects of the internet for young black women in the UK has been, and continues to be, vloggers. Although forums and blogs have been instrumental in teaching us haircare regimes and beauty techniques, reading up on how to do your hair and makeup is very different to *seeing* how to do it. Hundreds of black women are putting themselves out there to teach, advise and unwittingly befriend black girls who find themselves reflected in them. For many black women, YouTube has become the most public secret clubhouse in existence, with hundreds and thousands of members sharing tips on how to navigate and thrive on a high street stocked with products not created with us in mind. Vloggers search for, review and critique a range of products for their peers, often on a weekly basis. They find cost-effective deep conditioners and the darkest shades of concealer so that we don't have to. But this doesn't stop at winged-eyeliner tutorials and foundation swatches: they are teaching us so much more than how to do bantu knots or perfect a cut crease.

Videos focusing on how to dress, relationships, life experiences – any and everything – have found their way onto these channels. Their arrival marked the first time many black British girls not only saw black women who looked like them on such a platform, but also heard their own experiences being expressed on some form of media. Vlogging began as a movement from black women in the US, but it hasn't taken us long to find our own influencers from whom to gain outfit, and at times life, inspiration.

Some of the most popular and revered British beauty and lifestyle gurus have been at it for years, including Jennie Jenkins, Shirley B. Eniang and the most successful black British vlogger to date, Patricia Bright. Patricia has been YouTubing for the past eight years, creating beauty and lifestyle videos. But her fans have also watched her fall in love, quit her job, get married and even give birth through her channel, leading many of them to see her as a kind of big sister, the kind you only ever interact with on Skype. Her normality, humour and openness have earned her a similar amount of subscribers to the population of San Diego – the eighth-largest city in the United States. Although Patricia was not the first black female vlogger, she is aware that her mere presence online has given many unspoken permission to try something that for a long time had been seen as the sole preserve of white people: 'When I make videos, I'm the black female making videos, and other girls are going to see me and also want to do it. I think I know that I definitely made girls realise that there's an option for them to do it and I kind of opened that doorway. But I don't feel like I was the first – there were already so many people doing it when I did it.'

YouTubers, vloggers, influencers: they not only provide makeup, beauty, hair and fashion tips that have been one-shade-only for so long, but they reflect the black women many of us know or are ourselves. The black women who exist outside the biased imaginations of those who are neither black women – nor who know any – but still feel more than comfortable telling our stories.

'What the internet has done is that it has, again, [shown us] that power is in numbers,' Bola says. 'And it's a reminder that there are people who are like us who exist in the world. Especially when you're a black British woman, who lives in England. You're constantly reminded that you are a niche and that you are a minority. And I think that, somewhere along the line, it subconsciously affects us. Because people then go, "Your experience is limited, and so your viewpoint is limited and the way you think is limited and there's not that many people like you." Whereas the internet shows us that "no, wait a minute, there are millions of people that are like me." Like my major thing that I say is: "Just don't ever forget, as black people, we are a global majority."'

The Dark Web

On the World Wide Web, black women have created a space for themselves where they can be seen and heard outside of a real world that largely ignores them. When black actor Leslie Jones tweeted that no designers were willing to dress her for the *Ghostbusters* premiere, the internet roared. Within an hour, fashion designer Christian Siriano had stepped in. But following the film's opening weekend, Jones also found herself singled out for a hate campaign of racially charged slurs, in which she received hundreds of threatening and racist tweets in a coordinated attack.

Sadly our sanctuary is also a safe haven for the bigoted and cowardly. A 2014 study[13] focused on a nine-day period in November 2012 and found 'approximately 10,000 uses per day of racist and ethnic slur terms' in English on Twitter. Female MPs from ethnic minorities are significantly more likely than their white male and female peers to be subject to abuse and attacks by members of the public, according to the parliamentary authorities responsible for security. Aside from the economic and social barriers that hinder black women entering politics, the ease of online threats and abuse is another thing that bars us.

In 2016, Seyi Akiwowo, a Labour councillor in Newham, received reams of violent and racist abuse after a video of her suggesting former empires pay reparations to countries they once colonised went viral.

Last year, Diane Abbott, the country's first black woman MP and currently Shadow Home Secretary, finally spoke out about the violent messages she has received, and continues to receive, from members of the public, especially online (see 'Watercooler Microaggressions'). The messages are so serious that Abbott's staff often fear for her safety.[14] In a leaked letter,[15] they criticised the police for not acting on death threats made towards Abbott, while similar messages sent to white female MP Anna Soubry resulted in an arrest. During the last election, analysis by BuzzFeed News showed that 10 per cent of the most viral right-wing news stories were attacks aimed at Abbott.[16] A survey also found that she had been the victim of ten times as much abuse as any other MP, with 45 per cent of all abusive tweets directed at her.[17] As mentioned earlier, she eventually stepped down temporarily during the 2017 election for health reasons. One half of the internet responded with cruel jokes, the other, filled predominantly with black women, responded with a hashtag of support – #AbbottAppreciation – under which they tweeted messages of support and clips of her best speeches. The originator of the hashtag, Stephanie Ouzo, organised an event in

Abbott's honour with the help of others on the internet who wanted to support her. In a speech on the night, Abbott admitted that the deluge of abuse had taken its toll. 'Even strong black women cry, even strong black women feel alone, even strong black women wonder, is this all really worth it? Even strong black women think, maybe I should just bail out?' she told the crowd.

These attempts to silence us not only affect black women in politics, but also any black woman who is visible and vocal about our plight. In 2014, while Malorie Blackman was Children's Laureate, she found herself on the receiving end of racist vitriol after a piece by Sky News was given an inaccurate headline, claiming Blackman had said that children's books 'have too many white faces', when she had simply been appealing for more diversity.

'I got all kinds of death threats and threats against my family. And it was one of those things where I just thought, again: social media. Maybe there were people who *would* say it to my face, but an awful lot of people love the anonymity of being able to come out and threaten you, and they have the anonymity of social media to do it. In a way it's kind of like this constant thing of closing people down and trying to take your voice away from you, and you can't let them. By the time they changed the headline, it was reported in an Indian paper that UK Children's Laureate says "too many white people in books" – and that's not what I said at all! Again, it's this thing of lies spreading around the world by the time the truth is still pulling on its boots! If you are a woman and you raise your head above the parapet, they try to close you down. I was watching a programme just recently where there was a woman MP saying that a number of her friends who were thinking of entering politics are seriously thinking no – because of all the abuse they see other women get. It's sad and it's unfortunate and it is a way of almost trying to keep women "in their place", keep black people "in their place". Because as soon as you open your mouth, these other people will try to close you down, and you can't let them.'

Once something is online there is usually no taking it back. And the lack of fact-checking that is now common culture in online journalism leaves black women vulnerable to attack for things they haven't even said. But they also come under attack for things they do, or are perceived not to do. Over the last few years, Charlene White has received a torrent of racist abuse on social media sites around her decision not to wear a poppy on air, despite being a supporter of the Poppy Appeal. She has explained publicly several times the reasons behind her choice. She wears one off-screen on Armistice Day, and her father and uncle served in the RAF and the Army respectively. But every year the same 'debate' is stirred up:

'The poppy stuff is interesting, because it's now year five of it being an issue. But I was not wearing it for a number of years before then, because of impartiality – I support so many charities and I want to appear even with all of the charities. And it's important always for people to know it's not just because I just flagrantly decided not to wear it; there are reasons behind it. It was difficult, that first year, and it was a member of the EDL who told his followers to abuse me in any which way they could find me, which is exactly what they did. Jon Snow on Channel 4 news doesn't wear it for exactly the same reasons, and doesn't get anything like the abuse I get, and that is because I'm female, and also because I'm black, and also I'm not supposed to take a stand on those things. I am supposed to sit meekly and quietly and do as I'm told. Women generally, if you put your head above the parapet, in this day and age now, you are ripe for abuse online. A lot of my friends have retreated as a result, and don't do nearly as much telly stuff as they should do because of abuse they've received in the past and because of their hair or something they've said that someone may not agree with. But that's not how I was raised in terms of visibility at work. I've never ever ever been someone to purposely not be seen in the workplace. Because that's not what I know, and that's not how I've ever acted.'

These attacks on black women are usually not about what has been said or done – and not even about what has *not* been said or done, in Charlene's case. If they were, then Jon Snow, a white male presenter, would have received similar amounts of abuse. They occur because their targets are black women, and they are deliberate attempts to silence, gaslight and, most importantly, keep black women 'in our place'. The internet has amplified our voices in a way that is unprecedented, and now the very types who have for so long intentionally kept our voices out of the mainstream media are trying to do the same in this new space, where everyone can be heard.

Platforms like YouTube have particularly hateful comment sections, which Patricia Bright has borne the brunt of during her time as a vlogger:

'The pros are creating and sharing in part of what I love and what I'm passionate about and what I enjoy. The cons are the fact that you are open to public scrutiny – as a black woman, as a white woman, you're open to public scrutiny. I think one of the things I do notice is that if you are going to be seen in the mainstream, people are going to make racial comments. So if I end up on a YouTube trending page, there will be one, "Who's this n-word?" and it's just part and parcel of the fact that it's a public profile that is open to so many people from around the world who aren't as socialised as we are. That's the scary thing, is that we would all assume that everyone's got the same level of socialisation, they know how to respect other people. But no, that's an assumption.'

On the internet, bigoted men throw their toys out of their proverbial prams over many things. Their uniform is often an avi of anything other than their actual faces. Their line of attack? To hurl expletives and racial slurs until they are reported to moderators, who mostly do next to nothing. Their victims? Disproportionately black women. I've been writing on the internet since 2011 and the vast majority of insults I have received have either been about my race, my gender or both – even when I'm writing about neither. But when I *am* writing about them together, which is often, the comments intensify in both their volume and their cruelty. It's clear that the topics I write about and choose to amplify anger many who feel they shouldn't be written about at all. Black women are not being attacked solely because we are black or because we are women: it's the fact that we occupy both identities that puts us at risk of more vitriol. This is why intersectional feminism – a concept popularised online that acknowledges how different identities interconnect – matters so much.

Digital detox

When black women lament how unsafe online spaces can be for us, we are often advised to simply 'stay offline'. But that is to misunderstand the other side of the internet for us. The web can be as simultaneously empowering as it is alienating. It is both our scourge and our saviour, for where we find scorn, we also find solace. Twitter, the same social media site that sees black women scrutinised and criticised, also sees support garnered for us in droves. For every YouTube comments section filled with eye-watering racism and nosebleed-inducing sexism there's an empowering hashtag created by black women that effects real change.

Slowly but surely, the law is modernising to reflect the different forms that hate crime can now take. In 2017, the Crown Prosecution Service committed to treat online hate crime as seriously as offline offences, taking into account the impact of actions carried out on the wider community, as well as the victim. It published public statements explaining how it will prosecute hate crime and support victims, and confirmed those who experience online abuse on the basis of their ethnicity, religion, disability, gender or sexuality will be treated the same as victims of the same crimes IRL. These changes, the CPS said, were made 'in recognition of the growth of hate crime perpetrated using social media'.[18] In a similar bid to tackle online trolling, Seyi Akiwowo created Glitch,[19] an online platform committed to ending hate speech and online violence against young women and girls. She hopes to 'start a conversation about the importance of our generation being responsible citizens online' and provide workshops, coaching and assemblies. These changes are important but they are also new and still in their early stages. As it still stands, social media remains an often toxic environment and for the sake of your sanity, a regular detox is not only advised, but necessary.

'Twitter, I think, is full of fanatics and everyone gets radicalised on there,' says Susan Wokoma. 'Gone are the days when I used to tweet about, "Oh, I got a really nice coffee." Now it's just like, "I hate everyone." And that's why I sort of constrain that for work, and talking about my work, which is so difficult because there's so much going on politically that I am absolutely engaged with, but there's self-care and there's your mental health.'

Patricia uses her platform for work, too, and her role as an influencer requires her to be online far more than average. Yet even she is sure to focus on what matters *offline*, in order to put things into perspective.

'I have a very good personal life. I understand that it's the internet but I'm married with a baby. I'm very happy, so I try and keep my focus on those things that are important to me, which is my family, my baby. That's what's important to me. I mean, it can sting for a moment and then I bring everything back into perspective to what's important to me.'

Our ability to continue to take up space on a medium so many are hellbent on driving us from, is illustrative of our resilience. It's indicative of our ability to take a tool so often used to taunt us and make it into something that works for us. In the wake of Trump and Brexit, the outpourings of social media solidarity against a backdrop of seething, baseless hatred reminds us all that for black women, the internet is truly a tale of two cities. Trolls want black women with opinions – hell, just black women being black women – to be driven off the internet for good, and very little is being done to give us an incentive to stay. Here's hoping that the internet we love so much finally does something for us in return and makes itself, and ultimately us, safer.

DATING

'We might make lists of the most desirable attributes for our potential future husbands – 6 foot or over only, money longer than his height, beard as consistent as his texts – but do we prioritise that they should understand black women's position societally?'

Yomi

....

'Alongside your degree certificate, and once you get your foot in the career door, marriage is seen as the next big achievement, a social benchmark. It is the final signifier to say "Hi world, I have made it, I am worthy." The Holy Grail.'

Elizabeth

Does He Like Black Girls?

YOMI

'But you stay right, girl. And when you get on,
he'll leave your ass for a white girl.'
Kanye West, Goldigger

Watching the TV programme *Take Me Out* is often a cringeworthy experience for black women. For much of the population it offers a light-hearted Saturday night diversion from the weekly grind, but the continual rejection of its black female contestants can make it feel like a reflection of the realities of dating in darker skin. White-toothed, glowing-skinned black women answer innuendo-laden questions with a wink and a nudge and a perfectly crafted pun. They stand, shoulders back, hands on buzzers, part of the parade waiting for the man of their dreams to make his way down that love lift. They play the game, grin in the eyeline of the many men – of many races – and week after week their lights are turned out by Jack from Bath, Gary from Plumstead, Keith from Shropshire, Maj from Bethnal Green, Ade from Tottenham.

When a black woman *is* picked on *Take Me Out* it sparks something of a national holiday on black Twitter, especially if she has been chosen not simply because she is the only one who has kept her light on. It's bittersweet: the dating show is one of TV's more diverse offerings, but it also means we end up watching black women being dumped over and over again. A similar problem persisted with the US dating show *The Bachelor*, which would see black women usually filtered out within the first few episodes. It was a problem so severe that producers took to casting a black *Bachelorette* in 2017 and flipping the narrative so that whatever the outcome, the black woman came out on top. Hit British show *Love Island* hasn't yet included many black male contestants but it has *never* had a black female contestant, and has featured only three mixed-race women. With reality TV, real-life preferences mess with the script.

But even in fiction, black women are so often told that we are undeserving of love. In rom-coms black women are always the sassy bridesmaid and never the bride. A seminal moment for me as a young black Brit came when the character of Lavender Brown in the *Harry Potter* films was recast for *Harry Potter and the Half-Blood Prince*. Initially a minor, non-speaking character in both the books and films, Lavender was originally played by two different actors – Kathleen Cauley in *Chamber of Secrets* and Jennifer Smith in *Prisoner of Azkaban* – both of whom were black. By the time the plot had moved on to *The Half-Blood Prince*, Lavender's character had evolved into a love interest for Ron Weasley, one of the main protagonists. It was in this film that the decision was made to recast the role, this time with Jessie Cave, a white actor. I'm not really sure what could have sent a stronger message to young black women that love is only for white girls.

Personally, I have always taken a simple approach to dating. I like what I like and what I like is good-looking men with heart and brains by the bucket load. What colour they come in is something that's never really bothered me: when someone asks me my type, I usually respond with 'attractive and nice'. The idea of people excluding entire racial groups from their dating pool is something I've always considered odd, but not something I had ever considered relevant to me, as a somewhat in-love-with-myself twenty-something. At least, not until one night out when I was at university, and an overconfident, underdressed boy sidled up to me with the usual chat. He asked me what I was studying, whether I came here often, where I was from. After I answered, he enthusiastically replied, 'You know, you're the prettiest black girl in this club.' How strange, I thought, that in this wall-to-wall white club I'd been told I was the 'prettiest girl' (but with an asterisk), given a compliment (that came with a prefix), as if 'prettiest girl' would be a step too far, a bit too much, even for someone so clearly trying to get into my knickers. For him, in a room where there were also white girls, calling me the 'prettiest girl' wasn't possible. He didn't understand my less-than-positive response; I didn't understand his need for categorisation. I understood it even less because he was black, too.

Dating is complex enough, but dating as a black woman can be a whole different type of complex, requiring us to navigate bullshit from men of all colours and creeds and for all different kinds of reasons.

Pretty hurts

It's impossible to talk about dating without talking about one of the pervading myths that plagues black womanhood: that black women are ugly. Patriarchy has tied woman's worth almost entirely to their outward appearance, so relationship prospects are immediately contingent on perceived desirability. This is something that sucks for all women, even conventionally attractive ones. It sucks even more, however, when the concept of what is beautiful and desirable has been created in total juxtaposition to what you are. To be exclusive, whiteness requires something to be opposed to it, and so blackness must become what is ugly. So, if slim noses are beautiful, broad noses cannot be. If straight hair is what's considered beautiful, then the kinkier the hair, the uglier it is. The lighter your eyes, the more attractive you are and, of course, the fairer your skin, the better you look. As Patricia Hill Collins put it in *Black Feminist Thought*, 'Blue-eyed, blonde, thin white women could not be considered classically beautiful without the Other – Black women with classical African features of dark skin, broad noses, full lips, and kinky hair.' In order for western features to be put on a pedestal, black features must be denigrated.

In *Psychology Today*, evolutionary psychologist Satoshi Kanazawa published a piece confidently titled, 'A Look at the Hard Truths About Human Nature', which stated as an undeniable 'truth of human nature', that black women are less attractive than other women. Kanazawa, 'Reader in Management' at the London School of Economics, stated that we are heavier, less intelligent, and have higher levels of testosterone – making us more masculine and thus unattractive. While this might sound like an extract from an essay promoting eugenics written in 1922, it was actually published in 2011.

It's true that a deviation from this pattern has occurred in recent years. Fuller lips, for instance, are now fashionable, along with the shapely behinds that were once considered too big for fashion magazines. But when those traits that are more common amongst black women are celebrated, it tends to be only when they belong to white women. The 'ideal woman', according to popular culture, is currently Kim Kardashian: someone whose family have made good by wearing the bits of black culture they like. Certain physical characteristics are only stomached and even applauded because they are perceived as 'black bits' on non-black women. If big noses are ever to be considered pretty, they will no doubt have to be popularised on the faces of white women first.

As we saw in 'Being Susan Storm', when black women *are* represented or celebrated it is because they are considered to be more in line with white beauty standards. A study conducted by Kevin L. Keenan revealed that black women in magazine adverts were found to be more Caucasian in appearance than your average black woman, having 'lighter complexions, lighter eyes, and smaller nose and lip ratios'.[1] The same study found that these women were also more likely to have 'Caucasian attributes' than their male counterparts, another example of how the western standard of beauty is gendered and how it affects black women to a more significant degree.

With black women on the bottom rung of the idealised beauty ladder, proximity to whiteness can become the next best thing to whiteness, even within our own community. Susan Wokoma explains how, for her, the idea of dark skin as unattractive was embedded from when she was primary school age.

'I was born light. And I know this because my mum kept fucking telling me! "Oh, you were such a light baby, oh my God you were so pretty, you were the prettiest baby, pretty, pretty, pretty, pretty!" And then, of course, you get older, and you get your colour. I'd go and play out with [my brother], and Mum would get so angry when I'd go and play out in the sun, because I'd get dark. None of that bothered me. I couldn't give a shit. But there was a boy in my primary school who I was absolutely in love with, a black boy. I was smitten. He was smart, he was athletic, all of it. And then it got to that weird stage in primary school where everyone was like, we should just get a boyfriend or girlfriend. I must have been about six or seven, and this boy turned around to me, and he went, "I can't ask you to be my girlfriend." And I was like, ooh – ouch! Okay. He went, "Because people will laugh if you're my girlfriend." And then he ended up dating my best friend, who was white, blonde, very very pretty. And I was like, aah. I think I know what it means. At six, seven, is when I learnt that lesson. And I talk about this with my girlfriends a lot, about that moment, and I didn't realise until a few years ago that that was seminal.'

Nightclubs also show this theory in action. They are our millennial mating ground: complete with sensual music, dimmed lighting and Dutch courage, all designed to set the scene for some sexy time. Women are often awarded free entry to clubs and bars, in accordance with the famous saying: 'if you're not paying, it's because you are the product.' Men pay entry in the hopes of meeting women to buy drinks for and eventually get a number, or something more, from. Racism against both black men and women is rife in certain exclusive clubs but it is well documented that in many establishments black women specifically are not allowed entry, free or paid, because of the assumption that they are a 'product' that can't be shifted. In elite establishments, only the *crème de la crème* will do and, according to the logic of many managers, this immediately discounts black women.

In 2015, national uproar was caused when four women arrived at DSTRKT nightclub in London's West End after receiving an invitation from one of the promoters. Despite being assured a place on the guestlist, two of the women were asked to step outside the queue and stand across the road. They were allegedly told they were 'too dark' and 'overweight' to be allowed inside, something the club denied. After a social media outcry (see '#RepresentationMatters'), London Mayor Sadiq Khan has since promised to investigate the continuing accusations of a discriminatory door policy at DSTRKT.

The idea of black women being undeserving of love begins with the notion that beauty is what makes women deserving of love and that black women cannot be beautiful. But in my admittedly biased opinion, many of the most beautiful women I've ever seen are black. Black women are not beautiful *in spite* of their blackness but rather *because* of it. Even more important than this, though, is the fact that beauty is not something that we as black women, or indeed as women, owe the world, and it is not something that makes us more or less deserving of love. Beauty is subjective and not an absolute truth – and objectively, the world is pretty racist anyway. It's therefore no wonder that black women are continually internalising the idea that we are unattractive, despite us having eyes and common sense. Thankfully, as we have discussed in '#RepresentationMatters', the internet provides an antidote to this claim, offering visibility to all types of beauty.

'We're doing black things and black is beautiful and we're promoting positive images,' Jamelia says.

'I'm glad that my daughter has started to get on Instagram and stuff like that, when I see the pages that she follows, natural hair this and melanin this and I'm just like, yeah! I love that she has that to go to and to look at and to see these positive images portrayed to her. I do not want my daughter to be in any relationship but you see a few beautiful little black boys at the school and they, and they just think that she's the most beautiful girl in the world, and I'm just like, yaaaaas honey! 'Cause when I was at school, no one was looking at me. At school, you had the light-skinned girls and you had the girls with the long hair.'

What? White girls are evolving!

'I'd jump over ten nigger bitches just to get to one white woman. Ain't no such thing as an ugly white woman . . . There's softness about a white woman, something delicate and soft inside of her. But a nigger bitch seems to be full of steel, granite-hard and resisting . . . I can't analyse it, but I know that the white man made the black woman the symbol of slavery and the white woman the symbol of freedom. Every time I'm embracing a black woman, I'm embracing slavery, and when I put my arms around a white woman, well, I'm hugging freedom.'

These are the words of Eldridge Cleaver, an early leader of the Black Panther Party (and self-confessed rapist), in his book *Soul On Ice*. Since a woman's worth is tied up in how she looks and black women's looks are continually denigrated, it leaves us worth 'less' in the eyes of white society, but also, often, within our own communities. A worthwhile woman must be attractive, and the most attractive women, by society's standards, are white women, so for some men, the end goal and strongest signifier of success, along with a nice car, well-paid job and big house, is a white wife. Think of the wives and girlfriends of many black footballers, for instance – if anyone signifies the ultimate trophy for the man that already has a shelf full of them, it's the WAG. For a trophy wife to be a trophy, she must be desired, and white women are widely deemed the most desirable. It can often feel as though there is an unspoken belief that black women have no place in a successful man's world.

When black video vixens began to be replaced by white ones in music videos, it was a bittersweet experience for many black women. On the one hand, it was nice not to see black women as mute sex objects, but on the other we were now hardly seen at all. We weren't being swapped out because of increased respect for us, but because we were no longer the group musicians wanted to objectify. White women were the ultimate goal for the man who had it all.

A society in which black women feel slighted because they are at the bottom of the pecking order of women objectified by men of their own race is a society that is letting down black women. White women do not care if they are not featured in rap videos, because they live in a world that assures them they are not ugly because of their whiteness.

'I'm not saying that it's wrong for a black man to fall in love with a white woman, or a black woman in love with a white man,' VV Brown explains.

'I'm with a white partner. But I'm just sort of saying that in some capacity there is this sense in some couples [that] the black man goes for the white woman because he feels like the white woman is better. So that really affects black women and dating. And then there's the ideas of what it means to be beautiful with advertisements and all these kind of things – "to be beautiful is be blonde with blue eyes". That is thrown at us on a daily basis. So, of course, if you're going to be on a dating app, subconsciously you're going to gravitate toward what you've been told is beautiful, which is awful and it's so wrong.'

According to a 2014 study by AYI (now FirstMet), black men are 16 per cent more likely to contact a non-black woman than a black woman online in the UK.[2] Data from OKCupid says black women receive the fewest messages of all users, and men are least likely to respond to 'likes' from black women.[3] Christian Rudder, OKCupid's founder, said 'Essentially every race – including other blacks – [gives black women] the cold shoulder.' When it comes to dating apps, the biggest problem for black women is that the apps are inherently flawed, basing attraction on a superficial level. The emphasis on 'types' and on the visual as opposed to other characteristics, values and personality, makes users more prone to racial filtering than in the real world, and daters stick more stringently to what they know and like.

Men in general are aware of black women's position in the pecking order, and many often use this as a way of putting those women in 'their place': at the bottom. Men, and that includes black men, are happy to remind black women that they are not generally desired and that they should feel flattered – honoured even – that they still prefer black women.

A phrase that comes up in online spaces, which seems to be more about denigrating black women than uplifting white women, is 'white girls are evolving'. Videos of white girls twerking or blessed with the 'slim-thick' body idealised within the black community are commented on or captioned with a 'warning' to black women that they may soon find themselves obsolete. The threat is clear: if you're not careful, if you don't shrink yourselves and stay in your lanes, then we'll go elsewhere; you can't trap us with the parts of you we like, because white women have them, too. If it weren't for your asses and dancing and sexuality we'd be with white women, but now they have them, you are rendered redundant. Who needs black women anyway?

Rapper Trick Daddy perfectly summarised the idea of black women being replaceable in an Instagram post in 2016. 'These Spanish, these white hoes, they done started getting finer than a muthafucka,' he said in a video. 'Y'all black hoes better tighten up. I'm telling you, tighten up. Y'all doing all this extra shit for nothing . . . Tighten up, hoe. These Spanish and these white hoes is getting very spiffy on y'all. They fuck around and learn how to fry chicken, you hoes is useless.' While I can only speak from the black female experience, as far as I know, threats of finding 'another you in a min- ute' don't tend to be centred on race in many other communities. But from Facebook pages to Kanye lyrics, black women are pitted against women of other races, and we almost invariably come off worse.

When this frankly uncomfortable subject arises in conversa- tion, it is often met with the retort of 'preference'. Preferences are completely understandable and almost entirely unconscious, but they do not form within a vacuum and they should be critiqued and questioned like all assumptions. It would be insane to force men to date women they are not attracted to, but it is in all our interests to find ways to give upcoming generations a fighting chance at a less skewed, less racialised dating scene.

Almost one in ten people living in Britain is married to or living with someone from outside their own ethnic group[4] yet only one in 25 white people have settled down with someone from outside their own racial background. Of course, this can be explained by the fact that we live in a majority-white country, so it makes sense that white people would be over-represented in any type of couple. But this is also down to preference as well as population – a third of white people say they would never date a black person, compared to just 10 per cent of black people who say they'd never date a white person.[5] Out of 11 skin shades ranging from lightest to darkest, 80 per cent of people are happy to date a person of the lightest shade, while fewer than 40 per cent of people would date a person three shades away from the darkest. And while we generally assume that we are becoming more integrated and diverse as a society, only 5 per cent of 18–24-year-olds in the UK had had a date outside of their race, compared to 11 per cent of 25–34-year-olds.

The fact that white people as well as minorities seem to favour whiteness is more likely to come down to hundreds of years of denigration of non-white people instead of white people just being great. So preference itself isn't an issue, but the factors behind that preference are – especially as some black men remain unable to profess their preference for white women without slandering black women in the process. I rarely hear or read about white women who date black men explaining their choices by listing negatives about white men; or Asian men who date white women denigrating Asian women. More often their focus is on what attracts them to someone from another race. But online you can find post after post detailing what makes black women unattractive to black men to explain their choice to date interracially. Clara Amfo has experienced the online war on black women's self-esteem first hand:

'Being online it's been great to see how black women and girls have come together but it's heartbreaking to see the trash that is spoken about them. I've seen "Black girls trying to be Barbie. I told you black girls years ago there's no such thing as a black Barbie." "Take me Out always have the worst black girls on show." "Hoping it rains every day the Carnival is on just to fuck up the black girls' weave LOL." Every day it's easy to come across colourism based comments whether you choose to or not!'

I wish I didn't have to include this disclaimer, but for the record: I love black men, I support black men and it is because I do that this is so frustrating. Imagine a white man saying he doesn't date white women because he doesn't like greasy hair. Imagine a white club-goer telling someone she was the 'prettiest white woman' in there. This may not apply to the majority of black men, but it has to be said, it happens enough to make it into this book. Most women of other races do not have to wonder when they look at a man of the same race as them whether that man dates within their race or not. But, shockingly, this is a question we often find ourselves asking when catching the eye of a handsome melanated gentleman. Even AJ Odudu, TV presenter and all-around-stunner, has had to ponder:

'Is he into black girls? You do always have to think. And even black guys with me have been like "oh, I see that you date white boys", and I'm like, no, I would date you. I'm black, you're black, it's fine. But I find that so interesting, actually, because I obviously find anyone attractive, so I'm literally like, I don't know why . . . who wouldn't?'

In the Channel 4 documentary *Is Love Racist?*, an experiment took place in which the multiracial subjects were given glasses to track their eye movements and were then placed in a room full of similarly diverse people. Regardless of their own race or preconceived prefer-ences, all subjects looked overwhelmingly more at the white people in the room. The next exercise involved semi-nude models parading in front of the participants, who were later asked to rate them. As expected, the subjects demonstrated a preference for whiteness and an aversion to other skin tones. But interestingly, when sight was taken out of the equation and people were told to choose by smell and voice, everyone, including previously ignored non-white sub-jects, was able to find a match.

Aside from general white favouritism, anti-blackness is some-thing to bear in mind specifically. Considering most racial groups prefer to date within themselves, it is of note that black people date each other less than most other ethnic groups. The black community dates interracially more than other ethnic groups – after white Brits at 4 per cent, the next least likely group to date interracially are

Bangladeshi (7 per cent),[6] Pakistani (9 per cent) and Indian (12 per cent) compared to 43 per cent of Black Caribbeans and 62 per cent of those who identify as 'Other black'. Africans buck the trend with 22 per cent.

But looking closely at these stats, it's primarily black men in the UK who date interracially, with black women slightly lagging behind;[7] 25 per cent of Black African men are in an interracial relationship, versus 19 per cent of women; 48 per cent of Black Caribbean are compared to 37 per cent of women and 64 per cent of 'Other black', compared to 59 per cent of women. Here it's worth comparing our data to that from the US, where interracial relationships are less common and have only been legal for 50 years (I vividly remember the video to Craig David's 2000 banger 'Fill Me In', starring a white love interest in the original video, only for her to be recast as mixed-race in the US version). In the US, African-Americans have had the largest increase in interracial relationships, rising from 5 to 18 per cent since 1980.[8] Despite this increase, they are the second group least likely to marry outside their race, after white Americans. Black Brits are more open to interracial dating than their American counterparts, but again white people remain the most likely to date/ marry each other. But the most interesting similarity is that while white Americans have similar rates of intermarriage between men and women, black men in America are twice as likely to marry another race as black women – 24 per cent to 12 per cent.

Many black women in Britain are catching up with their black male peers and have opened up to the idea of interracial dating, but some still seem to be unwilling to date outside of their race, closing them off to a number of potential partners.

'There were quite a few black women who were adamant that they would never ever ever ever ever ever date outside their race, ever, ever!' Charlene White says, 'which I always think is really interesting, because, you know, we're the minority here, so you're just making your life so much more difficult! And a friend of mine was really really adamant that she would never ever ever ever ever ever date outside of her race, and ended up meeting her forever after in an

Ikea car park years and years and years ago, and he was a white guy, and she fought it and she fought it and she fought it, you know, emotionally, everything – was fighting it, fighting it, fighting it. They've been together over ten years now, and they have beautiful twin boys who are five, five or six now, but she was very like, "I am never ever dating anyone outside of my race!" and blah, blah blah. No one could have been more shocked than her when she realised that the person she fell in love with and was gonna end up building a life with was someone outside of her race. And I think we just generally as human beings should be open to whoever ends up taking our heart. And that goes for whether you're black, or Asian, or white, you're Christian or you're Catholic, or you're Muslim or you're Jewish, whatever! I think it's a real good testament to humanity that you're able to open your heart to whoever it is, because you actually fall in love with the person, not their colour or their religion, or even their sex, it's just down to whoever takes your heart really.'

Strong black woman who don't need no man

Whether we are dating outside our race or within it, a heap of stereotypes plague black women on the dating scene, in and outside of their communities, which pins the blame squarely on them.

'It's all about perception and stereotypes, and I think with black women it's either we're hypersexual or we've got an attitude,' says Clara Amfo.

'Or we're mammies, just here to care-give, really modest church girls, super freaky, all in extreme, the list goes. I grew up with and still know black guys who have openly told me "Oh, I couldn't date a black girl, it would be like dating my sister." The bottom line is black women are not a monolith. Of course we can be modest, caring, sexually free, sassy loud, quiet and whatever we feel.'

Black women are strong, by necessity rather than nature. This strength allows us to thrive against all odds, find the beauty in ourselves in a world that says we're anything but, and take up space never built with us in mind. This same strength, however, is often weaponised by those who should be nurturing it; our partners. Because of what we face and stand up against, we are not perceived as being as 'soft' as women of other races. We're told we lack 'feminine energy' and sweetness. White women are heralded for being 'laidback' and 'calm' by men, who in doing so denigrate both black and white women by assuming white women are easier to mug off. Thus the strength that gets black women through a white man's world often ends up being diluted for fear of alienating and emasculating potential partners. Black women who are educated, talented and who know their self-worth are expected by men to hold back in order to hold on to whichever man they're 'lucky' enough to get.

Black women are also held largely responsible for the apparent disintegration of the black family, despite being the most likely group to date within their race; 59 per cent of Black Caribbean and 44 per cent of Black African children grow up in single-parent families in the UK, while the overall proportion of children living with a lone parent in the UK is 22 per cent.[9] Nine in ten lone-parent families are headed by a woman.

Another accusation constantly levelled at black women is that we are more materialistic than other races and less likely to stick things out when the going gets tough. Rather than us 'shooting in the gym', we're apparently outside of it, waiting for another guy with bigger arms and a bigger pay cheque to save us from the broke boy out back. Black women are often stereotyped as being less supportive, less patient and creating stress by the bucket load. Black women are some of the most fiercely loyal people I know, but there is a perception that we bring 'black girl drama' to the table before anything else.

If we have any standards at all we are often seen as being high maintenance, 'too picky' and, of course, 'too stoosh'. We are policed from all sides: for not having straight hair, then for not being natural. For being ambitious, then for not being supportive. The Obamas, the Carters and various other couples are often wheeled out on social media as the walking embodiments of when black excellence merges with black love. However, they are also too often used to taunt black women about what we're apparently not – 'if you were a bit more like Michelle maybe you'd catch yourself an Obama!', is a popular quip. But many forget that after her first year as an associate at Sidley Austin, a 25-year-old Michelle Obama was assigned to mentor summer associate, 27-year-old Barack Obama, by their corporate law firm. She did not dilute herself – she was his boss. Men cannot continue to shout about #BlackExcellence and cower when they meet it. Black women's strength can be intimidating, but the problem lies with the intimidated, not us, as VV explains:

'We are strong, we are so strong – we are the strongest on the planet as far as I'm concerned, with what we have to go through. I think the strength is intimidating, with what we have to bear and how we have to cope, and the way we elegantly cope, but the strength can be intimidating to men. My partner, I keep telling him every day, "You just need to deal with the strength, it's just how it is. I'm a black woman." And he laughs and he loves it, thank God. But for a lot of men, that is intimidating. They feel emasculated.'

In response to the teaching that she should not do anything to emasculate a man, Chimamanda Ngozi Adichie once famously wrote in her book *We Should All Be Feminists*, 'Of course I am not worried about intimidating men. The type of man who will be intimidated by me is exactly the type of man I have no interest in.' A man who is afraid of ambition or drive or emotion isn't a man you want. Our strength is what makes us who we are. Those who implore you to tone it down in pursuit of a man do not want you to be loved in your entirety. And what's the point of that? No one asks us to scale back your worth when negotiating at work – why should we do it in relationships? When it comes to dating and loving men – white, black, Asian, whatever race they might be – the priority should be them loving and understanding all parts of you.

We might make lists of the most desirable attributes for our potential future husbands – 6 foot or over only, money longer than his height, beard as consistent as his texts – but do we prioritise that they should understand black women's position societally? That they should be 'woke'? Spending hours trying to explain to someone why touching your hair without permission makes you feel like you're a zoo attraction, or why the descriptor 'sassy' makes your eyes roll, is not only draining but takes its toll on a relationship of any kind. Everyone just wants to be understood by their other half. And it cannot be assumed that this is something black men understand by virtue of being black either. In the same way that white men can be blind to systemic racism, there are some black men who believe misogynoir is fantasy, and who put racial issues before sexist ones, ignoring the ways in which the two combine.

I don't want to have children with someone who'll tell them we live in a 'post-racial society', or someone who thinks it's okay to tell them to relax their hair because their natural hair is 'nappy'. I want someone invested in empathising with the complexities of my identity and experience, and that is something nobody, black or white, is born with an understanding of. Some men will match you in your 'wokeness' and you'll never need to worry about explaining why reverse racism isn't a thing. But a lot of men aren't quite there. Building a relationship in this case isn't impossible, but it requires giving your partner space to learn, if they're willing. It's worth giving the right person a chance – none of us wake up with the term 'intersectionality' in our vocabulary. How 'woke' were you when you were captioning #teamlightskin under Instagram posts or referring to someone's dark skin tone as an insult?

We all have to start somewhere. But it's about finding someone who is willing to listen, learn and unlearn – and preferably within their own time and using their own resources, because no one wants an unpaid internship as a 'man whisperer'. Point those you care enough about towards the things that taught you and hopefully you will grow in awareness together.

So where do you find this person, especially in the face of such damning data? Well, while it can be easy to get bogged down with numbers, it also is worth noting that though there are apps and sites with the odds stacked against you, there are those where the odds are stacked in your favour, too.

'It can depend according to what sort of site you're going on to,' Charlene says. 'There are so many – I remember seeing that advert for if you fancy dating people in the emergency services. I'm like "people actually . . . that's a *thing?* Wow." My friend Emma is Jewish and she's on a Jewish dating site and stuff, so there are so many different [sites] according to what it is that you're looking for. I just wouldn't suggest looking at data in any shape or form, to be honest. I have never looked at dating in a race way. I've looked at it in terms of who I am sexually attracted to, and who I get on with, that's how I've always looked at it. And I think I'm really lucky that that's come in so many different guises, because I've learnt so many things about different cultures, I think I'm really lucky in that way. My partner – I am the first black girl my partner has ever, ever dated, I don't know if in his sphere if he ever thought he'd end up settling down with a black girl, probably not, but that's what happens sometimes.'

There are dating sites and spaces that cater to what people particularly like, and there are plenty of people out there who like black women. BYP (Black Young Professionals) Network app, launched by Kike Oniwinde, is the first of its kind in the UK, a space for black Brits on the dating scene. It is a networking and socialising app, which also has a dating service, and as many in the black community can be quite wary of dating apps and sites, its multipurpose approach appeals to many black singles.

'If we just use Tinder as an example, it is seen as a hook-up app and can be deemed embarrassing to join,' Kike says.

'Furthermore, it takes countless swipes to finally see a black person, and that doesn't mean they'll be your type. The BYP Network app allows users to connect for job opportunities, entrepreneurship opportunities, friendships and relationships within the black community. This platform can help with the talk on diversity in the workplace and at the same time meet the needs for singletons.

'Social media has driven the concept that black love is dying because of the way black men and women treat each other online. Black men are labelled as trash or "demons", while black girls are pitted against each other based on skin tone. I don't think it's dying out, I just think there are problems that need resolving. People have had bad experiences with a black girl/guy and generalise it for everyone. That's the problem. There is also a disconnect where the world is telling us that black women are too successful and the black men that are successful don't want them. All these opinions thrown out into the media have provided the notion that "black love" is dying, but it's our choice to allow that view or fight it. Black love is wanted, and we should remember that.'

'Go where you're celebrated,' Bola adds.

'Why would you waste your time? If a man is like "Oh, I don't like black women," first of all, why are you gonna waste your time trying to convince them to like you as a black woman? And then you're gonna have a relationship and it doesn't work, you're just gonna feel bad about yourself. You see it online all the time, there's debates about "Oh, there's this guy that says he doesn't date black women and, oh, it's such a shame," and so I'm like, "Why are you focused on him!?" Because for every guy who doesn't like a black woman, there are millions who do. The world is so much bigger than that one person or those few handfuls that just don't like you . . . Search for what is for you, rather than what isn't for you.'

'I've always wanted to taste chocolate.'

As I've said above, talking about preference within dating makes for an uncomfortable conversation. People like what they like. But there are some preferences that come from an unhealthy place. Men of other races who like black women exclusively are understandable – we're fabulous – but we mustn't be blind to the fact that this can sometimes be more complicated than sheer attraction. People outside of the black female experience may eye-roll; 'So you moan when you're not liked and then moan when you are? Talk about black girl drama!' But black women are too used to fetishisation to know it isn't simply about being 'fancied'. In Merriam Webster's Medical Dictionary fetishisation is 'the pathological displacement of erotic interest and satisfaction to an object or bodily part, whose real or fantasised presence is psychologically necessary for sexual gratification'. It is used to describe the sexualising of or sexual fascination with things that are not inherently sexual. For instance, some people like to accompany sex with sides. Some people like to fuck feet. Many fetishes are weird, funny and generally harmless; but when it comes to the fetishisation of things that are not objects – namely, people – it is rarely funny or harmless. In fact, it's harm*ful*: weird at best and dehumanising at worst.

Fetishisation and objectification go hand in hand; they are about removing any sense of individuality and personhood from the one being fetishised. A man who gets off licking chocolate off his partner is very different to a man who gets off to his partner *because* she's 'chocolate'. Chocolate is not a person: a black woman, however, is.

'Robert De Niro came up to me after a show and he was like, "I love chocolate girls,"' Jamelia laughs.

'And I was like, mnmnhnm, okay, bye! I was just like, I don't know what to do with this 'cause I was a fan, before that point, and then I was like, okay, that's weird. You know, we are beautiful, we are the only race that has our attributes, so to me it's . . . I get it. But I don't think anyone should be treated in that way.'

Racial fetishes are often difficult to explain and usually have to be defined on a case by case basis. On paper, it essentially means a person having a somewhat unnatural or excessive preoccupation with the physical and cultural differences of another race. In real life, it's often something defined more by a creeping, churning feeling a few minutes into a date during which the sensual beauty of the language 'Twi' has been mentioned more than three times before starters, and you're not even Ghanaian. It's hard to summarise where a preference and something more problematic begins and ends, but one thing is for sure: just because black women don't want to be discarded because they are black, it does not mean they want to be dated because they are black either. No more than a white woman would want to be told by a potential partner that he was with her solely because she was ginger.

Fetishisation remains one of the more complicated elements of racism. It's difficult enough to explain to white people that good old-fashioned thinking-someone-is-unattractive-because-of-their-blackness is discriminatory, let alone thinking someone is attractive because of it. Many white people with a 'thing' for black women think we should be flattered by the fact they're opting out of the mainstream and into the 'niche'. They're doing us a favour via their unwanted fantasies. Some see it as some form of antidote to a world in which blackness is juxtaposed against what is considered attractive.

On the flip side, it can be difficult for black women to wrap our heads around the idea, because in the plethora of microaggressions to be offended by, someone saying that the very thing society hates about you is what attracts you to them can seem like an odd battle to pick. I mean, it beats being called a gorilla, I guess? But fetishising can be as insulting as it is flattering, leaving us confused and embarrassed at our own involuntary blushing.

Like tokenism, fetishisation can be both racist and sexist but it is easy to dismiss, because it is complex and can be construed in a positive light. This form of positive racism sees white men patting themselves on the back for generalisations about black women, because they're 'good' generalisations. 'All black girls can cook.' 'You guys can dance.' 'Black women are better in bed.' 'You guys have the best asses.' Ascribing positive attributes to an entire group and seeing them as integral to that group may feel like a good thing, but even 'positive racism' is still, well, racism.

Another take on fetishisation and interracial dating more generally is that you can't be racist if you date black people. So many people genuinely believe that deeply entrenched, centuries-old prejudices are deleted from one's subconscious with each Tinder date. In 2017, the UKIP candidate for Great Yarmouth was so sure she wasn't racist (despite her standing for a far-right, racist political party) that she brought along a large framed photograph of her husband, who is black, to a hustings to prove it. 'There are millions of people who voted out [of the EU] and are not racist, including myself,' she bristled. 'I sleep with somebody who is black, who is, you know, of Jamaican origin! So I am 100 per cent not racist.'[10]

By this very feeble logic, you cannot be sexist if you have a wife, or homophobic if the son you love but repeatedly send to conversion camp is gay. Plenty of racists get off to cuckolding porn or would happily 'bang a black bird'. Those who hold up mixed-race babies like Rafiki over Pride Rock as the saving grace of a generation blighted by division or the union of Prince Harry and Meghan Markle as the pathway to a post-racial utopia, are clearly unaware that, had mixed-race couples been the answer to crossing society's racial divide, then we'd have done so hundreds of years ago. White slavers raped their black female slaves all the time – some even acknowledged their biracial children as their own – and yet . . . here we are.

With fetishisation, in the same way that men who 'love' women can weaponise our sex and be misogynists, the same thing can happen to black women, with regards to sex and race. Women have long become accustomed to being dubbed a bitch for politely declining to trade a topless shot for a picture of a stranger's privates. For black women, however, when things turn sour that 'bitch' is often prefixed with 'black'. Dating a black girl doesn't mean a guy won't use the very thing that attracted him to her to degrade her the next moment.

The issue with people who believe that who they choose to have sex with is illustrative of their politics, is that it is often even harder to explain racism to them, because they believe you're preaching to the choir. Some of the most problematic people I have ever met are those who have exclusively dated black women, and who have been even more resistant to the calling-out of discriminatory behaviour because they assume they need it least. They conflate wanting to have sex with someone with genuine anti-racism. But black women were and still are seen as hypersexual, and a similar mindset fuels the fetishism of today. There are men who seem to think there is a colour-coded chart for sexual prowess, and the darker the berry, the better you are at deepthroating. Like our allegedly well-endowed black brothers, black women have been sexualised to the point where just having brown skin can be enough to give some guys a semi.

From the tragic Hottentot Venus to Jean-Paul Goude's 1980s book *Jungle Fever*, featuring photographs of young black women for white people to gawp at, to rap videos featuring young black women for white people to gawp at – black women's insatiable sexuality is a stereotype that plagues us as much as the 'Angry Black Woman'. One of the biggest problems with racial fetishism is how it furthers the 'othering' of black women. It is seen as a deviation from the 'standard' and a foray into the 'exotic'. It is not so much 'it don't matter if you're black or white,' more, 'it matters that you're black, because I heard you guys can go for hours.' White straight men have been the long-established norm, so everything else is kooky, quirky and exciting. White men are Fanta and BAME women can provide that zingy, zany 'fruit twist' to a standard orange. Whether it is for our different cultural or physical traits, black women are sometimes pursued in the same way that someone might visit a psychic medium, or get a temporary tattoo of the tattoo they're too afraid to actually get: a curiosity, we're a 'totally random' night, an experience, an exploration, a line on a bucket list.

Fetishisation strips black women of what actually makes us, us: our individuality. We become one homogenous brown, big-bummed, chicken-eating glob, twerking in unison. No one ever likes to feel as if they are one of many – less still when it comes to romantic scenarios – but a fetisher doesn't know black women, they don't know *you*, which is why they try to draw connections through things they think you should like and know based on stereotypes ('hey, Beyoncé, you listened to the new Kendrick yet?'). Fetishim relies heavily on assumption and it reduces black women to their skin tone and the several problematic tropes that come along with it. It makes us one-dimensional, and instead of our skin being a facet of us that someone likes, it becomes the focal point of their attraction. It also gives power to the fetisher by denying us our humanity – our sexuality becomes for their pleasure and not our own.

'Oh my God. Your tits are so gorgeous.
They're so black.'
Ash, Chewing Gum

On dating sites, black skin can lead dudes to talk about you as if you just vine-swung your way here from a jungle, when you're actually from Surrey. 'I've never been with a black girl before,' a Tin-duh brain will cyber smirk. Most black women really couldn't care less if a guy has been with a black woman before or not. It's not going to make them any more or less compatible with her because he's been with 'one of our kind' before. At best, it means he will know the rules about hair-pulling in the bedroom if you have a wig. At worst, it means he will never shut up about it.

But how can you tell the difference between someone who just knows you're cool af and someone who thinks you're cool af in the same way they thought Dalston was cool af before they gentrified it beyond recognition? It's a tricky one. But we thank God for our gut. It's usually quite apparent when there's something a bit off. The first port of call is language, as Clara Amfo explains:

'Behaviour is one thing but I think the bigger signifiers exist in language. I want you to appreciate me and see the beauty of a black woman but there are always those words and killer sentences that immediately let you know you're being fetishised. "Exotic" or "I just loooooove how our skin looks against each other" will always make my eyes roll. It happens on all sides – I've heard black women express their desire to have babies with Asian men so that "my baby has good hair" or white men who show sexual curiosity in black women because "black girls are freaks". I think you just know it in your gut in certain language that is used and how they treat you.

'I remember I used to work with a guy and he was gassed that he was going out with a black girl and he would tell me at every opportunity regaling stories such as, "Oh yeah we walked through Manchester, I've had fist bumps from guys saying 'yeah respect brother, touch one time,'" and I remember thinking, "Shut up. She's not your fucking pet to show off, she's a human being!" Honestly, I didn't have the energy or confidence at that time to confront him.

'I was DJing at a party recently and the sound technician guy couldn't wait to tell me that he was married to a black woman. Like, gagging – GAGGING. He came up next to me and said, "Oh digging your 'fro vibe" and l replied politely "thank you", and he then proceeded to say, "I keep telling my wife that she's got to do her hair like that," and I said to him, "Your wife can do with her hair what she wants because she's her own person LOL." I'm sure he was a bit embarrassed but what he really wanted from that exchange was to let me know that he is married to a black woman. I wish I could say that's the only time something like that has happened, it will always be a source of entertainment at the very least.'

The difference between a fetish and a preference is essentially necessity and would-be-nice. A racial fetish is when your skin and the stereotypes associated with it outweigh the importance of you as an individual. It's when you feel your partner wouldn't be with you but for the fact that you are black. You become their Black Girlfriend™. A preference is when your partner themselves matters more than whatever trait initially drew you to them. Your blackness simply increases their attraction to you. It's not a prerequisite for them to keep finding you attractive: they love you for you, and your Black Magic simply elevates it.

Speaking of Black Magic, it feels ironic that while Lavender Brown was infamously whitewashed in the Harry Potter movies, Hermione Granger's character is now widely interpreted as a black character in fan art and fan fiction, even being cast so in the play *Harry Potter and the Cursed Child*? Looks like the black girl got Ron after all! But all jokes aside; there is someone out there who will fall under your spell despite the potential hurdles ahead (when is dating ever easy?). Hopefully through broadening your horizons, knowing your worth and practising discernment, you won't have to kiss quite as many frogs along the way.

No Scrubs

ELIZABETH

'When will you marry?'

Like most young girls I grew up watching Disney movies. Over and over again I'd watch the beautiful yet naive damsel in distress be rescued from the evil villain by a prince in search of a wife. They would subsequently fall in love, he'd propose, she'd say yes, they'd have a fairy-tale wedding and live happily ever after. The End. Or so I thought.

I began to have doubts about this fantasy around the time I had my first playground crush. When he chose to pursue my friend instead of me in a game of kiss-chase, I had an inkling love wasn't going to be as straightforward as I thought.

Yet I was still somehow under the spell of the Disney romances and, like Cinderella, I still believed it was boy meets girl, boy and girl like each other and then they build a life together. I remained optimistic about my version of prince charming throughout my teenage years. Even watching the daily unfolding of dysfunction on soaps like *EastEnders* didn't put me off this thing called love. However, the potion well and truly started to wear off when I hit my twenties and realised finding 'the one' was quite the complicated pursuit, and that the countless 90s rom-coms I'd watched hadn't prepared me for the harsh reality of dating. In your twenties, you spend your time bumping into guys and hoping they're not assholes only for them, after a date or two, often to reveal themselves to be just that. Navigating the dating world and settling down is challenging, as Yomi has discussed. But the pressure to find 'the one' is made worse by the expectations that society has about women and marriage. Chimamanda's iconic quote is something that has always struck a chord with me; she noted, 'Because I am female, I am expected to aspire to marriage. I am expected to make my life choices always keeping in mind that marriage is the most important.'

Growing up, when I did something wrong my dad would say, 'Is this how you will be misbehaving in your husband's house?' This started when I was ten; by the time I was 16 and had started venturing out with friends, he would say, 'Do you think you'll find a husband gallivanting like this?' Conversely, when I did something well it would be: 'Elizabeth will make a good wife.' It's really no wonder that, thanks to a combination of the films and media I consumed and the messages coming from my parents, I grew up thinking that becoming someone's wife and then mother was the ultimate goal every girl should aspire to.

If it were up to a lot of African parents, many of us would be engaged by 25, married by 26, and have had kids by 28. Being single is seen as some sort of problem and something that increasingly concerns your parents as you get older. I have friends who are often reminded that 'Your age mates are all getting married' so, 'when will you marry?' Alongside getting your degree certificate and a foot in the career door, marriage is seen as the next big achievement: a social benchmark. The Holy Grail. It is the final signifier that says, 'Hi world, I have made it, I am worthy.' With every year that passes without a proposal, you're made to feel like *you* are the problem. 'Why doesn't anyone want to marry her?' relatives start to whisper, 'she's past her sell-by date now.' At some point, towards the end of your twenties, Beyoncé's 'Single Ladies' goes from being an anthem you would happily sing at the top of your lungs to an anxiety-inducing trigger, as you remember that Beyoncé is tucked up with Jay Z and very much married.

It is frustrating that, as a woman, no matter how much you may achieve or contribute to the world, many people still believe that the most important thing you can do is get married, settle down and raise beautiful babies. Shonda Rhimes, accomplished as she is, describes the experience of having this narrative placed on her, noting: 'I have never gotten so much approval and accolades and warmth and congratulations as when I had a guy on my arm that people thought I was going to marry. It was amazing. I mean nobody congratulated me that hard when I had my three children. Nobody congratulated me that hard when I won a Golden Globe or a Peabody or my 14 NAACP Image Awards. But when I had a guy on my arm that people thought I was going to marry, people lost their minds like Oprah was giving away cars. It was unbelievable. I was fascinated by it because I thought, like, I am not Dr Frankenstein, I didn't make this guy – he just is there. Everything else I actually had something to do with.'[11]

Because it's traditionally men who do the asking and therefore the 'choosing', I've often found myself forgetting that marriage is a choice. Society can make us feel that our worth is only measured by the value placed upon us by someone who chooses to marry us. In an ideal world we would have our own agency and free will to make what is nothing less than a life-changing decision as part of a two-way process. Marriage, when it is good, can be beautiful and a source of mutual support, and if you've met someone who is good for you, and if marriage is important to you, by all means go for it. However, we shouldn't assume marriage will be easy, or indeed that everyone wants to get married. Marriage *is* a life choice, but it's not the *only* choice, and it's not necessarily a better one either: just a different one. If we let ourselves be coerced into seeing marriage as the ultimate goal and pin our hopes, dreams and ambitions on this one thing, then there's a danger that if it doesn't happen for us, we will think it's because we're not good enough. We need to remember that it isn't the be-all and end-all of womanhood.

In a refreshing plot twist in 2016, Disney took a step away from the usual princess clichés in *Tangled: Before Ever After*. Rapunzel became the first Disney princess to reject a marriage proposal from the suitor she loved. Okay, she did say yes in the end, but hear me out. Her reason for initially turning him down was something I can very much relate to: she was petrified of making the commitment to share her life with another person in case it held her back from fulfilling her potential. This rarely seems to be a fear felt by men.

There is a troubling double-standard when it comes to age and the right time to marry which allows men to wait until they consider themselves to be mature enough, with an established career and financial security, before they decide to get married. Why should it be different for women? Many of us want to take time to travel the world, explore a multitude of opportunities and build our careers. Sometimes, when I've chosen not to carry on dating a particular man, my friends will ask, 'What was wrong with him?' And my reply will be: 'nothing'. But 'nothing wrong' doesn't mean I necessarily want to pursue a relationship with him right now. I have high expectations for marriage: I believe it takes time, maturity, patience and effort and I want to spend time working on myself, to figure out who *I* am, before I enter into a union with anybody.

It is important that little girl viewers (like me, all those years ago) could see Rapunzel making a conscious decision and not blindly accepting her prince like the other Disney princesses before her. Marriage should not be the last item on a bucket list. Rapunzel exerted her free will and reminded us all that marriage is a choice and, as women, we do have a say when – and if – we want to enter into it.

We all know how hard it can be to offer advice to a friend about a guy. No matter what you suggest they'll probably end up doing the opposite. We won't pretend that this chapter has all the answers to the 'tangled' and complicated questions of love and commitment, but we hope it will help empower you when it comes to making your own choices about them.

June Sarpong speaks eloquently about marriage and choice: 'I think a lot of women feel that pressure, but I think it's an individual choice. I'm not one of these people who says "Don't have kids at 25" or whatever. Do what feels right. If you're a woman who actually just wants to get married and have kids, that's cool. If you're a woman who wants to have a career, that's cool, too. It's up to you, it's what feels authentic, and for me the choices I've made feel authentic.'

'If someone doesn't make you feel like
you can take over the world, then they're
not the person for you. If they feel that you
are too career focused and you need to
become less than you are, they're
not the person for you.'
Charlene White

When I was at university there was this boy I thought I liked. It was the end of our first year and everybody was soon going to be on their way home. Because we both lived in South London, he assured me that he would make the effort to see me over the summer. Summer came and went: he didn't make any effort. 'Odd,' I thought, and by the end of the holidays I had definitely stopped liking him. However, when we got back to university in the autumn he was quick to try to rekindle things. He apologised profusely and offered numerous excuses. I was naive, I thought 'Let me give him a chance.' Then, over the next few weeks he blew hot and cold, until eventually I was so over it that I confronted him on a night out. I questioned his motives and he replied, 'Don't give me the black-girl chat.' I was like, 'Pardon?' I was so angry; I walked away in the biggest huff. What the hell did he mean 'Don't give me the black-girl chat'? He had reduced my feelings and behaviour to the stereotype of the angry black girl. The irony is, he was a black boy himself. By putting that label on me he thought it would make me adhere to the respectability politics of how I should behave. He clearly believed that if a woman wants to be considered wifey material she must turn herself into whoever it is that her prospective guy wants.

It may seem a ridiculous notion, but interestingly, according to a study by researchers at the National Bureau of Economic Research, young professional women tend to downplay their career goals and ambitions around men only when they were not in relationships. Women who were already in serious relationships were upfront about their career goals; those who were single tended to modify their ambitions.[12] It's sad that young women feel compelled to minimise their accomplishments and ambitions in order to be seen as marriage material. Chimamanda again: 'We teach girls to shrink themselves, to make themselves smaller. We say to girls, you can have ambition, but not too much.'[13] I've been on dates during which I've immediately tried to suss out whether the guy is easily intimidated and I've then adapted accordingly, because I didn't want to come across as an overbearing 'ambitious' girl. However, over the years I've realised that the kind of man I will attract if I play down or minimise myself is really not the type of man I want to be with in the first place.

It's counterproductive, as Charlene White explains, 'One of the reasons that I completely fell in love with my other half is because he pushes me at every single level, and he doesn't see the fact that I'm focused and wanting to get further and bigger and better at what it is that I'm doing at work as a problem, he just thinks that's one of the most amazing things about me. We'll come home and I do exactly the same for him and sort of say, you know, maybe you should try doing this, and maybe you should try doing that, and perhaps that wasn't such a good idea, and he'll tell me where I'm going wrong, and I'll tell him where he's going wrong.

'I have never had to be less than I am by nature of being in a relationship, I've never, ever had to do that. When I'm pumping Jay Z out of the house in the middle of Richmond at three o'clock on a Saturday afternoon, that doesn't always go down so well! He pushes me more than anyone has ever pushed me before in a relationship. My friends pushed me all the time, but in terms of being in a relationship he's pushed me more than anyone and just makes me believe that if I want to take over the world, I can take over the world.'

> '**I only realised after I got married how
> important it was to have somebody that will
> encourage you, that will support you and that's
> interested in me winning. I will take that over
> a 6-foot-5 guy for sure, I would take that
> over the guy that drives the Bentley.'**
> *Vannessa Amadi*

My friends and I have often lamented that the problem with the dating game isn't so much finding a guy, but finding the right kind of guy. It's hard not to sound shallow when describing what we would like from a partner. We've all imagined our ideal person, the person we eventually settle down with: someone who neatly fits into our expectations, who is understanding, who puts us first and loves us for who we are. The majority of my friends, of all races, seek partners from similar backgrounds to them; we are pretty much all looking for someone with equal or greater income and education. In our eyes, this is the bare minimum we would expect from the dating world. After all, if on paper I have a lot to offer, then why can't I date someone who also meets these 'reasonable' requirements? So when a US report revealed that university-educated black women in America are less likely than other groups to marry a man with a similar level of education[14] my curiosity was piqued. While there is no like-for-like stat in the UK, it's telling that Cambridge University recently revealed that of the 3,449 students it accepted during the 2015/2016 academic year, 38 defined themselves as black, and only 15 of those 38 students were men. Similarly, at Warwick University I always noticed that there were more girls in every year group at African-Caribbean Society events. There is a general trend in many countries for more women to go to university than men. The Higher Education Policy Institute (HEPI) has published research examining this increasingly polarised gender divide as women in the UK are now 35 per cent more likely than men to go to university and the gap is widening every year.[15] There are plenty of educated, ambitious women, but is it the case that there may not be enough educated men to go around?

It's as though men are a precious commodity, and we're all scrambling for the good ones who are left, the ones who meet our high standards. Because the thought of settling for scraps isn't an option. After all, we are the 'you can have it all generation', aren't we? The independent-women-then-it's-time-to-find-a-husband-and-have-a-baby-before-your-eggs-expire generation, too. None of us want to short-change ourselves and, through succumbing to the pressure to find a husband, risk marrying the wrong person. This can, however, cause a great deal of anxiety around the question of whether we will *ever* meet THE guy? Will he be good-looking? Will he be smart? Most importantly, will he be good enough? Granted, I may not want to be Cinderella waiting patiently for her unrealistic prince, but in *Grease* Sandy got her Danny, Beyoncé got Jay Z, and Michelle got Obama.

Throughout this book we have looked at the challenges of navigating work and life in general as a black girl, breaking down the ways in which ours is a singular experience. And I have come to realise that the thing that has become the most important to me when I think about settling down with anyone is whether that person is someone who understands the unique struggles that black women face. Empathy within a relationship is vital. We need to be able to have honest conversations with our partners, tell them about our days, tell them about the microaggressions we've experienced: all of the good, the bad and the ugly. And for them to empathise and understand, to help us with it. We should be able to ask, 'How do I deal with this?' or, 'This happened,' and for them to say, 'You know what, I understand, but how about this?' Our feelings and whatever we're going through need to feel important to both of us. And we have to be willing to do the same for him as well.

The meaning of 'finding your forever after' changed for me once I understood that it is this that really matters in a relationship. Vannessa Amadi went through a similar realisation: 'Whoever you end up with, if you end up with a partner that you marry or not, whoever that person is that you choose – it's a partnership. This life that we live, every day you have to wake up, and whoever it is that's there with you, that's the person that you have the conversations with and they have to be able to inspire you, if possible, and it's a big ask. It's not easy to find that kind of person. Sometimes you have to change your mindset to be able to have that type of person in your life. It's key. I think if everyone could have that it would be an incredible world that we live in, just to have someone that's on your team supporting you, not even financially, just mentally giving you that energy to say yes, you can do it. Because it's not easy, you know, to every day get up and go and do whatever it is you do and to have someone like that is a huge blessing.

'I think I maybe only realised that after I got married actually, how important it was to have somebody that will encourage you, that will support you and – I mean, he reads my press releases, and rewrites them sometimes, and those kinds of things, because he's interested in me winning. I will take that over a 6-foot-5 guy for sure, I would take that over the guy that drives the Bentley or whatever.'

We live in a society that encourages an unrealistic quest for perfection. But the older I get, the more I realise that my dating non-negotiables can't be based on a checklist of ideals, and if I only want to date men who have the right star sign and the right job, who have gone to the right university and who are 6-foot-2, then I've got to admit defeat now. So, rather than prioritising a degree: don't jump out of the window for someone who isn't going to even walk out of the door for you. I'm the last person to encourage 'settling', but I've come to realise that settling and compromising aren't the same thing. Compatibility is about far more than what's on the surface, or what might be on a notional checklist. A long-lasting relationship requires more than good looks, fun dates and many of the other things I once thought were important and now realise are not. But this doesn't mean I'm choosing to settle. I think instead it means I'm growing up, and I'm finally understanding that relationships don't have to come from a list, or even from a storyline on *Love Actually* . . .

Not being married by a certain age isn't something we should fret over or rush into. It's far more worthwhile to spend time seeking a partner who complements you, not *completes* you. Don't be in a rush about getting it, it's more important to get it right. If the right person comes along, they come along. If not, it doesn't mean we have failed at being women. You don't need to find someone else to define your existence. As Amma Asante says, 'In terms of him not necessarily being your financial equal, or your equal when it comes to education, or your equal when it comes to ambition, and all of those things, if that's what matters to you, it's not for me to tell you to marry "beneath you", but I had a thought process when I was a kid about who I might end up married to. None of what I thought matched on the surface to who my husband is today. On the surface, right? But when you dig deep he is those things.

'One day I thought, "If this world were mine, what would I give? What would I do for my husband? What would I give for my husband?" and there isn't anything that I wouldn't do or give to my husband if this world were mine, because he has as much value for me as I have for myself. And he treats me with that level of value. He treats me with that level of importance in his life.

'So, ultimately, though I might have had all these other little things – "He must have a degree, and he must have this, and he must have that" – if I'm really honest with you, I'm not quite sure what my husband's degree is in, because he got it in Denmark. My point is, you can put all those things down, but ultimately what I want is someone who treats me in the way that I know I deserve. That's the bottom line.

'I think about my dad in his last few days, as we knew that he was going to pass away within that month, he was just becoming weaker and weaker. The last time he saw my husband, my dad was sitting in a wheelchair because they had put him in it for the day to just kind of get him up out of the bed – and my dad had dementia and Alzheimer's when he passed away. But, actually, the closer he got to death, the more he knew who everybody was.

'My dad was just that typical African dad, "Who are you? Are you worthy of my child?" you know, all of the stuff that we kind of know and recognise, and who would've loved me to have married not just an African man, but an African man from Ghana, not just from Ghana but from his village, that's what he would've loved.

'But I remember my husband walking in through the door and my dad being quite hunched over, and slowly looking up – slowly his eyeline came up to reach my husband's – and I remember my dad, with all the effort it took in the world, lifting his hand up and putting his hand out to shake my husband's hand. What he was saying in that moment is, "I'm trusting you with this. You take this with the responsibility that I'm putting in your hands."

'I knew how important and how much effort that would've taken from my dad physically, but I also know the message he was giving to my husband in that moment. I knew that was because he knew that my husband treats me with the importance that I deserve. Now that my dad has gone, my biggest cheerleader in life is my husband and that's all that I would wish for. Regardless of what his degree is, and if he earns as much as me. There's some years I earn more than my husband, and there's some years he earns more than me!

'We didn't know what it was going to be like when we were getting together, we didn't know who was going to earn the most. I didn't ask him what his degree was because that's not what attracted me to him. It was his heart and soul. I always say, to the best of my knowledge [that] I'm not a lesbian, but if my husband had come in the shape of a woman, I know that we would be in the same relationship because that's what I fell in love with, ultimately, and that's what we should be looking for.'

People often say that true love comes from knowing a person's every flaw and still choosing to love them all the same. This kind of acceptance requires compromise, so holding on inflexibly to an unrealistic version of a Disney hero is unlikely to bring you happiness. Settling down, rather than settling *for*, is a state of mind, and the one who has to live with that choice is you. So when you feel that the time is right, just make sure you're not settling because of your parents' expectations of when you should get married, or because you're worried that society will render you undesirable once you hit your thirties.

When will you marry? When – and if – you bloody well choose to.

HEALTH

'Admitting I might have depression felt like I would
have been admitting defeat, succumbing to failure
in a culture that preached strongly about
the importance of success.'

Yomi

....

'As a society we also applaud working yourself
into the ground as a sign of strength, admirable
determination and resilience. But blind resilience
can be very detrimental.'

Elizabeth

Black Girls Don't Cry

YOMI

'Caring for myself is not self-indulgence,
it is self-preservation, and that is an
act of political warfare.'
Audre Lorde, A Burst of Light

One day, after reading up on depression and mental illness, I came up with what I thought was a thoroughly groundbreaking theory. The idea was simple: everyone in the entire world should technically be mentally ill, and if they're not, it's a miracle. Even those who grow up sheltered by white picket fences and the unwavering support of family and friends, those who have enough money to be comfortable – but not the kind of vast wealth that is often accompanied by various personality disorders – those who have been loved and looked after unconditionally: it still should boggle our frankly fragile minds that they're okay.

Because just existing in and of itself, even in the best circumstances, is enough to make anyone mentally ill. We're thrust onto an orbiting rock and given no choice in the matter, no idea how long for, no understanding of why we have to exist, with no obvious purpose or obvious point to it all. Even for those who are religious, many things remain unexplained or unanswered, and that should be enough to throw anyone into an existential breakdown. Existence itself is conducive to mental illness.

I was soon informed that this 'theory' of mine was actually a common belief shared by various philosophers and thinkers. It wasn't as groundbreaking or niche as I had thought. But since it's by no means a new train of thought, why then do we continue to subscribe to the belief that there must be a 'reason' behind someone needing support when it comes to their mental health?

I'm not a doctor, nor am I psychiatrist. I am, however, someone who has suffered from depression. I spent much longer at university than was probably good for me because I couldn't come up with a distinct, tangible 'reason' that would legitimise me seeking real help. On the surface, there was no particular basis for the feelings I was experiencing, but this didn't stop me feeling them. The idea that there had to be something specific occurring for me to feel sad or bad made me believe I was ungrateful, self-pitying and selfish.

Even when there *is* an obvious 'reason' we often don't consider it 'sufficient' to have caused these feelings. Of course, there are many well-recognised triggers that can affect our mental health, and the toll taken by work stress, relationship breakdowns, grief and the state of the world (as documented by a never-ending news cycle) is often acknowledged. But the impact of racism or sexism, and of the two combined, on mental health is rarely examined. According to statistics, people from black and ethnic minority groups living in the UK are more likely than their white counterparts to be diagnosed with mental health problems. But they are also more likely to experience a poor outcome from their treatment and to disengage from mainstream mental health services, leading to social exclusion and further deterioration in their mental health.[1]

It is astonishing that most of us *aren't* walking around in a constant state of worry, confusion and angst for 'no reason', but more of us *are* feeling this way than we might think, and that's okay. What is not okay is how difficult we continue to make it for us to talk about it.

I'm no Super(wo)man

Black women's 'strength' is a double-edged sword. The continued reminders of our resilience help us to thrive in all manner of situations where the odds are stacked against us, and to make our way over hurdles with perceived ease. But 'perceived' is the operative word. We are championed and celebrated for being strong, but we are not always beneficiaries of this trait. It can lead people to believe that we are immune to any slight or obstacle that comes our way, and as a consequence, any acknowledgement of emotional trauma is read as 'weakness': a wasteful and self-indulgent distraction. We internalise this and become hesitant in revealing our problems to others and to ourselves, and more importantly, in seeking much-needed help. Mental health is often seen as 'white people problems'. Black people don't get depressed, they have demons in need of exorcising, or they are simply being swept up with the whims of the western world. At least, this is what we are told by society and what we often tell each other. In the era of #BlackExcellence, #BlackGirlJoy and #BlackGirl-Magic, #BlackGirlSadness is something of a downer; the remit of #BlackGirlProblems extends only to a failed twist out, or not finding your foundation shade on the high street. Many of us feel that in the face of so much strength we do not want to be the weak link.

In 2010, it was found that black girls are more likely to self-harm than any other group surveyed in the emergency rooms of three major UK cities.[2] In Manchester, the rate for self-harm among black women was 10.3 per 1,000, compared to 6.6 per 1,000 for white people as a whole. Almost more revealing was the fact that black British girls were the least likely to receive assessment or specialist care. According to the lead author of the report, Dr Jayne Cooper, young black women 'may not communicate their distress to clinical staff as much, and be less likely to admit to depression'. This was very much my experience: admitting I might have depression felt like I would have been admitting defeat, succumbing to failure in a culture that preached strongly about the importance of success. It would have meant revealing weakness in a society that told me I should be infinitely strong. I believed that with enough self-censoring and chastising I would eventually get over it; I would pull myself up by my bootstraps and trudge onward, however weary I felt.

Often, if we are willing to take note at all of our mental state it is simply because of the physical toll it takes on our bodies. In the end,

I only took pause when I couldn't physically drag myself through it any longer. In a 2010 National Institutes of Health study,[3] it was found that black women in the US between the ages of 49 and 55 are 7.5 years biologically 'older' than white women. The reason? Unattended-to stress. The study went on to say that the impact of overexposure to stress takes a toll on the body and contributes to the development or progression of such ailments as 'cardiovascular disease, obesity, diabetes, susceptibility to infection, carcinogenesis, and accelerated aging'. Despite the infamous and proudly worn adage 'black don't crack', black women's bodies suffer at the hands of stress and, considering how much we tend to bottle up our anxieties, it's almost fitting that the damage doesn't show on the outside.

Rapper Lady Leshurr is well known for her upbeat, often comedic music and videos on social media, and, as a female grime artist 'strength' is infused in her brand. But last year she deviated from her usual banter to post a video on social media outlining her struggles with depression and anxiety. It was a huge step-change and one that continued when she decided to rap about it in her personal and poignant song, '#Unleshed 2': 'My anxiety's killing me, making my mind go mad/I'm scared to go to the shop cus people know who I am/ And I know some kids wanna do dumb things record it on cam/So I lock myself away/But I still feel trapped/I'm a human being with a broken heart and a soul that's cracked/I tried to take my life in my own flat/A few months ago I got assaulted for being black/So why would I want to live?/Why would I want to stay?'

The stigma of mental health in the black community often means many sufferers are silent about it, even to their close friends and family. Leshurr took perhaps the most public route possible to opening up, and she explains why:

'I want people to know that having music is cool but we go through things that everyone goes through. I think a lot of people just think we're robots or something – we just get on the stage and we get off the stage. But we're still human beings, you know what I mean? I just wanted people to know that they're not alone and if people do have anxiety, depression it's something I've battled throughout my career, battling demons. This industry is a cold industry and a lot of people don't know about it. I got so many messages and I replied to the majority of them; it made me feel so much better and I didn't want to just post that video and get props, it wasn't nothing like that. I wanted people to know what I'm going through and that this is why I'm not releasing music.'

In '#Unleshed2', Leshurr touched on a contributing factor to mental illness that is also rarely discussed: discrimination. It's almost as if black people think it is just part and parcel of life – we often haven't experienced any other way of living – and therefore we rarely think about what it is doing to us mentally on a day-to-day basis. A 2015 study[4] showed that some of the sexism faced by women makes them generally more fearful and anxious. Researchers found a substantive 'link between physical safety concerns and psychological distress'. Clear links have also been established between racism and depression.[5] Two UK-based studies released in 2001 revealed that minorities living in majority-white areas in London were twice as likely to suffer from psychosis as their counterparts in diverse communities.[6] Another UK study found that minorities were more likely to attempt suicide if they lived in areas lacking ethnic diversity.[7]

This shouldn't be surprising: assimilation is a full-time job (see '***Flawless') and one that can leave us feeling emotionally drained. Black women often feel as though we are playing a role, and that we could be exposed for playing it at any given time. We compartmentalise, shrink and diminish traits that are deemed unacceptable, yet which are often at the core of our identity. The combined experiences of racism, sexism and cultural alienation result directly from our experiences as black British women. The resulting impact on our confidence and mental state cannot be downplayed, as Gloria Boadi, a counsellor who specialises in issues surrounding racism and cultural identity, explains:

'A lot [of black women] come to seek help when they go into the workplace. A lot of high-achieving women who have done well academically – they've got their grades, they've got their As in their A-levels, they've gone to the red brick unis. They've gone through all the hurdles required. They've gone through all these really tough exams and all these internal recruitment processes to get to the top companies, and then when they get there, they're blocked and then they realise, "Oh, gosh, this barrier really does exist." Things are unsaid – me and you would know, you can tell, but you can't name it. It's those subtleties that are blocking you – when you're not invited, when you're given extra workload, when you're judged harshly. They come to seek help become sometimes you come to think, "Is it me? Am I being extra sensitive?" and they just need confirmation and affirmation that, no, you're right, you're not going mad, it is really happening and you deserve better.'

Racism in Britain is an ailment that white people will never suffer from, and sexism a scourge men do not have to endure. In a world dominated by white men, it's no surprise that research into the effects of both on mental health is severely lacking (despite endless annual studies designed to validate the size of the average penis). While there are currently very few studies focusing on their specific impact on women who occupy a racial minority, it can be assumed that sexism, racism and the combination of the two affect us in ways we may not be actively aware of. Cal Strode of the Mental Health Foundation acknowledged this in an article, saying there is still not enough research into why black British women are commonly experiencing more mental health problems yet receiving less mental healthcare. 'On the whole, our research tells us that black women are more exposed to harmful experiences and stressors than non-BAME women,'[8] she concluded. Josefien Breedvelt, research manager at the Mental Health Foundation, agrees with this sentiment, speaking of how black women's specific plight is often invisibilised in discourse: 'Little is known about black women and mental health as these individuals have been largely absent from research. The majority of the research has looked at ethnic minorities as a whole, rather than providing a focus on the challenges faced by black women.'[9]

The needs of black British women are not considered a priority, which explains the lack of readily available research. But when we look at the black community as a whole, the problem persists, with little explanation offered as to why we tend to be worse off. In 2007, an article co-authored by Chris Heginbotham and Kamlesh Patel summarised it like this: 'No one has yet provided an adequate explanation for the very high rates of admission and detention for some of these groups – notably for Black African, Black Caribbean and Black Other (Black British) people . . . Either there is an epidemic of mental illness among certain Black groups or there are seriously worrying practices that are leading to disproportionate levels of admission. Wherever the answer lies on the spectrum between the two extremes it is essential that we find out as a matter of urgency.'[10]

There is a clear problem regarding black people and mental health that seems to be unique to this country. There are no studies showing that black people are biologically more prone to mental illness, yet we are startlingly over-represented in the UK's long-term psychiatric care. According to the NHS website, mental health is compromised for black people who move to predominantly white countries – and the risk is even higher for their children. African-Caribbean people living in the UK are more likely to be diagnosed with severe mental illness than any other ethnicity in the UK.[11] Mental illness is no more common in Africa or the Caribbean than it is in the UK as a whole, but it's a bigger problem for these communities living in the UK. Stigma may well skew these stats, as Africans and Caribbeans may struggle with accessing services in their home countries, but it may also be that something is causing these problems in Britain that we are yet to properly interrogate.

It is no coincidence that 93 per cent of black and ethnic minorities with mental illnesses have experienced discrimination, yet 80 per cent feel unable to speak about these experiences.[12] A big reason for this is the lack of groups and services in the UK created to address the specific mental health needs of minorities in this country. As I mentioned earlier, mental health issues are often difficult to diagnose, because black women tend to underplay the gravity of their problems. As a result, they often end up seeking help only much later in life or when their illness becomes quite severe. A lack of freedom in speaking openly, honestly and comfortably about mental health is stopping us identifying its specific causes for black women, but also, crucially, from seeking the help we need.

Lost in translation

There is a cultural and generational clash that can make discussion around mental health hard. Many of our parents, grandparents and great grandparents came to this country with less than we have now and went through unimaginable difficulties to set up the lives that many of us are privileged to lead. Many have lived through overt state-sanctioned racism and hate, where there was no recourse to be found in law, nor the comfort of having others to turn to who were experiencing the same thing. When they hear we are suffering from depression and anxiety, some wonder what on earth we could have to be depressed or anxious about. This can lead to irritation or even anger. And those reactions can lead to shame in those who are suffering. Gloria notes that this is often a problem that arises with several of her black clients:

'There tends to be the generational gap. So issues that have come from the current black British [generation], their parents and their parents' parents . . . You have this general view of "I've gone through worse. I've had to go through maybe war, divorce, I've been displaced, I never stayed with my mum so what's all these issues? Pull yourself together!"

'A lot of families are now split, and if they're not, in many families they're together but separate. They're living like a family but inside, they don't have really anything to do with each other. So they've got the view of "we need to be together at all costs," but they're living totally different lives, sometimes not even talking to each other. [There are] lots of internal conflicts and that has an impact on the children.'

At times, family members may attest that you have no reason to feel the way you do, because they have been through more and have never been mentally ill. But I sometimes wonder just how many of our older relatives have probably had their lives blighted by mental health ailments that have gone unchecked?

In a 2013 survey,[13] a third of BAME people reported experiencing either a moderate amount or a lot of discrimination from within their own communities because of their mental health issues – Caribbeans at 33 per cent and Africans at 31 per cent. A third of respondents said they felt they were treated less favourably by their own communities. And sadly, only a fifth of BAME people felt able to speak to people about their mental health, suggesting a large and important part of their lives goes undiscussed completely, either with loved ones or with health and social services.

Musician Laura Mvula was formally diagnosed with clinical depression and sought treatment last year. She believes the first step to breaking the stigma around mental health in the black community is conversation – one she has helped to start, and hopes to continue:

'I was raised by a mother, aunties and uncles and a father who didn't have the idea of our mental health being something that even exists. There wasn't even a vocabulary in our household. If there was, it was drenched in spirituality and the church and things that I wouldn't diminish their significance and relevance at all – that stuff is a part of who I am – but I do remember being told by my mum when I complained that I was having a panic attack one time to "Have a bath, have a hot meal, go to your bed." It's something that's totally alien to her.

'I've been so overwhelmed with the feeling of being charged with a new responsibility to just expose that stigma. It's so old-fashioned, that's the other thing. It's outdated. We are mind, body and soul, it's so basic. Maybe there needs a balance to be struck, but I think for the most part I don't think you can be too vulnerable with trustworthy people. If it's a necessary sacrifice for me to expose myself in order that somebody else just speaks to their local therapist in the NHS, then do it. So be it, then I'll be that person.

'The cost is too high now to be suffering in silence, and the myth that we're alone in that particular struggle is rampant. That's one of the things that doesn't stop surprising me – that we all think that we're somehow totally alone in that struggle and there's nobody else that [would] understand or can relate. And there's a sense of shame with that. Just all things that I recognised, more so over the last five to six months. It is an opportunity here for me to use my foghorn to call people out.

'I've been just amazed, more so than my music over here, this story about my struggle seems to be causing waves amongst a community that's felt so neglected and like we're outsiders, misfits. It's a human condition, we're all susceptible. [We] might have different experiences of it – it manifests itself in different ways – but everybody's got their shit, you know?

'I wouldn't be being a true artist if I didn't speak openly about what life feels like and looks like. Because music is great and metaphors are wonderful, but at the end of the day sometimes people want to know, "What does that song mean?" or, "Where were you when you wrote that in your mind and in your heart?" I want to be able to be accountable to the audience.'

Pray it away

Religion can be more than just a crutch to lean on during difficult times. When I was depressed, my own prayers and those of my loved ones gave me strength and peace. But often religious faith and professional help are positioned as opposing and competing solutions, instead of as two valuable aids that can work in conjunction. The stigma around mental illness paralyses people from opening up about mental health, but when we do, often the only remedy prescribed to us is scripture. If our 'demons' do not flee, it is because we haven't prayed properly or fasted long enough. But if we can acknowledge that most medical treatments were created to help God's people, why not therapy?

A large proportion of us and our families are religious – 69 per cent of black Britons identified as Christian during the last census, and black Muslims make up 10.1 per cent of the British Muslim population.[14] Because mental health is 'unseen', it can be considered otherworldly; depression is frequently explained as demonic and many assume that spiritual attacks can be healed through fervent prayer and unshakeable belief. But even if you believe this to be the case, there is nothing in the Bible that suggests counselling is in any way a contradiction to turning to God for help. This is a fallacy that must be abandoned for all our sakes. While many of us are finally embracing other solutions alongside faith, there are huge numbers of people in our community who continue to suffer unnecessarily. Religious sects such as The Followers of Christ, in the US, preach faith healing, which, despite an alarming child mortality rate, sees people refusing medical help in the name of religion. Many of the same people who would balk at this, steer those suffering with their mental health away from help, not truly considering them 'unwell'.

VV Brown is from a Christian family, and while prayer gave her strength, the fact it was touted as the only solution to her mental health problems also left her depression sidelined for some time:

'I was raised in the church where every single cure was "Pray about it", right? You can be hearing all kind of voices or be going through some serious psychoses, and the only thing that was talked about was "Pray about it". Now I'm not saying that prayer doesn't work, because I was raised in church and I do believe in the power of prayer, that's my belief. But I also believe that it's more than prayer and some things are psychological. And I think because a lot of black families are rooted in church, we ignore the psychological aspect and we don't talk about it. There's almost a stigma of shame when you talk about mental illness, and not a real understanding of it.

'I'm quite open about it because I think a lot of people are going through something. When you open up about it you'd be surprised how much it helps somebody else to be like, "Oh my God, I went through something similar." I'm a loudmouth anyway, so I don't mind. And my parents – my mum works in education, so I think our household is quite open. But I think that in black communities we need to be a little bit more open with each other. I know I always harp back to those days, but the manuscript with how to break a slave was to put them against each other, and be suspicious of each other, and not communicate with each other, and be fragmented. And I think that has got a huge part to play in the way that we communicate our emotions in our lives, and our beliefs and dreams with each other. The competitiveness which has been put into our consciousness from slavery and is still there. And it's also lack of education as well of what [depression] means. We can't always just say "pray about it". Sometimes it's more. We have to do more.'

Trust issues

Unconscious bias does not have a pause button. The prejudices and stereotyping that plague the workplace permeate everywhere, including where they should least: healthcare. When black people do decide to take the first steps to treatment for mental health, or if things worsen to a point where we have no choice but to seek help, many of us worry that a diagnosis may be missed or misinterpreted as a result of miscommunication. It sounds incredible, but the stats speak for themselves: in the UK, mental health staff, including psychiatrists, are more likely to perceive black patients as being potentially dangerous, even though there is no evidence that they are any more aggressive than other patients from different racial groups.[15] Black people are three times more likely to be admitted to hospital and up to 44 per cent more likely to be detained under the Mental Health Act than white people,[16] and due to the belief that black people are more dangerous, they are also more likely than white people to be given physical treatments, such as medication and ECT, as well as to be prescribed higher doses of medication. Minorities are more likely to use crisis mental health care, and for many, long-term care is denied in favour of sectioning and medication, with little or no support after they are released. Statistics also show that black people are more likely to be physically restrained on a psychiatric ward.[17]

Conversely, they are less likely to be offered psychotherapy, counselling and other non-medical interventions,[18] which leaves many distrustful of medication, full stop.

The most harrowing data shows that compared with white patients, black patients are less likely to be referred to mental health services by a GP, and are more commonly referred by a criminal justice agency.[19] Services such as the police, A&E, social services and the benefit system are not well known for working together to help people affected by mental illness, which sees many people suffering from mental illness caught in a cycle, without the support they need to work towards recovery.

One of the most famous and tragic examples of this was the case of Sarah Reed, who died, aged 32, at Holloway prison while awaiting trial for assault. Prison staff told her family she had strangled herself while lying on her bed. Her arrest occurred after an altercation while Sarah was detained in a hospital in South London. Her family say she was acting in self-defence, and questioned why a woman with a documented history of severe mental health problems was removed from care under a mental health team in the community and transferred to prison. They also claim she was denied treatment for her condition while there.

Reed had suffered from mental health issues since the sudden death of her newborn baby in September 2003. After her child died at Beckton children's hospice, she and the child's father were forced to carry the body in their own car to an undertaker's, an ordeal her family say she never recovered from. For 12 years, Reed suffered from bouts of severe mental illness and relatives say that it was while she was detained under Section 3 of the Mental Health Act that the altercation occurred that led to her arrest.

Reed had been let down by police before – in 2012, she was a victim of a widely publicised incident of brutality after she was thrown to the ground, grabbed by the hair and punched three times in the head by PC James Kiddie. She had been arrested on suspicion of shoplifting. The attack had been so brutal that fellow officers who had seen the CCTV footage reported Kiddie to the police's directorate of professional standards. Two years later he was found guilty of assault over the incident, sentenced to 150 hours of community service, then suspended. Sarah's case reverberates as an example of how racism can be a barrier to individuals getting the help they desperately need. How did they get it so wrong?

When you choose to get help, you are likely to feel vulnerable. And for those who have had generally bad experiences within the system, they are likely to be left feeling disempowered and afraid. A 2010 paper confirmed this, stating that black and ethnic minority groups 'May find themselves disillusioned with the services they receive, and so be reluctant to return to hospital if they self-harm again.'[20]

Aside from covert and overt racism, many struggle with mental health treatment, as the remedies often require a great deal of talking, opening up and effective communication. We can find ourselves wondering what an old, white man will make of our black, female problems. For me, the idea of having to spell out cultural intricacies that made conversations around mental health at home difficult made me wince. I thought it would be like doing an unpaid presentation on my life, to someone whose job it was to feign interest. 'Women of black ethnic backgrounds do not receive the support and interventions needed, which impacts BME (black and minority ethnic) women's well-being,' Cal Strode states. But alongside this, Strode acknowledges that the healthcare system could be improved to provide tailored solutions for minorities. 'Services are not culturally aware enough and BME communities hesitate to access services due to stigma.'

Lord Avebury, a former Liberal Member of Parliament, spoke about cultural differences affecting quality of care in the House of Commons all the way back in 1982, and very little seems to have changed since then: 'It is said by the West Indian community that psychiatrists in the prisons, and indeed in the hospital service as a whole, are not properly trained in recognising the different cultures of ethnic minorities, and that as a result people may be wrongly diagnosed as suffering from mental illness when they talk, for instance, as the Rastafarians frequently do about God.'[21] Certain cultural nuances are easily lost in translation. Mainstream mental health services are often not equipped with services that are acceptable and accessible to BAME individuals and that meet their particular cultural needs. A 2013 report by mental health charity Mind found that the majority of respondents said staff weren't diverse enough within mental health[22] and the effect of this is often felt throughout the system.

Institutional racism plagues the mental health system, just as it plagues many public bodies. It was defined by the Macpherson Report[23] in 1999, after the inquest into the murder of black teenager Stephen Lawrence, as 'the collective failure of an organisation to provide an appropriate and professional service to people because of their colour, culture or ethnic origin. It can be seen or detected in processes, attitudes and behaviour which amount to discrimination through unwitting prejudice, ignorance, thoughtlessness, and racist stereotyping which disadvantage minority ethnic people.' Despite the admission that institutional racism continues to ravage Britain, accusations of racism often bother people more than racism itself, in and outside of mental health. As Kamlesh Patel wrote in his paper on institutional racism in psychiatry,[24] mental health workers who complain that psychiatry and psychiatrists are being accused of racism 'misunderstand the concept of institutional racism and dismiss the legitimate concerns of the Black community'.

....

F.U.B.U.

....

The lack of racial diversity in mental health has led to black people creating our own spaces where we can help each other and ourselves. For several years in Britain, black community-based groups have operated from psychiatric wards, old community centres, libraries, parks and anywhere else they have been able to find. Canerows and

Plaits, for instance, is one such project – a ward visiting service providing weekly visits to local mental health wards, offering support to inpatients, and consulting them about ways that their experience in hospital could be improved. It was founded by mental-health service users from a charity called Sound Minds with the aim of improving mental healthcare, particularly for people from BAME backgrounds. Mama Low's Kitchen is another, also started by Sound Minds, which is open to all people recovering from mental health issues, and it is free to attend.

These black-led organisations have created a welcome alternative to mainstream services. They come to the aid of those who often do not have the financial requirements to gain access to other solutions, considering NHS counselling can take months to secure and the quality varies widely. As we have discussed elsewhere, 40 per cent of ethnic minority women live in poverty – twice the proportion of white women. Poverty extends to more than a third of black women in Britain[25] and 50 per cent of black Britons live in low-income families.[26]

Aside from other barriers to mental health, one of the biggest is funding, as public services are being increasingly cut by the government. Day centres were once a strong support system that minorities relied on in terms of mental health services, and they are increasingly important as other services continue to buckle under the pressure of austerity. But they are often funded by local authorities and Mental Health Trusts,[27] which are also suffering from cuts and struggling to cover increasing costs. Various services that were once centralised in a single day centre have now been scattered across different organisations, meaning, for example, that if someone required counselling, a hot meal and something recreational such as art lessons, they would be required to visit several different venues instead of one. Paul Burstow, a former Liberal Democrat MP, mentioned the problem in a parliamentary debate in 2013, saying: 'It is concerning that services are being withdrawn where they involve providing peer support or reaching into harder-to-reach communities, particularly black and minority ethnic communities, which often get left behind and often are most prone to being subject to the most coercive parts of our mental health system.'[28]

Cuts to local services and projects provided by voluntary organisations affect those in need most, and they are often black and female. Many minorities feel more comfortable being helped by these types of organisations instead of the state and their continued erosion only consolidates the idea that our mental health is not a priority.[29]

In pursuit of the #CarefreeBlackGirl

I am not a doctor, as I've said, but even doctors are often unsure about how to properly tackle mental health within the black community. As with so many things, systemic change is required first and foremost, because the inequalities that black people experience in mental health services are heavily influenced by how these services operate and are organised. Occupational psychologist Delroy Constantine-Simms explains that the problems are on more than just an interpersonal level – they are historic, entrenched and woven into the very fabric of the Union Jack:

'There is little credence to the argument that what happens to black people within mental health services is simply a product of individual racism or, a consequence of cultural ignorance on the part of practitioners. The roots of racism within psychiatric care can be traced to the conceptual and theoretical framework of what constitutes modern psychiatry.'[30]

Despite this, there are several different things that can be done to tackle the very different levels of mental health problems. It doesn't mean that you are unable to be effectively treated through these services. I say this as someone who owes a lot to counselling provided to me, for free. We as a country may still have far to go with mental health in broader society, let alone within the black community, but although the system may be flawed, it still saves lives.

The most important thing if you're seeking help is to take control as soon as you're able, and find out what works for you. If you want to try a talking therapy, ask your GP. They will know what's available locally and can help you decide which treatment is best for you. Many GP surgeries provide counselling or therapy services on the NHS and you can often self-refer for counselling or therapy. Which therapy you are referred for depends on what emotional or mental health problem you have and its severity – not everything works for everyone, nor does it work immediately. The support can range from guided self-help, computerised cognitive behavioural therapy, anti-depressant medicine, cognitive behavioural therapy, group support meetings and more. Some charities also offer cheap or free talking therapies or group support, such as Cruse for bereavement care,[31] Mind for mental health problems[32] and Relate for relationship counselling.[33] There are a few free youth-counselling services that run locally, but also often services you can inquire about at university, and even sometimes through your job. For some, professional help is the difference between life and death; for many, it's simply the difference between struggling and being okay. Very few of us or our loved ones know exactly what works – even professionals can be flawed – but with the right guidance and knowledge of what is on offer, it can be utilised to make a real difference.

It isn't always easy for black girls and women to navigate the system of mental healthcare in Britain, and it may take some research, but there are definitely services available that are more well-suited to your particular needs. For instance, if you are someone of faith, support groups can often be found in places of worship. Furthermore, there are Christian and Muslim counsellors and psychotherapists, who use scripture to consolidate counselling. A counsellor who knows about the specific nuances of the black British and female experiences is often preferred and can be requested, but they are hard to come by. Organisations such as The Black and Asian Therapist Network have tried to rectify this by introducing schemes such as pairing black service users to black staff. There are also specific services available throughout the UK that offer free counselling specifically set up to serve the BAME community, which can easily be located online, such as the Maya Centre, a free multi-ethnic women-only counselling service with all-female counsellors. There is often an assumption that 'black' is the same as 'African' is the same as 'Caribbean', but cultural attitudes and a great manner of things differ dependent on background, upbringing and various other factors. A good counsellor, especially one located in an ethnically diverse area, will make it their job to be aware of these differences.

When I settled in for my first ever therapy session, I was hesitant to explain to the older white man in front of me the specific nature of my experience. I wanted to talk about how I felt without having to explain who I was and why. But when he recognised my Nigerian name and proceeded to discuss the cultural specificities of West African culture, I immediately felt at ease. Not all counsellors are as well versed in cultural differences, but when they are, it works wonders.

Black women have also taken action at a grassroots level to create spaces for ourselves to navigate mental health. Unmasked Women is a series of exhibitions that aims to document the experiences of black British women through the lens of mental health and it has helped launch a much-needed conversation surrounding black women's mental health in the UK. Black Blossoms is another organisation that, through safe spaces, has allowed black women to discuss self-care and mental health without the fear of shame or stigma.

'Self-care' accompanied by professional help is also massively important. Self-care involves general lifestyle changes that can help manage the symptoms of many mental health problems, improve physical health or well-being. It can also help to prevent some problems developing or getting worse, and it means different things to different people. But essentially it is about looking after yourself. We should be as dedicated to scheduling time for things that make us feel better and happier as we are to work-related commitments. For Laura Mvula, leaving time aside just for herself, alongside dedicating herself to fitness, helped her greatly on her path to recovery:

'I'm always in awe of people who are disciplined, even in small ways, about how they spend their time – what time is taken just for you, the individual. Whether it's, you know, developing a routine where every week you take a walk in the park.

'Fitness is definitely changing my life, I'll admit a lot of my motivation has been in the past – and there's still the dregs of it there – about getting down to some ridiculous size and feeling like Naomi Campbell or something. More now it's about [how] I can feel, how my body is stronger, and so mentally I feel better and better equipped to deal with the days and events.

'The other day I was on the treadmill, I mean, before, I couldn't run on the treadmill for five minutes without worrying that I was going to have a panic attack or stepping off or feeling dizzy. A few days ago I did 40 minutes straight, which feels miraculous, but actually the psychology of it is pretty basic, it's just built up over time. I think even what can feel like small adjustments to a routine can make a world of difference further down the line.'

Cynthia Erivo also discusses the importance of 'me-time'. She has also found herself through fitness but she encourages everyone to find whatever it is that takes them to their happy place:

'I've been more busy than I've ever known in my life, but what you do is you discover the things that will take care of the inside, because there's a lot of stuff going on outside, and you have to learn to figure out what makes you happy inside, what moves you from the inside so you can keep going. For me it was fitness. Find the thing that takes care of your mind and your brain – maybe it's yoga, maybe it's breathing, maybe it's fitness, maybe it's working out, maybe it's taking yourself to the cinema every weekend, reading a book. I think that young people probably don't know very much about innate care, like, taking care of the inside, because it's hard when you're young. You're trying to impress people on the outside constantly at full validation, but you really have to search for validation within yourself before you seek validation from anyone else. It's a case of looking for the thing that will serve you first or make you pleased. So maybe you look in the mirror and you think you don't like the way your body is – you have to find out whether or not that's because someone else said you don't like it, or because you yourself need to feel healthier, you yourself need to listen to more music, you need to take an hour every weekend to just listen to the kind of music you like, or you want to write stuff down. If there are feelings you don't get to say, write them down, if there's music you don't get to hear or there are things that inspire you, write it down. Remember the things that fill you from the inside first.'

Getting better is often about taking each day as it comes and as best as you can. I learned to do what I can, when I can, especially when it comes to pressing tasks, where I start with smaller, more manageable things until I'm capable of properly doing the slightly bigger things. Getting better often also requires simply slowing down or stopping altogether, if you're able to. I had to take time out of university in order to get myself back on track, but that wouldn't be necessary for everyone; sometimes a few days off spent taking care of yourself, recharging and resting, can do a great deal, or at least help clarify in your mind about what steps you should take next, as Mvula helpfully explains:

'I feel very much at the beginning of a new era for me. I feel like I'm having minor breakthroughs every other day, and I think it's coming as a result of stopping, first of all. And I don't mean giving up, I mean taking time out. I recently just blocked out time, this month, the rest of the week and weeks coming I've made the decision to just step back and give myself a chance. I recognise that not everybody has the luxury of doing that – we have to get out and earn – but I do think that the way we manage time is almost like an art form really.'

Another aspect of self-care can be sharing the load, though it's often not easy due to the stigma and fear that we've looked at already. As 'strong black women', we often fall into the trap of believing we can bring ourselves out of every and any thing, but we also need the care, support and strength that we readily give to others. In order to be helpful to our loved ones, we have to love ourselves and ensure we are okay, too. And despite the difficulty in talking about these things, sometimes the best support is provided by our own networks, as was the case for Alexis Oladipo. Within the space of a few weeks,

Alexis, who was then working as a cleaner, had come out of a serious relationship, had two medical procedures carried out and had been victimised online for her job by people she knew on social media. She was in severe physical and emotional pain and she couldn't see a way out, but her best friend could:

'I started going to a deep depression. I just wouldn't get out of bed, I'd just cry all day,' Alexis says. 'My best friend would call me and I wouldn't even answer, I wouldn't answer the phone to anyone but my mum. Then she would call me, I could hear she was trying not to cry because I'm upset. She'd be begging me like, "Please, get out of this, get up, go and bath, wash your hair, do something. Don't just lay in bed all day upset." But nobody could talk me out of my situation. I was just so disappointed in everything. I thank God for my best friend, because she came to my house one day with her son, and she was banging down my door, like, "I know you're there. Come out, it's me outside." So I opened the door and she was just like, "Woah." She looked me up and down just like, "Nah, we're not doing this. Get in the bath, I'm taking you to my house. Even if it's just to go and sit down in my living room, I'm not leaving you here by yourself anymore." So I went and bathed, got dressed, kind of dragged myself, she drove to her house. My hair was all matted down to my head because, like, that's how much tears were in my hair. I went to her house and we just kind of spoke about it all, I cried – again. She doesn't really know this, but our relationship really helped me get through a lot of what I was going through. Because even though she was going through her problems, she always supported me, always had my back, always was there when I needed a shoulder to cry on. I'm really trying not to get emotional, but it was one of those things where I was in so much pain that I'd even inflicted it on her. I wasn't the best friend to her at that time. That's why now she can call me for anything in this life. I would die for that girl because she had my back so much. She just had me, and she was heaven-sent. I do thank God for her life, because a lot of what I went through, she helped me with. I really don't want to cry – a lot of it she helped me through.'

People can rarely talk you out of your bad place, but talking to them can help a great deal. If you are blessed enough to have someone in your life who cares about you, let them do what friends are supposed to. A therapist I once had offered me a simple but useful analogy: that several straws were going into me from different avenues – work, relationships, money, family – sapping away my mental and physical energy, and because I never sought support, I was never replenished. I simply continued until I completely dried out, and I was unable to be of use to anyone around me or to myself. It sounds basic, but it really hit home.

We are all in need of a refill sometimes, but it cannot all come from ourselves, as explained by Lady Leshurr:

'Whether it is, you know, to your closest friends or family or it's just writing it down, you need to get it out, because when you keep it in it's bottled and you can get to a point where it blows up in your face. That's what happened to me; I kept so much in, I was scared to say anything and because of the pressure of being signed. "Oh I shouldn't post that tweet because it's not going to look good." I bottled it and it just made me burst. That was the main reason for a breakdown – you have to express, you have to get it out so it's out there. Speak it out, pray it or say it to the Lord, you have to definitely tell somebody, don't ever bottle it up because it makes it ten times worse. Try be positive, try to meditate, try to read a book, try and do something you don't really do. Turn all music off, the TV, listen to the silence – do things you don't really do, do things you're comfortable with – try and find different things that make your life a little bit better. You're going to feel the same way all the time, so it's good to change. That's what I did.'

Everybody comes to help in different ways. My route to getting help for depression was characteristically peculiar. I had explained to my dad that I had been feeling low, and in typical Nigerian father fashion, he decided to tell me a story. It was a Persian adage, about a king who called on his wise men to provide him with a quote that would be applicable to whatever situation, good or bad, that he found himself in. After racking their brains, the men came back with 'this too, shall pass' inscribed on a ring. My dad told me the point was that the highs as well as the lows in life were ephemeral and I'd eventually find myself on the other side. It was simple, but it helped.

Months later, at university, curled up on the bed I hadn't moved from for several days, I had forgotten all about that story. My mind had been too crammed with the fact that I was almost certainly going to fail my looming exams and the fact that I didn't care – something that would have shocked me, had I had the energy to be shocked. I hadn't been eating and was fretting over what TV series I could now watch, since I'd binged all then-nine series of *American Dad* in a week. I was in a particularly bad way. I had been attempting to stream *Shutter Island* for three days straight and even the time it was taking to buffer wasn't enough to jolt me into some sort of feeling. On my thousandth refresh, the captcha cropped up like clockwork and I sat up to type in the code that would finally let me conclude what had now become something of an ordeal. But that day, instead of 'TyP3-meat' or 'weathe4 – cAt!', the captcha scrambled up something familiar: 'This too shall pass.'

It was a coincidence, granted, but one that made me feel like something was shouting at me through my computer screen to get some breakfast and crack a window, for goodness sake. A few days after that, I booked my first counselling session. A month after that, I took a year out of university – still one of the best decisions I ever made. It took me some time (and a weird conversation with my own laptop) but eventually I was able to take the steps to getting better. And while those steps were shaky and sometimes even went backwards, the most important thing was that they were being taken.

Perhaps this chapter will be someone else's captcha – a weirdly prescient message that freaks them out enough to eventually book some days off work. Maybe it's a conversation with a friend, maybe it's simply feeling fed up with feeling the way you're feeling. But whenever you're ready to take those first steps, know that you don't have to take them alone and unaided. There are many things that can help you along the way.

TLC

ELIZABETH

'I had found a lump in my neck when I was
about 24 and I just felt it was nothing at first,
and it was actually vanity that made me go
and check it out properly. Thank God I did,
it turned out to be cancerous and I had
to have treatment.'
Vannessa Amadi

As I entered my twenties I was repeatedly told to make the most of this time and seize every opportunity. These years weren't the years for comfort living but instead the decade for challenging myself; the time to break down barriers and live my life to the absolute fullest. But in order to live your best, you need to ensure that you are on your A game when it comes to your health. This starts with knowing your body, being aware of any changes to it and taking care of yourself.

We all have different approaches to our health; there are those who, at the smallest sign of an ache and pain, book an appointment to see a doctor. Then there are people like me, who put off seeking medical attention unless I'm in such physical pain that I can't carry out my everyday tasks, which then forces me to go to the hospital. We say 'health is wealth', but we need to be proactive in seeking help and advice about it.

However, we live in a time where it can be difficult to keep on top of health advice, and a study by E45 recently revealed that we are bombarded with conflicting health messages. British women are in a constant state of confusion when it comes to their health and well-being. From 'how much water should we drink every day?' to 'Is red meat healthy?', the majority of UK females (79 per cent) admit they are worried about getting it wrong in terms of their health and well-being.[34] Not surprisingly, 81 per cent of women feel baffled by information overload and 49 per cent of women said that they turn to the internet for guidance, with 14 per cent scrolling through social media for the best advice. But if you're like me and have ever googled your symptoms when you're ill, then almost had a mini panic attack from your subsequent self-diagnosis, you know how unhelpful it can be.

There is more to a healthy life than eating brown bread and hitting the gym. Our health is determined by a lot of factors: things like biology, genetics, culture and, of course, lifestyle. There is no harm in occasional tiredness, but when it becomes a pattern and you're bordering on exhaustion, that's a warning sign. Different groups of people have different health considerations and risks, and for black women it's important for us to know about the diseases that can affect us. It's about taking care of yourself and your body, in all ways possible. After all, the best advocate for your health is you.

> **'We need to be better at understanding our bodies and understanding the changes in our bodies.'**
> *Charlene White*

When I was younger, I would look at the children's medical encyclopaedia and flick through it, learning about the various illnesses. But when it described symptoms of various conditions and showed images of those symptoms, I couldn't always relate to them. Often the description would refer to symptoms that were only visible on white skin, with a red patch denoting pain, and – having dark skin – I didn't think it applied to me, even though I was a child just like them.

Knowledge is power, and when it comes to your health, knowing what to do, what to look out for and how to take positive steps can save your life. Cancer affects all communities, but according to

Cancer Research UK, black women in England are almost twice as likely to be diagnosed with advanced breast cancer compared to white women. Shockingly, late-stage disease is found in about 25 per cent of Black African and 22 per cent of Black Caribbean breast cancer patients. In white breast cancer patients, the figure is 13 per cent. Experts say there are various reasons for this, but a low awareness of symptoms and screening (meaning abnormal cells or tumours are found at a later, more advanced stage) is one of the key issues.

Black women are less likely than white women to go for a mammogram when invited by the NHS. Spotting the early signs of cancer is very important, as the sooner it's detected and treated, the better the outcome. Heather Nelson, from BME Cancer Voice, says: 'Women, especially women of colour, are less likely to go for screening. You'll get leaflets through your door and they will predominantly show white middle-class women. There's no representation of South Asian, African descent etcetera. If you get information like that, you're going to look and think, "That's not about me."'[35]

But unfortunately it *is* about you and me. How can we safeguard ourselves against diseases, if we don't take the necessary preventative actions in the first place? Ask yourself when was the last or the first time you went for a mammogram? Or if you even know what mammogram means? If your answers to questions like these are erring on the negative, it should really be a wake-up call. Regular screening is the best way to find breast and cervical cancers early in most women. Talk to your doctor about what screening tests are right for you.

Like breast cancer, the awareness and prevention of cervical cancer is lower amongst women from an ethnic minority background. Research shows that these women may face different barriers to screening than white women. A study by Jo's Cervical Cancer Trust revealed that a third more black, Asian and minority ethnic (BAME) women of screening age (12 per cent) compared to white women (8 per cent) said they had never attended a cervical screening appointment and only 28 per cent of BAME women said they would feel comfortable talking to a male GP.[36]

Charlene White is the patron of the charity Bowel Cancer UK, and is dedicated to raising awareness of the disease. Her mum was diagnosed with bowel cancer and she stresses the importance of early detection; a lack of awareness of the symptoms in the young causes delays in diagnosis and treatment. 'We need to be better at understanding our bodies and understanding the changes in our bodies, and I don't think that we are that great at doing it. Yes, it's because we take for granted that we have an amazing health service, so we just kind of assume, well, if something happens, then it's all right, the NHS will fix me and I'll be fine, but unfortunately it doesn't work like that, it doesn't always work in that way. When it came to my mum's diagnosis, the doctors didn't necessarily spot what it was as soon as they should have done, and by the same token she didn't necessarily go to the doctors as soon as she realised she was having symptoms. I think it's really important for people to understand, yes, the symptoms of bowel cancer, but just cancer, full stop. With women checking their boobs, with men checking their prostate, all of those things, and not really see it as being like an icky thing that no one really wants to talk about, because not talking about icky things can kill you.' Bowel cancer is the third most common cancer in the UK, and as Charlene's experiences prove, checking for changes in your body and being aware of the state of your health can be life-saving.

The lack of health literacy among black women leads to us being less likely to get ourselves checked. Ask yourself: when you received your cervical screening invitation, did you go? Did your first cervical cancer screening happen at the age of 25? It should have. As Heather Nelson said, it doesn't help that the leaflets and information about cancers predominantly affecting women mainly feature white women, further exacerbating the notion within BAME communities that these issues affect 'them' and not 'us'. But it is vital that we become more aware of these diseases and what they can do to us, because refusing to acknowledge them will not make them go away.

Black people are the most likely to suffer from blood-related diseases such as sickle cell, diabetes and hypertension – conditions that often require blood transfusions and in the case of diabetes (which affects black people in higher numbers) can also lead to organ transplants. Out of a population of roughly 4.4 million black people (according to the last census),[37] about 15,000 people and counting suffer from sickle cell, a disease caused by irregularly shaped red blood cells, which have a shorter lifespan than normal red blood cells and can get trapped in blood vessels, leading to a heightened risk of infections, strokes, lung problems, anaemia and severe pain when blood cells get stuck.[38]

Sickle cell is a disease that predominantly affects people like ourselves, of African and Caribbean origins, so we need to know more about it and how to treat it. Right now, it could be said that in the black community, we are failing our brothers, sisters, children, mothers and fathers who suffer from this disease because we are not donating enough blood. This is critical because people with sickle cell disease, as well as other blood-related illnesses, such as diabetes, rely upon regular blood transfusions (every 3–4 weeks for sickle cell sufferers) for survival and to be able to live an ordinary life. In addition, stem cell and bone marrow replacement treatments are also used to treat blood-related diseases, yet without regular black donors how can the doctors do this? At the moment only 1 per cent of black people in the UK are active donors (roughly 10,000 people), which means that fewer people are registered donors than suffer from sickle cell alone. Here's another sobering stat: only 20 out of 1,282 people who passed away in 2015 were registered as black organ donors, even though there are 600 people on the waiting list.

The effects of these shortfalls can cost lives – most sickle cell carriers have a shortened lifespan (40–60 years), but this can be significantly compromised by a lack of blood used for transfusion; and black people are more likely than white people to need organ donations due to our heightened risk of suffering diseases that can lead to organ failure.[39]

This is why it's so important that we become more clued up about the need to donate blood and organs. These shortfalls can only be met by a massive increase in donations from within our own community.

We cannot rely on others to solve it for us, because similar blood types are more likely to be found within ethnicities, and because certain rare blood types in black people can only be found within those of the same ethnic background, the lack of organs and blood available currently means that black people have only a 20 per cent chance of finding a suitable match from an unrelated donor.[40]

The dearth of black blood and organ donation is so stark that government health officials and NHS Blood and Transplant have launched several campaigns targeting the African and Caribbean community,[41] such as the Be There campaign in 2015, and most recently #ImThere. The Be There campaign offers some simple steps to become a more proactive donor, steps which are as easy as reapplying a coat of nail varnish. Really simple actions, such as visiting the national www.blood.co.uk website, can help to make regular blood donation routine in our lives, and to also learn more about organ donation and how to sign up as a donor.

The NHS website also offers easily digestible information, such as how often to donate blood, where to go to do it and apps that will enable you to be kept in the loop of available blood donation sessions and centres, so it really is worth a look. Often the idea of donating blood seems like a chore, but it doesn't need to be.

The fact that campaigns such as this have been repeated over the years, despite raising awareness, shows that there is still a long way to go before our community normalises and fully embraces blood and organ donations. Acting upon the knowledge we now have is the only thing that will make these life-saving donations within the black community commonplace, in the way they should be.

Hair done, nails done, everything did

When was the first time you had a relaxer? I had mine when I was six. I was told my hair was too tough, too hard to manage. Several burning scalps later, I had a relaxer every year until I was 16.

Fast-forward to years later, and if you ask any black woman: 'What is the most damaging beauty product they could use?' the resounding answer would be 'relaxers'.

Health issues affecting black women are not only restricted to diseases and infections, but also to products that we have been using and that have been marketed to us for centuries. Cosmetics targeting black women are more likely to contain potentially harmful ingredients than those marketed to the general public, according to a study by the Environmental Working Group. As we have discussed in the Representation chapter, black women have fewer beauty products available to them, and it's shocking that these products are more likely to contain hazardous chemicals. But the negative effects of products like relaxers aren't restricted to how they make your hair look and feel but also to what they may be doing to our bodies in the long term. To say 'pretty hurts' would be putting it mildly, how about 'pretty kills'? The cocktail of chemicals used in relaxers and hair dyes reads like an ingredients list for a DIY chemical bomb. Relaxers are laced with corrosive chemicals like sodium hydroxide – used in drain cleaners – and women who have been exposed to them for prolonged periods have been known to develop ailments such as cancer, asthma and fibroids.[42] Suddenly a bit of dry scalp and hair breakage seems like the least of our hair-routine-induced worries.

Among the most serious of health concerns associated with the chemicals used is uterine fibroids. Another recent study into the use of hair relaxers found that the condition is estimated to affect 80 per cent of black women who use them over their lifetime. When you look at the ingredients – which can include formaldehyde, ammonia, bleaching agent, DMDM hydantoin, linalool methylparaben and propylparaben – we shouldn't necessarily be surprised. Other dangerous side-effects of popular products range from dermatitis to occupational asthma.[43] The products also often contain EDCs (endocrine-disrupting chemicals), which have been linked to various reproductive and birth defects,[44] along with breast cancer and heart disease.

This is genuinely scary because these are everyday products marketed to and used en masse by black women, which can and do lead to life-threatening diseases. Sadly, it doesn't just stop at relaxers and dyes, which a lot of us have already been made aware of. The dangers to our health, masked by our cosmetics culture, are a lot more insidious, and products that have been a staple in the black-girl haircare regime, such as Olive Oil Sheens and Pink Luster, contain higher levels of toxins, steroids and hormone-disrupting chemicals than cosmetics made for non-black women.

Out of more than 1,000 different products and ingredients researched, relaxers unsurprisingly came out as some of the most hazardous, but hair dyes marketed to black women were also shown to be very dangerous.[45] Ingredients used in these dyes, such as ammonia, have also been linked to asthma and rare lymphatic cancers, bladder cancer and multiple myeloma (cancer in the white blood cells).[46]

For centuries black women have been encouraged to undertake so-called 'health and beauty regimes' and to use products that compromise our health. Douching and the use of products such as talcum powder are habits that have been passed down through the (black) generations. I remember when I was younger how my white friends would ask why I moisturised every day, and to me it just seemed obvious; I moisturise because that's what I've always done, and because my skin feels ashy without my daily cocoa butter. This is similar to the relationship that many of us black women have with practices such as douching and using vaginal deodorising products. It's just something we've always done.[47] But the roots of some of the most harmful black-dominated practices, such as douching and using talcum powder to maintain intimate hygiene, are sadly intertwined with historical misogynoir, which should be a red light in itself. Misogyny deems that vaginas are taboo and racism narrates that black people are dirty,[48] so add those together and, voilà, we have a highly toxic mix. And this heightened scrutiny of black female hygiene breeds insecurities and compulsions that are in turn capitalised upon by multinational cosmetic companies.

A chilling example of how dangerous this can be is the case of

Jacqueline Fox from the US. In 2013, before losing her battle to ovarian cancer, Jacqueline sued Johnson & Johnson for $72 million. She believed that talcum powder, which contains carcinogenics such as phthalates, was linked to her illness. While she won her legal action, Johnson & Johnson successfully appealed the first ruling. Soon after her death more than 1,000 women also sued Johnson & Johnson.

It is often these dangerous, potentially deadly, products that are the most vigorously marketed to black women. Are you feeling the need to have a spontaneous cupboard clear out now? Me too. Racial targeting is in no way unique and it is sadly very much in keeping with the overall theme of the disregard of black women's health by the beauty industry. But this isn't as simple as black women only having a higher number of dangerous products marketed at them. The questionable ingredients in beauty products is a universal phenomenon affecting women of all races. But the crucial difference is the fact that there are fewer products available to black women which are deemed as safe and healthy to use. The report by the Environmental Working Group last year, illustrates this by showing that less than 25 per cent of products marketed to black women got high safety ratings, compared to 40 per cent of products aimed at the general public.[49]

The point of bringing this all to light is to demonstrate how toxic racism, which isn't always explicit, is genuinely diminishing our ability as black women to live long and healthy lives. It really is a bitter pill to swallow, that we are exploited and compromised in industries that rely upon our hard-earned cash, especially as we pump so much more into hair and beauty than our better-catered-for non-black counterparts (estimated at about six times more than women of other ethnicities).[50] The cosmetics industry continues to show a marked lack of respect for our race, and studies show that manufacturers are less likely to spend the money on putting products used by black women through the same robust testing regimes as they are for white women.[51]

So what is the solution? It is a difficult one to remedy, as the onus shouldn't be on us to control what goes into the haircare products that we buy, nor is it even feasible to expect this. Also, I don't know about you, but the ingredients list on the back of packages looks like Latin to me. However, it is useful to google what is in your cream or shampoo and to ensure that none of the products in there have been blacklisted elsewhere. And, as Yomi has discussed, the natural hair movement has meant that plenty of hair and beauty bloggers are also able to offer advice on what is good to use and what is not.

....

**'I had to learn to put the brakes on
everything and take care of myself because
at one point, I was shaking every day, and I was
like, "Yo, if I'm not here tomorrow, the world
will continue. I want to be here; I want
to be around it all."'**
Estelle

....

Being busy and building an empire in your defining twenties is often seen as winning at life. But too often our pursuit of success can compromise our health. As we have discussed in the previous chapters, many of us live by the mantra that we have to work twice as hard to get half as much, whether that's in the form of aiming for a promotion, proving yourself at your new job or studying for exams. When I am in work mode, I find myself almost allergic to resting, seeing procrastination not only as the thief of time, but rest and sleep as hostage-takers of progress and harbingers of failure. Being black and female, we can feel more pressure to overwork ourselves compared to our white peers, because we are blighted with the double disadvantage of race and gender – triple if we are from lower economic backgrounds. It's great to strive for social, occupational and economic elevation, but unless we're careful, the price of this can compromise our quality of life and our ability to actually attain success. So, for starters, you should make sure you are able to get that minimum of six hours or more of sleep a night, rather than relying upon coffee and caffeine-laden energy drinks.

As black women, we can push ourselves too hard, but – as Yomi has said – we also often refuse to show weakness, despite being well aware of the injustice of our station as black women, who must dodge the slings of sexism and arrows of racism in a world that wants to keep us at the bottom of that societal pyramid. This can, of course, make us into formidable women and many of us, like Denise Lewis, look up to our first examples of an unshakeable work ethic in the face of adversity, which often come in the form of our mothers. Denise recounts, 'My mum was a great inspiration to me. We grew up in a very small family. My mum was a bit of a powerhouse, and she was my world. I watched her pretty intensively, working two jobs just to keep everything running smoothly; she has always, always been a hard-working woman. So I guess she was my primary source of inspiration as a person that really taught me that you have to work for anything that you want in life, and when it seems like the odds are stacked against you, with perseverance and commitment and a need and willingness to push yourself, you can make things work.'

The strong black female figure striving despite the weight of the world on her shoulders. Sounds familiar, no? Many of us grew up with strong female figures in our lives who grinded night and day, and often did so without complaint or regard for their health, determined to put their families first. This really is inspirational and we should emulate the drive of these women. However, we also need to do a better job of acknowledging the pressure we put ourselves under to be strong women who never break down or show signs of struggle, and we need to acknowledge that this can be very harmful to us. A study published by the University of Georgia, in the US, gives a worrying exposé into how race and socioeconomic disadvantage can genuinely affect our path to success, our health and our overall life expectancy. The study looked specifically at black youth in the US and their struggles to succeed, but the experience of working against the limitations of systemic racial and class imbalance are paralleled by black youth (and adults) in the UK.

The study found that 'white blood cells among the strivers were prematurely aged relative to those of their peers' and suggested that those (black youths) with an 'unrelenting determination to succeed' were more likely than their white peers to get sick or contract illnesses in the process of working towards their goal.[52] Stress doesn't only cause insomnia, anxiety or depression (which in themselves are extremely worrying states), but the study also showed that there was an alarming correlation between strivers and problems with cardiovascular and metabolic health, as well as diabetes, hypertension and arthritis.[53] White Americans, in the study, seemed relatively immune to the negative effects of the pursuit for success. This is not because they are naturally more resilient, but because in a world that orbits on an axis of white privilege, they don't have to *be* as resilient.

Of course, stress is something that all people of all races are exposed to and race is not the only determining factor. Class and gender in particular also play a massive role. However, the reason it is important to flag this up is for it to serve as a wake-up call for us to be more aware of when we are burning ourselves out. As we discussed in the microaggression chapter, black women can be especially vulnerable to the impacts of race-related stress.

Earlier we looked at the importance of going to the doctor when you notice changes in your body. In 2006, Vannessa Amadi was working on various different projects in her PR career and started to feel very stressed: 'It's hard to put your health first, I had found a lump in my neck when I was about 24 and I just felt it was nothing at first, and it was actually vanity that made me go and check it out properly because it was growing and I thought, I don't want a big old lump hanging out my neck. That's the only reason I went to the doctor, and thank God I did, it turned out to be cancerous and I had to have treatment.' Unfortunately, the lump turned out to be Hodgkin's Lymphoma and her doctor told her it was related to the excessive stress she had been under.

There are so many parallels between Vannessa's story and the stories of so many of us reading this book, living life, assuming we are invincible and ignoring signs of ill-health, especially when they are not inhibiting our day-to-day routines. Gloria Boadi agrees: 'At times people think "We've always done it this way, my parents did it this way and they came through. I'm the product of a strong black woman." A good friend of mine at work, at that time I was a housing officer, was doing two jobs, as we often do because we sometimes have to be the sole breadwinner, we've got to clothe our kids, plus look after extended families – we take on these roles. She came back from holiday and she wasn't well. I said to her, you need to relax, just take a day off, because, trust me, if you drop dead they will replace you tomorrow. She said – she actually used this term – "I'm a strong black woman. I'm fine." Three days later, she was dead.'

Managing stress is something I've had to get better at over the years. Rather than seeing it as rite of passage in the pursuit of success, I've had to take self-imposed breaks in order to manage it. I've learned that being good at my work is great and working hard is essential to this, but not at the expense of my health. Sometimes it's as simple as me declaring verbally, 'I can't come and kill myself!' to remind myself to put things into perspective. Estelle's approach has been similar: 'I had to learn to take self-imposed time off. I remember taking almost a year off one year, and it was partly because I was just exhausted, had nothing to write about, had nothing to talk about, and I was just tired. I remember getting on the internet one week and someone had been like, "Oh, Estelle's lazy, she should've done this, that and the rest," and I was like, "Do you realise that I haven't slept in three years, physically, been to sleep for more than four hours, for three years? Let alone the ten years prior to this that I had spent trying to get to this point? I'm going to take a break. I don't care if you don't like it."' She advises us to be resolute in our self-care and to be able to step back from stressful situations, or unrealistic expectations: 'It was forced on me because I got to a point where I was just shaking. Every time you saw me I'd be out here talking and doing what I was doing, but I was physically shaking, and then I decided that I was going to take a few days and nap. So every so often now, whenever I feel myself going to a point, I just make a decision, "All right, now I'm going to take the weekend off."'

However, Estelle acknowledges that this does require a level of discipline as well, especially when you have responsibilities and may not want to let anyone down. But setting fair boundaries is key to maintaining self-preservation: 'I had to learn to put the brakes on everything and take care of myself . . . I was like, "Yo, if I'm not here tomorrow, the world will continue. I want to be here; I want to be around it all. I'm not going to die, you're not going to have me out here on drugs, drunk, strung out, after all this work and everything I've put into my career, and also how much I mean to myself, let alone everyone else, so will my mum be crying because her daughter collapsed?" So I went on a self-imposed, "Promise yourself, whenever you feel like you're about to lose it, you're going to take a break," and that's what I do. There is success and there is drive, and absolutely, do it while you're young, do it in your twenties, but know that you need to take some time off. Yes, "We have to get it while we still can," but it's your life, it's your career, it will still be here. Take your time. You will be okay. The world is not going to implode on you, people will not forget you, do your work, just do great work.'

If you sacrifice yourself in the pursuit of success, you will have done it for an undeserving and ungrateful world. So rest, say no to too much work, but also take a step back and allow yourself to disengage and detox. Go on holiday, actually take your permitted leave when you can and when you're away from work genuinely switch from work mode to holiday mode: but properly, no peeking at work emails. Lady Leshurr describes suffering from similar burnout effects, induced by the non-stop demands of being a rising rapper; 'Last year I had over a hundred shows, and I didn't know that I was going to get burnt out. I was thinking, yes, let's do these shows! I've done it, but I burnt out at the end because I'm hardly eating, I'm losing weight, I'm just the opposite to who I was at the start of the year, so it's something that I just had to experience to realise that, wow, I actually need a break, because it's going to help my mind, my body, my soul: physically, mentally, emotionally. So yeah, it means a lot to have breaks and just relax every now and again.'

What do these women have in common? Three black women,

confident in their craft and deserving of success, yet damaging themselves due to the insurmountable burden of expectation from themselves and the demands that the world places upon them. What else do they all have in common? They are only human and they all eventually had to stop because their physical and mental health was being severely compromised. And what is notable in each case, is that working too hard actually inhibited their ability to do their best at their roles at that specific time.

Their examples reassert the need for self-care. Often we find ourselves alone on our journeys to achievement, without moderators there to remind us to stop and rest. As a society we also applaud working oneself into the ground as a sign of strength, admirable determination and resilience, but unrelenting resilience can be very detrimental. Succumbing to the need to give your body a rest should in no way be seen as weakness.

It's also okay to ask for help, as Yomi discussed in the previous chapter. As black women, we have to be more open and proactive in doing what we can to help ourselves mentally, which involves trying to limit the effects of stress and societal pressures on ourselves. Combatting burnout is simple, but it does take a lot of mental rewiring of priorities. It is important to acknowledge when the expectations placed on you by yourself and others become too much, and to know that you are not undermining your ability by taking a step back for the sake of your own regeneration. As we have seen, overworking doesn't only make you tired, it can lead to depression, anxiety and other medical issues. This isn't about 'slacking off' and compromising the trajectory of your success, it's about encouraging us to be able to say no to unrealistic expectations and to instead be more time-efficient and use the time we do have to work more effectively.

It's important, as Estelle and Lady Leshurr say, to physically take yourself away from the surroundings that you associate with stress, and then use that time to clear your head, rewire and get back into an effective mode. Work incredibly hard, yes, but also work hard to take that weekend off where you relax, sleep and regroup. It is this that will make you as productive as possible when you get back into work mode; after all, everything we use – our cars, our electronic appliances, even our phones! – need to be recharged at some point, so why wouldn't this be the case for our minds and bodies? Looked at this way, you're actively making your holiday or break a necessary but bloody enjoyable element of your overall mission.

Always put your health first, strive for the best and work hard. So let's live our best lives, but do so in moderation and without jeopardising our health.

AFTERWORD

YOMI

This book is by black women, for black women, and could not have come to fruition without the support of black women. Our photographers, our stylists, our cover designer, our supporters and so many others – they are black women without whom this would not have been possible. Elizabeth and I started this process, as mentioned earlier, with a focus group of young black Brits from different backgrounds, with different interests and jobs, who took time out of their day to tell us why they wanted this book and what they wanted from it. We then met and interviewed black women whom we have looked up to for years, finding new heroes along the way and also, as clichéd as it may sound, finding ourselves in the process.

The women we spoke to gave up their time and their personal stories to aid us, and you. The willingness of so many to share their experiences in the hope that black British women and girls might take something – anything – from them, is a perfect illustration of our ability to spin gold from what might at first seem like a heap of hay. There may have been moments in this book when you felt overwhelmed by gloomy stats, or bummed out by second-hand experiences that can seem out of place in this day and age, but we hope you also feel inspired by the words of wisdom from our interviewees, spurred on by their stories and, most importantly, optimistic about the future. We know we didn't need to sugarcoat situations that many of you are already familiar with, but while things for us are still not by any means perfect, there *has* been progress, and we should acknowledge that the women we spoke to, and others like them, paved the way for us through a more difficult set of circumstances than we can imagine.

Had we pitched this book ten or even five years ago, I'm not sure whether it would have found a publisher – certainly not nine publishers competing to acquire it. At that time it would have been just as important, just as necessary and just as sought-after by black women, but for so long, what black women *want* has never been enough. I like to think that the existence of this book is a sign that things are changing, but it's a change that has not occurred in a vacuum. It is those who came before us who have helped in so many ways to make it possible.

Here's to us making the best of an ever-changing world, one full of possibilities.

ELIZABETH

When I turned 21, and just after I had graduated, I wrote a note to myself about the approach I wanted to take in life. I knew I was entering a new chapter and that there would be bumps in the road along my journey. This note was a sort of promise, a manifesto that I could refer back to, that would reassure me whenever I lacked motivation, when a particular goal seemed impossible, when something I wanted didn't go to plan, or when someone let me down. A key part of this note was a quote from Maya Angelou: 'My mission in life is not merely to survive, but to thrive; and to do so with some passion, some compassion, some humor, and some style.'

Through ups and downs over the years I have gone back to this note and it has always reignited that spark in myself, helping to refocus my purpose. I hope that through these women's stories and, most importantly, their advice, *Slay In Your Lane* does something similar for you. Depending on where you are in your life, it will reassure you that, whatever you may experience, whatever it is you have to offer the world, and whatever *your* purpose, you're not alone. Because calling it the *Black Girl Bible* was intentional. We hope that by joining us on this journey you will come to realise that your personal mission is not only to survive in this world, but also to thrive within your own expectations, without limitations: to slay in your own lanes.

ENDNOTES

INTRODUCTION

1   National Literacy Trust. 'Children's and Young People's Reading in 2014.'
(20 May 2015). Retrieved from: https://literacytrust.org.uk/research-services/
research-reports/childrens-and-young-peoples-reading-2014/

EDUCATION

Lawyer, Doctor, Engineer

1   Social Mobility Commission. 'Asian Muslims and black people do better in school,
worse in work.' (28 December 2016). GOV.UK. Retrieved from: www.gov.uk/
government/news/asian-muslims-and-black-people-do-better-in-school-worse-in-
work

2   Pears, E. 'African pupils excel while their Caribbean counterparts sink.' (7 February
2015). *The Voice.* Retrieved from: www.voice-online.co.uk/article/african-pupils-
excel-while-their-caribbean-counterparts-sink

3   Curtis, P. 'Education: Black Caribbean children held back by institutional racism
in schools, says study.' (5 September 2008). *Guardian.* Retrieved from: www.the
guardian.com/education/2008/sep/05/raceineducation.raceinschools?INTCMP=
%20SRCH

4   BBC *Newsround.* '1 in 5 black kids feel skin colour could affect their job.' (30 June
2014). Retrieved from: www.bbc.co.uk/newsround/28060401

5   Villines, Z. 'Exclusion from School Linked to Poor Mental Health in Children.'
(13 September 2017). GoodTherapy.org. Retrieved from: www.goodtherapy.org/
blog/exclusion-from-school-linked-to-poor-mental-health-in-children-0913171

6   Boisrond, C. 'If Your Teacher Looks Like You, You May Do Better In School.' (29
September 2017). nprEd. Retrieved from: www.npr.org/sections/ed/2017/09/29/
552929074/if-your-teacher-looks-likes-you-you-may-do-better-in-school

7   https://www.theguardian.com/teacher-network/2015/nov/19/teaching-fails-
reflect-multi-cultural-student-population

8   In Shaw, B., Menzies, L., Bernardes, E., Baars, S., Nye, P., Allen, R., LKMco and
Education Datalab. *Ethnicity, Gender and Social Mobility.* (28 December 2016).
London: Social Mobility Commission.

9   Pells, R. 'Black and ethnic minority teachers face "invisible glass ceiling" in schools,
report warns.' (14 April 2017). *Independent.* Retrieved from: www.independent.co.
uk/news/education/education-news/black-asian-ethnic-minority-teachers-
invisible-glass-ceiling-racism-schools-report-runnymeade-nut-a7682026.html

10 BBC News. 'Black children have more concerns over job prospects than white.'
(30 June 2014). Retrieved from: www.bbc.co.uk/news/uk-28085152

11 Natasha Codiroli, 'Inequalities in Students' Choice of STEM Subjects', Working
Paper 2015/16, Centre for Longitudinal Studies, UCL Institute of Education,
September 2015.

12 Camden, B. 'Black girls take the lead in STEM subjects.' (27 January 2017). Schools

Week. Retrieved from: https://schoolsweek.co.uk/black-girls-take-the-lead-in-stem-subject

Black Faces in White Spaces

13 An unlicensed establishment or private house selling alcohol and typically regarded as slightly disreputable.

14 Bhugra, Dinesh, Cardiff University. 'Independent Review Panel Into Issues Of Racial Equality In The School Of Medicine.' (25 January 2017). Retrieved from: https://www.cardiff.ac.uk/__data/assets/pdf_file/0011/551837/Prof-Dinesh-Bhugra-report-Final.pdf

15 Sherriff, Lucy. 'Outrage As Students "Black Up" As Jamaican *Cool Runnings* Team.' (21 November 2013). *Huffington Post.* Retrieved from: www.huffingtonpost.co.uk/2013/11/19/york-university-students-black-up-cool-runnings_n_4300968.html

16 Sherriff, Lucy. 'Edinburgh University Law Students In Race Row After "Blacking Up" For Somalian Pirate Fancy Dress.' (18 November 2013). *Huffington Post.* Retrieved from: www.huffingtonpost.co.uk/2013/11/18/somalian-pirates-edinburgh-students-black-up_n_4294952.html

17 Davis, Anna. 'Blacked-up Reveller Wins Fancy Dress Prize, but Students' Union Pledges to Investigate "Racist Connotations".' (5 November 2013). *Evening Standard.* Retrieved from: www.standard.co.uk/news/london/blacked-up-reveller-wins-fancy-dress-prize-but-students-union-pledges-to-investigate-racist-8922057.html

18 Weale, S. '"Slave Auction" for Loughborough Freshers Leads to Outcry.' (14 September 2017). *Guardian.* Retrieved from: www.theguardian.com/education/2017/sep/14/slave-auction-for-freshers-outcry-loughborough-university

19 Durham University. 'Thought Leadership: Universities Must Aim Higher on Ethnic Equality and Diversity. (4 February 2015). Retrieved from: www.dur.ac.uk/research/news/thoughtleadership/?itemno=23570

20 Social Market Foundation. 'SMF and the UPP Foundation to Investigate Continuation Rates in Higher Education in London.' (27 February 2017). Retrieved from: www.smf.co.uk/smf-upp-foundation-investigate-continuation-rates-higher-education-london/

21 Stevenson, Jacqueline. 'Black and Minority Ethnic Student Degree Retention and Attainment.' Higher Education Academy. Retrieved from: www.heacademy.ac.uk/system/files/bme_summit_final_report.pdf

22 Press Association. 'White Pupils "Less Likely to Apply for University than Other Ethnic Groups".' (22 July 2013). *Guardian.* Retrieved from: www.theguardian.com/education/2013/jul/23/white-pupils-university-ethnic-groups

23 GOV.UK. 'University Challenge: How Higher Education Can Advance Social Mobility.' (October 2012). Retrieved from: www.gov.uk/government/uploads/system/uploads/attachment_data/file/80188/Higher-Education.pdf

24 2011 Census. Office for National Statistics (2011). www.ons.gov.uk/census/2011census

25 Boliver, Vikki. 'Hard Evidence: Why Aren't There More Black British Students at Elite Universities?' (1 March 2018). *The Conversation.* Retrieved from: theconversation.com/hard-evidence-why-arent-there-more-black-british-students-at-elite-universities-25413

26 GOV.UK. 'Investigating the Accuracy of Predicted A Level Grades as Part of the 2010 UCAS Admission Process.' Department for Business Innovation and Skills.

(5 November 2013). Retrieved from: www.gov.uk/government/publications/
accuracy-of-predicted-a-level-grades-2010-ucas-admission-process

27   Boliver, Vikki. 'How fair is access to more prestigious UK universities?' (28 May
2013). *British Journal of Sociology* 64(2): 344–364.

28   Adams, Richard. 'Black Students Still Struggle to Win Places at UK Universities.'
(25 January 2017). *Guardian*. Retrieved from: www.theguardian.com/education/
2017/jan/26/black-students-struggle-uk-university-places-ucas

29   Times Higher Education. 'Anonymise admissions, says race equality report.'
(3 February 2015). Retrieved from *Times Higher Education (THE)*, https://www.times
highereducation.com/news/anonymise-admissions-says-race-equality-report/2018
334.article

30   Boliver, Vikki. 'Hard Evidence: Why Aren't There More Black British Students at Elite
Universities?' (1 March 2018). *The Conversation*. Retrieved from: theconversation.
com/hard-evidence-why-arent-there-more-black-british-students-at-elite-
universities-25413

31   'Undergraduate Admissions Statistics: 2011 Entry.' Retrieved from Oxford University
Website, https://www.ox.ac.uk/media/global/wwwoxacuk/localsites/gazette/
documents/statisticalinformation/admissionsstatistics/Undergraduate_Admissions_
Statistics_2011.pdf

32   Grove, Jack. '"Small" Russell Group Racial Bias in Admissions: Ucas.' (27 May
2015). Retrieved from *Times Higher Education (THE)*, www.timeshighereducation.
com/news/small-russell-group-racial-bias-in-admissions-ucas/2003594.article

33   Shukman, Harry. 'How White Is Your Uni?' (14 November 2014). *The Tab*. Retrieved
from: thetab.com/2014/11/13/white-uni-24303

34   Study by the Institute for Policy Research at the University of Bath. Retrieved from:
www.bath.ac.uk/publications/diverse-places-of-learning-home-neighbourhood-
ethnic-diversity-ethnic-composition-of-universities/attachments/Appendix-of-
tables.pdf

35   Sutton Trust. 'Four Schools and One College Win More Places at Oxbridge than
2000 Schools Combined.' (4 July 2017). Retrieved from: www.suttontrust.com/
newsarchive/four-schools-one-college-win-places-oxbridge-2000-schools-
combined/

36   Alexander, Claire, and Arday, Jason. 'Aiming Higher: Race, Inequality and
Diversity in the Academy.' (February 2015). Runnymede Trust. Retrieved from:
www.runnymedetrust.org/uploads/Aiming%20Higher.pdf

37   Blandford, E., Brill, C., Neave, S., & Roberts Allison, A. *Equality in higher education:
statistical report 2011. Part 2: students.* (2011). Equality Challenge Unit. Retrieved
from: www.ecu.ac.uk/publications/equality-in-he-stats-11

38   'New HEFCE Analysis Shows Significant Link between Factors Such as Ethnicity,
Gender and School Type on Achievement in Higher Education.' (27 March 2014).
Higher Education Funding Council for England. Retrieved from: www.hefce.ac.uk/
news/newsarchive/2014/Name,94018,en.html

39   Blandford, E., Brill, C., Neave, S., and Roberts Allison, A. *Equality in higher education:
statistical report 2011. Part 2: students.* (2011). Equality Challenge Unit. Retrieved
from: www.ecu.ac.uk/publications/equality-in-he-stats-11

40   Alexander, Claire, and Arday, Jason. 'Aiming Higher: Race, Inequality and Diversity
in the Academy.' (February 2015). Runnymede Trust. Retrieved from: www.
runnymedetrust.org/uploads/Aiming%20Higher.pdf

41   Ibid.

42 Haslam, Rebecca. 'Staff at Higher Education Providers in the United Kingdom 2015/16.' (19 January 2017). Retrieved from: www.hesa.ac.uk/news/19-01-2017/sfr243-staff

43 HESA, UK Data Service, ONS Census 2011. Retrieved from: www.hesa.ac.uk/

44 Bhopal, Kalwant. *The Experiences of Black and Minority Ethnic Academics: A Comparative Study of the Unequal Academy.* (Routledge, 2015).

45 Bhopal, Kalwant, et al. 'BME Academic Flight from UK to Overseas Higher Education: Aspects of Marginalisation and Exclusion.' *British Educational Research Journal,* vol. 42, no. 2, 2015, pp. 240–257., doi:10.1002/berj.3204

46 Bhopal, Kalwant. *The Experiences of Black and Minority Ethnic Academics: A Comparative Study of the Unequal Academy.* (Routledge, 2015).

47 Ibid.

48 Birmingham City University. 'Black Studies – BA (Hons).' www.bcu.ac.uk/courses/black-studies-ba-hons-2018-19

49 Ackah, William. 'There Are Fewer than 100 Black Professors in Britain – Why?' (10 March 2014). *The Conversation.* Retrieved from: www.theconversation.com/there-are-fewer-than-100-black-professors-in-britain-why-24088

50 Equality in Higher Education: Statistical Report 2014. Retrieved from: www.ecu.ac.uk/wp-content/uploads/2014/11/2014-08-ECU_HE-stats-report_staff_v19.pdf

WORK

Work Twice as Hard to Get Half as Good

1 Bromwich, Kathryn. 'Destiny Ekaragha: "I've got to break two glass ceilings".' (28 September 2014). *Guardian.* Retrieved from: www.theguardian.com/film/2014/sep/28/destiny-ekaragha-ive-got-to-break-two-glass-ceilings-gone-too-far

2 Danielle, Britni. 'Michelle Obama's "twice as good" speech doesn't cut it with most African Americans.' (12 May 2015). *Guardian.* Retrieved from: www.the guardian.com/commentisfree/2015/may/12/michelle-obama-twice-as-good-african-americans-black-people

3 BBC News. 'Social mobility promise "broken" for ethnic minority children.' (28 December 2016). Retrieved from: www.bbc.co.uk/news/uk-38447933?ocid=socialflow_twitter&ns_mchannel=social&ns_campaign=bbcnews

4 BBC News. 'Ethnic minority women face jobs "catastrophe".' (2 December 2012). Retrieved from: www.bbc.co.uk/news/uk-politics-20571996

5 Acas. 'Minority ethnic women face compounded workplace discrimination, says report.' (2013). Retrieved from: www.acas.org.uk/index.aspx?articleid=4099

6 Anonymous. 'I applied for the same job using an English name and got the interview.' (24 March 2016). *Guardian.* Retrieved from: www.theguardian.com/media-network/2016/mar/24/british-journalism-female-ethnic-minorities-reporters-editors

7 Hewlett, Sylvia Ann. *Black Women: Ready, Willing and More Than Able to Lead.* (8 June 2015). Retrieved from: www.inc.com/center-for-talent-innovation/black-women-ready-willing-and-more-than-able-to-lead.html

8 Business in the Community. *Race at Work 2015.* (2015). London: Business in the Community. Retrieved from: https://race.bitc.org.uk/sites/default/files/bitc_race_at_work_recommendations.pdf

9 Ibid.

10   Ibid.

11   BBC News. 'Tesco chairman: White men "endangered species" in UK boardrooms.'
     (11 March 2017). Retrieved from: www.bbc.co.uk/news/business-39241630

12   Eddo-Lodge, Reni. '"You're talked to as if you are a junior" – employees on workplace
     racism.' (26 September 2017). *Guardian.* Retrieved from: www.theguardian.com/
     inequality/2017/sep/26/employees-on-workplace-racism-under-representation-
     bame

13   McGregor-Smith, R. 'Race in the workplace.' London: Department for Business,
     Energy & Industrial Strategy. (2017). Retrieved from www.gov.uk/government/
     uploads/system/uploads/attachment_data/file/594336/race-in-workplace-
     mcgregor-smith-review.pdf

14   Lebowitz, Shana. 'Why black women are more ambitious than white women – but
     have a harder time getting ahead.' (23 April 2015). *Business Insider UK.* Retrieved
     from: http://uk.businessinsider.com/new-report-on-black-women-leaders-2015-4

15   Peck, Emily. 'Black Women Are Leaning In And Getting Nowhere.' (27 September
     2016). *Huffington Post.* Retrieved from: www.huffingtonpost.co.uk/entry/black-
     women-are-leaning-in-and-getting-nowhere_us_57e98908e4b024a52d29b0e8

16   Business in the Community. *Mentoring for Success.* (2012). Business in the
     Community. Retrieved from: https://race.bitc.org.uk/leading_change/mentoring-
     success

17   Business in the Community. *Race at Work 2015.* (2015). London: Business in the
     Community. Retrieved from: https://race.bitc.org.uk/sites/default/files/bitc_race_at_
     work_recommendations.pdf

18   Rosenberg, Alyssa. 'Shonda Rhimes's "Year of Yes" and the price of breaking
     barriers.' (10 November 2015). *Washington Post.* Retrieved from: www.washington
     post.com/news/act-four/wp/2015/11/10/shonda-rhimess-year-of-yes-and-the-
     price-of-breaking-barriers/?utm_term=.0c5f69b7a5b8

19   Rankine, Claudia. 'The Meaning of Serena Williams.' (25 August 2015). *New York
     Times.* Retrieved from: www.nytimes.com/2015/08/30/magazine/the-meaning-of-
     serena-williams.html?_r=0

Water Cooler Microaggressions

20   Liu, Anni. 'No, You're Not Imagining It: 3 Ways Racial Microaggressions Sneak into
     Our Lives.' (25 February 2015). *Everyday Feminism.* Retrieved from: https://everyday
     feminism.com/2015/02/ways-racial-microaggressions-sneak-in/

21   Sue, Derald Wing, PhD. 'Racial Microaggressions in Everyday Life.' (5 October
     2015). *Psychology Today.* Retrieved from: www.psychologytoday.com/blog/
     microaggressions-in-everyday-life/201010/racial-microaggressions-in-everyday-life

22   Dishman, L. 'How To Shut Down "Microaggressions" At Work.' (3 July 2017). *Fast
     Company.* Retrieved from: www.fastcompany.com/3068670/how-to-shut-down-
     microagressions-at-work

23   Business in the Community. *Race at Work 2015.* (2015). London: Business in the
     Community. Retrieved from: https://race.bitc.org.uk/sites/default/files/bitc_race_at_
     work_recommendations.pdf

24   Ashe, S. D., and Nazroo, J. 'Equality, Diversity and Racism in the Workplace: A
     Qualitative Analysis of the 2015 Race at Work Survey.' (2015). Manchester: ESRC
     Centre on Dynamics of Ethnicity, University of Manchester.

25   TUC. '1 in 3 British BME workers have been bullied, abused or singled out for unfair

treatment, finds TUC poll.' (13 September 2017). Retrieved from: www.tuc.org.uk/news/1-3-british-bme-workers-have-been-bullied-abused-or-singled-out-unfair-treatment-finds-tuc-poll

26 Naftulin, Julia. 'How Gaslighting Affects Your Mental Health.' (20 June 2017). *Motto.* Retrieved from: http://motto.time.com/4825032/gaslighting-mental-health/?utm_campaign=time&utm_source=twitter.com&utm_medium=social&xid=time

27 Taylor, D. 'Eni Aluko: "The minute you are brave enough to talk about race you are in a difficult situation."' (21 August 2017). *Guardian.* Retrieved from: www.theguardian.com/football/2017/aug/21/eni-aluko-interview-race-difficult-situation

28 Abbott, Diane. 'I fought racism and misogyny to become an MP. The fight is getting harder.' (14 February 2017). *Guardian.* Retrieved from: www.theguardian.com/commentisfree/2017/feb/14/racism-misogyny-politics-online-abuse-minorities?CMP=twt_g

29 TUC. '1 in 3 British BME workers have been bullied, abused or singled out for unfair treatment, finds TUC poll.' (13 September 2017). Retrieved from: www.tuc.org.uk/news/1-3-british-bme-workers-have-been-bullied-abused-or-singled-out-unfair-treatment-finds-tuc-poll

30 Holder, Aisha, M. B. 'Black women often suffer microaggressions at work.' (27 February 2016). Retrieved from LSE USAPP blog: http://blogs.lse.ac.uk/usappblog/2016/02/27/black-women-often-suffer-microaggressions-at-work/

31 Williams, Joan C., and Phillips, K. W. 'Double Jeopardy? Gender Bias Against Women of Color in Science.' (2014). WorkLife Law. UC Hastings College of the Law.

32 Prowess Women in Business. (n.d.). 'UK Female Entrepreneurship: key facts.' Prowess Women in Business. Retrieved from: www.prowess.org.uk/facts

33 Cooney, Samantha. 'Michelle Obama Reveals the Most Difficult Part of Her Time as First Lady.' (26 July 2017). *Motto.* Retrieved from: http://motto.time.com/4874387/michelle-obama-first-lady-racism/

***Flawless

34 Wikipedia. 'Respectability politics'. (22 February 2018). Retrieved from: https://en.wikipedia.org/wiki/Respectability_politics

35 Gardiner, Becky, et al. 'The Dark Side of Guardian Comments.' (12 April 2016). *Guardian.* Retrieved from: www.theguardian.com/technology/2016/apr/12/the-dark-side-of-guardian-comments

36 Business in the Community. *Race at Work Report 2015.* (5 November 2015). Retrieved from: race.bitc.org.uk/system/files/research/race_equality_campaign_yougov_report_nov_2015_vfull_vfinal_e.pdf

37 Project 28-40 Report. (1 April 2014). Retrieved from: Business in the Community, https://gender.bitc.org.uk/all-resources/research-articles/project-28-40-report

38 Woolcock, Nicola. '"Wrong" Accent and Clothes Keep Poor out of Top Jobs.' (6 March 2017). *The Times.* Retrieved from: www.thetimes.co.uk/edition/news/wrong-accent-and-clothes-keep-poor-out-of-top-jobs-9v0mm52wz

39 'Diversity & Inclusion Framework.' Hyatt in Action. Retrieved from: www.hyatt.com/corporate/Programs/diversity/en/diversity/hyatt-in-action.html

GETTING AHEAD

Independent Women

1 Beaty, Zoe. 'Some women are being left behind by pay gap progress.' (6 March 2017). *The Pool*. Retrieved from: www.the-pool.com/work/work-news/2017/10/racial-inequality-in-the-pay-gap

2 Goodfellow, Maya. 'A toxic concoction means women of colour are hit hardest by austerity.' (28 November 2016). *Guardian*. Retrieved from: www.theguardian.com/commentisfree/2016/nov/28/toxic-concoction-women-colour-pay-highest-price-austerity?CMP=share_btn_tw

3 Woodhams, C., Lupton, B., and Cowling, M. 'The Snowballing Penalty Effect: Multiple Disadvantage and Pay.' *British Journal of Management*, 63–77. (2015). Retrieved from: http://onlinelibrary.wiley.com/doi/10.1111/1467-8551.12032/full

4 Beaty, Zoe. 'We need to talk about our differences to see the true scale of the pay gap.' (10 November 2016). *The Pool*. Retrieved from: www.the-pool.com/work/work-news/2016/45/zoe-beaty-equal-pay-intersectionality

5 Breach, Anthony., and Li, Yaojun. 'Gender Pay Gap by Ethnicity in Britain – Briefing.' (2017). The Fawcett Society. Retrieved from: www.fawcettsociety.org.uk/Handlers/Download.ashx?IDMF=f31d6adc-9e0e-4bfe-a3df-3e85605ee4a9

6 Acas. 'Minority ethnic women face compounded workplace discrimination, says report.' (2013). Retrieved from: www.acas.org.uk/index.aspx?articleid=4099

7 BBC News. 'One in 13 ethnic minority workers are in insecure jobs, says TUC.' (2 June 2017). Retrieved from: www.bbc.co.uk/news/business-40117388

8 The Womens Resource Centre.org. Retrieved from: www.womens.cusu.cam.ac.uk/campaigns/bem/fawcett_ethnicminoritywomen.pdf

9 Rawlinson, Kevin. 'Minority ethnic families earning up to £8,900 less than white Britons.' (7 August 2017). *Guardian*. Retrieved from: www.theguardian.com/money/2017/aug/07/minority-ethnic-families-earning-less-white-britons-uk-pay-gap?CMP=Share_iOSApp_Other

10 O'Connor, Sarah. 'UK companies "holding back black and ethnic minority workers".' (28 February 2017). *Financial Times*. Retrieved from: https://www.ft.com/content/6037bea4-fd06-11e6-8d8e-a5e3738f9ae4

11 Fidelity Investments. 'Fidelity Investments Money FIT Women Study.' (2015). Retrieved from: www.fidelity.com/bin-public/060_www_fidelity_com/documents/women-fit-money-study.pdf

12 Cooper, Marianne. 'Why Financial Literacy Will Not Save America's Finances.' (2 May 2016). *Atlantic*. Retrieved from: www.theatlantic.com/business/archive/2016/05/financial-literacy/480807/

13 Khan, Omar. 'Why do Assets Matter?'. (2009). Runnymede Trust. www.runnymede trust.org/uploads/publications/pdfs/WhyDoAssetsMatterv8.pdf

14 Ibid.

15 The Womens Resource Centre.org. Retrieved from: www.womens.cusu.cam.ac.uk/campaigns/bem/fawcett_ethnicminoritywomen.pdf

16 Savage, Michael. '100 tenants a day lose homes as rising rents and benefit freeze hit.' (22 July 2017). *Guardian*. Retrieved from: www.theguardian.com/society/2017/jul/22/100-tenants-a-day-lose-homes-rising-rents-benefit-freeze

17 Simms, Jane. 'Stop sexual harassment at work – for good.' (12 December 2017). *People Management*. Retrieved from: www2.cipd.co.uk/pm/peoplemanagement/b/

weblog/archive/2017/12/04/bame-employees-twice-as-likely-to-say-discrimination-holds-back-their-careers.aspx

18 North, Anna. 'Who Gets a Raise?' (26 January 2015). *New York Times.* Retrieved from: https://op-talk.blogs.nytimes.com/2015/01/26/who-gets-a-raise/

19 Ibid.

20 Dionne, Evette. 'Pay Me What You Owe Me: "Insecure's" Yvonne Orji Talks Black Women's Equal Pay Day.' (31 July 2017). bitchmedia. Retrieved from: www.bitch media.org/article/yvonne-orji-interview-black-women-equal-pay-day

21 North, Anna. 'Who Gets a Raise?' (26 January 2015). *New York Times.* Retrieved from: https://op-talk.blogs.nytimes.com/2015/01/26/who-gets-a-raise/

22 Ibid.

When Life Gives You Lemons, Make Lemonade

23 Workneh, Lilly. 'Black Millennials Most Optimistic About Future In Face Of Racial Oppression: Study.' (20 March 2017). *Huffington Post.* Retrieved from: www.huffingtonpost.co.uk/entry/black-millennials-most-optimistic-about-future-in-face-of-racial-oppression-study_us_58cf1d9ae4b0ec9d29dcf283

24 Quittner, Jeremy. 'How African American Entrepreneurs Can Power the Economy.' (3 August 2016). *Fortune.* Retrieved from: http://fortune.com/2016/08/03/african-american-startups/

25 Carter, Sara, et al. 'Supporting ethnic minority and female entrepreneurs.' (February 2015). Economic & Social Research Council. Retrieved from: www.esrc.ac.uk/files/news-events-and-publications/evidence-briefings/supporting-ethnic-minority-and-female-entrepreneurs/

26 Devenport, Andrew. 'Challenging Times – Finance Is Not the Only Barrier for Ethnic Minority Businesses.' (9 September 2013). *Huffington Post.* Retrieved from: www.huffingtonpost.co.uk/andrew-devenport/uk-business-ethnic-minorities_b_3874229.html

27 Brown, Sonia. 'Women Doing the Business.' (12 March 2012). *The Voice.* Retrieved from: www.voice-online.co.uk/article/women-doing-business

28 Sanusi, Victoria. 'This Total Legend Went From A Sales Assistant At Selfridges To One Of Its Suppliers.' (23 October 2016). BuzzFeed News. Retrieved from: www.buzzfeed.com/victoriasanusi/she-did-it-her-way?utm_term=.pswz9PB9w#.iynXVQKV9

29 Scott, Matthew. 'Entrepreneur Tristan Walker Talks About Taking a Startup from 0 to 100.' (11 November 2015). *Ebony.* Retrieved from: www.ebony.com/career-finance/entrepreneur-tristan-walker-talks-about-taking-a-startup-from-0-to-100#axzz4q6QqgGAU

30 Grant, Adam. 'Good News for Young Strivers: Networking Is Overrated.' (24 August 2017). *New York Times.* Retrieved from: www.nytimes.com/2017/08/24/ opinion/sunday/networking-connections-business.html?mcubz=1&_r=0

31 Chan, Rosalie. 'Why More Women of Color Than Ever Are Starting Their Own Businesses.' (10 August 2016). *TIME.* Retrieved from: http://time.com/4408900/latina-women-business-owner-entrepreneur/

32 GOV.UK. 'Nick Clegg calls on banks to do more to support ethnic minority business.' (30 July 2013). GOV.UK. Retrieved from: www.gov.uk/government/news/nick-clegg-calls-on-banks-to-do-more-to-support-ethnic-minority-business

33 Prowess Women in Business. *Facts.* (2012–17). Prowess Women in Business. Retrieved from: www.prowess.org.uk/facts

REPRESENTATION

Being Susan Storm

1 Egere-Cooper, Matilda. 'Young, Gifted and Black – and Ignored.' (27 January 2011) *Independent*. Retrieved from: www.independent.co.uk/arts-entertainment/ music/ features/young-gifted-and-black-ndash-and-ignored-2196311.html

2 Hannon, Lance, et al. 'The Relationship Between Skin Tone and School Suspension for African Americans.' (5 September 2013). *SpringerLink*, Springer US. Retrieved from: www.csun.edu/sites/default/files/ColorismSuspension.pdf

3 Creative Skillset. 'Employment Census of the Creative Media Industries.' (2012). Retrieved from: https://creativeskillset.org/assets/0000/5070/2012_Employment_Census_of_the_Creative_Media_Industries.pdf

4 CIF & MOBO Creative Diversity Report. (28 September 2015). Retrieved from: http://www.mobo.com/press/diversity-report-launch-cif-mobo

5 BBC News. 'London's black male graduates less likely to get jobs.' (22 March 2017). Retrieved from: http://www.bbc.co.uk/news/uk-england-london-39302804

6 Williams, Oscar. 'British journalism is 94% white and 55% male, survey reveals.' (24 March 2016). *Guardian*. Retrieved from: https://www.theguardian.com/media-network/2016/mar/24/british-journalism-diversity-white-female-male-survey

7 Bahr, Lindsey. 'Diversity in Hollywood Films Remains Largely Unchanged.' (31 July 2017). *TIME*. Retrieved from: motto.time.com/4881052/diversity-hollywood-films-unchanged/

Fifty Shades of Beige

8 Russell, Akilah. 'Out Now – a Plaster That Matches Brown Skin.' (26 September 2010). *Guardian*. Retrieved from: www.theguardian.com/theguardian/2010/sep/26/plaster-matches-brown-skin. This was rectified in 2010 by a range of plasters that come in different tones.

9 BBC News. 'Clara Amfo Quits L'Oreal Campaign in Support of Munroe Bergdorf.' (6 September 2017). Retrieved from: www.bbc.co.uk/newsbeat/article/41178624/clara-amfo-quits-loreal-campaign-in-support-of-munroe-bergdorf

10 *Ebony*. 'Relaxers Linked to Early Puberty.' (24 February 2012). Retrieved from: www.ebony.com/wellness-empowerment/relaxers-linked-to-early-puberty#axzz48R5NoPAS.

#RepresentationMatters

11 Mintel. 'Hair Relaxer Sales Decline 26% over the Past Five Years.' (5 September 2013). Mintel.com. Retrieved from: www.mintel.com/press-centre/beauty-and-personal-care/hairstyle-trends-hair-relaxer-sales-decline

12 Nielsen. 'African-American Women: Our Science, Her Magic.' (21 September 2017). Nielsen.com. Retrieved from: www.nielsen.com/us/en/insights/reports/2017/african-american-women-our-science-hermagic.html?afflt=ntrt15340001&afflt_uid=ghmzuRUHXD4.RFW4CEVPseZus1rtPhUZEnh5QQNIiQZe&afflt_uid_2=AFFLT_ID_2

13 Bartlett, Jamie, et al. 'Anti-Social Media.' (7 February 2014). Demos. Retrieved from: www.demos.co.uk/project/anti-social-media/.

14 Mason, Rowena. 'Diane Abbott on abuse of MPs: "My staff try not to let me go out

alone".' (19 February 2017). *Guardian.* Retrieved from: www.theguardian.com/politics/2017/feb/19/diane-abbott-on-abuse-of-mps-staff-try-not-to-let-me-walk-around-alone

15 Asthana, Anushka, and Halliday, Josh. 'Conservative Official Suspended over Racist Tweet Aimed at Diane Abbott.' (9 February 2017). *Guardian.* Retrieved from: www.theguardian.com/politics/2017/feb/09/alan-pearmain-conservative-official-suspended-over-racist-tweet-aimed-at-diane-abbott

16 Phillips, Tom, and Waterson, Jim. 'Not Even Right-Wingers Are Sharing Positive Stories About Theresa May On Facebook.' (3 June 2017). BuzzFeed. Retrieved from: www.buzzfeed.com/tomphillips/not-even-right-wingers-are-sharing-positive-stories-about?utm_term=.evd517l7OO#.snGxaO3Okk

17 Peck, Tom. 'Diane Abbott Received Almost Half of All Abusive Tweets Sent to Female MPs before Election, Poll Finds.' (5 September 2017). *Independent.* Retrieved from: www.independent.co.uk/news/uk/politics/diane-abbott-abuse-female-mps-trolling-racism-sexism-almost-half-total-amnesty-poll-a7931126.html

18 Crown Prosecution Service. 'CPS Publishes New Public Statements on Hate Crime.' (21 August 2017). Retrieved from: www.cps.gov.uk/news/cps-publishes-new-public-statements-hate-crime

19 https://seyiakiwowo.com/GlitchUK/

DATING

Does He Like Black Girls?

1 Keenan, Kevin L. 'Skin Tones and Physical Features of Blacks in Magazine Advertisements.' *Journalism & Mass Communication Quarterly,* vol. 73, no. 4, 1996, pp. 905–912., doi:10.1177/107769909607300410

2 'Interracial Dating: Which Ethnicity Is Most Preferred in the UK?' (24 January 2014). FirstMet.com Blog. Retrieved from: www.firstmet.com/dating-blog/united-kingdom-interracial-dating-ethnicity-preference/

3 'How Your Race Affects The Messages You Get.' (1 October 2009). *OkCupid.com Blog.* Retrieved from: theblog.okcupid.com/how-your-race-affects-the-messages-you-get-39c68771b99e

4 Office for National Statistics. (2011). '2011 Census.' www.ons.gov.uk/census/2011census

5 *Is Love Racist? The Dating Game.* Channel 4 Documentary. First aired 17 July 2017.

6 Office for National Statistics. (2011). '2011 Census.' www.ons.gov.uk/census/2011census

7 Ibid.

8 Livingston, Gretchen, and Brown, Anna. 'Intermarriage in the U.S. 50 Years After Loving v. Virginia.' (18 May 2017). *Pew Research Center's Social & Demographic Trends Project.* Retrieved from: www.pewsocialtrends.org/2017/05/18/intermarriage-in-the-u-s-50-years-after-loving-v-virginia/

9 Runnymede Trust. 'Fact Sheet.' Retrieved from: www.runnymedetrust.org/projects-and-publications/parliament/past-participation-and-politics/david-lammy-on-fatherhood/fact-sheet.html

10 Koshy, Yohann. 'A UKIP Candidate Brought a Photo of Her Black Husband to Hustings to Prove UKIP Isn't Racist.' (17 May 2017). *Vice.* Retrieved from: www.vice.com/en_uk/article/d7aegq/a-ukip-candidate-brought-a-photo-of-her-black-husband-to-hustings-to-prove-ukip-isnt-racist

No Scrubs

11 MPR News. 'For a year, Shonda Rhimes said "yes" to all the things that scared her.' (9 November 2015). Retrieved from: www.mprnews.org/story/2015/11/10/npr-books-shonda-rhimes

12 Zarya, Valentina. 'Study Finds That Single Women Act Less Ambitious Around Guys.' (25 January 2017). *Fortune*. Retrieved from: http://fortune.com/2017/01/25/single-women-ambition/

13 Adichie, Chimamanda Ngozi. *We Should All Be Feminists*. (Fourth Estate, 2014).

14 White, Gillian B. 'Marrying Your Peer, a Tougher Prospect for Black Women.' (28 April 2015). *The Atlantic*. Retrieved from: www.theatlantic.com/business/archive/2015/04/marrying-your-peer-a-tougher-prospect-for-black-women/391586/

15 Coughlan, Sean. 'Why do women get more university places?' (12 May 2016). BBC News. Retrieved from: www.bbc.co.uk/news/education-36266753

HEALTH

Black Girls Don't Cry

1 Mentalhealth.org.uk. 'Black, Asian and Minority Ethnic (BAME) Communities.' (10 November 2017). Mental Health Foundation. Retrieved from: www.mental health.org.uk/a-to-z/b/black-asian- and-minority-ethnic-bame- communities

2 Chavis, Selena. 'Greater Risk for Self-Harm in Young Black Women.' (6 October 2015). *Psych Central News*. Retrieved from: psychcentral.com/news/2010/09/03/greater-risk-for-self-harm-in-young-black-women/17607.html

3 Geronimus, Arline T., et al. 'Do US Black Women Experience Stress-Related Accelerated Biological Aging?' *Human Nature*, vol. 21, no. 1, 2010, pp. 19–38., doi:10.1007/s12110-010-9078-0. www.ncbi.nlm.nih.gov/pmc/articles/PMC2861506/

4 Watson, Laurel B., et al. 'Understanding the Relationships Among White and African American Women's Sexual Objectification Experiences, Physical Safety Anxiety, and Psychological Distress.' (15 January 2015). *SpringerLink*, Springer US. Retrieved from: link.springer.com/article/10.1007%2Fs11199-014-0444-y#page-1

5 Ong, Anthony D., et al. 'Racial Discrimination and the Stress Process.' (20 January 2009). *Journal of Personality and Social Psychology*. Retrieved from: www.research gate.net/publication/26241102_Racial_Discrimination_and_the_Stress_Process

6 Chakraborty, Apu, and McKenzie, Kwame. 'Does Racial Discrimination Cause Mental Illness?' (1 June 2002). *The British Journal of Psychiatry*, The Royal College of Psychiatrists, bjp.rcpsych.org/content/180/6/475

7 Ibid.

8 Igbokwe, Sharon, et al. 'Black British Girls Most Likely to Self Harm, Least Likely to Receive Help.' (19 May 2016). *Women's Enews*. Retrieved from: womensenews.org/2016/05/black-british-girls-most-likely-to-self-harm-least-likely-to-receive-help/.

9 Ferguson, Anni. '"The Lowest of the Stack": Why Black Women Are Struggling with Mental Health.' (8 February 2016). *Guardian*. Retrieved from: www.theguardian.com/lifeandstyle/2016/feb/08/black-women-mental-health-high-rates-depression-anxiety

10 Patel, Kamlesh, and Heginbotham, Chris. 'Institutional Racism in Mental Health

Services Does Not Imply Racism in Individual Psychiatrists: Commentary on . . . Institutional Racism in Psychiatry.' (1 October 2007). *BJPsych Bulletin*, The Royal College of Psychiatrists, , pb.rcpsych.org/content/31/10/367

11 Mental Health Foundation. 'Black, Asian and Minority Ethnic (BAME) Communities.' (10 November 2017). Retrieved from: www.mentalhealth.org.uk/a-to-z/b/black-asian-and-minority-ethnic-bame-communities

12 'Tackling Stigma with Black and Minority Ethnic Communities.' *Speak Out – Summer 2014 Issue*, Time to Change, 2014, www.time-to-change.org.uk/sites/default/files/Speak%20Out%20Summer%202014%20issue%205.pdf

13 Owen, David, and Rehman, Hamid. 'Mental Health Survey of Ethnic Minorities.' (October 2013). *Time to Change*, ETHNOS, www.time-to-change.org.uk/sites/default/files/TTC_Final%20Report_ETHNOS_summary_0.pdf

14 2011 Census. Office for National Statistics (2011). www.ons.gov.uk/census/2011 census

15 Nazroo, J. and King, M. 'Psychosis – symptoms and estimated rates', in Sproston, K., Nazroo J. (eds). *Ethnic Minority Psychiatric Illness Rates In The Community* (EMPIRIC), Quantitative Report, London: Stationery Office (2002).

16 Healthcare Commission. 'Count Me in: Results of a National Census of Inpatients in Mental Health Hospitals and Facilities in England and Wales.' (November 2005). Retrieved from: www.diversecymru.org.uk/wp-content/uploads/count-me-in-2005.pdf

17 Care Quality Commission. 'Care Quality Commission looks ahead as last Count me in census is published.' (6 April 2011). Retrieved from: www.cqc.org.uk/content/care-quality-commission-looks-ahead-last-count-me-census-published

18 Keating, Frank, and Robertson, David. 'Breaking the Circles of Fear: A Review of Mental Health Services to African and Caribbean Communities.' *PsycEXTRA Dataset*, doi:10.1037/e427032008-011

19 Morgan, Craig, et al. 'Pathways to Care and Ethnicity. 2: Source of Referral and Help-Seeking.' (1 April 2005). *The British Journal of Psychiatry*, The Royal College of Psychiatrists, bjp.rcpsych.org/content/186/4/290

20 Chavis, Selena. 'Greater Risk for Self-Harm in Young Black Women.' (6 October 2015). *Psych Central News.* Retrieved from: psychcentral.com/news/2010/09/03/greater-risk-for-self-harm-in-young-black-women/17607.html

21 Mental Health (Amendment) Bill [H.L.]. (Hansard, 19 January 1982). Retrieved from: hansard.millbanksystems.com/lords/1982/jan/19/mental-health-amendment-bill-hl-1#S5LV0426P0_19820119_HOL_474

22 Cooper's research was followed by a 2013 MIND report: Mind.co.uk. Annual Review 2012/13. Report.mind.org.uk/2013/

23 Macpherson, William. 'The Stephen Lawrence Inquiry.' (24 February 1999). GOV. UK, Home Office. Retrieved from: www.gov.uk/government/publications/the-stephen-lawrence-inquiry

24 Patel, Kamlesh, and Heginbotham, Chris. 'Institutional Racism in Mental Health Services Does Not Imply Racism in Individual Psychiatrists: Commentary on . . . Institutional Racism in Psychiatry.' (1 October 2007). *BJPsych Bulletin*, The Royal College of Psychiatrists. Retrieved from: pb.rcpsych.org/content/31/10/367

25 Moosa, Zohra, and Woodroffe, Jessica. *Poverty Pathways: Ethnic Minority Women's Livelihoods.* (2009.) Fawcett Society. Retrieved from: https://www.scie-socialcare online.org.uk/poverty-pathways-ethnic-minority-womens-livelihoods/r/a11G 00000017vRmIAI

26 'Low Income and Ethnicity.' *UK: Low Income and Ethnicity – The Poverty Site*, www.poverty.org.uk/06/index.shtml

27 Omonira-Oyekanmi, Rebecca. 'Black and Dangerous? Listening to Patients' Experiences of Mental Health Services in London.' (27 September 2014). *Open Democracy*, www.opendemocracy.net/shinealight/rebecca-omonira-oyekanmi/black-and-dangerous-listening-to-patients-experiences-of-mental

28 Burstow, Paul. House of Commons Debates. (16 May 2013). *TheyWorkForYou*. Retrieved from: www.theyworkforyou.com/debate/?id=2013-05-16a.814.2

29 Jeraj, Samir et al. 'Mental health crisis review – experiences of black and minority ethnic communities.' (June 2015.) Race Equality Foundation. Retrieved from: raceequalityfoundation.org.uk/resources/downloads/mental-health-crisis-review-%E2%80%93-experiences-black-and-minority-ethnic-communities

30 Mind, 'Psychiatry, Race and Culture.' (2009). Retrieved from: www.mind.org.uk/media/192441/mind_think_report_4.pdf

31 Cruse.org.uk

32 Mind.org.uk

33 www.relate.org.uk

TLC

34 Response Source. 'British women are in a constant state of confusion about their health.' (28 July 2017). Retrieved from: https://pressreleases.responsesource.com/news/93683/british-women-are-in-a-constant-state-of-confusion-about/

35 BBC News. 'Breast cancer "more often advanced" in black women.' (16 November 2016). Retrieved from: www.bbc.co.uk/news/health-37991460

36 Jo's Cervical Cancer Trust. 'Black, Asian and Minority Ethnic women do not recognise the term "cervical screening".' (4 July 2016). Retrieved from: www.jostrust.org.uk/node/451856

37 Institute of Race Relations. (n.d.). Ethnicity and religion statistics. Institute of Race Relations. Retrieved from: www.irr.org.uk/research/statistics/ethnicity-and-religion/

38 NHS Choices UK. *Sickle cell disease*. Retrieved from: www.nhs.uk/conditions/sickle-cell-disease/

39 Give Blood. 'News: Call for black blood and organ donors to "Be There" for their community.' (6 October 2015). Retrieved from: www.blood.co.uk/news-and-campaigns/news-and-statements/news-call-for-black-blood-and-organ-donors-to-be-there-for-their-community/

40 *The Voice*. 'Sisters back campaign for more black bone marrow donors.' (17 February 2015). Retrieved from: www.voice-online.co.uk/article/sisters-back-campaign-more-black-bone-marrow-donors

41 Give Blood. 'News: Call for black blood and organ donors to "Be There" for their community.' (6 October 2015). Retrieved from: www.blood.co.uk/news-and-campaigns/news-and-statements/news-call-for-black-blood-and-organ-donors-to-be-there-for-their-community/

42 Osei-Bempong, Kirsty. 'Health risk link to black hair products.' (9 April 2016). *The Voice*. Retrieved from: www.voice-online.co.uk/article/health-risk-link-black-hair-products

43 Gan, Vicky. 'The Fight to Rid Black Women's Hair Salons of Toxic Chemicals.' (6 November 2015). City Lab. Retrieved from: www.citylab.com/life/2015/11/the-fight-to-rid-black-womens-hair-salons-of-toxic-chemicals/414430/

44 James-Todd, T., Senie, R., and Terry, M. B. 'Racial/Ethnic Differences in Hormonally-Active Hair Product Use: A Plausible Risk Factor for Health Disparities.' *Journal of Immigrant and Minority Health*, 506–511. (2012).

45 Miranda, Leticia. 'Black Beauty Products Are More Likely To Contain Risky Chemicals, Study Says.' (6 December 2016). BuzzFeed News. Retrieved from: www.buzzfeed.com/leticiamiranda/black-beauty-products-are-more-likely-to-contain-risky-chemi?utm_term=.wxO4prQpg#.lupl1351v

46 Osei-Bempong, Kirsty. 'Health risk link to black hair products.' (9 April 2016). *The Voice*. Retrieved from: www.voice-online.co.uk/article/health-risk-link-black-hair-products

47 Tinsley, Omise'eke Natasha. 'Profiting From the Myths About Black Women's Bodies.' (6 April 2016). *TIME*. Retrieved from: http://time.com/4280707/black-women-beauty-myths/

48 Ibid.

49 Miranda, Leticia. 'Black Beauty Products Are More Likely To Contain Risky Chemicals, Study Says.' (6 December 2016). BuzzFeed News. Retrieved from: www.buzzfeed.com/leticiamiranda/black-beauty-products-are-more-likely-to-contain-risky-chemi?utm_term=.wxO4prQpg#.lupl1351v

50 Osei-Bempong, Kirsty. 'Health risk link to black hair products.' (9 April 2016). *The Voice*. Retrieved from: www.voice-online.co.uk/article/health-risk-link-black-hair-products

51 Ibid.

52 Hamblin, James. 'Why Succeeding Against the Odds Can Make You Sick.' (27 January 2017). *New York Times*. Retrieved from: www.nytimes.com/2017/01/27/opinion/sunday/why-succeeding-against-the-odds-can-make-you-sick.html?_r=5

53 Ibid.

BIBLIOGRAPHY

INTRODUCTION

National Literacy Trust. 'Children's and Young People's Reading in 2014.' (20 May 2015). Retrieved from: https://literacytrust.org.uk/research-services/research-reports/childrens-and-young-peoples-reading-2014/

EDUCATION

Lawyer, Doctor, Engineer

BBC News. 'Black children have more concerns over job prospects than white.' (30 June 2014). Retrieved from: www.bbc.co.uk/news/uk-28085152

BBC *Newsround*. '1 in 5 black kids feel skin colour could affect their job.' (30 June 2014). Retrieved from: www.bbc.co.uk/newsround/28060401

Boisrond, C. 'If Your Teacher Looks Like You, You May Do Better In School.' (29 September 2017). nprEd. Retrieved from: www.npr.org/sections/ed/2017/09/29/552929074/if-your-teacher-looks-likes-you-you-may-do-better-in-school

Camden, B. 'Black girls take the lead in STEM subjects.' (27 January 2017). Schools Week. Retrieved from: https://schoolsweek.co.uk/black-girls-take-the-lead-in-stem-subject

Curtis, P. 'Education: Black Caribbean children held back by institutional racism in schools, says study.' (5 September 2008). *Guardian*. Retrieved from: www.the guardian.com/education/2008/sep/05/raceineducation.raceinschools?INTCMP=%20SRCH

Pears, E. 'African pupils excel while their Caribbean counterparts sink.' (7 February 2015). *The Voice*. Retrieved from: www.voice-online.co.uk/article/african-pupils-excel-while-their-caribbean-counterparts-sink

Pells, R. 'Black and ethnic minority teachers face "invisible glass ceiling" in schools, report warns.' (14 April 2017). *Independent*. Retrieved from: www.independent.co.uk/news/education/education-news/black-asian-ethnic-minority-teachers-invisible-glass-ceiling-racism-schools-report-runnymeade-nut-a 7682026.html

Shaw, B. Menzies, L., Bernardes, E., Baars, S., Nye, P., Allen, R., LKMco and Education Datalab. *Ethnicity, Gender and Social Mobility*. (28 December 2016). London: Social Mobility Commission.

Social Mobility Commission. 'Asian Muslims and black people do better in school, worse in work.' (28 December 2016). GOV.UK. Retrieved from: www.gov.uk/government/news/asian-muslims-and-black-people-do-better-in-school-worse-in-work

Villines, Z. 'Exclusion from School Linked to Poor Mental Health in Children.' (13 September 2017). GoodTherapy.org. Retrieved from: www.goodtherapy.org/blog/exclusion-from-school-linked-to-poor-mental-health-in-children-0913171

Black Faces in White Spaces

Ackah, William. 'There Are Fewer than 100 Black Professors in Britain – Why?' (10 March 2014). *The Conversation*. Retrieved from: www.theconversation.com/there-are-fewer-than-100-black-professors-in-britain-why-24088

Adams, Richard. 'Black Students Still Struggle to Win Places at UK Universities.' (25 January 2017). Retrieved from *Guardian*, www.theguardian.com/education/2017/jan/26/black-students-struggle-uk-university-places-ucas

Alexander, Claire, and Arday, Jason. 'Aiming Higher: Race, Inequality and Diversity in the Academy'. (February 2015). Runnymede Trust. Retrieved from: www.runnymede trust.org/uploads/Aiming%20Higher.pdf

Bhopal, Kalwant. *The Experiences of Black and Minority Ethnic Academics: A Comparative Study of the Unequal Academy*. (Routledge, 2015).

Bhopal, Kalwant, et al. 'BME Academic Flight from UK to Overseas Higher Education: Aspects of Marginalisation and Exclusion.' *British Educational Research Journal*, vol. 42, no. 2, 2015, pp. 240–257., doi:10.1002/berj.3204

Bhugra, Dinesh, Cardiff University. 'Independent Review Panel Into Issues Of Racial Equality In The School Of Medicine.' (25 January 2017). Retrieved from: www.cardiff.ac.uk/__data/assets/pdf_file/0011/551837/Prof-Dinesh-Bhugra-report-Final.pdf

Birmingham City University, 'Black Studies – BA (Hons).' www.bcu.ac.uk/courses/black-studies-ba-hons-2018-19

Blandford, E., Brill, C., Neave, S., & Roberts Allison, A. 'Equality in higher education: statistical report 2011. Part 2: students.' (2011). Equality Challenge Unit. Retrieved from: www.ecu.ac.uk/publications/equality-in-he-stats-11

Boliver, Vikki. 'How fair is access to more prestigious UK universities?' (28 May 2013). *British Journal of Sociology* 64(2): 344–364.

Boliver, Vikki, Lecturer in Sociology and Social Policy, School of Applied Social Sciences, Durham University. 'Hard Evidence: Why Aren't There More Black British Students at Elite Universities?' (14 December 2017). Retrieved from *The Conversation*, the conversation.com/hard-evidence-why-arent-there-more-black-british-students-at-elite-universities-25413

Davis, Anna. 'Blacked-up Reveller Wins Fancy Dress Prize, but Students' Union Pledges to Investigate "Racist Connotations".' (5 November 2013). *Evening Standard.* Retrieved from: www.standard.co.uk/news/london/blacked-up-reveller-wins-fancy-dress-prize-but-students-union-pledges-to-investigate-racist-8922057.html

Durham University. 'Thought Leadership: Universities Must Aim Higher on Ethnic Equality and Diversity. (4 February 2015). Retrieved from www.dur.ac.uk/research/news/thoughtleadership/?itemno=23570

Equality Challenge Unit. 'Equality in higher education: statistical report 2014.' Retrieved from: www.ecu.ac.uk/wp-content/uploads/2014/11/2014-08-ECU_HE-stats-report_staff_v19.pdf

Gamsu, Dr Sol, and Donnelly, Dr Michael. 'Diverse Places of Learning? Home neighbourhood ethnic diversity & ethnic composition of universities.' (August 2017). University of Bath Department of Education. Retrieved from: www.bath.ac.uk/publications/diverse-places-of-learning-home-neighbourhood-ethnic-diversity-ethnic-composition-of-universities/

GOV.UK. 'Investigating the Accuracy of Predicted A Level Grades as Part of the 2010 UCAS Admission Process'. Department for Business Innovation and Skills. (5 November 2013). Retrieved from www.gov.uk/government/publications/accuracy-of-predicted-a-level-grades-2010-ucas-admission-process

GOV.UK. 'University Challenge: How Higher Education Can Advance Social Mobility.' (October 2012). Retrieved from: www.gov.uk/government/uploads/system/uploads/attachment_data/file/80188/Higher-Education.pdf

Grove, Jack. '"Small" Russell Group Racial Bias in Admissions: Ucas.' (27 May 2015). *Times Higher Education (THE)*. Retrieved from: www.timeshighereducation.com/news/small-russell-group-racial-bias-in-admissions-ucas/2003594.article

Haslam, Rebecca. 'Staff at Higher Education Providers in the United Kingdom 2015/16.' (19 January 2017). *Staff at Higher Education Providers in the United Kingdom 2015/16 | HESA*. Retrieved from: www.hesa.ac.uk/news/19-01-2017/sfr243-staff

HESA, UK Data Service, ONS Census 2011. Retrieved from: www.hesa.ac.uk/'New HEFCE Analysis Shows Significant Link between Factors Such as Ethnicity, Gender and School Type on Achievement in Higher Education.' (27 March 2014). Higher Education Funding Council for England. Retrieved from: www.hefce.ac.uk/news/newsarchive/2014/Name,94018,en.html. 2011 Census. *Office for National Statistics* (2011). www.ons.gov.uk/census/2011census

Press Association. 'White Pupils "Less Likely to Apply for University than Other Ethnic Groups".' (22 July 2013). *Guardian*. Retrieved from: www.theguardian.com/education/2013/jul/23/white-pupils-university-ethnic-groups

Russell Group Comment on Access Research. (2013) Retrieved from: www.russellgroup.ac.uk/russell-group-latest-news/154-2013/5485- russell-group-comment-on-access-research/

Sherriff, Lucy. 'Outrage As Students "Black Up" As Jamaican *Cool Runnings* Team.' (21 November 2013). *Huffington Post*. Retrieved from: www.huffingtonpost.co.uk/2013/11/19/york-university-students-black-up-cool-runnings_n_4300968.html

Sherriff, Lucy. 'Edinburgh University Law Students In Race Row After "Blacking Up" For Somalian Pirate Fancy Dress.' (18 November 2013). *Huffington Post*. Retrieved from: www.huffingtonpost.co.uk/2013/11/18/somalian-pirates-edinburgh-students-black-up_n_4294952.html

Shukman, Harry. 'How White Is Your Uni?' (14 November 2014). *The Tab*. Retrieved from: thetab.com/2014/11/13/white-uni-24303

Social Market Foundation. 'SMF and the UPP Foundation to Investigate Continuation Rates in Higher Education in London.' (27 February 2017). Retrieved from: www.smf.co.uk/smf-upp-foundation-investigate-continuation-rates-higher-education-london/

Stevenson, Jacqueline. 'Black and Minority Ethnic Student Degree Retention and Attainment.' The Higher Education Academy. Retrieved from www.heacademy.ac.uk/system/files/bme_summit_final_report.pdf

Study by the Institute for Policy Research at the University of Bath. Retrieved from: www.bath.ac.uk/publications/diverse-places-of-learning-home-neighbourhood-ethnic-diversity-ethnic-composition-of-universities/attachments/Appendix-of-tables.pdf

Sutton Trust. 'Four Schools and One College Win More Places at Oxbridge than 2000 Schools Combined.' (4 July 2017). Retrieved from: www.suttontrust.com/newsarchive/four-schools-one-college-win-places-oxbridge-2000-schools-combined/

Times Higher Education. 'Anonymise admissions, says race equality report.' (3 February 2015). Retrieved from *Times Higher Education (THE)*, https://www.timeshigher education.com/news/anonymise-admissions-says-race-equality-report/2018334.article

'Undergraduate Admissions Statistics: 2011 Entry.' Retrieved from Oxford University website, https://www.ox.ac.uk/media/global/wwwoxacuk/localsites/gazette/documents/statisticalinformation/admissionsstatistics/Undergraduate_Admissions_Statistics_2011.pdf

Weale, S. '"Slave Auction" for Loughborough Freshers Leads to Outcry.' (14 September 2017). *Guardian.* Retrieved from: www.theguardian.com/education/2017/sep/14/slave-auction-for-freshers-outcry-loughborough-university

WORK

Work Twice as Hard to Get Half as Good

Acas. 'Minority ethnic women face compounded workplace discrimination, says report.' (2013). Retrieved from: www.acas.org.uk/index.aspx?articleid=4099

Anonymous. 'I applied for the same job using an English name and got the interview.' (24 March 2016). *Guardian.* Retrieved from: www.theguardian.com/media-network/2016/mar/24/british-journalism-female-ethnic-minorities-reporters-editors

BBC News. 'Ethnic minority women face jobs "catastrophe".' (2 December 2012). Retrieved from: www.bbc.co.uk/news/uk-politics-20571996

BBC News. 'Social mobility promise "broken" for ethnic minority children.' (28 December 2016). Retrieved from: www.bbc.co.uk/news/uk-38447933?ocid=socialflow_twitter&ns_mchannel=social&ns_campaign=bbcnews

BBC News. 'Tesco chairman: White men "endangered species" in UK boardrooms.' (11 March 2017). Retrieved from: www.bbc.co.uk/news/business-39241630

Bromwich, Kathryn. 'Destiny Ekaragha: "I've got to break two glass ceilings"'. (28 September 2014). *Guardian.* Retrieved from: www.theguardian.com/film/2014/sep/28/destiny-ekaragha-ive-got-to-break-two-glass-ceilings-gone-too-far

Business in the Community. *Mentoring for Success.* (2012). Business in the Community. Retrieved from: https://race.bitc.org.uk/leading_change/mentoring-success

Business in the Community. *Race at Work 2015.* (2015). London: Business in the Community. Retrieved from: https://race.bitc.org.uk/sites/default/files/bitc_race_at_work_recommendations.pdf

Danielle, Britni. 'Michelle Obama's "twice as good" speech doesn't cut it with most African Americans.' (12 May 2015). *Guardian.* Retrieved from: www.theguardian.com/commentisfree/2015/may/12/michelle-obama-twice-as-good-african-americans-black-people

Eddo-Lodge, Reni. '"You're talked to as if you are a junior" – employees on workplace racism.' (26 September 2017). *Guardian.* Retrieved from: www.theguardian.com/inequality/2017/sep/26/employees-on-workplace-racism-under-representation-bame

Hewlett, Sylvia Ann. *Black Women: Ready, Willing and More Than Able to Lead.* (8 June 2015). Retrieved from: www.inc.com/center-for-talent-innovation/black-women-ready-willing-and-more-than-able-to-lead.html

Lebowitz, Shana. 'Why black women are more ambitious than white women – but have a harder time getting ahead.' (23 April 2015). *Business Insider UK.* Retrieved from: http://uk.businessinsider.com/new-report-on-black-women-leaders-2015-4

McGregor-Smith, R. 'Race in the workplace.' London: Department for Business, Energy & Industrial Strategy. (2017). Retrieved from www.gov.uk/government/uploads/system/uploads/attachment_data/file/594336/race-in-workplace-mcgregor-smith-review.pdf

Peck, Emily. 'Black Women Are Leaning In And Getting Nowhere.' (27 September 2016). *Huffington Post.* Retrieved from: www.huffingtonpost.co.uk/entry/black-women-are-leaning-in-and-getting-nowhere_us_57e98908e4b024a52d29b0e8

Pells, Rachael. 'Black and ethnic minority teachers face "invisible glass ceiling" in schools, report warns.' (14 April 2017). *Independent*. Retrieved from: www.independent.co.uk/ news/ education/education-news/black-asian-ethnic-minority-teachers-invisible-glass-ceiling-racism-schools-report-runnymede-nut-a7682026.html

Prowess Women in Business. (n.d.). *UK Female Entrepreneurship: key facts*. Prowess Women in Business. Retrieved from: www.prowess.org.uk/facts

Rankine, Claudia. 'The Meaning of Serena Williams.' (25 August 2015). *New York Times*. Retrieved from: www.nytimes.com/2015/08/30/magazine/the-meaning-of-serena-williams.html?_r=0

Rosenberg, Alyssa. 'Shonda Rhimes's "Year of Yes" and the price of breaking barriers.' (10 November 2015). *Washington Post*. Retrieved from: www.washingtonpost.com/ news/act-four/wp/2015/11/10/shonda-rhimess-year-of-yes-and-the-price-of-breaking-barriers/?utm_term=.0c5f69b7a5b8

Shaw, B., Menzies, L., Bernardes, E., Baars, S., Nye, P., Allen, R., LKMco and Education Datalab. *Ethnicity, Gender and Social Mobility*. (28 December 2016). London: Social Mobility Commission.

Water Cooler Microaggressions

Abbott, Diane. 'I fought racism and misogyny to become an MP. The fight is getting harder.' (14 February 2017). *Guardian*. Retrieved from: www.theguardian.com/commentisfree/ 2017/feb/14/racism-misogyny-politics-online-abuse-minorities? CMP=twt_g

Acas. 'Minority ethnic women face compounded workplace discrimination, says report.' (2013) Retrieved from Acas: www.acas.org.uk/index.aspx?articleid=4099

Ashe, S. D., and Nazroo, J. 'Equality, Diversity and Racism in the Workplace: A Qualitative Analysis of the 2015 Race at Work Survey.' (2015). Manchester: ESRC Centre on Dynamics of Ethnicity, University of Manchester.

Cooney, Samantha. 'Michelle Obama Reveals the Most Difficult Part of Her Time as First Lady.' (26 July 2017). *Motto*. Retrieved from: http://motto.time.com/4874387/ michelle-obama-first-lady-racism/

Dishman, L. 'How To Shut Down "Microaggressions" At Work.' (3 July 2017). *Fast Company*. Retrieved from: www.fastcompany.com/3068670/how-to-shut-down-microaggressions-at-work

Eddo-Lodge, Reni. '"You're talked to as if you are a junior" – employees on workplace racism.' (26 September 2017). *Guardian*. Retrieved from: www.theguardian.com/ inequality/2017/sep/26/employees-on-workplace-racism-under-representation-bame

Holder, Aisha, M. B. 'Black women often suffer microaggressions at work.' (27 February 2016). Retrieved from LSE USAPP blog: http://blogs.lse.ac.uk/usappblog/2016/02/ 27/black-women-often-suffer-microaggressions-at-work/

Liu, Anni. 'No, You're Not Imagining It: 3 Ways Racial Microaggressions Sneak into Our Lives.' (25 February 2015). *Everyday Feminism*. Retrieved from: https://everyday feminism.com/2015/02/ways-racial-microaggressions-sneak-in/

Naftulin, Julia. 'How Gaslighting Affects Your Mental Health.' (20 June 2017). *Motto*. Retrieved from: http://motto.time.com/4825032/gaslighting-mental-health/?utm_ campaign=time&utm_source=twitter.com&utm_medium=social&xid=time

Prowess Women in Business. (n.d.). 'UK Female Entrepreneurship: key facts.' Prowess Women in Business. Retrieved from: www.prowess.org.uk/facts

Sue, Derald Wing, PhD. 'Racial Microaggressions in Everyday Life.' (5 October 2015). *Psychology Today*. Retrieved from: www.psychologytoday.com/blog/microaggressions-in-everyday-life/201010/racial-microaggressions-in-everyday-life

Taylor, D. 'Eni Aluko: "The minute you are brave enough to talk about race you are in a difficult situation".' (21 August 2017). *Guardian.* Retrieved from: www.the guardian.com/football/2017/aug/21/eni-aluko-interview-race-difficult-situation

TUC. '1 in 3 British BME workers have been bullied, abused or singled out for unfair treatment, finds TUC poll.' (13 September 2017). Retrieved from: www.tuc.org.uk/news/1-3-british-bme-workers-have-been-bullied-abused-or-singled-out-unfair-treatment-finds-tuc-poll

Williams, Joan C., and Phillips, K. W. 'Double Jeopardy? Gender Bias Against Women of Color in Science.' (2014). WorkLife Law. UC Hastings College of the Law.

***Flawless

Business in the Community. *Race at Work Report 2015.* (5 November 2015). Retrieved from: race.bitc.org.uk/system/files/research/race_equality_campaign_yougov_report_nov_2015_vfull_vfinal_e.pdf

'Diversity & Inclusion Framework.' Hyatt in Action. Retrieved from: www.hyatt.com/corporate/Programs/diversity/en/diversity/hyatt-in-action.html

Gardiner, Becky, et al. 'The Dark Side of Guardian Comments.' (12 April 2016). *Guardian.* Retrieved from: www.theguardian.com/technology/2016/apr/12/the-dark-side-of-guardian-comments

Project 28-40 Report. (1 April 2014). Retrieved from: Business in the Community, https://gender.bitc.org.uk/all-resources/research-articles/project-28-40-report

Wikipedia. 'Respectability politics'. (22 February 2018). Retrieved from: https://en.wikipedia.org/wiki/Respectability_politics

Woolcock, Nicola. '"Wrong" Accent and Clothes Keep Poor out of Top Jobs.' (6 March 2017). *The Times.* Retrieved from: www.thetimes.co.uk/edition/news/wrong-accent-and-clothes-keep-poor-out-of-top-jobs-9v0mm52wz

GETTING AHEAD
Independent Women

Acas. 'Minority ethnic women face compounded workplace discrimination, says report.' (2013). Retrieved from: www.acas.org.uk/index.aspx?articleid=4099

BBC News. 'One in 13 ethnic minority workers are in insecure jobs, says TUC.' (2 June 2017). Retrieved from: www.bbc.co.uk/news/business-40117388

Beaty, Zoe. 'We need to talk about our differences to see the true scale of the pay gap.' (10 November 2016). *The Pool.* Retrieved from: www.the-pool.com/work/work-news/2016/45/zoe-beaty-equal-pay-intersectionality

Beaty, Zoe. 'Some women are being left behind by pay gap progress.' (6 March 2017). *The Pool.* Retrieved from: www.the-pool.com/work/work-news/2017/10/racial-inequality-in-the-pay-gap

Breach, Anthony, and Li, Yaojun. 'Gender Pay Gap by Ethnicity in Britain – Briefing.' (2017). The Fawcett Society. Retrieved from: www.fawcettsociety.org.uk/Handlers/Download.ashx?IDMF=f31d6adc-9e0e-4bfe-a3df-3e85605ee4a9

Cooper, Marianne. 'Why Financial Literacy Will Not Save America's Finances.' (2 May 2016). *Atlantic.* Retrieved from: www.theatlantic.com/business/archive/2016/05/financial-literacy/480807/

Dionne, Evette. 'Pay Me What You Owe Me: "Insecure's" Yvonne Orji Talks Black Women's Equal Pay Day.' (31 July 2017). bitchmedia. Retrieved from: www.bitchmedia.org/article/yvonne-orji-interview-black-women-equal-pay-day

Fidelity Investments. 'Fidelity Investments Money FIT Women Study.' (2015). Retrieved from: www.fidelity.com/bin-public/060_www_fidelity_com/documents/women-fit-money-study.pdf

Goodfellow, Maya. 'A toxic concoction means women of colour are hit hardest by austerity.' (28 November 2016). *Guardian*. Retrieved from: www.theguardian.com/commentisfree/2016/nov/28/toxic-concoction-women-colour-pay-highest-price-austerity?CMP=share_btn_tw

Khan, Omar. 'Why do Assets Matter?' (2009). Runnymede Trust. Retrieved from: www.runnymedetrust.org/uploads/publications/pdfs/WhyDoAssetsMatterv8.pdf

North, Anna. 'Who Gets a Raise?' (26 January 2015). *New York Times*. Retrieved from: https://op-talk.blogs.nytimes.com/2015/01/26/who-gets-a-raise/

O'Connor, Sarah. 'UK companies "holding back black and ethnic minority workers".' (28 February 2017). *Financial Times*. Retrieved from: https://www.ft.com/content/6037bea4-fd06-11e6-11e6-a5e3738f9ae4

Rawlinson, Kevin. 'Minority ethnic families earning up to £8,900 less than white Britons.' (7 August 2017). *Guardian*. Retrieved from: www.theguardian.com/money/2017/aug/07/minority-ethnic-families-earning-less-white-britons-uk-pay-gap?CMP=Share_iOSApp_Other

Savage, Michael. '100 tenants a day lose homes as rising rents and benefit freeze hit.' (22 July 2017). *Guardian*. Retrieved from: www.theguardian.com/society/2017/jul/22/100-tenants-a-day-lose-homes-rising-rents-benefit-freeze

Simms, Jane. 'Stop sexual harassment at work – for good.' (12 December 2017). *People Management*. Retrieved from: www2.cipd.co.uk/pm/peoplemanagement/b/weblog/archive/2017/12/04/bame-employees-twice-as-likely-to-say-discrimination-holds-back-their-careers.aspx

The Womens Resource Centre.org. Retrieved from: www.womens.cusu.cam.ac.uk/campaigns/bem/fawcett_ethnicminoritywomen.pdf

Woodhams, C., Lupton, B., and Cowling, M. 'The Snowballing Penalty Effect: Multiple Disadvantage and Pay.' *British Journal of Management*, 63–77. (2015). Retrieved from: http://onlinelibrary.wiley.com/doi/10.1111/1467-8551.12032/full

When Life Gives You Lemons, Make Lemonade

Brown, Sonia. 'Women Doing the Business.' (12 March 2012). *The Voice*. Retrieved from: www.voice-online.co.uk/article/women-doing-business

Carter, Sara, et al. 'Supporting ethnic minority and female entrepreneurs.' (February 2015). Economic & Social Research Council. Retrieved from: www.esrc.ac.uk/files/news-events-and-publications/evidence-briefings/supporting-ethnic-minority-and-female-entrepreneurs/

Chan, Rosalie. 'Why More Women of Color Than Ever Are Starting Their Own Businesses.' (10 August 2016). *TIME*. Retrieved from: http://time.com/4408900/latina-women-business-owner-entrepreneur/

Department for Communities and Local Government. *Ethnic Minority Businesses and Access to Finance*. (2013). London. Retrieved from: www.gov.uk/government/uploads/system/uploads/attachment_data/file/225762/EMBs_and_Access_to_Finance.pdf

Devenport, Andrew. 'Challenging Times – Finance Is Not the Only Barrier for Ethnic Minority Businesses.' (9 September 2013). *Huffington Post*. Retrieved from: www.huffingtonpost.co.uk/andrew-devenport/uk-business-ethnic-minorities_b_3874229.html

GOV.UK. 'Nick Clegg calls on banks to do more to support ethnic minority business.' (30 July 2013). GOV.UK. Retrieved from: www.gov.uk/government/news/nick-clegg-calls-on-banks-to-do-more-to-support-ethnic-minority-business

Grant, Adam. 'Good News for Young Strivers: Networking Is Overrated.' (24 August 2017). *New York Times.* Retrieved from: www.nytimes.com/2017/08/24/opinion/sunday/networking-connections-business.html?mcubz=1&_r=0

Prowess Women in Business. *Facts.* (2012–17). Prowess Women in Business. Retrieved from: www.prowess.org.uk/facts

Quittner, Jeremy. 'How African American Entrepreneurs Can Power the Economy.' (3 August 2016). *Fortune.* Retrieved from: http://fortune.com/2016/08/03/african-american-startups/

Sanusi, Victoria. 'This Total Legend Went From A Sales Assistant At Selfridges To One Of Its Suppliers.' (23 October 2016). BuzzFeed News. Retrieved from: www.buzzfeed.com/victoriasanusi/she-did-it-her-way?utm_term=.pswz9PB9w#.iynXVQKV9

Scott, Matthew. 'Entrepreneur Tristan Walker Talks About Taking a Startup from 0 to 100.' (11 November 2015). *Ebony.* Retrieved from: www.ebony.com/career-finance/entrepreneur-tristan-walker-talks-about-taking-a-startup-from-0-to-100#axzz4q6QqgGAU

Workneh, Lilly. 'Black Millennials Most Optimistic About Future In Face Of Racial Oppression: Study.' (20 March 2017). *Huffington Post.* Retrieved from: www.huffington post.co.uk/entry/black-millennials-most-optimistic-about-future-in-face-of-racial-oppression-study_us_58cf1d9ae4b0ec9d29dcf283

REPRESENTATION

Being Susan Storm

Bahr, Lindsey. 'Diversity in Hollywood Films Remains Largely Unchanged.' (31 July 2017). *TIME.* Retrieved from: motto.time.com/4881052/diversity-hollywood-films-unchanged/

Egere-Cooper, Matilda. 'Young, Gifted and Black – and Ignored.' (27 January 2011). *Independent.* Retrieved from: www.independent.co.uk/arts-entertainment/music/features/young-gifted-and-black-ndash-and-ignored-2196311.html

Hannon, Lance, et al. 'The Relationship Between Skin Tone and School Suspension for African Americans.' (5 September 2013). *SpringerLink*, Springer US. Retrieved from: www.csun.edu/sites/default/files/ColorismSuspension.pdf

Fifty Shades of Beige

BBC News. 'Clara Amfo Quits L'Oreal Campaign in Support of Munroe Bergdorf.' (6 September 2017). Retrieved from: www.bbc.co.uk/newsbeat/article/41178624/clara-amfo-quits-loreal-campaign-in-support-of-munroe-bergdorf

Ebony. 'Relaxers Linked to Early Puberty.' (24 February 2012). Retrieved from: www.ebony.com/wellness-empowerment/relaxers-linked-to-early-puberty#axzz48R5NoPAS

Russell, Akilah. 'Out Now – a Plaster That Matches Brown Skin.' (26 September 2010). *Guardian.* Retrieved from: www.theguardian.com/theguardian/2010/sep/26/plaster-matches-brown-skin. This was rectified in 2010 by a range of plasters that come in different tones.

#RepresentationMatters

Asthana, Anushka, and Halliday, Josh. 'Conservative Official Suspended over Racist Tweet Aimed at Diane Abbott.' (9 February 2017). *Guardian*. Retrieved from: www.the guardian.com/politics/2017/feb/09/alan-pearmain-conservative-official-suspended-over-racist-tweet-aimed-at-diane-abbott

Bartlett, Jamie, et al. 'Anti-Social Media.' (7 February 2014). Demos. Retrieved from: www.demos.co.uk/project/anti-social-media/

Crown Prosecution Service. 'CPS Publishes New Public Statements on Hate Crime.' (21 August 2017). Retrieved from: www.cps.gov.uk/news/cps-publishes-new-public-statements-hate-crime

Mason, Rowena. 'Diane Abbott on Abuse of MPs: "My Staff Try Not to Let Me Go out Alone".' (19 February 2017). *Guardian*. Retrieved from: www.theguardian.com/politics/2017/feb/19/diane-abbott-on-abuse-of-mps-staff-try-not-to-let-me-walk-around-alone

Mintel. 'Hair Relaxer Sales Decline 26% over the Past Five Years.' (5 September 2013). Mintel.com. Retrieved from: www.mintel.com/press-centre/beauty-and-personal-care/hairstyle-trends-hair-relaxer-sales-decline

Nielsen. 'African-American Women: Our Science, Her Magic.' (21 September 2017). Nielsen.com. Retrieved from: www.nielsen.com/us/en/insights/reports/2017/african-american-women-our-science-hermagic.html?afflt=ntrt15340001&afflt_uid=ghmzuRUHXD4.RFW4CEVPseZus1rtPhUZEnh5QQNIiQZe&afflt_uid_2=AFFLT_ID_2

Peck, Tom. 'Diane Abbott Received Almost Half of All Abusive Tweets Sent to Female MPs before Election, Poll Finds.' (5 September 2017). *Independent*. Retrieved from: www.independent.co.uk/news/uk/politics/diane-abbott-abuse-female-mps-trolling-racism-sexism-almost-half-total-amnesty-poll-a7931126.html

Phillips, Tom, and Waterson, Jim. 'Not Even Right-Wingers Are Sharing Positive Stories About Theresa May On Facebook.' (3 June 2017). BuzzFeed. Retrieved from: www.buzzfeed.com/tomphillips/not-even-right-wingers-are-sharing-positive-stories-about?utm_term=.evd5171700#.snGxaO3Okk

https://seyiakiwowo.com/GlitchUK/

DATING

Does He Like Black Girls?

'Interracial Dating: Which Ethnicity Is Most Preferred in the UK?' (24 January 2014). *FirstMet.com Blog* Retrieved from: www.firstmet.com/dating-blog/united-kingdom-interracial-dating-ethnicity-preference/

Is Love Racist? The Dating Game. Channel 4 Documentary. First aired 17 July 2017.

'How Your Race Affects The Messages You Get'. (1 October 2009). *OkCupid.com Blog* Retrieved from: theblog.okcupid.com/how-your-race-affects-the-messages-you-get-39c68771b99e

Keenan, Kevin L. 'Skin Tones and Physical Features of Blacks in Magazine Advertisements.' *Journalism & Mass Communication Quarterly*, vol. 73, no. 4, 1996, pp. 905–912., doi:10.1177/107769909607300410

Koshy, Yohann. 'A UKIP Candidate Brought a Photo of Her Black Husband to Hustings to Prove UKIP Isn't Racist.' (17 May 2017). *Vice*. Retrieved from: www.vice.com/en_uk/

article/d7aegq/a-ukip-candidate-brought-a-photo-of-her-black-husband-to-hustings-to-prove-ukip-isnt-racist

Livingston, Gretchen, and Brown, Anna. 'Intermarriage in the U.S. 50 Years After Loving v. Virginia.' (18 May 2017). Pew Research Center's Social & Demographic Trends Project. Retrieved from: www.pewsocialtrends.org/2017/05/18/intermarriage-in-the-u-s-50-years-after-loving-v-virginia/

Office for National Statistics. (2011). '2011 Census.' www.ons.gov.uk/census/2011 census

Runnymede Trust. 'Fact Sheet.' Retrieved from: www.runnymedetrust.org/projects-and-publications/parliament/past-participation-and-politics/david-lammy-on-fatherhood/fact-sheet.html

No Scrubs

Adichie, Chimamanda Ngozi. *We Should All Be Feminists*. (Fourth Estate, 2014).

Coughlan, Sean. 'Why do women get more university places?' (12 May 2016). BBC News. Retrieved from: www.bbc.co.uk/news/education-36266753

MPR News. 'For a year, Shonda Rhimes said "yes" to all the things that scared her.' (9 November 2015). Retrieved from: www.mprnews.org/story/2015/11/10/npr-books-shonda-rhimes

White, Gillian B. 'Marrying Your Peer, a Tougher Prospect for Black Women.' (28 April 2015). *The Atlantic*. Retrieved from: www.theatlantic.com/business/archive/2015/04/marrying-your-peer-a-tougher-prospect-for-black-women/391586/

Zarya, Valentina. 'Study Finds That Single Women Act Less Ambitious Around Guys.' (25 January 2017). *Fortune*. Retrieved from: http://fortune.com/2017/01/25/single-women-ambition/

HEALTH

Black Girls Don't Cry

Burstow, Paul. House of Commons Debates. (16 May 2013). *TheyWorkForYou*. Retrieved from: www.theyworkforyou.com/debate/?id=2013-05-16a.814.2

Care Quality Commission. 'Care Quality Commission looks ahead as last Count me in census is published.' (6 April 2011). Retrieved from: www.cqc.org.uk/content/care-quality-commission-looks-ahead-last-count-me-census-published

Chakraborty, Apu, and McKenzie, Kwame. 'Does Racial Discrimination Cause Mental Illness?' (1 June 2002). *The British Journal of Psychiatry*, The Royal College of Psychiatrists, bjp.rcpsych.org/content/180/6/475

Chavis, Selena. 'Greater Risk for Self-Harm in Young Black Women.' (6 October 2015). *Psych Central News*. Retrieved from: psychcentral.com/news/2010/09/03/greater-risk-for-self-harm-in-young-black-women/17607.html

Cruse Bereavement Care, www.cruse.org.uk/

Ferguson, Anni. ' "The Lowest of the Stack": Why Black Women Are Struggling with Mental Health.' (8 February 2016). *Guardian*. Retrieved from: www.theguardian.com/lifeandstyle/2016/feb/08/black-women-mental-health-high-rates-depression-anxiety

Geronimus, Arline T., et al. 'Do US Black Women Experience Stress-Related Accelerated Biological Aging?' *Human Nature*, vol. 21, no. 1, 2010, pp. 19–38., doi:10.1007/s12110-010-9078-0. www.ncbi.nlm.nih.gov/pmc/articles/PMC2861506/

Healthcare Commission. 'Count Me in: Results of a National Census of Inpatients in Mental Health Hospitals and Facilities in England and Wales.' (November 2005). Retrieved from: www.diversecymru.org.uk/wp-content/uploads/count-me-in-2005.pdf

Igbokwe, Sharon, et al. 'Black British Girls Most Likely to Self Harm, Least Likely to Receive Help.' (19 May 2016). *Women's Enews*. Retrieved from: womensenews.org/2016/05/black-british-girls-most-likely-to-self-harm-least-likely-to-receive-help/

Jeraj, Samir, et al. 'Mental health crisis review – experiences of black and minority ethnic communities.' (June 2015.) Race Equality Foundation. Retrieved from: raceequality foundation.org.uk/resources/downloads/mental-health-crisis-review-%E2%80%93-experiences-black-and-minority-ethnic-communities

Keating, Frank, and Robertson, David. 'Breaking the Circles of Fear: A Review of Mental Health Services to African and Caribbean Communities.' *PsycEXTRA Dataset*, doi:10.1037/e427032008-011

'Low Income and Ethnicity.' *UK: Low Income and Ethnicity – The Poverty Site*, www.poverty.org.uk/06/index.shtml

Macpherson, William. 'The Stephen Lawrence Inquiry.' (24 February 1999). GOV.UK, Home Office. Retrieved from: www.gov.uk/government/publications/the-stephen-lawrence-inquiry

Mental Health Foundation. 'Black, Asian and Minority Ethnic (BAME) Communities.' (10 November 2017). Retrieved from: www.mentalhealth.org.uk/a-to-z/b/black-asian-and- minority-ethnic-bame-communities

Mentalhealth.org.uk. 'Black, Asian and Minority Ethnic (BAME) Communities.' (10 November 2017). Mental Health Foundation, . Retrieved from: www.mental health.org.uk/a-to-z/b/black-asian- and-minority- ethnic-bame- communities

Mental Health (Amendment) Bill [H.L.]. (Hansard, 19 January 1982). Retrieved from: hansard.millbanksystems.com/lords/1982/jan/19/mental-health-amendment-bill-hl-1#S5LV0426P0_19820119_HOL_474

Mind, the Mental Health Charity – Help for Mental Health Problems, www.mind.org.uk/ Mind Annual Review 2012/13. Report.mind.org.uk/2013/.

Mind. 'Psychiatry, Race and Culture.' (2009). Retrieved from: www.mind.org.uk/media/192441/mind_think_report_4.pdf.

Moosa, Zohra, and Woodroffe, Jessica. *Poverty Pathways: Ethnic Minority Women's Livelihoods*. (2009.) Fawcett Society. Retrieved from: https://www.scie-socialcare online.org.uk/poverty-pathways-ethnic-minority-womens-livelihoods/r/a11G 00000017vRmIAI

Morgan, Craig, et al. 'Pathways to Care and Ethnicity. 2: Source of Referral and Help-Seeking.' (1 April 2005). *The British Journal of Psychiatry*, The Royal College of Psychiatrists, bjp.rcpsych.org/content/186/4/290

Nazroo, J., and King, M. 'Psychosis – symptoms and estimated rates', in Sproston, K., Nazroo, J. (eds). *Ethnic Minority Psychiatric Illness Rates in the Community* (EMPIRIC), Quantitative Report, London: Stationery Office (2002).

Omonira-Oyekanmi, Rebecca. 'Black and Dangerous? Listening to Patients' Experiences of Mental Health Services in London.' (27 September 2014). *OpenDemocracy*, www.opendemocracy.net/shinealight/rebecca-omonira-oyekanmi/black-and-dangerous-listening-to-patients-experiences-of-mental

Ong, Anthony D., et al. 'Racial Discrimination and the Stress Process.' (20 January 2009). *Journal of Personality and Social Psychology*. Retrieved from: www.researchgate.net/publication/26241102_Racial_Discrimination_and_the_Stress_Process

Owen, David, and Rehman, Hamid. 'Mental Health Survey of Ethnic Minorities.' (October 2013). *Time to Change*, ETHNOS, www.time-to-change.org.uk/sites/default/files/TTC_ Final%20Report_ETHNOS_summary_0.pdf

Patel, Kamlesh, and Heginbotham, Chris. 'Institutional Racism in Mental Health Services Does Not Imply Racism in Individual Psychiatrists: Commentary on . . . Institutional Racism in Psychiatry.' (1 October 2007). *BJPsych Bulletin*, The Royal College of Psychiatrists. Bpb.rcpsych.org/content/31/10/367

raceequalityfoundation.org.uk/resources/downloads/mental-health-crisis-review-%E2% 80%93-experiences-black-and-minority-ethnic-communities

Relate | The Relationship People, www.relate.org.uk/

Sproston, Kerry, et al. 'Ethnic Minority Psychiatric Illness Rates in the Community (EMPIRIC): Quantitative Report.' (18 June 2003). *PsycEXTRA Dataset*, doi:10.1037/ e623492007-001

'Tackling Stigma with Black and Minority Ethnic Communities.' *Speak Out – Summer 2014 Issue*, Time to Change, 2014, www.time-to-change.org.uk/sites/default/files/ Speak%20Out%20Summer%202014%20issue%205.pdf

Watson, Laurel B., et al. 'Understanding the Relationships Among White and African American Women's Sexual Objectification Experiences, Physical Safety Anxiety, and Psychological Distress.' (15 January 2015). *SpringerLink*, Springer US. Retrieved from: link.springer.com/article/10.1007%2Fs11199-014-0444-y#page-1

TLC

BBC News. 'Breast cancer "'more often advanced" in black women.' (16 November 2016). Retrieved from: www.bbc.co.uk/news/health-37991460

Gan, Vicky. 'The Fight to Rid Black Women's Hair Salons of Toxic Chemicals.' (6 November 2015). City Lab. Retrieved from: www.citylab.com/life/2015/11/the-fight-to-rid-black-womens-hair-salons-of-toxic-chemicals/414430/

Give Blood. 'News: Call for black blood and organ donors to "Be There" for their community.' (6 October 2015). Retrieved from: www.blood.co.uk/news- and-campaigns/news-and-statements/news-call-for-black-blood-and-organ-donors-to-be-there-for-their-community/

Hamblin, James. 'Why Succeeding Against the Odds Can Make You Sick.' (27 January 2017). *New York Times*. Retrieved from: www.nytimes.com/2017/01/27/opinion/ sunday/why-succeeding-against-the-odds-can-make-you-sick.html?_r=5

Healthcare Commission Count Me In: 'Results of a national census of inpatients in mental health hospitals and facilities in England and Wales.' (2005) Retrieved from: www.healthcarecommission.org.uk (accessed August 2006)

Institute of Race Relations. (n.d.). Ethnicity and religion statistics. Institute of Race Relations. Retrieved from: www.irr.org.uk/research/statistics/ethnicity-and-religion/

James-Todd, T., Senie, R., and Terry, M. B. 'Racial/Ethnic Differences in Hormonally-Active Hair Product Use: A Plausible Risk Factor for Health Disparities.' *Journal of Immigrant and Minority Health*, 506–511. (2012).

Jo's Cervical Cancer Trust. 'Black, Asian and Minority Ethnic women do not recognise the term "cervical screening".' (4 July 2016). Retrieved from: www.jostrust.org.uk/ node/451856

Miranda, Leticia. 'Black Beauty Products Are More Likely To Contain Risky Chemicals, Study Says.' (6 December 2016). BuzzFeed News. Retrieved from: www.buzzfeed.com/ leticiamiranda/black-beauty-products-are-more-likely-to-contain-risky-chemi?utm_ term=.wxO4prQpg#.lupl1351v

NHS Choices UK. *Sickle cell disease*. Retrieved from: www.nhs.uk/conditions/sickle-cell-disease/

Osei-Bempong, Kirsty. 'Health risk link to black hair products.' (9 April 2016). *The Voice*. Retrieved from: www.voice-online.co.uk/article/health-risk-link-black-hair-products

Response Source. 'British women are in a constant state of confusion about their health.' (28 July 2017). Retrieved from: https://pressreleases.responsesource.com/news/93683/british-women-are-in-a-constant-state-of-confusion-about/

The Voice. 'Sisters back campaign for more black bone marrow donors.' (17 February 2015). Retrieved from: www.voice-online.co.uk/article/sisters-back-campaign-more-black-bone-marrow-donors

Tinsley, Omise'eke Natasha. 'Profiting From the Myths About Black Women's Bodies.' (6 April 2016). *TIME*. Retrieved from: http://time.com/4280707/black-women-beauty-myths/

2011 Census. Office for National Statistics (2011). www.ons.gov.uk/census/2011census

ACKNOWLEDGEMENTS

A huge thank you to: Everyone at 4th Estate, the Adegoke Family, Juliet Pickering, Sam Rico Batista, Clarissa Pabi, Sherida Kuffour, Chinwe Nnajiuba, Bosun Lewis, Derek Owusu, Nicola Hare, Philippa Ikhile, Heidi Mirza, Akwugo Emejulu, Smashbox, ASOS, Radiant Salon, Virgos Lounge, Scissor Edge, Lolade Lewis, Toby Bakare, Annabel Grace, Ife Akinroyeje, Tish Greenaway, Dorothy Oginni, Bengono De Besbeck, Katie Vowles, Nikesh Shukla, Emily Corfield, Ingrid Beazley, Philippa Mensah, Michelle Blackman-Asante, Tina Tan, Jon Laurence, Gloria Boadi.

4th Estate
An imprint of HarperCollinsPublishers
1 London Bridge Street
London SE1 9GF
www.4thEstate.co.uk

First published in Great Britain in 2018 by 4th Estate

This 4th Estate paperback edition published in 2019

1

Printed and bound by CPI Group (UK) Ltd, Croydon, CR0 4YY

MIX
Paper from
responsible sources
FSC™ C007454

This book is produced from independently certified FSC™ paper
to ensure responsible forest management.

For more information visit: www.harpercollins.co.uk/green